57

144

169f.

WHITE ON ARRIVAL

WHITE ON ARRIVAL

Italians, Race, Color, and Power
in Chicago, 1890–1945

THOMAS A. GUGLIELMO

UNIVERSITY PRESS

2003

OXFORD
UNIVERSITY PRESS

Oxford   New York
Auckland   Bangkok   Buenos Aires   Cape Town   Chennai
Dar es Salaam   Dehli   Hong Kong   Istanbul   Karachi   Kolkata
Kuala   Lumpur   Madrid   Melbourne   Mexico City   Mumbai
Nairobi   São Paulo   Shanghai   Taipei   Tokyo   Toronto

Copyright © 2003 by Oxford University Press, Inc.

Published by Oxford University Press, Inc.
198 Madison Avenue, New York, New York 10016
www.oup.com

Oxford is a registered trademark of Oxford University Press

Library of Congress Cataloging-in-Publication Data
Guglielmo, Thomas A.
White on arrival : Italians, race, color, and power in Chicago, 1890–1945 / Thomas A. Guglielmo
p.   cm.
Includes bibliographical references (p.) and index.
ISBN 0-19-515543-2
1. Italian Americans—Illinois—Chicago—Ethnic identity. 2. Race
awareness—Illinois—Chicago. 3. Chicago (Ill.)—Race relations. I. Title.
F548.9.I8 G84   2003
305.85′1077311—dc21   2002025828

9 8 7 6 5 4 3 2 1

Printed in the United States of America
on acid-free paper

In memory of my mother, Mary Loretta, and my grandfather, Angelo.

For the Guglielmo and Smith families.

ACKNOWLEDGMENTS

This book began as a dissertation and so thanks go first to my committee members, all of whom improved this manuscript in more ways than I could ever describe. Terry McDonald, my chair, was the ideal adviser— incredibly generous with his time, thoughtful and shrewd in his (continual) readings of my work, and tremendously supportive and friendly from the very start of this project. No other person had a more extensive and positive impact on the manuscript. Donna Gabaccia, for her part, willingly read early drafts of every chapter and gave me copious, incisive comments in record time. Earl Lewis and Tomás Almaguer also have supported my work from the beginning and have improved it at every turn.

Many thanks go as well to different institutions that made this book possible. First, I am deeply indebted to Oxford University Press, especially Susan Ferber, Jennifer R. Kowing, and Marie Milton. Special thanks to Susan for reading the entire manuscript several times, providing countless invaluable insights, and tightening my writing on every page. I also want to thank the University of Michigan's Department of History (especially Lorna Altstetter, Dawn Kapalla, Dorothy Marschke, and Sheila Williams), the University of Michigan Regents, the Mellon Foundation, the Michigan Society of Fellows, and the Society of American Historians for generous financial support throughout the research, writing, and revising stages. For providing me with the best support of all—a job—during final manuscript revisions, many thanks to the University of Notre Dame, the Department of American Studies there, and my wonderful new colleagues. Finally, I want to thank numerous archivists across the country, without whom this book's evidence base (and footnotes) would be a lot more limited. Deserving of special mention are Fr. Conrad Borntrager at Our Lady of Sorrows Basilica Archives, Wayne Johnson at the Chicago Crime Commission, Debbie King and Archie Motley at the Chicago Historical Society, Pat Bakunas at the University of Illinois at Chicago's Special Collections, Rodney Ross at the National Archives in Washington, and Marian Smith at the INS.

A host of professors and colleagues helped me in myriad ways—reading chapter drafts, sharing archival information and leads, challenging me to sharpen my ideas, and/or offering encouragement at crucial times. Sincere thanks to Eric Arnesen, Gabriela Arredondo, Jim Barrett, Giorgio Bertellini, Eduardo Bonilla-Silva, Mark Carnes, Matthew Countryman, Peter D'Agostino, Neil Foley, Grace Elizabeth Hale, Rick Halpern, Brad Hunt, Franca Iacovetta, Matthew Jacobson, Scott Kurashige, Matt Lassiter, Caroline Merithew, Gina Morantz-Sánchez, Tim Neary, Dave Roediger, Sonya Rose, Sal Salerno, J. Vincenza Scarpaci, David Scobey, Robert Self, Marty Sherwin, Richard Cándida Smith, Randi Storch, Rudy Vecoli, the members of the Newberry dissertation group and the Michigan Society of Fellows, and the engaged and thoughtful audiences at the North American Labor History Conference, 2001, and at the Defining Whiteness Symposium at the University of Toronto in the fall of 2000. Several of these scholars deserve special recognition: Dave Roediger, whose superb work inspired me to explore European immigrants and race in the first place, has graciously supported my work from the beginning, even as my views diverged slightly from his. Jim Barrett and Matthew Jacobson read the entire manuscript word for word, encouraged me with their enthusiasm, challenged me at points with their skepticism, and offered innumerable valuable suggestions (some of which, it should be stated in fairness to them, I have not followed). Many thanks as well to Anthony Sorrentino for generously sharing an afternoon and his many memories of early Italian Chicago with me; to Jonathan Glickstein at the University of California, Santa Barbara, whose advice to me at an early stage in my graduate career proved crucial; and to my two high school history teachers—Mr. Ritner and Mr. Tucker—whose love of history continues to inspire me to this day.

Deep gratitude and warm thanks go, as well, to the following friends, who taught me so much and sustained me during research, writing, and rewriting: Giorgio Bertellini, Gina Bloom, Connie Bright, Jason Chang, Sharad Chari, Becky Cheng, Tom Colt, Jeff Edelman, Tyrone Forman, Mike Galland, Will Glover, Bethany Grenald, Larry Hashima, Peter Kalliney, Nadia Kim, Richard Kim, Janxin Leu, Amanda Lewis, Shaun Lopez, Daryl Maeda, Rama Mantena, John McKiernan-Gonzales, Jonathan Metzl, Chris Mihm, Farina Mir, Dave Mizner, Andrew Needham, Anna Pegler-Gordon, Monica Prasad, Tom Romero, Laurie Romero-Blumberg, Mario Ruiz, Parna Sengupta, Jonathan Shar, Alex Sherwin, Jonathan Struthers, John Swerdlow, Rich Thomas, Stephen Weissman, Eben Wood, my great graduate student cohort at the University of Michigan, the folks on Isle-au-Haut, and my former colleagues and students at Westminster Middle School. Also many thanks to my co-conspirators in Academics for Affirmative Action and Social Justice, for continually reminding me why I became interested in history in the first place. Special thanks to Amelia Gavin, whose love, patience, and good cheer have made my life in the final months of manuscript preparation more enjoyable than I could have ever hoped.

Finally, there is my family on the Guglielmo and Smith sides. From my grandmother, Grace Porcelli Guglielmo, proudly showing off my modest journal articles at family reunions, to my brother's careful reading of so much of this book; from my father's infectious intellectual curiosity, to my sister's never-ending collaboration with me, support of me and my work, and sharing of ideas, contacts, sources, and so much more; this book would simply not have been possible without my family's faith in and love for me from day one. This book is for them, and for those members of my family—especially my mother and grandfather—for whom the completion of this work did not come soon enough.

CONTENTS

WHITE ON ARRIVAL

"Yusuf rest in peace,
Let the hate cease."
Manifest

INTRODUCTION

In January 1942, Ed Peterson, an African American from Chicago, wrote a letter to the *Chicago Defender*. With America's wartime propaganda machine glorifying the nation's past, Peterson was irritated that this past so often ignored African Americans. Instead, thrifty, hard-working European immigrants supposedly made America—settling its untamed wilderness, laboring in its factories, and farming and peopling its vast frontier. "One would imagine," wrote Peterson, "that the colored race never did any thing to build up the country." Moreover, he argued, European immigrants arrived in the United States with privileges that most African Americans could only dream of:

> The immigrants had all the advantages of coming to the open American white freedom while Negroes had to continue in bondage, at least of thought—for a long while due to the prejudices of the native whites. The immigrant was given encouragement and in time full opportunity to share in the social life of the whites anywhere. . . . The white immigrant found his unions and his white congressional politician. . . . The white immigrant finds his way to the top social ranks, though at one time he was a pal of the colored youths who might have lived in his neighborhood. Friends in childhood, in maturity the white one lives in the quiet, healthful suburbs, while the colored one lives in the dusty, dirty restricted neighborhood and can never leave it.[1]

Other African Americans shared these sentiments. In one typical editorial cartoon from the *Chicago Defender*, an African-American man attempts in vain to open an "equal rights" safe. In the background, Uncle Sam whispers to "the foreigner" (a man with stereotypically Italian features—handle-bar mustache, dark, curly hair, dark eyes): "He's been trying to open that safe for a long time, but doesn't know the combination—I'll give it to *you*."[2]

3

Chicago Defender, September 27, 1924.

This study is, in part, an exploration of the ideas expressed by Peterson and the *Defender* cartoon. Were Italian immigrants and their children readily accepted as whites with easy access to America's "equal rights" safe? Were they "given encouragement and in time full opportunity to share in the social life of the whites anywhere?" Was it only in childhood that they befriended "Negroes" in the neighborhood and that over time they escaped these areas in search of "quiet, healthful suburbs"? Most broadly, this study explores Italians' encounters with race in Chicago. I am interested in questions of identity—how Italians came to understand

Chicago Defender, November 29, 1924.

themselves racially over time—and questions of power—what Italians' precise location was in Chicago's developing racial structure; whether this location changed much over time; and what consequence this location had on their everyday lives, opportunities, and social relations.

Beginning in earnest with the onset of mass migration from Italy (particularly southern Italy) in the late nineteenth century and continuing well into the twentieth century, racial discrimination and prejudice aimed at Italians, South Italians, Latins, Mediterraneans, and "new" European immigrants were fierce, powerful, and pervasive. Italians had their defenders, to be sure, but their detractors—from individuals in particular Chicago neighborhoods to powerful institutions like the U.S. federal government, newspapers, and race science—were more vocal and numerous. And some of this anti-Italian sentiment and behavior questioned Italians' whiteness on occasion. This questioning occurred at the highest levels of national power when, for instance, congressmen in 1912 seriously debated and doubted whether Italians were "full-blooded Caucasians." It also occurred in Chicago where in 1910, one local anthropologist informed newspaper readers: "If you don't like the brunette, if you prefer a pure white skin . . . and feel certain that the future welfare of the United States depends on the prevalence of this type, then you will be justified in favoring the exclusion of Italians."[3]

All of this said, however, Ed Peterson's remarks contained more than a kernel of truth. In the end, Italians' many perceived racial inadequacies aside, they were still largely accepted as white by the widest variety of people and institutions—naturalization laws and courts, the U.S. census, race science, anti-immigrant racialisms, newspapers, unions, employers, neighbors, realtors, settlement houses, politicians, and political parties. This widespread acceptance was reflected most concretely in Italians' ability to naturalize as U.S. citizens, apply for certain jobs, live in certain neighborhoods, marry certain partners, and patronize certain movie theaters, restaurants, saloons, hospitals, summer camps, parks, beaches, and settlement houses. In so many of these situations, as Peterson and the *Defender* well recognized, one color line existed separating "whites" from the "colored races"—groups such as "Negroes," "Orientals," and sometimes "Mexicans." And from the moment they arrived in Chicago—and forever after—Italians were consistently and unambiguously placed on the side of the former. If Italians were racially undesirable in the eyes of many Americans, they were white just the same.

They were so securely white, in fact, that Italians themselves rarely had to aggressively assert the point. Indeed, not until World War II did many Italians identify openly and mobilize politically as white. After the early years of migration and settlement, when Italy remained merely an abstraction to many newcomers, their strongest allegiance was to the Italian race, not the white one. Indeed, one of the central concerns of this book is to understand how *Italianita'*, as both a racial and national consciousness, came to occupy such a central part of many Italians' self-understandings. For much of the turn-of-the-century and interwar years, then, Italians were white on arrival not so much because of the way they viewed themselves, but because of the way others viewed and treated them.

To make better sense of these arguments, two conceptual tools are critical. First is the simple point that we take the structure of race seriously. Race is still too often talked about as simply an idea, an attitude, a consciousness, an identity, or an ideology.[4] It is, to be sure, all these things— but also much more. It is also rooted in various political, economic, social, and cultural institutions and thus very much about power and resources (or lack thereof). Particularly helpful on this point is sociologist Eduardo Bonilla-Silva, who argues that we use "racialized social system" as an analytical tool. In all such systems, he argues

> the placement of people in racial categories involves some form of hierarchy that produces definite social relations between the races. The race placed in the superior position tends to receive greater economic remuneration and access to better occupations and/or prospects in the labor market, occupies a primary position in the political system, is granted higher social estimation . . . often has a license to draw physical (segregation) as well as social (racial etiquette) boundaries between itself and other races, and receives what Du Bois calls a "psychological wage." The totality of these racialized social relations and practices constitutes [a racialized social system].[5]

Such a system existed throughout the nineteenth- and twentieth-century United States. Whether one was white, black, red, yellow, or brown—and to some extent Anglo-Saxon, Alpine, South Italian, or North Italian—powerfully influenced (along with other systems of difference such as class and gender) where one lived and worked, the kinds of people one married, and the kinds of life chances one had. Thus, race was not (and is not) completely about ideas, ideologies, and identity. It is also about location in a social system and its consequences.

To understand fully these consequences, one more conceptual tool is critical: the distinction between race and color. Initially, I conceived of my project as a "wop to white" study, an Italian version of Noel Ignatiev's *How the Irish Became White*. I quickly realized, however, that Italians did not need to become white; they always were in numerous, critical ways. Furthermore, race was more than black and white. If Italians' status as whites was relatively secure, they still suffered, as noted above, from extensive *racial* discrimination and prejudice as Italians, South Italians, Latins, and so on.

Nor was this simply "ethnic" discrimination. To be sure, few scholars agree on how best to conceptually differentiate between race and ethnicity. Some have argued that whereas race is based primarily on physical characteristics subjectively chosen, ethnicity is based on cultural ones such as language and religion. Others have maintained that "membership in an ethnic group is usually voluntary; membership in a racial group is not." Still others have argued that "while 'ethnic' social relations are not *necessarily* hierarchical, exploitative and conflictual, 'race relations'" almost always are.[6] None of these distinctions, while all valid in certain ways, is very helpful for our purposes. None of them, that is, helps us to better understand Italians' social experiences in the United States. After all, a group like the "South Italian race" was purported to have particular cultural *and* physical characteristics; included both voluntary *and* involuntary mem-

Joseph Imburgia's Declaration of Intention form to naturalize, Chicago, July 25, 1939. National Archives and Records Administration, Great Lakes Branch, Chicago, Illinois.

bers; and was a category created in Italy and used extensively in the United States to explicitly rank and exploit certain human beings.

How, then, to navigate between Italians' relatively secure whiteness and their highly problematical racial status, without resorting to unhelpful conceptual distinctions between race and ethnicity? The answer, I contend, is race and color. I argue that there were primarily two ways of talking about and structuring race between the mid-nineteenth and mid-twentieth centuries. The first is color (or what might be called "color race" since this is what many Americans think of as race today): the black race, brown race, red race, white race, and yellow race. Color, as I use it, is a social category and not a physical description. "White" Italians, for instance, could be darker than "black" Americans.[7] Second is race, which could mean many things: large groups like Nordics and Mediterraneans, medium-sized ones like the Celts and Hebrews, or smaller ones like the North or South Italians.

This race/color distinction was, of course, never absolute. Even the most astute sociologists could pass unknowingly between discussions of, on the one hand, Alpines and Anglo-Saxons, and on the other hand, blacks and browns. Still, some people and institutions were very clear on the distinction. For example, the federal government's naturalization applications throughout much of the early twentieth century asked applicants to provide their race and color. For Italians, the only acceptable answers were North or South Italian for the former and white for the latter. And other examples abound: the race/color distinction helps explain why "undesirable Dagoes" were never the target either of violence during Chicago's "Negro"/"white" riot in 1919 or of the city's countless all-"white" restrictive covenants; why politicians could both rail against "the one race [Italians] that has more killers in it than any other" and at the same time openly welcome them into the Democratic Party's all-white electoral coalition; and why famous racialist Lothrop Stoddard could condemn southern and eastern Europeans as "lower human types" and at the same time concede that "if these white immigrants can gravely disorder the national life, it is not too much to say that the colored immigrant [from Asia, Latin America, and Africa] would doom it to certain death." Most important, then, for all of its discursive messiness, the race/color distinction was crystal clear when it came to resources and rewards. In other words, while Italians suffered greatly for their putative *racial* undesirability as Italians, South Italians, and so forth, they still benefited in countless ways from their privileged *color* status as whites.

These systems of difference, however, did change from the mid-nineteenth to the mid-twentieth centuries. In time, after immigration restriction in 1924, the rise of Nazi racialism in the 1930s and early 1940s, and the migration of several million African Americans from the U.S. South to the North and West in the interwar and World War II years, many Americans lost interest in delineating the racial distinctions between Alpines and Anglo-Saxons; the "American dilemma" or color line became their primary concern. By World War II, race and color came to mean the same thing and new terms like "ethnicity" and old ones like "nationality" emerged to explain differences previously thought to be based on race but not color. With some exceptions, Italians became an ethnic or nationality group, as race increasingly referred solely to larger groups like "whites" and "Caucasians," "Negroes" and "Negroids," "Orientals" and "Mongoloids."[8]

Like all history books, this one owes much to existing scholarship. Indeed, without the groundbreaking work on race, immigration, and whiteness of the last few decades, this study would not have been possible. My hope, nonetheless, is to build on and challenge these literatures in certain ways. Regarding race studies, scholars in numerous disciplines have embraced the notion of race as a social construction, but few studies have fully explored the intricacies of the construction process. We have excellent studies on race-making and the state, science, medicine, mass culture, empire, urban space, and so forth.[9] However, few studies have attempted to explore the interaction of many of these sites and institutions in a particular place and time. I attempt to do this here by paying particularly close attention to the "cultural" and "material," as well as to the micro- and macrolevels of human experience.

My work also draws on European immigrant historiography, which has made great advances in the last several decades. Still, historians in this field have often discussed immigrants' incorporation into the American polity, economy, and society without any reference at all to race and color issues. This blind spot is particularly glaring given the fact that immigrants to the United States entered a world in which every resource imaginable was distributed, at least to some degree, according to race and color considerations. Following scholars like Matthew Jacobson, Robert Orsi, and David Roediger, I argue that race and color deeply structured Italians' everyday lives. Indeed, when it came to *fare l'America*—making it in America—Italians' whiteness was their most prized possession. Therefore, to understand Italian immigrant experiences—indeed any immigrant experiences—one must talk about race and color. These are not optional "variables" but central to the story.[10]

Finally, this study is deeply indebted to whiteness historiography and the indispensable work of David Roediger, James Barrett, Theodore Allen, Alexander Saxton, and many others.[11] Nonetheless, I challenge several key arguments in much (though not all) of this historiography, especially the claim that European immigrants arrived in the United States as "in-between peoples" and only became fully white over time and after a great deal of struggle.[12] Numerous scholars in a wide range of disciplines have uncritically accepted this argument.[13] I contend that challenges to Italian immigrants' color status were never sustained or systematic and, therefore, Italians never occupied a social position "in between" "colored" and "white."[14] Often failing to understand the distinctions between race and color, some scholars have assumed that challenges to a group's *racial* desirability as, say, Latins or Alpines, necessarily called into question their *color* status as whites. This was not the case. Italians, for instance, could be considered racially inferior "Dagoes" *and* privileged whites simultaneously.[15] This point is vividly apparent when one compares their experiences with those of groups whose whiteness was either really in question (e.g., Mexican Americans) or entirely out of the question (e.g., African Americans and Asian Americans).

Studying these sorts of race and color issues in Chicago offered several advantages. Along with New York and Philadelphia, it was one of the three great American destinations of Italian immigrants throughout the late nineteenth and early twentieth centuries. Chicago's first and second generation Italian population always paled in comparison to that of New York but was roughly equal to Philadelphia's throughout these years.[16] Chicago also offers an extremely rich set of source materials thanks to a prolific group of settlement workers, the University of Chicago's sociology department, and the 118 oral histories in the Italians in Chicago Project. Chicago Italians shared churches, schools, workplaces, saloons, parks, and settlement houses with people from all over the world and of all race and color classifications—Asians, Mexicans, myriad European groups, and native-born Americans of all hues. This kaleidoscopic mix makes an Italian race and color story in Chicago rich and exciting. Finally, Chicago, more than any other city, stands at the heart of America's urban North color narrative. The city was always among the most popular destinations for southern African-American migrants and the site of major events like the "Race Riot" of 1919 and postwar violence in places like Cicero and Trumbull Park. Furthermore, scholars—beginning with the Chicago Commission on Race Relations, the Chicago School of Sociology, and Horace Cayton and St. Clair Drake, and continuing on through the years with Lizabeth Cohen, James Grossman, Arnold Hirsch, Thomas Philpott, Allan Spear, William Tuttle, and others—have kept Chicago at the center of questions about race, color, and the urban North.[17]

My study begins in the late nineteenth century when Italian mass migration to the United States began in earnest and when southern Italian immigrants began to significantly outnumber their northern compatriots. It ends in World War II when race and color collapsed and Italian Americans began openly mobilizing around a white identity. There are limitations to this time frame. It would be interesting, for instance, to know something about Italians' race and color experiences prior to mass migration and the enormous influx of southern Italians, as well as after the Second World War when deeply racialized and colorized New Deal policies took root, millions of "white" Americans fled to the suburbs, the "second ghetto" emerged, decolonialism spread abroad, and social justice movements led by people of "color" gained power and prominence. I leave these questions, gladly, to another historian.

The book opens with a general chapter on Italian immigrants' race and color experiences in Italy and Chicago between the late nineteenth century and World War I—the era of migration and settlement. The book then examines the postwar years through a series of overlapping stories about Italians' encounters with race and color in Chicago at different historical moments. These stories, organized more or less chronologically and each having its own chapter, deal with the following: the Chicago Color Riot of 1919 and neighborhood race and color relations in its aftermath (chapter 2); the debate over and restriction of "new" immigration in the early 1920s (chapter 3); the rise of Italian organized crime—represented by gangsters like Al Capone and Johnny Torrio—during the era of Prohibition (chapter 4); mayoral politics in the late 1920s and early 1930s (chapter 5); the rise of fascism and the Italian-Ethiopian War of 1935–1936 (chapter 6); industrial and craft unionism as well as left-wing politics during the Depression and World War II (chapter 7); and, finally, private and public housing in Chicago's Italian neighborhoods from the late 1930s through World War II, when major African-American migration to Chicago resumed (chapter 8).

In the end, this study is about both stasis and change. Italians arrived in Chicago white and remained that way for the rest of their time in America. This part of the story is very much about stasis, power, and privilege. One of the more disturbing things I discovered in the many oral histories of Chicago Italians was a deeply distorted sense of the past. Many interviewees—often contrasting themselves explicitly with African Americans—spoke proudly of the ways in which they pulled themselves up by their bootstraps by working hard and shunning government assistance.[18] And, of course, these narratives have some truth to them. Many Italians did work hard and their success in America is, in part, a testament to this fact. However, the idea that they, unlike groups like African Americans, did it all by themselves without government assistance could not be more inaccurate. Indeed, the opposite was often the case. Italians' whiteness—conferred more powerfully by the federal government than by any other institution—was their single most powerful asset in the "New World"; it gave them countless advantages over "nonwhites" in housing, jobs, schools, politics, and virtually every other meaningful area of life. Without appreciating this fact, one has no hope of fully understanding Italians' experiences in the United States.

But this study is also about change and about how Italian immigrants and their offspring came to understand themselves in new ways—first as Italians and Italian Americans, then as whites. And related to these changes, particularly those regarding color, were shifting social relations between Italians and their various neighbors and co-workers in Chicago. In the early years of migration and settlement, many observers remarked on Italians' tolerance and openness on color issues. This was certainly the case in the South where white supremacists often denounced Italians for wholly lacking "the instinct . . . against mingling with the negroes." This was the case in Chicago too where numerous observers from settlement house workers to sociologists commended Italians for their refreshingly underdeveloped color consciousness and their harmonious relations with African Americans and other "colored" groups.[19]

These virtues, sadly, did not last long. As Italians learned more about the color line and their precise location along it, heretofore harmonious relations became less so and color consciousness increased. Of course, there were exceptions to the rule and I hope to highlight some of these in the pages that follow. But this general shift in Italian behavior and thinking is unmistakable. Having grown up not far from Howard Beach, Queens, and Bensonhurst, Brooklyn, where Italian Americans were at the center of "racial" violence in the late twentieth century, I want more than anything else to better understand this fateful shift. These events, more than any historiographical or theoretical debates, brought me to this project. This book—though about another time and place—still seeks to shed light on these tragic events, as well as remind us of an earlier, more promising time.

1

EARLY ITALIAN CHICAGO

Nineteenth-century Chicago was the quintessential boom town. When incorporated in 1833, it was a lonely, swampy outpost of several hundred people located where a small river ran into Lake Michigan. No more than fifty years later, it was one of the largest cities and most important manufacturing and commercial centers in the world. With jobs aplenty in any number of industries—steel, clothing, timber, packing, mail-order, railroads—workers flocked to the city from all over the United States, much of Europe, and, at different times, parts of Asia and Latin America. As a result, the city's population exploded, going from just over 100,000 in 1860 to over ten times that number thirty years later. By 1920, Chicago had just over 2.7 million inhabitants, making it the second most populous city in America and one of the largest in the world. And while roughly an equal share of native-born Americans and immigrants made Chicago's spectacular growth possible, the city increasingly became a foreign-born Mecca during the late nineteenth and early twentieth centuries. By 1900, immigrants and their children constituted almost 80 percent of Chicago's inhabitants.[1]

Among the many immigrant groups coming to Chicago were Italians, whose communities were transformed in these years both quantitatively and qualitatively. With its roots in the mid-nineteenth century migration of a handful of Genovese fruit sellers, saloonkeepers, and restaurateurs, Chicago's Italian population soared between 1880 and World War I. Continually fed by an ever-increasing number of immigrants, new Italian communities sprouted up all over Chicago and older communities burst their boundaries. In 1870, there were 552 foreign-born Italians in Chicago, by 1890, the population had grown to 5,685; by 1920, it had grown another ten times to 59,215. By this year, Italians were the fourth largest foreign-born group in Chicago behind Poles, Germans, and Russians. But these years were hardly about population growth alone. Also extremely important was the changing origin of these immigrants. Starting around 1880, northern Italians became increasingly outnumbered by their southern *connazionali* (compatriots), who, by virtually all accounts, were poorer, less educated, less skilled, and darker in complexion. By 1919, a Department of Public Welfare study estimated that more than three-quarters of Chicago's Italians had come from the *Mezzogiorno* (southern Italy).[2]

The years from the late nineteenth century through World War I were a complicated and difficult time for many Italian immigrants—particularly those from southern Italy. Many Chicagoans and their various institutions, often drawing extensively on ideas from Italy, degraded *meridionali* (southern Italians) mercilessly and viewed and treated them as racial undesirables. Italians did, however, have their allies in Chicago—among them settlement house workers, ward politicians, and Catholic priests—who defended them faithfully. More important, for all of the racial discrimination and prejudice that many Italians faced as Latins, Mediterraneans, southern Italians, and "new" immigrants, they were still accepted as white.

Italians may not have viewed matters in quite the same way. Chicago's main Italian-language newspaper, *L'Italia*, agreed with this general color categorization but did not openly or often advertise the point. Instead, it appeared far more interested in *la razza italiana* (the Italian race) than in *la razza bianca* (the white race). The mass of everyday Italians, on the other hand, may not have immediately grasped either the importance of Chicago's color line or their precise location along it. As for Italians and race, again "community" perspectives differed. *L'Italia*, for one, along with some middle-class leaders, worked tirelessly in these years to build a more unified Italian racial/national community, in part, to defend its members from the vicious and frequent racialist attacks directed against them. However, these efforts had only a minimal effect on the racial/national consciousness of many everyday Italians. By World War I, Italy remained for many a distant abstraction at best. Town and regional loyalties reigned supreme.

Migration and Settlement

From 1870 on, more than twenty-six million Italians officially declared their intention to emigrate.[3] Of these millions, a fraction went to Chicago; still a smaller fraction eventually settled there. Who were these Italians arriving and settling in Chicago, and why and how did they come? In the early years, Italian immigration to Chicago (as to so many other U.S. cities) consisted primarily of two groups: First, and most numerous, there were young men primarily from the *Mezzogiorno* who were in search of temporary work and who had little intention of settling in the United States permanently. They wanted to find work, save their earnings, and send them back home to their families.[4] Some of these men would travel back and forth between Italy and the United States annually; others would stay in the United States for several years, make enough money to buy land back home, and then return to Italy. As Alessandro Mastro-Valerio, an Italian-language newspaper editor from Chicago's Near West Side, noted in 1895, "Italians do not come to America to find a home, as do the British, Teutons, Slavs, and Scandinavians, but to repair the exhausted financial conditions in which they were living in Italy. . . . They leave the mother country with the firm intention of going back to it as soon as their *scarsellas* shall sound with plenty of *quibus*." And statistics bear this observation out. Between 1908 and 1923, close to 60 percent of all Italian immigrants to the United States eventually returned home. In 1908 alone, returnees outnumbered immigrants by almost two to one.[5]

But, as Mastro-Valerio himself admitted, many migrants stayed. No doubt having talked the matter over with their spouses, parents, siblings, and/or children, a good number of Italian "birds of passage" eventually chose to settle in America and to arrange for their families to join them there in the future. These families were the second major group of Italian migrants. Many years later, scores of Chicago Italians—men and women like Philomena Mazzei, Valentino Lazzaretti, Marietta Interlandi, Lawrence Spallitta, Domenic Pandolfi, Antoinette De Marco, and many others—recalled in oral interviews that this was the way their families had come to the United States.[6]

But why did these Italians choose Chicago? As an industrial center, a fast-growing city, and the busiest of U.S. railroad hubs, Chicago offered immigrants interested in making money innumerable opportunities. Italians found jobs in Chicago's many bustling factories and construction projects, as well as in the city's vast hinterlands in mines and on railroads. Just as important, Italians went to Chicago because their family members and *paesani* were already there. The vast majority of Italian immigrants to Chicago carefully constructed intricate migration chains from particular towns in Italy to particular neighborhoods in the United States. And prior to the transatlantic trip, they were often in close contact with family members, who in many cases found jobs and housing for them in advance and arranged to meet them at the Dearborn Station in downtown Chicago upon their arrival.[7]

As an increasing number of Italian migrants chose to make Chicago their home, older Italian settlements grew and many newer ones came into being. By World War I, the Chicago area had nearly two dozen distinct Italian communities both close to downtown in the river wards, as well as farther away in Kensington, Melrose Park, and Chicago Heights.[8] The river ward communities housed by far the largest number of Italians in these early years. The two oldest of these were a Genovese settlement on the Near North Side and Polk Depot just south of the Loop. Peddlers, saloonkeepers, and restaurateurs developed the former in the mid-nineteenth

Chicago's Italian Communities, c. 1920

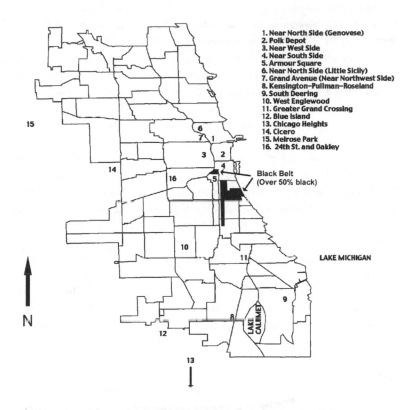

1. Near North Side (Genovese)
2. Polk Depot
3. Near West Side
4. Near South Side
5. Armour Square
6. Near North Side (Little Sicily)
7. Grand Avenue (Near Northwest Side)
8. Kensington–Pullman–Roseland
9. South Deering
10. West Englewood
11. Greater Grand Crossing
12. Blue Island
13. Chicago Heights
14. Cicero
15. Melrose Park
16. 24th St. and Oakley

Black Belt
(Over 50% black)

LAKE MICHIGAN

N

century just to the north and east of where the Chicago River and its north branch meet. Organized around the Church of the Assumption, which was built in 1881, this North Italian enclave had 455 residents in 1884 and never grew to much more than twice that number.[9] South of this settlement, around Dearborn Station amid Chicago's vice district, was another small Italian colony, Polk Depot. Many of this neighborhood's first Italians came from Potenza in Basilicata as early as the 1870s; but, by the end of the nineteenth century, it quickly became the destination of many other southern Italians from towns and cities in Calabria, Campania, Abruzzo, and Molise. Although known to many Chicagoans as the "Dago District," Polk Depot was also home to African Americans and an assortment of European groups. Regarding the neighborhood's Jones School, one housing reformer noted in 1913: "Probably more nationalities are represented [there] than in any other school in Chicago."[10]

As both migration and settlement increased in the early years, Italian Chicago expanded well beyond these two initial colonies. Spilling out of Polk Depot to the west across the southern branch of the Chicago River,

Italians clustered on the Near West Side, creating Chicago's largest Italian neighborhood. Well-known for Hull-House, Johnny Powers's raucous aldermanic campaigns, and the "Old World" flavor of Taylor Street, this area—the old Nineteenth Ward—had twenty-five thousand Italian residents by 1910, a full third of all Chicago's Italians at the time. By 1920, more than fifteen thousand Italians lived in five adjacent census tracts alone in the heart of the Near West Side.[11] Some Italian women did piecework at home or labored as tailoresses and seamstresses at many of the neighborhood's large garment factories. The majority of the men were common laborers in these years, working seasonal jobs in construction or on railroads, though a good number were also barbers, bakers, candy makers, cobblers, saloonkeepers, peddlers, and tailors.[12] Like Polk Depot, this neighborhood was extremely heterogeneous. Coming from all over the *Mezzogiorno* and settling according to strong regional and town loyalties, Italians shared the neighborhood with Jews, Bohemians, Greeks, Germans, Irish, and, beginning during World War I, African Americans and Mexicans.[13]

Many Italians settled west of Polk Depot, but a good number went south into the Near South Side and Armour Square areas. Southern Italians, by and large, populated both neighborhoods—Riciglianese in Armour Square and Sicilians from Nicosia and Termini on the Near South Side. Working mainly as seamstresses, pieceworkers, bootblacks, street sweepers, peddlers, and common laborers (depending mainly on one's gender and town or region of origin), Italians numbered close to five thousand in 1910, and, according to one estimate, over double that number by 1918.[14] And while many of these *meridionali* attended the same church—Santa Maria Incoronata—*campanalismo* (loyalty to one's region, town, or clan) still reigned supreme in these neighborhoods. As historian Rudolph Vecoli has pointed out, "Among the Riciglianese it was considered a scandal for anyone to marry out of the village group." Italians first lived among Swedes, Germans, Czechs, and Irish, all of whom slowly moved out in these early years. In their place came Croatians, Chinese, who created Chicago's biggest Chinatown nearby, and growing numbers of African Americans, whose fast expanding Black Belt bordered these Italian neighborhoods on its northwestern corner.[15]

The final two major Italian colonies of the river wards were "Little Sicily" on the Near North Side and the Grand Avenue community just to its west across the north branch of the Chicago River. The former, located a dozen or so blocks north of the early Genovese settlement, grew immensely in the first decade of the twentieth century as Sicilian immigration to the United States soared and as many *Siciliani* migrated north to Chicago from the sugar cane plantations of Louisiana. By 1910, this small neighborhood had nearly thirteen thousand Italians, making it the second most populous Italian colony in Chicago.[16] Although the Italians of this neighborhood shared much in common—virtually everyone was from

Sicily, a vast majority were unskilled laborers, and many attended the neighborhood church, St. Philip Benizi—the community was far from unified. Well into the 1920s, numerous commentators and residents described the neighborhood as "a mosaic of Sicilian towns."[17] The neighborhood also maintained the most unsavory of reputations for its "death corner," where Italian "black hand"[18] murders and kidnappings were reported by the Italian- and English-language presses weekly (if not in some cases daily). Regardless, many different people called the Near North Side their home, especially Swedes and Irish in the late nineteenth and early twentieth centuries and African Americans during and after World War I. In addition, to the neighborhood's east lived a diverse group of Persians, Filipinos, hoboes, and Chicago's Gold Coast elite.[19]

The Grand Avenue community on the Near Northwest Side was the third largest of Chicago's Italian colonies with 11,500 Italians in 1910. With residents coming at different times from Genoa, Tuscany, Basilicata, Rome, Venice, Campania, Abruzzo, Apulia, and Sicily, this neighborhood featured perhaps a greater variety of Italians than any other section of Chicago. Clustering around the Chicago Commons settlement house and the Italian Catholic church, Santa Maria Addolorata, Italians, as in other neighborhoods, maintained close ties with and resided near their *paesani*. As Graham Taylor, head resident for many years at Chicago Commons, noted in 1930, "these neighborly folk literally transplant old-country neighborhoods across the sea. Many Italian societies bear the name of the old-country town from which most of their members came and in or near which their relatives and former neighbors live." In addition to its wide range of Italians, this area also had many Irish, Scandinavian, and German immigrants and then toward the 1910s larger and larger numbers of Poles. Some Italians worked in the neighborhood's many small factories, which manufactured everything from furniture and shoes to bottles and brooms. The vast majority, however, worked outside the neighborhood as common laborers in construction, street-sweeping, and railroads, or in the case of some women, as garment workers on the Near West Side. A small number of neighborhood Italians were also proprietors of small businesses like grocery stores and barber shops.[20]

These seven river ward colonies constituted the core of early Italian Chicago, providing homes for two-thirds of its population in 1910. But Italians also formed vibrant communities in other areas inside and just outside of Chicago. On the Far South Side, for instance, different settlements sprung up around the Kensington-Pullman-Roseland area, South Deering, West Englewood, Greater Grand Crossing, and Blue Island. With roughly four thousand Italian residents in 1910, the first of these communities was the most populous.[21] Drawn to the area by work in the Pullman shops, the Illinois Central Railroad yards, and construction, Italians from various regions—first, Veneto, then Piedmont, Calabria, and Sicily—settled in this semirural area according to their regional and town identities. A sprinkling of Poles, Lithuanians, Swedes, Dutch, Irish, Germans, and Russian Jews accompanied them there.[22]

Even farther south of these communities and south of Chicago's city limits lay another important Italian colony in Chicago Heights. First populated by Marchegiani and then by migrants from Sicily, Calabria, Abruzzo, and Lazio, this town's two Italian neighborhoods—East Side and Hungry Hill—had over three thousand Italian residents in 1910, making up 20 percent of the town's population at the time. Many women and children, like those in the Kensington area, worked in onion fields during the harvest season, while many men were employed in local companies like Inland Steel, the National Brick Company, and Canedy-Otto Machine Tools. Italians shared their neighborhoods with Poles, Greeks, Slovaks, Germans, and Rumanians, and, beginning in the 1920s, increasing numbers of African Americans.[23]

Another important set of Italian communities were located west of the river wards in places like Cicero, Twenty-fourth and Oakley, and Melrose Park. The two most populous of these were Melrose Park and Twenty-fourth and Oakley. The latter, like Chicago Heights, was located outside of Chicago's city limits, eleven miles west of the Loop. Unlike Chicago Heights and many of the other communities already mentioned, however, Melrose Park was a secondary settlement community populated mainly by Italians moving not from Italy but more likely from another part of Chicago. By 1910, the town had over one thousand Italians from a variety of regions like Basilicata, Campania, Sicily, Calabria, and the Marches. The community became best known for its annual feast of *La Madonna del Carmine*, which drew record numbers of Italians from all over Chicagoland and quickly became the most popular of its kind in the area.[24]

Twenty-fourth and Oakley, located several miles due west of Armour Square, was different from every other Italian community in Chicago. Most of the Italians here came from the North—almost exclusively from Tuscany. (They shared the neighborhood with sizable numbers of Lithuanians, Swedes, and Germans). Most of the community's men had industrial factory jobs at the nearby McCormick Plant or the National Malleable Casting Works factory. (The local women who worked outside the home had more typical jobs in garment factories on the Near West Side.) Finally, socialists dominated the neighborhood in many respects by holding annual and popular May Day parades, by organizing their own mutual aid societies and social clubs, and by displaying a fierce anti-clericalism. Many of the neighborhood's churchgoers had to find alternative routes to mass to avoid their radical neighbors' pestering. As local resident, Lena Tarabori, later recalled, "when we would go to church we were told . . . [not to] come down Oakley Avenue, because all the Socialists were out. . . . We didn't want to be harassed and we didn't want to give them a chance to harass us."[25]

Taken together, Italian immigrants settled in a wide variety of communities during their early years in Chicago. But there are three unifying themes critical to later discussions of race and color issues. First, "Italian communities" were never exclusively Italian. Blocks existed here and there that were 90 percent or more Italian in, for instance, Little Sicily and around Polk Depot, but most Italians shared their streets, stores, buildings, saloons, and workplaces with the most cosmopolitan of groups.[26] Second, even if Italians' population density had been higher in particular neighborhoods, these areas would still not have been "Italian" in any meaningful sense. Although some Chicagoans (Italians and non-Italians) viewed them as such, the vast majority of these neighborhoods' inhabitants knew little of the Italian nation and cared about it even less. Coming from isolated hill towns in southern Italy, the mass of Italian immigrants in these years could communicate with and trust a Chinese person or a Czech as much as a "connazionale" from another region or town than their own. Therefore, Italian neighborhoods more closely resembled loose federations of Italian village and regional groups than unified, national communities.[27] Third, these were neighborhoods in motion, continually experiencing tremendous turnover from constant immigration and return migration, high rates of local residential mobility, and the on going seasonal labor migration of thousands of Italian men back and forth between their homes in Chicago and their workplaces in mines and on railroad gangs in Colorado, Pennsylvania, Minnesota, New Mexico, downstate Illinois, and many other places.[28]

Aryans and Africans: Race in Turn-of-the-Century Italy

A rough sense of the origins and geography of early Italian Chicago makes it possible to examine Italians' race and color experiences there. But any such discussion must begin in Italy, from which many Americans received their first ideas about the millions of *contadini* (peasants) reaching their shores, and where many Italian immigrants themselves learned some of their earliest racial lessons.

Most important are beliefs about southern Italian inferiority, which, while extant for centuries prior to mass migration, received their fullest articulation and exposure during Italy's long and difficult process of nation-building. Between 1848 and 1870 and led by the Kingdom of Sardinia, Italy became a nation through the political integration of several other kingdoms, smaller states, and principalities. While many social groups in the new nation welcomed and celebrated these events, many peasants in the South and in other regions did not. By and large, they were either unaware that unification had occurred (until, as historian Dino Cinel noted, "new tax collectors showed up in different uniforms") or were openly hostile to the idea, seeing Garibaldi and his troops as simply the latest in a long line of foreign colonizers. Those of the latter camp staged peasant rebellions throughout the *Risorgimento* period and all across Italy—but particularly in the South—to resist their integration into the Italian nation.[29]

But these uprisings, quickly suppressed by the nascent Italian state, proved to be the least of the new nation's problems regarding the *Mezzogiorno*. Much more challenging in the end was bringing the South—deeply destitute and disorganized due to centuries of political subjugation and economic and social mismanagement—within the fold of the developing Italian national economy and culture. With this as its goal, the Italian state tried numerous measures throughout the late nineteenth century, such as administrative centralization, colonization in Africa, and a program of national improvements. As each of these programs failed more miserably than the next, the South appeared more and more as *the* central stumbling block to Italy's nation-building project. By the turn of the century, then, Italians of all kinds searched desperately for answers to the confounding *questione meridionale* (southern question).[30]

Precisely at this time and in this context, an influential group of positivist anthropologists, like Cesare Lombroso, Giuseppe Sergi, Alfredo Niceforo, and Paolo Orano, emerged on the scene with scientific "proof," explaining the intractable problems of the South and confirming the suspicions of a good number of northern Italians (among others).[31] The people of the *Mezzogiorno*, argued these scholars, were racially distinct from and hopelessly inferior to their northern *connazionali*. Sergi, for instance, using skull measurements to trace the various origins and desirability of the Italian people, argued that while northern Italians descended from superior Aryan stock, southerners were primarily of inferior African blood. Similarly, Niceforo argued in his widely read study, *L'Italia Barbara Contemporanea*, that two Italies existed, whose fundamental racial differences made unification impossible. After all, "one of the two Italies, the northern one, shows a civilization greatly diffused, more fresh, and more modern. The Italy of the South [however] shows a moral and social structure reminiscent of primitive and even quasibarbarian times, a civilization quite inferior."[32]

Such ideas were by no means restricted to the academy; a great deal of Italian mass culture and many public officials absorbed and disseminated them as well. For instance, Italy's leading illustrated magazine of the time, *Illustrazione Italiana*, repeatedly and "patronizingly celebrate[d] the South's anomalous position between Italy and the Orient, between the world of civilized progress and the spheres of either rusticity or barbarism." As one of the magazine's reporters noted after a trip through Sicily in 1893, "in the fields where I interviewed many peasants I found only types with the most unmistakable African origin. My how much strange intelligence is in those muddled brains." Similarly, Filippo Turati, a Socialist Party leader at the turn of the century, no doubt spoke for many of his *connazionali* when he referred to the "Southern Question" as a battle between "an incipient civilization and that putrid barbarity."[33]

These theories never went completely unchallenged, of course. A highly articulate and vocal group of southern intellectuals—*meridionalisti* like Gaetano Salvemini and Napoleone Colajanni—defended the *Mezzogiorno* throughout this time by offering nonracialist sociological answers to the Southern Question.[34] But even these defenders would at times draw careful distinctions between the peasant and the intellectual classes of the South and admit to the former's overall degradation and backwardness. By the early twentieth century, then, theories of southern Italian racial inferiority—now with scientific imprimatur—were more widely accepted in many parts of Italy than ever before. Thus, when the Italian state began dividing at this time its emigrants into northern and southern categories for the purpose of statistics-gathering, it was merely institutionalizing further a set of racial ideas already widely prevalent in turn-of-the-century Italy.[35]

Keltics and Iberics: Race in Chicago

Just at this moment—at the height of the scientific and popular racialist assault on the *Mezzogiorno* and its people—the origins of Italian immigration to the United States shifted dramatically from the North to the South. As hundreds of thousands of these much-maligned *meridionali* arrived in America each year, a wide variety of American institutions and individuals, alarmed by this massive influx, made great use of Italian positivist race arguments. The U.S. Bureau of Immigration, for instance, began in 1899 recording the racial backgrounds of immigrants and distinguishing between "Keltic" northern Italians and "Iberic" southern Italians.[36] The U.S. Immigration Commission, throughout its highly influential forty-two volume report, made a similar distinction. Citing the works of Niceforo and Sergi, it argued that northern and southern Italians "differ from each other materially in language, physique, and character, as well as in geographical distribution." While the former is "cool, deliberate, patient, practical, as well as capable of great progress in the political and social organization of modern civilization," the latter is "excitable, impulsive, highly imaginative, impracticable" and has "little adaptability to highly organized society."[37]

Social scientists like Edward Ross, also citing the work of Italian positivists, made a similar set of arguments. In popular magazine articles and books, Ross warned that while northern Italians were well-fitted for citizenship, their southern counterparts certainly were not because of their horrifying "propensity for personal violence," "inaptness" for team work, strong dose of African blood, and "lack of mental ability." Deeply anxious about many of these characteristics, the popular magazine, *World's Work*, went so far as to urge the federal government in 1914 to pass an exclusion law "aimed specifically at the southern Italians, similar to our immigration laws against Asiatics," since southern Italians "are a direct menace to our Government because they are not fit to take part in it."[38]

A wide range of Chicago's newspapers shared these anti-*meridionali* racialist ideas. In 1910, for instance, the *Chicago Tribune*, having viciously and regularly attacked southern Italians as criminally inclined mongrels from the late nineteenth century on, sent anthropologist George A. Dorsey to the *Mezzogiorno* (among other places) to study immigrants in their homelands. Traveling from one small hill town to the next and writing daily columns for months on his impressions, Dorsey offered, in the end, the most damning view of southern Italians. They were, he claimed, unmanly and primitive barbarians, who had clear "Negroid" ancestry, shared much more in common with the East than the West, and were "poor in health, stature, strength, initiative, education, and money." "They are," concluded Dorsey after five months of daily investigations, "of questionable value from a mental, moral, or physical standpoint."[39] The *Chicago Daily News* wrote in 1891 that southern Italian neighborhoods in Chicago were "honey-combed with crime and lawlessness" and that their inhabitants were "cowardly worshipers of power as are the Chinese or any barbarian tribe."[40] The *Chicago Record-Herald*, perhaps the friendliest of Chicago's major newspapers to Italians, still published frequent articles about Italians' grisly, criminalistic "nature" and about the frequent riots among themselves due to trivial matters like "a long-standing feud" or the boast of one gang of workers that it could dig faster than another.[41] Similarly, if a bit less degradingly, the *New World*, Chicago's archdiocesan weekly, often portrayed southern Italians as a religiously challenged, racialized "problem" desperately in need of church guidance.[42]

Even social settlement workers—often immigrants more loyal defenders—could at times reveal a contempt for *meridionali*. In her famous book, *Twenty Years at Hull-House*, Jane Addams remarked that "possibly the South Italians more than any other immigrants represent the pathetic stupidity of agricultural people crowded into city tenements." Marie Leavitt, the head resident at the Eli Bates House on the Near North Side, portrayed local Sicilians as the perfect picture of pathology: "We have about us many hopelessly dependent families, either broken down by disease, or of so low a grade mentally that they cannot compete with normal persons. These huddle together in the cheapest tenements, sinking in the social scale, but bearing children whom we must hope to inspire with a desire for better things."[43]

Finally, the University of Chicago's widely renowned sociology department conducted many studies of local Italian communities; their findings, like those of Dorsey, were rarely flattering. Graduate student Gertrude Sager, for example, noted in her master's thesis that southern Italians "are very impractical, they let their imagination run away with them. They are impulsive and excitable. They would rather sit and sing all day than do any work and improve their surroundings."[44]

Everyday Chicagoans shared many of these racialist critiques of southern Italians, a fact that most often and most visibly manifested itself in day-to-day neighborhood relations. On the Near North Side, bloody battles involving sticks, guns, knives, and blackjacks occurred regularly between Swedes and Sicilians. The former also held homeowner meetings to devise more genteel ways of ridding the neighborhood of the dreaded "dark people." The problem, in the words of one local Swedish pastor, was that Sicilians "do not keep their places clean; they tear up the cedar blocks of the sidewalk; and they also bring the district into disrepute in many other ways." Meanwhile children engaged in similar battles on the playgrounds and streets of the neighborhood as Swedish girls kept Sicilians off the swings and sandboxes at Seward Park by exclaiming: "Get out! Dagoes! Dagoes! You can't play here!"; and Irish and Swedish boys regularly engaged in street battles with their Sicilian counterparts. On one occasion an Italian youngster led a charge of his *connazionali* against their neighborhood aggressors on horseback.[45]

Nearby in the Grand Avenue community around the same time, Norwegians and Irish immigrants, also distressed about declining property values, asked local settlement house workers for police protection to prevent Italians from flooding and destroying the neighborhood. As one Norwegian at the time confessed, "I don't think I can live in a block with an Italian family." Well aware of this ill will, one neighborhood Italian remarked that "de Norwegian peoples dey mova out fast. Dey no get along with Italianos. Dey afraid of dem. Dey say Italianos blackhands and dey mova quick." In the first decade of the twentieth century, neighborhood tensions ran so high that a full-scale riot nearly erupted when an Irish family's wash line snapped and dropped clothes into an Italian neighbor's tomato sauce stewing below. Lea Taylor, resident of the nearby Chicago Commons, later recalled that this incident "was our first community war and it was very vocal and vigorous."[46]

Similar friction accompanied Italians' movement into certain neighborhoods on the South Side as well. As one old-time resident of South Chicago remarked in the 1920s, "the Italians have been coming in here for twenty years but most of them live north of the tracks. There weren't many down in our section. We wouldn't let 'em come south of the tracks. They were afraid of getting pelted with stones and we would have done it too. . . . It is bad enough to work with 'Dagoes.' I wouldn't think of living next to one." As a result of such battles, one Italian resident of the area later recalled moving fast because "that was an Irish neighborhood . . . and it was not any too pleasant for the Italians."[47]

Taken together, many Chicagoans, like other Americans in these early years of migration and settlement, harbored serious doubts about southern Italians' racial fitness and desirability. *Meridionali*, however, were not without their loyal defenders in prominent institutions like city newspapers, settlement houses, churches, and city government, as well as in many of their neighborhoods around Chicago. One Irish Catholic priest, who ministered to *meridionali* on the Near West Side, praised his parishioners for being "honest, industrious, and temperate, pure in their domestic lives and law-abiding in their civic-relations." Similarly, a Chicago Department of Welfare report noted that an Italian's "racial psychology must be known and respected as has not been heretofore. His love for democracy, fine family control and other points of peculiar strength must be conserved. They should even be capitalized and given publicity for the sake of the general good. There is much that the children of Dante and Cavour can teach us." And these ideas were not completely lost on some of the Italians' neighbors. As one Swede from the East Side neighborhood told an interviewer in the 1920s, "the Italians started coming in up around 95th and 97th Streets about 1900. . . . There wasn't any real friction. Mother always said that they were as clean as any others." A German woman from the Near North Side agreed: "Italians are settling the whole district. They are a very industrious class of people and save their money and many of them have bought property here." Another immigrant from northwestern Europe and from the same neighborhood remarked similarly that "I like Italians fine, they are good neighbors and mind their business."[48]

Equally important to keep in mind is that anti-southern Italian racial prejudice was not like some infectious ideological germ, which *meridionali* carried with them from the "Old World" and which quickly insinuated itself into the minds of Americans. Some such infecting did, of course, occur occasionally. But many of these anti-southern Italian ideas became popular in America because they made sense to people by reflecting—not just affecting—the social structure of America (and Chicago) at the time.[49] Certainly in Chicago, Italians occupied one of the lowliest of social positions: They worked menial "Dago" jobs as street sweepers, rag pickers, and ditch diggers; they practiced, at best, a questionable brand of spirituality in the eyes of Catholics and non-Catholics alike; they were extremely poor and uneducated; they lived alongside other "new" European immigrants and "colored" races like African Americans and Chinese (and later Mexicans) in some of the most dilapidated and dangerous of Chicago's neighborhoods; and they wielded virtually no electoral power, for they either abstained from naturalizing or failed to vote. Taken together, southern Italians faced a racial antagonism that was both ideological and embedded in the social structure of Chicago. If *meridionali* emigrated from Italy in part to escape a racialized social system that relegated them to the bottom tier, they entered America fairly close to the bottom again.

The White City: Color in Chicago

In some critical respects, however, the social systems of turn-of-the-century Italy and the United States were quite different. Most important, unlike in the "Old World," southern Italians never occupied the lowest of social positions in America. This was because America (and Chicago, more particularly) had both racial *and* color hierarchies, and if Italians were denigrated and exploited in the former, they were still generally accepted as white in the latter and reaped the many rewards that came with this status.

This statement needs serious qualification, for at no other time in Italian-American history has the color status of *meridionali* been more hotly contested. In 1903, for instance, the Democratic Party attempted to exclude Italians (and Mexicans) from voting in their "white primaries" since they did not qualify on color grounds. Eight years later, the U.S. House Committee on Immigration and Naturalization openly debated and seriously questioned whether one should regard "the south Italian as a full-blooded Caucasian"; many representatives did not seem to think so. And a range of Americans shared such suspicions. From the docks of New York to railroads out west, some native-born American workers carefully drew distinctions between themselves—"white men"—and foreigners like Italians. In 1891, for instance, a West Coast construction boss testified before a congressional committee that an Italian was "a Dago," not a "white man."[50]

Similarly in the South, one Mississippi Delta town attempted to bar Italians from white schools, while state legislators in 1898 fought to disenfranchise Italians along with African Americans at the state constitutional convention. As one local newspaper at the time wrote, "when we speak of white man's government, they [Italians] are as black as the blackest Negro in existence." In the sugar cane fields of Louisiana, one Sicilian-American recalled that "the boss used to call us niggers" and "told us that we weren't white men."[51] And, of course, lynchings—a punishment often reserved for African Americans—were none too rare an occurrence for Italians throughout the South, West, and Midwest at this time. The most infamous and shocking of these took place in New Orleans in 1891, when an angry mob, bent on avenging the murder of Police Chief David Hennessy, lynched eleven Sicilian suspects in one night. As late as 1915, an armed posse in Johnston City, Illinois, a mining town only three hundred miles from Chicago, lynched Sicilian Joseph Strando for his alleged murder of a prominent town resident.[52]

Various Chicago institutions and individuals also had their questions about Italians' proper color status. The city's newspapers, for instance, sometimes drew connections between southern Italians and the "colored races": The former, it was thought, were at least partially the descendants of "Negroid" people; were as frugal, exploitable, and undesirable as the Chinese (and thus had a reputation in the "Old World" as being the "Chinese of Europe"); hailed from a part of the globe thought to be far more "Oriental" in ways of thinking and living than European; and had swarthy enough features to warrant frequent remark. In one typical front-page story about an Italian murder on the Near North Side, the *Chicago Tribune* described the neighborhood crime scene: "Squat two-story buildings, apparently crammed to bursting with dark skinned men and women and overflowing with dark skinned children, were giving off odors of garlic from midday meals." At other times, newspapers could be more direct. *Tribune* guest columnist, George Dorsey, in an essay entitled "Ideas of East and West Rub Elbows in Naples," stated openly that "a brunette from the south of Italy looks like a white man in the heart of Africa. [But] the same man in Chicago might be taken for mulatto."[53] In the end, economist Robert Foerster no doubt had a point when he noted in 1919: "In a country where yet the distinction between the white man and black man is intended as a distinction in value as well as in ethnography it is no compliment to the Italian to deny him whiteness, yet that actually happens with considerable frequency."[54]

Foerster overstated the point, however, because color challenges were never sustained or systematic. If U.S. congressmen openly debated whether southern Italians were "full-blooded Caucasians," they never went so far as to deny *meridionali* naturalization rights based on their doubts; if magazines like *World's Work* called for the exclusion of Italian immigration, Congress never seriously considered the matter; and if some Louisianans tried to disenfranchise Italians, their efforts, in direct contrast to those regarding African Americans, failed miserably.

In Chicago, Italians' privileged color status was equally visible in myriad ways. When famous African-American boxing champion, Jack Johnson, attempted to marry a "white" woman in 1912, a rowdy and menacing crowd of a thousand "whites" protested on the Near North Side by hanging Johnson in effigy. Meanwhile a nationwide legal and popular campaign was launched to prevent the "interracial" union from occurring. Italians, by contrast, could marry members of most any group without anywhere near this level of resistance.[55]

Regarding housing, battles took place to prevent Italian infiltration in places like the Near North Side, the Grand Avenue area, and the South Side, as noted. These efforts, however, were never as organized or persistent as were those in places like Hyde Park, Kenwood, and West Woodlawn, where scores of "neighborhood improvement associations" sprouted up to restrict the movement of even the fewest African Americans into their neighborhoods; nor were these efforts as violent as those in areas just west of the Black Belt, where bombings, rioting, and gang attacks against African Americans became regular occurrences, particularly as the Great Migration got underway during World War I. Furthermore, while the few wealthy Italians could move to any Chicago neighborhood they could afford (some Asians, it appears, may have enjoyed similar privileges), African Americans were forced to live in the most blighted of Chicago's neighborhoods regardless of their wealth, income, or education level. As a result, African-American residential segregation was extraordinarily high even as early as 1900 and always much higher than that of any European immigrant group.[56]

Italians faced a good deal of workplace discrimination from both unions and employers in these early years. They nonetheless enjoyed more employment options and opportunities than did African Americans or Asians, who worked almost exclusively in their own communities or in the domestic and personal service trades, since better-paying jobs in commerce and industry were effectively closed to them.[57] Finally, as for public accommodations and private agencies, southern Italians were refused admission to a movie theater or restaurant on occasion, but they were not subjected to systematic exclusion from or segregation in countless Chicago restaurants, theaters, hotels, bars, prisons, hospitals, settlement houses, orphanages, schools, and cemeteries, as African Americans and some Asians were.[58] To be sure, none of these points is meant to suggest that Chicago's color line enjoyed some sort of transhistorical coherence and continuity. As a number of scholars have pointed out, the city's color boundaries and rules remained somewhat fluid prior to the Great Migration. Still, even in this early period when the "colored races" remained a small fraction of the city's population, a distinct and pervasive color line existed separating "whites" from "nonwhites." And for all their alleged racial inadequacies, Italians were placed firmly among the former.

Why was this the case? Given the widespread doubts about (chiefly) southern Italian *racial* fitness and desirability, why was their *color* status as whites not undermined? First, scientists, for as long as they had attempted to construct racial/color taxonomies, placed Italians firmly within the white category.[59] The weight of scientific opinion in the United States supported some variation of Johann Friedrich Blumenbach's classification scheme from the late eighteenth century, which divided humankind into "five principal varieties": the American ("red"), Caucasian ("white"), Ethiopian ("black"), Malay ("brown"), and Mongolian ("yellow"). As the U.S. Immigration Commission's *Dictionary of Races and Peoples* noted in 1911,

in preparing this dictionary . . . the author deemed it reasonable to follow the classification employed by Blumenbach. . . . The use of this classification as the basis for this present work is perhaps entirely justified by the general prevailing custom in the United States [to follow Blumenbach], but there is equal justification in the fact that recent writers, such as Keane and the American authority Brinton, have returned to practically the earlier [Blumenbach] classifications.

Significantly, Blumenbach placed Italians (both southerners and northerners) within the Caucasian "variety." To question Italian whiteness, then, required one to challenge widely accepted theories in race science as well.[60]

Second, the history of the Italian peninsula—particularly that of the Roman Empire and the Renaissance—also supported the classification of Italians as white. As Eliot Lord argued in the early twentieth century, "the far-reaching ancestry of the natives of South and Central Italy runs back to the dawn of the earliest Greek civilization in the peninsula and to the Etruscan, driving bronze chariots and glittering in artful gold when the Angles, Saxons and Jutes, and all the wild men of Northern Europe were muffling their nakedness in the skins of wild beasts." As a result, asked Lord in conclusion: "Upon what examination worthy of the name has the Southern Latin stock, as exhibited in Italy, been stamped as 'undesirable'? Is it undesirable to perpetuate the blood, the memorials and traditions of the greatest empire of antiquity, which spread the light of its civilization from the Mediterranean to the North Sea and the Baltic?"[61] Given these points, racialists had to exercise caution in their color-questioning of Italians, for if Italians were not white, a good deal of Western civilization might not have been either.

Finally, if various branches of the American state deeply institutionalized the *racial* differences between northern and southern Italians in their immigration statistics, studies, and applications, they just as surely secured the two groups' *color* commonalities. For one, American naturalization laws during this time allowed only "free white male persons" or "aliens of African nativity or persons of African descent" to become U.S. citizens; and American courts repeatedly denied Asian and some Middle Eastern immigrants access to American citizenship because of the color stipulation in the law, Italians never once encountered any problems. An examination of the naturalization applications of Chicago's Italians at this time reveals that while Italians were defined *racially* as northerners or southerners, their *color* status was always "white." And, of course, the right to naturalize gave Italians at least the potential for electoral power that could be used to protect this privileged color status.[62]

Just as important as naturalization laws was the U.S. census. The color/race category and the kinds of answers the census requested changed many times between 1880 and 1920; the census, for instance, alternated frequently between asking for people's "color," "race," and "color or race." At some points they also asked enumerators to distinguish between "whites" and "Mexicans," between "mulattos," "octoroons," "quadroons," and so forth. Throughout all these variations, however, Italians were always listed as foreign-born or native-born "whites." Because the census represented the federal government's final word on color categories, this classification was no small thing. Indeed, census categorization schemes must have had an immense influence on everyday Americans and their color conceptions. With the largest collection of social data on Americans anywhere, the U.S. census offered invaluable information to countless people—from social scientists and politicians to government bureaucrats and journalists. When using this information, one often unwittingly reproduced the various ways the census organized it—and, in the process, reproduced Italian whiteness.[63]

Encountering Race and Color

While censuses and science, newspapers and neighbors, are crucial to race and color categorization, so too are those people being categorized. Chicago Italians, sometimes consciously and sometimes not, actively encountered race and color from the moment they arrived in the United States. But because class, regional, gender, generational, and racial differences cross-cut the Italian "community," the nature of these encounters could vary greatly.

Some Italian individuals and community institutions, in part as a critical defense strategy, attempted to build a more unified Italian national/racial community in Chicago. Most important in this effort were Italian-language newspapers, particularly the most-widely read Chicago weekly, significantly titled *L'Italia*. This newspaper, published throughout this period by Neapolitan immigrant, Oscar Durante, helped to construct an Italian racial/national identity in several ways: It was written in standard Italian rather than in some regional dialect; it reported constantly on news from, and the glories of, the Italian nation and race; it routinely downplayed regional or town identifications; and it did what it could to ease tensions created by these and other intra-"community" divisions.[64] Also helping Italians to "imagine" themselves as one community were annual Columbus Day parades in Chicago; the organization of Italian-language locals in labor unions, as well as left-wing groups of anarchists, socialists, and communists; statues of prominent Italians like the one of Garibaldi in Lincoln Park; Italy's involvement in wars against Turkey in the early twentieth century; and Americans' and other immigrants' discrimination and prejudice against Italians.[65] By the end of this early period of migration and settlement, the national/racial identity of Italians as Italians grew more salient as their Chicago communities matured, as they marched off alongside the Allies to battle the Central Powers in World War I, and as nationwide institutions emerged like the Order of the Sons of Italy and the Italo-American National Union, which served *all* Italians, not simply those from particular regions or towns.[66]

All these points notwithstanding, even as late as the Great War, many Italians remained divided along numerous lines. First, a pervasive spirit of *campanalismo* was embedded in the geography of virtually every Chicago Italian neighborhood and in the organization and membership of the city's hundreds of "Italian" mutual aid societies, as well as the *feste* and other events that they sponsored. Second, many northern Italians never tired of professing their superiority over their southern *connazionali*. One northerner in the 1880s declared that *meridionali* were "on a level with the Chinese, and in some respects not as good, as they are more vicious." By the 1920s, the president of the Chicago Italian Chamber of Commerce informed an interviewer: "The early Italians were all North Italians. It is only in the last 30 or 35 years that you find the Neapolitan and Sicilian coming to this country. They seem to me to be an entirely different race, and we do not even speak the same language." One southern Italian woman, recalling the prevalence of such views during her childhood on the Near North Side, admitted many years later that the "Genovesi considered themselves superior to us. And naturally we were bitter about that."[67] These sorts of ideas, like those of *campanalismo*, became embedded in Italian neighborhood geography and institutions such that northern and southern Italians rarely lived together in the same neighborhoods, almost never intermarried, and seldom socialized. On the Near North Side, within walking distance of each other, were two Italian churches: Assumption for the North Italian Genovesi and St. Philip Benizi for the Sicilians. Even when Italians attempted to cross the North-South divide to work in common cause, conflict sometimes ensued. In 1899, when various Italians launched a campaign to raise money to honor Garibaldi, many *meridionali* soon boycotted the effort after a North Italian leader in the movement scorned them as "ignorant, stupid, [and] anti-patriotic."[68] Finally, Italians could also draw distinctions between themselves that were not exactly along common North-South or *paese* lines. One woman, whose family came from Amaseno in the south of Italy and who grew up on the Near West Side, recalled how "my mother forbid me to even have anything to do with any Sicilian kids." When the woman started dating a Sicilian man, this information had to be kept from her mother because "that would have been holy hell"—"that was just not allowed." Similarly, an Italian man from Chicago Heights noted that as a kid he and his friends, all Marchegiani from Central Italy, were "hostile to . . . the Sicilians. . . . We [Marchegiani and Sicilians] were separated like two communities." And, of course, class differences could militate against the development of a strong Italian identity. In the wake of a crushing Italian defeat at the hands of the Ethiopians in 1896, for instance, different Chicago Italians met to determine ways of assisting their beleaguered *connazionali* abroad. The meeting ended prematurely, however, when a fight nearly erupted between the working- and middle-class Italians in attendance.[69] In the end, these many divisions were both cause and consequence of a deeply underdeveloped national and racial consciousness among the majority of Chicago's Italians in these early years.

Italians were no more unified on issues of color. *L'Italia*, for one, clearly viewed Italians as white. Perhaps once every few years the newspaper, usually in a story involving a "colored" group, would label Italians as members of *la razza bianca* (the white race). And this labeling would often be indirect, as in the case of one short story about a San Francisco Chinese man's inability to marry an Italian woman because "in California marriages between whites and orientals are not permitted"; or in a blurb on a "bloody battle" between "bianchi e neri" (whites and blacks) around Armour Square in 1911, which involved Edoardo Concimi on the white side; or in a story on Italian immigrants in the South, in which the paper cited the Italian ambassador discussing how "foreign workers of the white race" (presumably Italians among them) would soon come to supplant African Americans in the labor force there.

The newspaper's discussion of Italian whiteness became more explicit only when this status was directly challenged. Thus, in 1903, when the Executive Committee of the Democratic Party tried to exclude Italians (and Mexicans) from their primaries for being "inferior to white men," *L'Italia* furiously assailed the Democrats for the "gravest insult" that Italians had *ever* sustained in America and wondered how Italians' color status could be questioned when they were the glorious compatriots of Garibaldi. Similarly, six years later when an obscure newspaper in Santa Rosa, California listed crime statistics for "whites," "Italians," and "Indians" separately, *L'Italia* was outraged at this "odio di razza" (race hatred) and this senseless attempt to deny Italians their "rightful" membership in the white race.[70]

Although *L'Italia* assumed and at times even asserted Italian whiteness, the newspaper was hardly engaged in some sustained and coherent campaign to secure for Italians this status. For one, it talked about *la razza italiana* always and *la razza bianca* almost never. It also published articles on occasion that challenged Italian whiteness just as much as the Santa Rosa newspaper's listing of statistics. In 1903, for instance, *L'Italia* ran a short front-page story about an Italian woman from Ferrara who gave birth to twins—"one of which is white with blonde hair, the other is completely black with all the distinctive signs of the negro race."[71] Evidently, the newspaper was not overly anxious about Italians being "wrongly" positioned along Chicago's color line. And this was not because the newspaper cared little about color; to the contrary, its impassioned responses to the Santa Rosa newspaper and to the Democratic Party clearly demonstrate the newspaper's keen appreciation for the "wages of whiteness." One can only assume, then, that *L'Italia* felt safe featuring articles about, for instance, Italian women giving birth to "negro" children, because it considered Chicago Italians' color status secure.

L'Italia hardly spoke for the mass of Chicago's Italians, however. The most widely read Italian-language newspaper in Chicago, it was still controlled by one man and most likely represented the views of only a small minority of better-educated, middle-class Italians. So what were the thoughts and actions of everyday Italians on issues of color? It should, first, be understood that these sorts of issues may not have been completely foreign to some Italian immigrants. Africa, for instance, was not a mysterious "dark continent" to all *meridionali*. Around the turn of the century, it was the destination of thousands of Italian male migrants and the site of several Italian imperialist adventures, which virtually all Italian newspapers covered closely and which many popular novels reproduced in fictional form. Some male *meridionali*, moreover, volunteered or were enlisted to fight in these African wars, and no doubt returned to their southern towns with stories to tell about their experiences. Much of southern Italy, furthermore, is closer to Africa than to Rome let alone Florence or Milan, and thus has always had some contact with this part of the world. In this way, it should be no surprise that many social scientists at the time considered *meridionali* part African—in many cases they were (and are). Finally, some Italians may have learned first about "colored" people from migrants returning from sojourns in North and South America.[72]

If some Italians encountered or heard about "colored" people prior to emigration, however, such encounters had to have been rare indeed. The bulk of Italian immigrants at this time came from isolated hill towns, had little formal education, could not read, and often knew little about surrounding villages, let alone other people on other continents. Moreover, Italians would have known very little about the colorized social system in America that produced and was reflected by the dispossession of land from and mass slaughter of "reds," the enslavement, segregation, and disenfranchisement of "blacks," and the exclusion of and denial of citizenship to "yellows." Such a social system had to have been very new to most Italian immigrants.[73]

The migration and settlement process offered Italians at every stage numerous lessons about this system. Many Italian immigrants traveled far and wide before ultimately settling in Chicago, and in some of these places, they lived and worked closely with "colored" groups and thus witnessed the workings of the color line intimately. As the Dillingham commission reported on a steel mill and its motley group of workers in Birmingham, Alabama: "Two distinct racial lines are drawn in association of a social nature. One of these is the color line between whites of all races and negroes, and the other is the line drawn between native whites and northern European races on the one hand and southern European races on the other. These are well defined and practically universal." Many of the Sicilians, who eventually settled on the Near North Side of Chicago, first worked alongside African Americans on sugar cane plantations in Louisiana, where they would have become well acquainted with Jim Crow ideas and practices.[74]

Opportunities to learn color lessons continued in Chicago, even though African Americans and "other races" (i.e., Asians) were never more than a miniscule percentage of Chicago's population prior to World War I (2 percent and 0.1 percent, respectively). The color line was plenty visible to Italians in the geography of their neighborhoods; in the kinds of people accepted—and not accepted—into the local school, settlement house, bar, restaurant, hotel, church, theater, workplace, and union; in the many stories of African-American lynchings in their Italian-language newspapers; in the massive riots against African Americans that took place not far from Chicago in Springfield in 1908 and East St. Louis in 1917; and in the minstrel shows held at community centers like Gads Hill near Armour Square.

How quickly did immigrants learn these lessons, claim whiteness, and/or denigrate blackness, yellowness, and so forth? A wide variety of scholars have suggested very quickly indeed. Gunnar Myrdal argued in his classic, *An American Dilemma*, that for most European immigrants the "development of prejudice against the Negroes is usually one of their first lessons in Americanization." And numerous African-American commentators have heartily agreed. While Ralph Ellison noted that "one of the first epithets that many European immigrants learned when they got off the boat was the term 'nigger,'" Du Bois argued similarly that the United States "trains her immigrants to this despising of 'niggers' from the day of their landing, and they carry and send the news back to the submerged classes in the fatherland." Sociologists Horace Cayton and St. Clair Drake noted that "the foreign-born . . . were not slow to adopt the prevailing stereotypes about the Negroes. 'Foreigners learn how to cuss, count and say "nigger" as soon as they get here.'"[75]

Some evidence on Chicago Italians supports these arguments. In the early years, for instance, Italian–African-American conflict was not unheard of. In the winter of 1905, a ferocious fight erupted in two stages between scores of Italians and African Americans in the Armour Square area. The first stage ended only after numerous knifings and shootings, and after the police intervened and made thirty arrests. The following day fighting broke out again when the young wife of an Italian shot in the previous day's fracas attempted to avenge her husband's injury by charging a group of African Americans with a pick. *L'Italia* reported that this attack caused the neighborhood once again to resemble "un vero campo di battaglia" (a true battlefield). Similarly, five years later, *L'Italia* reported "sanguinose risse" (bloody brawls) between African Americans and Italians on Chicago's North and Near South Sides.[76]

Colorful tales of brawls and ice picks hardly tell the entire story, however. For one thing, color conflict is not the same as color consciousness. In none of these stories did Italians express a white consciousness of any kind, and *L'Italia* rarely attributed "odio di razza" (race hatred) to battle causes.[77] Throughout these years, furthermore, Italians fought most often with themselves or with other "white" groups, as the Italian- and English-language press documented weekly.[78] Finally, some conflict between Italians and African Americans seems to have resulted from close contact and fraternization, not a heightened color consciousness or hatred. In 1901, for instance, an Italian saloonkeeper and an African-American patron engaged in a vicious altercation only after drinking and socializing together for hours.[79]

There were also many instances of amicable relations between Italians and "colored" groups in Chicago. Italians lived with the small number of

Chinese and African Americans in Chicago and open conflict, the few stories cited above notwithstanding, was rare. It should be stressed as well that living in the same building—as Italians and their cosmopolitan neighbors did—often meant the most intimate of contact. As one appalled housing reformer noted in 1915 about a typical Polk Depot tenement, "the toilet was situated in the hall and used by both the Chinese men and the Italian children."[80] Intimate contact naturally led on occasion to intimate relations. For example, *L'Italia* reported casually of marriages or sexual liaisons between Italians and African Americans at times. And, of course, living in close proximity to one another brought about close contact of a purely social nature, as neighbors frequented the same bars, shops, and passed each other on the street. *L'Italia* noted in 1912, for instance, that an Italian band had played at a Chinese wedding and the newspaper featured regular advertisements around this same time of a Chinese doctor—"Signor Chan"—who presumably had Italian patients.[81]

In addition, some Italians seemed to associate with different people of "color" in various ways. At a time when Italian lynching was not uncommon, *L'Italia* carried stories almost weekly about brutal killings of African Americans in the South and elsewhere, in which the newspaper often condemned the United States for its rank hypocrisy and bankrupt "Civilita' Americana" (American Civilization). The newspaper would similarly associate itself with Asians on occasion. In one editorial from 1906 on the "Japanese Question," *L'Italia* scolded Californians for their race prejudice against the Japanese and admonished the United States to treat all immigrants equally, regardless of their background. And some individual Italians, not just their newspapers, drew similar connections with "colored" groups. One man, for instance, ridiculed Professor Dorsey for his fear of "the size of our race, seeing in the Italian immigration the future physical degeneration of the American people. . . . After the lesson given by the little Japanese to the gigantic Russians, to state that bulk is the standard of superior manhood, would be simply ridiculous. Where is your Anglo-Saxon physical superiority when the negro subdues your champion pugilists, and the Indians are winning your marathons?"[82]

In the end, I do not wish to romanticize these early years as some golden era of color relations. Not enough evidence exists to make such an argument. Moreover, Italians, like many immigrants in their early years of settlement, were largely an insular group, preferring to be around people as similar to themselves as possible, especially family members and *paesani*. Nonetheless, it appears that many Italians treated African Americans and the Chinese no differently than anyone else. And in a country where color lines were so ruthlessly and meticulously maintained—even in early twentieth-century Chicago where people of "color" remained few and far between—this sort of indiscriminate treatment *is* notable.

Such behavior suggests that many everyday Italians may not have nec-

Italian and African-American men in a bar at Twenty-ninth Street and Federal near the Armour Square neighborhood and in the Black Belt, n.d. Italian-American Collection, Department of Special Collections, The Richard J. Daley University Library, University of Illinois at Chicago.

casarily seen themselves as white. To be sure, scant evidence makes any argument about color self-identification speculative at best. Still, that many newcomers seem to have treated "colored" and "white" groups similarly suggests that many Italians may not have viewed their social world as such. Instead of seeing one color line dividing all humanity, Italians may have seen any number of alternative lines based, depending on the individual and the situation, on *paesi*, *regioni*, nationality, gender, class, race (e.g., Bohemian, Chinese, Irish), and so forth. Such a conclusion may seem hard to believe today, but in the early twentieth century, it most certainly was not. Jane Addams, for instance, noted on several occasions how neighborhood Italians in these early years "held no particular animosity toward Negroes for those in the neighborhood were mostly from South Italy and accustomed to the dark-skinned races." At another time, she praised the local "Mediterranean immigrants" for being "less conscious than the Anglo-Saxon of color distinctions, perhaps because of their traditional familiarity with Carthage and Egypt."[83]

Taken together, Italians were hardly a unified group when it came to race and color. While some Italians and their various institutions insisted on drawing North-South and regional distinctions, others worked tirelessly to construct a less divided national/racial consciousness. The majority of Italian immigrants at this time ignored these debates entirely and clung instead to family and town loyalties. For these people, up until World War I and often beyond, the Italian race/nation remained a remote abstraction at best. Regarding color, Chicago's main Italian-language newspaper and presumably a portion of its educated readership assumed Italians to be white, though they never flaunted the identity much. By the end of the Great War, the mass of Italian immigrants still had not yet fully understood the workings and importance of the color line. There were certainly instances of learning but probably more signs of ignorance.

2

RIOT AND RELATIONS

In the fall of 1929, the *Chicago Evening Post* wrote a glowing, full-page tribute to the city's Italian population. It praised "Our Modern Romans" for being the "sons of the men who founded the empire of Caesar . . . [and who] carried the conquering eagles over all Gaul, and across the sea to Ultima Thule." The newspaper was equally impressed with Italians' more recent success in Chicago—their speedy assimilation, strong work ethic, and impressive social mobility. Offered as proof positive of the first of these virtues was the following statement: "Today it does not matter whether his [an Italian's] neighbors are Irish, Germans or Swedes. It is very seldom that he inquires who are the owners of adjacent property, so long as they belong to the Caucasian race."[1]

This chapter examines neighborhood relations in Chicago between the Color Riot of 1919 and the mid-1930s, a period when the first wave of African-American and Mexican migration (i.e., non-"Caucasians") arrived during and after World War I, and when, because of restriction laws, Italian immigration effectively ended and more stable Chicago communities emerged. On the one hand, the *Evening Post*'s observation was accurate. This time period witnessed—some local variations notwithstanding—the rising importance of color lines, not European racial ones, in neighborhood relations. On the other hand, within this context Italians continued to avoid using terms like "Caucasian" and "white" in defining themselves and their interests publicly. Instead, *Italianita'* was becoming, in neighborhood relations and in other contexts, an increasingly salient social identity.

The Color Riot of 1919

Throughout the summer of 1919, Chicago had been simmering with color tensions. Mass migration from the South had doubled Chicago's African-

American population between 1916 and 1919, touching off bitter color conflict and competition in local politics, the South Side housing market where the Black Belt expanded, and the workplace, particularly the meatpacking industry, where a large number of migrants first found jobs.[2] On July 27, Eugene Williams, an African-American teenager, drowned after being stoned by "white" bathers at the Twenty-ninth Street beach for swimming across an imaginary color line in the water. When a "white" police officer on the scene refused to arrest the people responsible for the young Williams's death, arguments ensued, tempers flared, and rumors spread quickly about the stoning and the officer's negligence. Within hours, a full-scale riot was well underway, which, over the course of five days, swept uncontrolled throughout Chicago's South Side, the Loop area, and parts of the Near West and Near North Sides. In the end, the riot's casualty list was staggering: "Thirty-eight persons killed, 537 injured, and about 1,000 rendered homeless and destitute."[3] The vast majority of these victims were African Americans.

These facts are familiar. Much less familiar is what Italians' role in and response to the riot was. If, by World War I, many Chicago Italians remained relatively oblivious to the hardening color line in Chicago, did this orientation withstand the enormity and fury of the riot? In most cases it did—but there were exceptions to the rule.

L'Italia covered the riot quite similarly to the way it had discussed lynchings of African Americans: it clearly sympathized with African Americans, expressing hope that a reconstruction of the riot-torn Black Belt would begin soon and that African-American victims would quickly receive the milk and bread they needed to survive. The paper related a tragic story, for instance, about "una poveretta"—African American Mrs. L. Kirkpatrick—who lay on her deathbed ill from malnutrition. *L'Italia* also scolded Americans for their hypocrisy when it came to issues of race and color. In response to one congressman's denunciation of an Italian murder of an innocent African American during the riot, the newspaper ridiculed those critics who readily exaggerated Italians' shortcomings, while ignoring the common lynchings of African Americans in the South. Chicago's other popular Italian-language newspaper, *La Tribuna Italiana Transatlantica*, also criticized America for its arrogant insistence on the assimilation of its immigrants while "barbaric" race riots raged, but it showed less sympathy for African Americans. It suggested that by invading "white" neighborhoods, depreciating property values, and acting insolently, African Americans were in part responsible for the outbreak of violence.[4]

As for actions on the street, many South Side Italians in the Armour Square area lived along Wentworth Avenue, the key east-west dividing line between "whites" and "Negroes." It therefore stood at the center of a great deal of riot violence, in which some Italians certainly took part. On July 31, for instance, Sam Cardinelli of 2330 S. LaSalle Street was arrested for having shot at an African-American passerby, while two days before Giustino

Mustiore was shot in a brawl between "whites" and "Negroes" that erupted on the corner of Wentworth and Thirty-first Street. A middle-aged Italian peddler, Casimiro Lazzeroni, was stabbed to death by four African-American boys on July 28 near Thirty-sixth and South State Streets.[5]

Meanwhile, on the Near West Side, a group of Italians perpetrated what the Chicago Commission on Race Relations (the group of prominent Chicago citizens—"white" and "Negro"—appointed by Illinois Governor Frank Lowden to investigate the riot) called "the most atrocious murder" of the entire riot.[6] On the evening of July 29 near the corner of Taylor and Loomis Streets, only several blocks from Hull-House, Italians of the neighborhood were enraged by a rumor that a young Italian girl had been shot and killed earlier that day by an African-American employee of a local mattress factory. Just at this moment an innocent African American, Joseph Lovings, rode his bicycle through the neighborhood on his way home from work, and a mob of Italians, having mistaken him for the murderer, chased him through back alleys and streets. When they finally found Lovings hiding in a local basement, they dragged him out into the street, beat and stabbed him repeatedly, and then riddled his body with bullets. The murder—initially thought to have been a lynching and a burning—was, in the words of the coroner's jury, an "atrocious, savage crime" just the same.[7]

In the Sicilian section of the Near North Side, tensions ran high as well. With rumors circulating that African Americans from the South Side were coming to "shoot up" their neighborhood, some Italians armed themselves and shot and threw stones from their roof-tops at random African Americans below. Meanwhile select Italian children, caught up in the riot excitement, "pushed through windows and doors pictures of skulls and coffins inked in red." Over sixty years later, one Italian-American woman still vividly recalled the mayhem of the moment: My friends and I "were at the Sidney Theatre on Sedgewick . . . sitting so quiet watching the silent movie and here my brother and sister-in-law came in and they [had] guns in their hands . . . and they said come on girls come on let's get out. They get [sic] out of the car and there were all colored people, with trucks full of colored people and people were looking out the windows in the streets. There were squad cars and the patrol wagon." Another Italian from the neighborhood, Joseph Loguidice, remembered a similarly tense situation: "I recall vaguely a lot of policemen comin' in trucks. . . . And I remember . . . a man running down the middle of a street and hollering. . . . I'm White, I'm White. . . . But he was so dirty that he thought people would mistake him for being colored and shoot him down."[8]

These episodes notwithstanding, the vast majority of Italians do not appear to have taken part in the Color Riot of 1919. On the South Side, the area west of the Black Belt between Twenty-second and Sixty-third Streets has long been considered the heart of anti-African-American violence prior to, during, and long after the riot. Often described as Irish, Polish, or both, it was actually home to more Italians than to any other group.[9] Given this fact, it is certainly noteworthy that, judging by injury and death lists, Italians were only a small fraction of the rioters. Two of the thirty-eight riot deaths were of Italians (one was of an innocent peddler noted above; the other was of a man involved with a mob in stoning the home of an African-American woman in the south Loop area); and of the 277 people listed among the officially injured in the first three days of rioting, there were only three men with Italian surnames.[10] On the West and Near Northwest Sides, where many Italians and some African Americans (among others) shared neighborhoods, rioting was sporadic and minor compared to that on the South Side, the brutal Lovings murder notwithstanding. For instance, speaking of Italians' Grand Avenue community, which bordered on a sizable African-American neighborhood around Lake Street between the Near West and Near Northwest Sides, Lea Taylor of Chicago Commons later recalled that the riot "did not affect our community too much." Finally, on the Near North Side in "Little Sicily," the Chicago Commission on Race Relations noted that the results of local rioting were "not serious" and that "immediately after the fracas the Negroes and Italians were again on good terms."[11]

Italians' relative lack of involvement makes eminent sense. Some of the key sources of color tension in preriot Chicago—competition over housing, jobs, and political patronage—affected Italians much differently than they did other groups like the Irish and native-born "white" Americans. As for politics, most Chicago Italians did not follow aldermanic and mayoral campaigns too closely, as nearly two-thirds of them were unnaturalized in 1920.[12] As for labor issues, most color conflict in this area occurred in the meat-packing industry, where large numbers of African-American migrants first found jobs in Chicago, and where different strikes before (and after) the riot had deeply divided many unionized "whites" and nonunionized African Americans. Significantly, however, few Italians worked in the stockyards and, therefore, few knew about these issues.[13] Regarding housing, Italian neighborhoods around Armour Square and the Near South Side bordered the Black Belt on its north and west sides, but every other major Italian colony was well removed from the district and thus removed too from the bloody, color housing conflicts of the late 1910s in places like Hyde Park, Woodlawn, and Kenwood.[14]

Equally important was that Italians still had much to learn about the color line. Examining the backgrounds of those men who died during the riot, historian Dominic Pacyga has recently argued that Polish Americans largely abstained from participating in the riot, believing that it was a battle between "whites" and "Negroes," in which they had no direct stake. And no doubt a large number of Italians—not yet fully aware of Chicago's colorized social system—felt similarly. Interestingly, L'Italia covered the riot between "bianchi" and "neri," but devoted just as much time to defending Italians against a senator's accusation that they were in part responsible for the violence. Denying that evidence existed to implicate Italians in the murder of Joseph Lovings, the newspaper scolded people like Senator MacKellar of Tennessee for trying to "incite more race hatred against the Italians" by blaming them for the massacres of African Americans. Indeed, for many Italians, like the writers and publisher of *L'Italia* in this case, "race hatred" against Italians—not "colored" groups—remained their primary concern.[15]

But many Italians would become more aware and concerned about these groups in time and the Color Riot, in several important ways, no doubt powerfully facilitated this process. First, the riot divided the entire city unmistakably between "whites" and "Negroes," and most people at the time seem to have understood it in these terms. Newspapers—both foreign- and English-language—spoke of the riot in these terms and the Riot Commission perpetuated these "white"/"Negro" understandings several years later in its 672-page report. Everyday people engaged in the riot on the street in this manner as well. When Joseph Schoff, "white," came across a certain Jose Blanco in the Back o' the Yards neighborhood on July 30, Schoff did not know how to treat Blanco until the latter answered the former's question "Are you a Negro?" Indeed, much of the riot's activity revolved around this very question and of course its corollary: "Are you white?"[16] Mr. Loguidice's memories from the Near North Side surely confirm this point. Second, the riot taught Italians more than simply that the color line existed; it just as surely taught them their "proper" position along it. Indeed, no one seemed to question Harold Brignardello's rightful membership in the "white" mob that stoned an African American's home or that the Lovings' murder on the Near West Side was just another example of "white" rage against "Negroes." In all accounts of the riot at the time and since in newspapers, books, and so on, Italians—whether as perpetrators or victims of color violence—were (and are) always categorized as white. Finally, the riot taught Italians that in the face of color conflict, even some of the deepest racial divisions among whites faded fast. For some of the few Italians who partook in the riot, and for others who followed the events closely in their newspapers or from their window sills, the unity of purpose of an otherwise polyglot group of Europeans must have seemed remarkable. Indeed, when it came to attacking African Americans, former enemies—Poles, Irish, Swedes, Jews, Italians, and others—quickly found common cause.

Race and Color Neighborhood
Relations in the Postriot Era

The learning of some of these riot lessons—particularly the rising significance of color and declining significance of European race—represents the key story of Italians' neighborhood relations in Chicago's postriot era. Curiously, however, these developments did not seem to have an immediate effect on Italians' still-underdeveloped color consciousness. These points are especially clear at the local level in numerous Italian neighborhoods throughout the Chicago area.

"Little Sicily"

Beginning with "Little Sicily" on the Near North Side, this area witnessed fierce turf struggles between Swedes and Irish, on the one hand, and Sicilians, on the other, in the first decade or so of the twentieth century. By World War I, however, these tensions had subsided some, as the immigration of Sicilians slowed, and "old" immigrants left the neighborhood, learned to grudgingly tolerate the "dark people," or became their friends and, in some cases, their family members through intermarriage.[17] At this moment, the neighborhood received a new crop of migrants, as some four thousand African Americans moved to the area between the end of World War I and the middle of the 1920s. In 1912, a house-to-house canvas of 1,393 neighborhood families showed the area to be 53 percent Italian and 0.4 percent African American. A similar canvas conducted twelve years later revealed that Italians' proportion of the population had not changed while that of African Americans had risen to almost 22 percent. In the late 1920s, even more African Americans arrived in the neighborhood, as they replaced Italians fast fleeing the intensification of organized crime violence.[18]

Initially, it appears that many Italians, no doubt remembering the struggles they had endured with the "old" immigrants of the neighborhood, showed little animosity toward their new African-American neighbors and in some cases became quite friendly with them. In 1922, the Riot Commission noted that "friendly relations exist between the Sicilians, who predominate [on the Near North Side] and their Negro neighbors. Some Negroes live harmoniously in the same tenements with Sicilians. Their children play together, and some of the Negro children have learned Sicilian phrases so that they are able to deal with the Sicilian shopkeepers." Italian residents had similar recollections in oral interviews many years later. Paul Penio grew up in the neighborhood and recalled a relationship he had with an African-American childhood friend: "Color of skin didn't mean nothing to us guys. We would just play together. I used to go to his house, he used to go to my house, and we got to be pretty good friends." Mr. Penio also recalled another African American from the neighborhood, whom people called "St. Louis" (because "he might have been a saint") and who "would talk Italian . . . almost as good as my mom. . . . He knew all the people in the neighborhood—everybody—I guess they respected him." And these rosy memories are not necessarily incongruous with what some African Americans observed and felt at the time. A private Urban League report on the area noted in 1925 that "Negro families often reported their Italian neighbors as being very friendly, visiting and even rendering assistance in some few cases of sickness and poverty."[19]

During the 1920s, however, relations seemed to worsen over time. In her 1925 master's thesis on the area's housing conditions, sociologist Esther Quaintance observed that "the Italians of the district resent the coming of the negro and frequently appealed to the investigator to 'Chase the niggers out,' and 'Tell 'em to move on, we don't want 'em here.'" Four years later, Harvey Warren Zorbaugh painted a similar picture in his classic sociological study of the neighborhood, *The Gold Coast and the Slum*:

> The Sicilian has not retired before the Negro without a show of resistance. On the school and public playgrounds are re-enacted the scene of a generation ago when the Sicilian was forcing out the Swede. The Negro child is often mistreated and ostracized. There are gang fights on playground and street. The police patrol clangs along the streets of Little Hell in answer to not infrequent riot calls. Sicilian fathers protest to the schools against admitting Negro children. Sicilian landowners band together to keep the Negro from acquiring property.[20]

Indeed, many Italians were not shy about expressing their distaste for their new African-American neighbors. One prominent Italian resident warned a social worker in 1931 that many of his *connazionali* "would like to get out their shotguns and drive the Negroes out. Hardly a day passed that someone does not come in here madder than a boil and complain about the low property values and the negro prostitutes." Another Italian of the neighborhood, speaking around 1930, bemoaned the recent changes in "Little Sicily" this way: "Yes, this was surely a lively neighborhood about six or eight years ago. . . . There weren't any niggers here then. I can remember how scared a nigger would be when he would walk up Orleans Street. He would even tip his hat or some of the fellows would beat hell [*sic*] out of him. . . . But things are altogether different now." Another Italian, speaking of local *paesani* willing to rent to African Americans, asked bewildered and bitter: "What kind of people are these? They live under the same roof as the negroes—and let their children play with them. No respect. They are terrible. . . . No decent Italian family would do a thing like that."[21]

Italians certainly did more than talk. One social worker from the area noted in 1933 that "on certain streets the Italian boys had so damaged the property in which colored people lived that they moved out and will not be permitted to return." The *Chicago Defender* reported several incidents at this time of Italian violence against African Americans that appear to have been motivated by neighborhood animosities. In 1925, four Italians knocked on the door of Eleanor Seymour, an African-American woman living at 656 Elm Street. When the woman answered the door the Italians attacked her, beating, kicking, and stabbing her repeatedly over the heart and in the arm and back. The newspaper concluded the story by adding that "numerous cases of a similar nature have been called to the attention of policemen who have [simply] warned the persons attacked that they should 'move out of the district'." Some Italians sought the removal of African Americans from "their" neighborhood using more organized means. Prominent Italian neighborhood residents, with the help of the local Catholic church, St. Philip Benizi, fraternal orders like the *Unione Siciliana*, and even the Italian consulate, formed the North Side Improvement Association in the late 1920s in an attempt to restrict African Americans from moving to and purchasing property on the Near North Side.[22]

Well aware of this hostility, many African Americans fought back with words and deeds. One resident of the area noted in the 1930s, "over here, there is not much mixing among the grown-ups. Small children play together at times all right. Dagoes call the children 'niggers' once in a while. These Dagoes over here is rotten. They think they is better than you, especially the young women. On Clark in some of the restaurants they are not particular about serving you." Another African American speaking about the neighborhood around the same time agreed: "This place is ruined. Nothing is around here but these old Italians from New Orleans. You will hear one telling his neighbor, 'Don't visit niggers in their houses.' I would send them all back to Italy where they belong. I hate them folks." A local community group observed in 1929:

> The Negroes have been conscious of the growing resentment and seem determined not to be driven out of the district. On several recent occasions, usually following a fight or a minor beating between Italians and Negroes, there have been a great number of negro men "imported" into the neighborhood. For three or four days about a hundred Negro men were around the corner of Elm and Larrabee Streets. Then they vanished for two weeks. Then another group appeared on west Division street and filled the streets for several days again.[23]

These tensions came to a head in the spring of 1935 when a group of Italian property owners, led by prominent neighborhood residents like Father Luigi Giambastiani, pastor of St. Philip Benizi, and backed by a local real estate association, attempted to evict 4,700 African-American tenants from the area. Giambastiani justified the effort by stating: "the Italians resented the invasion of the neighborhood by the colored people, since the neighborhood has always belonged to them. . . . The landlords were protecting their property values as they had a right to do." A month after the eviction drive was first exposed, the *Chicago Defender* reported that the neighborhood was on the "brink of a . . . riot" as many African Americans were furious about the campaign to rob them of their homes and were equally determined to resist it. In the end, no riot appears to have occurred, in large part due to the successful campaign on the part of the Chicago Urban League and other organizations in defeating the eviction drive.[24] Deep tensions, however, remained between African Americans and Italians in the area and conflict would resurface in the 1940s around local public housing issues.

The Near West Side

The Near West Side, with a more complex set of neighborhood groups than "Little Sicily," had its own distinct history. Up until World War I, this area was predominantly Italian, Greek, Jewish, Irish, and Polish, but beginning during the war and continuing well after it, the neighborhood received large numbers of Mexicans and African Americans. Continuing to flock to Chicago from the South throughout the 1920s, African Americans developed a settlement between Roosevelt Road to the north, Sixteenth Street to the south, Laflin Street to the west, and Canal Street to the east. In 1920, African Americans in the area numbered less than 150 people; ten years later, they had become more than half of all area residents and numbered over eleven thousand. Mexican immigrants, recruited to work on railroads, began arriving on the Near West Side in 1916. By the end of the 1920s, this area counted some seven thousand Mexicans, many of whom settled among Italians around the intersection of Taylor and South Morgan Streets and Blue Island Avenue.[25]

Of all neighborhoods in Chicago, it was this one over which Italians enjoyed the greatest control. They had a long history in the neighborhood, a substantial population, and strong Italian political representation from the area at the local, state, and, later, national levels. As a result, they had become by the 1930s, in the words of one social worker, "the big frogs in the near-west Side puddle." Well into the 1930s, however, they continued to face a great deal of antagonism from other European groups. In oral interviews many years later, several Italians recalled Irish families refusing to rent homes to them, Jewish parents prohibiting their kids from playing with them, and regular street battles and fights in school. Having grown up in the area in the 1920s and 1930s, Anthony Sorrentino, an important community activist, later remembered schoolyard taunts like "dago, dago, eats nothing but potatoes." "The feeling was always there," admitted Sorrentino many years later, that Italians were "considered the least desirable of all immigrant groups."[26]

Italians' relations with African Americans and Mexicans were different. Italians shared with the latter some real cultural similarities and relations seemed quite friendly initially. Jane Addams noted that in the early days of Mexican migration to Chicago, Italians received the newcomers "almost as a group of their own countrymen. We had, for instance, a large Latin Club of young men at Hull-House, a membership fairly represented of both nationalities." And some Mexican Americans at the time confirmed this rosy picture. Mrs. Quintero of 759 Bunker Street told an interviewer in the early 1920s that "the Italians are very nice. . . . Whenever they passed by, the Italians would invite [us] to come into their homes and talk with [us]. The boys have trouble with the Polish boys, but the Italian boys always defend them and escort them home. Upstairs lives an Italian family and whenever one of the girls sees one of the Polish boys bullying a Mexican boy, they chase him out." Indeed, as one Mexican-American sociology student noted in 1924, "in the majority of the cases the conflicts are with the Poles—not with the Italians. The Italians readily fraternize with the Mexicans. It is possible that general features—language, folkways, mores, and other similarities—make for better feeling between the Mexicans and the Italians."[27]

But as in Little Sicily, "better feeling" often did not last long. These changes appeared particularly dramatic to Jane Addams, who noted that the deteriorating relations between the two "Latin" groups reached a low point in the mid to late 1920s when "a committee of Italians came to Hull-House with the threat that if we continued to rent Bowen Hall to the Mexicans, the Italians would discontinue to use it for their wedding receptions and other festivities. It was not that they would necessarily meet the Mexicans but that the hall would lose its prestige if it were being used by people of color!" By the late 1920s and early 1930s, relations may never have become irreparably hostile—Italian and Mexican children still went to the local Chicago Boys Club summer camp together, many Italian and Mexican families continued to share the same buildings and churches, and intermarriage occurred on occasion—but tensions and conflict did occur. Speaking of the late 1920s, one Mexican woman from the neighborhood recalled that Italians "were very bad to us and some of the other Mexican families had trouble with them. They were always trying to do something to us. They called us dogs and threw things when we were not looking. They would crowd us off the sidewalks and make insulting remarks at us when we went by." Similarly, one social worker of the area noted in these years that "though the Mexican has penetrated the Italian district, they are not accepted. The hard fact is that there were no Italians to rent the flats. However, no self-respecting Italian would live in a rear flat or rent a front flat to a Mexican."[28]

Italians' thoughts on and treatment of African Americans were slightly different. According to Jane Addams, relations between the two groups soured as early as the Color Riot of 1919, when Joseph Lovings was savagely murdered. The Chicago Commission on Race Relations noted that "in the September following the riot, she [Addams] said the neighborhood was still full of wild stories so stereotyped in character that they appeared to indicate propaganda spread for a purpose." However, according to some sources, Italians and African Americans were able to settle their differences and get along well after the riot. One director of a Near West Side community center told an interviewer in 1930: "the Jew and the Italian seem to be the only people who will live in the same house with the Negroes. I think that is why the Italians are coming into this neighborhood—they follow right on the heels of the Negroes." Similarly, the Riot Commission reported in 1922 that at a local park kids mingled freely and that "animosity between the Negro and white groups was entirely lacking."[29]

Unlike Mexicans who lived among Italians in the heart of the Near West Side's "Little Italy," however, the vast majority of African Americans lived south of the neighborhood's most prominent color boundary, Roosevelt Road, which many Italians knew well and were determined to maintain. In 1925, the *Chicago Defender* reported a vicious attack by a "rowdy bunch of [Italian] hoodlums" on two young African-American women, because one of the Italians "has been very hostile since she moved into the neighborhood and has made several threats." Similarly, a local Italian many years later recalled that Arrigo Park was off-limits to many non-Italians, but particularly to certain groups: "Colored fella[s] . . . weren't allowed to go in the park. And for those [who] tried to come in there . . . they used to fight." By the 1930s, one local social worker noted that "Negroes are driven from the Italian district with out and out terrorism. The fact that the Negroes will soon be the political bosses of the ward and that a Negro family living on an Italian block seriously challenges the Italians' growing sense of social importance makes the Negro the Italians' greatest irritant." As on the Near North Side, these relations continued to be a source of tension as the federal government completed public housing projects on and around Roosevelt Road in the late 1930s.[30]

Armour Square

Italians' Armour Square neighborhood, bordering on both the Black Belt and Chicago's largest Chinatown, had its own unique demography and set of neighborhood relations. Up until the Great Migration, this was where the largest number of Italians and African Americans came regularly into contact, and conflict was rare even up through the Color Riot of 1919, which swept most intensely through this and other nearby neighborhoods. Following this event, some locals emphasized the peaceful nature of their community. As one social worker in the mid-1930s stated, "there is no trouble and the Italians get along very peaceably with all peoples." An Italian agreed, recalling years later that "colored people were around our neighborhood. We never discriminated. I never discriminated against anyone in my whole life. Why? Because . . . we had dark complected Italians amongst our midst." An Italian woman similarly recalled that Italians and African Americans were "always very close. I think our problems today in Chicago is that we don't have the mixture in the neighborhood."[31]

But, of course, "mixture" also led to conflict. One Chicago Park district official remembered that around Armour Square "the Italian kids used to love to catch a Negro boy in their territory and beat his head. Those little guys were tough and they didn't like outsiders, especially Negroes." Some newspaper stories confirm this observation. In 1924, the *Chicago Defender* reported that a gang of three Italian boys attacked Forrest Harris, a 17-

year-old African American, with sticks and bricks around Thirty-seventh Street and Wells, just west of the Black Belt and in the heart of the local Italian neighborhood. The same year, a left-wing Italian-language paper featured a short story on the killing of Antonio Lascola, who had been involved in a brawl between "neri e bianchi" at a schoolyard around Forty-seventh Street and Wentworth.[32] Indeed, that Wentworth Avenue—the key neighborhood color boundary—remained throughout this time period such a bulwark against African-American expansion (without the aid of restrictive covenants), suggests not only that this area had undesirable real estate that even many destitute and desperate African Americans did not want, but it also suggests that east of Wentworth European groups—Italians among them—fiercely defended this boundary.

Italians' relations with the Chinese seemed less contentious than those with African Americans. While Chinatown extended several blocks south of Twenty-second Street, an area in which few Italians lived, large numbers of both Italians and Chinese shared the area between Twenty-second and Twenty-sixth Streets, and between the south branch of the Chicago River and Federal Street. This area, census tract 524, had in the early 1930s some two thousand Italians and seven hundred Chinese.[33] Within this area, some members of the two groups came to know each other—and their personal business—quite well. One Chinese man of the area complained in the early 1930s that his Italian neighbors often "have too much gossip" about him. More positively, around the same time a sociology student, analyzing a part-Chinese "unadjusted girl" of the neighborhood, wrote the following field notes: "She has some Italian children as her chums. . . . Last year I saw her play tennis in Hardin Square with an Italian girl. . . . I saw Helen went with a White boy, probably Italian, walking down in Archer Avenue. Looked very intimate to each other. I saw two boys with her some other time in the Italian section of Wentworth Ave."[34] Evidence from oral histories suggests that Italians held a range of opinions on their Chinese neighbors. While one recalled having positive impressions of Chinese while growing up—that their neighborhood was safe and that they were smart people—other Italians recalled making fun of Chinese as kids (one woman noted that she and her friends would taunt their Chinese neighbors by singing "ching ching chinaman . . . wash my shirt for a penny") and being fearful of them (another woman recalled hearing stories as a child that the Chinese would cut up little kids and put them in their chop-suey).[35] Nonetheless, I have found no evidence of serious conflict between Italians and Chinese.

Local race relations were often just as complex as color relations. One Italian-American woman recalled in an oral interview many years later that "from listening to those people who grew up on the West Side, Taylor Street," things were quite a bit different around Armour Square. The Italians on the West Side "said they were ostracized in school by other ethnic groups. They were looked down upon. They were ashamed. We never had that here. We always felt we were better than the other ethnic groups, not worse." And, in some ways, this recollection seems correct. As another local Italian noted some years later, "The Croatians . . . didn't have as much culture. I don't know. I shouldn't say that. . . . They are just never . . . people I became friendly with. You know, they were just on the other side of the tracks." Still, other Italians remembered mixing rather freely with other European immigrants like the Croatians and much intermarrying. Also, Italians of the neighborhood may not have been entirely spared the discrimination and prejudice that their West Side *connazionali* faced. A number of Italians later recalled being denigrated as "dumb dagoes" on the street and in school. At this time, one social worker, from the heavily Irish, Polish, and German Bridgeport section just to the west of Armour Square, noted: "Now the 'Dagoes' are east of Halsted. The term includes Italians, Mexicans, Gypsies, mulattos. A few Italian families and two or three American Indian families have moved into the area and have been accepted, but the community is determined to prevent any important population change."[36]

The Near Northwest Side

The Italian community on the Near Northwest Side—a thin, though populous, sliver between Chicago Avenue to the north and Austin (later Hubbard) and Grand to the south—had, like other areas, its own particular neighborhood relations story. While many Italians first settled closer to the north branch of the Chicago River, throughout the 1920s and 1930s they migrated west and north along Grand Avenue toward Austin, Humboldt Park, and Belmont Cragin. Italians' sliver lay between a massive Polish settlement to the north, which leaked south of Chicago Avenue and blended with the Italian communities there, and an established African-American enclave just south of Grand Avenue. Of course, there were many other people in this neighborhood, but the Poles to the north and the African Americans to the south were, in addition to Italians, the most populous groups.[37]

African Americans seemed less a part of Italians' day-to-day lives than were Poles. As was the case around Armour Square and on the Near West Side, neighborhood boundaries seem to have been a lot less permeable when it came to African Americans. While many Poles lived among Italians in this area, the vast majority of African Americans did not. Significantly, when an Italian-American woman was asked many years later about boundaries in her neighborhood, she could not recall any for European groups, but knew that "south of Grand there were some Blacks." Boundaries did not necessarily mean tense relations, however. One Italian resident of the area later noted that while African Americans and Italians did not interact much, there were rarely any problems. "I remember going to work and walking through those [African-American] neighborhoods years ago. And . . . very nice. Nobody bothered us. . . . They minded their own business and we minded ours. And they respected us and we respected them." In the mid-1930s, the Chicago Commons began accepting larger numbers of African Americans into their summer camp, which previously had been overwhelmingly Italian. And while there were some concerns about how children would get along, Lea Taylor later noted that "the [African-American] children were accepted immediately. . . . The fact that they were living together in cabins was apparently accepted without difficulty by the children." Some people were so impressed with this peaceful intermingling that the Chicago Commons, with the help of the B'nai B'rith, made a film of the camp, which was "used often in the city at the beginning of the inter-racial problem when large numbers of Negroes moved from the South into Chicago [during World War II]." In the end, Italians of the neighborhood were not completely free of some of the color prejudice and discrimination they exhibited in other neighborhoods. In 1934, for instance, one social worker at the local Erie Neighborhood House remarked: "The Italians especially have a tendency toward looking down upon everyone, especially the negro, because they think Italians are the best." Still, relations between Italians and African Americans were relatively peaceful in these years.[38]

Italians and Poles seem to have interacted more frequently on the Near Northwest Side and their relations were more contentious. Few between the two groups seem to have had much love or respect for one another. One Italian man from the area stated that "oh, I like the neighborhood, but some of these 'Polacks' around here are so darn stupid—yeah, they're vulgar too." In the late 1920s, one local Polish mother admitted to an interviewer that "some of de Italianos dey good, and some dey bad. I scart of dem, dey sticka wit de knife. My Joey and my John dey no come here, dey afraid of dey Italianos. . . . De Italiano boys dey fight my Joey and John, and broke dere clothes. I no lika de Italianos, dey bad."[39]

Harboring these ill feelings, many Poles and Italians—particularly teenagers it seems—battled frequently with one another throughout much of the 1920s and 1930s. In the late 1930s, one social worker reported the following incident in the area:

> I was supervising a dance at the park. The crowd was Polish. Later that evening three nice-looking Italian fellows came in. I heard the undertone of dissention [sic] and went over and told the young men it would be best for them to leave. They refused saying they would behave. They did behave but soon I noticed a crowd in one corner and heard a bang, biff, boom. Switching on all the lights I dashed over and found the three Italian boys on the floor. I stopped the fight but the point is these Polish boys didn't want the Italians here.

Italians engaged in their share of aggression as well. At the Chicago Commons, where they had for years numerically dominated, they were particularly territorial. One Polish boy in the late 1920s stated that "I went down to the Commons wid all dem Dagoes and dey bounced me, called me Pollack and told me to get the hell out of dere. Dere tough over dere, but just wait until they come over here on our street and den see who'se tough." One Italian boy confirmed this story when he stated that "the Pollacks" "always come to gym but dey don't stay long. Every year dey try to come to our gym class, but we always meet dem outside and kick de hell out of dem." Similarly, another Commons worker in 1929 observed that the Polish Busy Bees Club "began operations with a group of Italian girls, but after a few weeks during which the Poles had sat on one side of the room and the Italians had sat on the other, and a large part of the conversation . . . had consisted of 'Dirty Polocks!' from Italians to Poles, and equally uncomplimentary remarks from Poles to Italians, the situation had become impossible. The two groups were separated."[40]

All of this conflict notwithstanding, Italian-Polish relations did seem to improve with time. As one Chicago Commons worker noted in 1937, "as is usually the case, the Italians express great antagonism towards the other nationality groups, particularly the Polish and Greek, that is, when speaking of them generally, but many have particular friends from both of these groups. Almost all club groups have one or two members of another nationality in these intimate groupings. Many mixed marriages are taking place."[41]

Other Neighborhoods

Some of the most populous Italian communities in the 1920s and 1930s, the Near North, West, and Northwest Sides and the Armour Square area, reveal a great deal about neighborhood relations, but other areas had their stories as well. Battles between Italians and other European groups, for instance, took place all over Chicago. In the Calumet Park district on Chicago's Far South Side, one observer noted around the late 1920s that "the Slavs are the only ones who fraternize with the Italians. The Swedes regard the 'Wops' as they call them, as sneaky and vicious, and they are continually fighting with one another." In nearby South Deering, a sociology student observed in 1929 that "north of 106th Street is occupied by the last immigrants, at the present time Mexicans and a few Italians. . . . The latest immigrants are looked down upon and thought to be spoiling the neighborhood." Further south in Chicago Heights, numerous oral interviews reveal a good deal of hostility against Italians in the 1920s and 1930s. One longtime resident, Nick Zaranti, recalled that "we were second class citizens without a doubt . . . you couldn't even go downtown, 'cause they just wouldn't allow you, think you would be stealing." In Melrose Park, one Italian resident, Mildred Bonevolenta, recalled that Nineteenth and Twentieth Streets were the boundaries between Italians and Germans that none of the former dared cross because Germans "didn't like so much the dagos." Meanwhile, in other places like Burnside, Austin, Twenty-fourth Street and Oakley, and Roseland, Italians struggled with other groups like Jews, Poles, and the Irish.[42]

Significantly, many of these conflicts were said to have improved over time. In Chicago Heights, long-time resident Nick Tieri recalled school as being a struggle initially: "It was a bad situation for awhile. . . . I was called all kinds of names. . . . You're a dago, guinea, wop and everything. But after I went to school here for a while, we [the Italians] began to get along with the boys and [we had] . . . no problem." Around Twenty-fourth and Oakley, immigrant Sylvio Petri had almost an identical experience: schoolmates initially called him "Dago" and other kinds of epithets, but over time these same kids became his best friends.[43]

Italians also encountered Mexicans and African Americans in several of these smaller neighborhoods. Though scarce, evidence suggests that relations with African Americans were quite peaceful in certain locations. One Italian, for instance, recalled growing up, living near, and going to school with African Americans in Melrose Park in the 1930s and "we thought nothing of it." Perhaps most representative of relations in these years (in areas removed from significant numbers of African Americans) was the memory of Nick Zaranti. He recalled that in the 1930s, while Italians and African Americans generally got along well together, "after you went home and ate supper, we didn't socialize. We went out on a date or to a show or something, we didn't go with the blacks. We didn't mix with them. During the day [we did] and then they went their way and we went ours."[44]

As for Mexicans, there is little evidence of their interactions with Italians outside of the Near West Side, despite the fact that they shared certain neighborhoods on the Far South Side of Chicago in places like South Deering and South Chicago. From the scant evidence available, however, relations may have been relatively congenial. In 1930, a Spanish-language newspaper, *Mexico*, mourned the passing of one Victor Lapiano, who "was a well-liked and highly esteemed member of our [South Chicago] colony. The deceased was one of the founders of the most worthy *Sociedad Mutual-ista Obreros Lebres Mexicanos de South Chicago* in which he distinguished himself by his untiring efforts. . . . We cannot do more than express our grief for the loss of this fellowman who was Italian by birth." In addition, in his master's thesis on "Delinquency among Mexican Boys in South Chicago," Edward Baur noted that while Mexicans seemed to group Italians with other Europeans using the indiscriminate label—"Los Pollacos"—there were still instances of Mexican-Italian intermarriages and of gangs that included Mexicans and Italians (among other groups) in the area.[45]

Patterns, Explanations, Meanings

Some local variation notwithstanding, a general pattern of race and color neighborhood relations does emerge. Regarding the latter, where large numbers of people of "color" and Italians shared neighborhoods without a prominent boundary, relations, often quite friendly initially, deteriorated over time. Therefore, in boundaryless Little Sicily, where sizable numbers of Italians and African Americans lived together, relations eventually became most hostile and tense. Whereas in places like Armour Square and the Near Northwest Side, where boundaries were best defined, respected, and protected, relations remained less contentious longer.[46]

Italians did not treat all "colored" groups equally, however. Chinese, for instance, were always something of an anomalous group—heavily male, insular, largely self-sufficient, without citizenship rights, and thus without formal political power of any kind, and unable to grow significantly because of exclusionary immigration laws. For these reasons, the Chinese community in Armour Square never occupied a very prominent or visible position in Chicago's color structure or seemed much of a concern to Italians. While the two groups shared a neighborhood, neither conflict nor much close interaction seems to have occurred. Italians, at least in certain areas, had more everyday contact with Mexicans, as they shared a great deal of the Near West Side neighborhood with one another. Mexicans, like the Chinese, were also a far less visible part of Chicago's largely "black"-"white" color structure. This fact helps to explain why, by the mid-1930s, Italians' concerns about "blacks" always far outweighed those about "browns."

Indeed, these concerns began increasing in the 1920s and early 1930s. Italian–African-American relations, to be sure, never became universally hostile. Having written a dissertation on Chicago's various "cultural groups" and their patterns of neighborhood relations and succession during the 1920s, Paul Cressey concluded that African Americans "are usually found in close associations with Jewish or Italian communities. These two groups are, on the whole, the most recent immigrant groups in the city and they do not seem to have acquired the marked prejudice against the Negroes which characterizes many of the older immigrant and American groups in the city."[47] Still, if in the early years of migration and settlement Italians treated all groups more or less the same with little regard to color, these days faded fast in the 1920s and 1930s, when some Italians actively and openly resisted the movement of African Americans into their neighborhoods on the Near North Side, the Near West Side, and in Armour Square.

As for European groups, these years hardly brought about a universal rapprochement. Fierce battles continued throughout Chicago between Italians and Poles, Jews, Swedes, and the Irish. Still, even the worst conflicts never resulted in eviction drives or in the formation of prorestriction neighborhood associations as on the Near North Side. Indeed, Italians' neighborhood boundaries were always much more fluid when it came to European groups. In their neighborhoods, then, as Italians grew more concerned about color boundaries—particularly those restricting "Negroes"—they became less concerned about European racial ones.

Improving race relations reflect, in part, the fact that, in the 1920s and 1930s, European immigrants and their children were coming to share an increasing number of common experiences, many of which this book will discuss—finding and working a job, buying a home, joining a union, going to the movies, eating at a local restaurant, and especially living and socializing in a neighborhood. As we saw with the Color Riot, European groups exhibited remarkable unity when it came to opposing "colored" groups (mainly African Americans), and this would continue throughout the postriot years. Even former enemies like the Sicilians and Swedes of the Near North Side joined forces to fight African Americans. For all their differences, various European groups could often agree at least on this—that the "colored" races needed to be kept out of "their" communities.[48] Working toward this common cause must have significantly improved some erstwhile rocky race relations.

As for color relations, explaining them is made easier, in part, by three (sometimes overlapping) theories on the matter: what we might call the competition, becoming American, and becoming white schools. All schools agree that relations between "colored" groups and European immigrants deteriorated over time; they differ on what explains this. The first group points to increasing competition over jobs, housing, and status;[49] the second to an insidious form of Americanization, by which immigrants absorbed U.S. "racial attitudes," "prejudice," and/or "racism";[50] the third, closely related to the second, stresses a particular kind of Americanizing process, whereby immigrants came to better understand the color line and their position along it, and, therefore, "to insist on their own whiteness" and their differentiation from blackness (and in some cases, yellowness, browness, and redness).[51]

While all these theories have their strengths, none alone is adequate, in my view, for explaining the Italians' neighborhood relations story. The competition group is right that Italians and "colored" groups competed for various scarce resources in Chicago. However, it is of little help in explaining why color relations were generally more contentious than race relations, when Italians competed for housing and jobs far more often with other European races than with anyone else. As for the becoming American crowd, groups like Italians did not just learn some disembodied collection of disparaging ideas about, say, African Americans and celebratory ones about "whites"—ideas that together might be called "racism," "racial attitudes," and so forth. They learned these for sure, but they also learned about how "whites" and "Negroes"—because of these ideas *and* because of Chicago's color structure—occupied different places in society. They learned that as Italians they belonged to the "white race," and that by virtue of this fact they were a very different kind of human being from, say, African Americans, and deserved to live in better and separate neighborhoods, work better and separate jobs, marry "better" and different people, and so forth. It was this sort of realization at the macrolevel, this growing awareness of Chicago's color structure and their privileged position within it, that led to Italians' deteriorating neighborhood color relations. That this system revolved most of all around African Americans also helps to explain Italians' differential treatment of "colored" groups.[52]

Of course, microlevel factors were important too. Thus, some critical variables were how well-defined and respected neighborhood color boundaries were; what the relative population numbers of different groups were; what the specific histories of particular communities were; how willing and able groups were to outmigrate; what rates of home ownership were like; and what sorts of local institutions like Catholic churches existed. Still, these questions must be placed in a larger structural context to make sense. For instance, increased "mixing" or intensifying housing competition in neighborhoods with high home ownership rates could have contributed to color conflict but could not have produced it. After all, Italians "mixed" with, competed against, and invested in homes with other Europeans much more than with or against "colored" groups. Indeed, it was precisely the fact that these groups were defined and positioned as "colored"—and thus *not* along with Italians as "whites"—that residential mixture with or competition against them became so intolerable to some Italians.[53]

This argument owes much to whiteness scholars—with one exception. Contrary to what much of whiteness historiography suggests, I have found that Italians began neighborhood mobilizing against African Americans and in some cases Mexicans *before* they developed a public white consciousness.[54] As we have seen, when a mother on the Near North Side scolded her neighbors for their friendliness to African Americans, she complained that "no decent *Italian*"—rather than no decent *white* person—would act like that. Similarly, on the Near Northwest Side, when Italians looked down on African Americans it was, according to one social worker, because they thought Italians—not whites—were "the best." And when Father Giambastiani mobilized his community behind the anti-African-American eviction drive, he did this by appealing to their *Italianita'* rather than to their whiteness. As Giambastiani told the *Chicago Defender*, it was Italians—not whites—who resented the influx of African Americans and the putatively plunging property values. Within the context of postriot neighborhood relations, *Italianita'* and not whiteness was becoming most Italians' identity of choice.

Why many Italians opted to advertise the former more publicly than the latter is one of the key concerns of this book. Important to note here, however, is that neighborhood relations were critical to issues of identity. Throughout the 1920s and 1930s, certain neighbors had their doubts about Italians' general desirability, manifesting themselves in any number of ways: an Irish man's refusal to sell his house to Italians on the Near West Side; a Jewish family's decision to move from the same area when "the Italian people . . . moved in and the neighborhood became unsafe"; Germans' general insistence in Melrose Park that Italians stay on their side of the Nineteenth-Twentieth Street boundary; and the similar determination on the part of many Bridgeport "old" immigrants to stem the influx of "Dagoes." Italians' consciousness as Italians was forged, in part, through this conflict. Just as historian Linda Colley has argued that Britishness "was an invention forged above all by wars," so too was Italianness the product, in part, of everyday street struggles with any number of non-Italian "others"—the Irish, Jews, Poles, Swedes, Slavs, and so on.[55] It was here where many Italians—whether being excluded or doing the excluding, whether being derided or doing the deriding—received daily reminders about who they were and who they were not. *Italianita'* flourished in such an environment.

The same could be said for whiteness, of course. The neighborhood hostility Italians faced in these years was never nearly as violent, organized, or relentless as what the "colored races" endured, particularly African Americans. No evidence exists that any all-"white" covenants ever restricted Italians from residing in particular Chicago neighborhoods. Similarly, no powerful property owners associations, like those that emerged in places like Park Manor, Hyde Park, Woodlawn, and Uptown to ward off the "Negro invasion" (among others), ever emerged to deal with any similar invasion of Italians. And the waves of anti-African-American house bombings and gang violence that swept across Chicago in the late 1910s and 1920s always made the neighborhood resistance that Italians faced seem like welcoming parties in comparison. In the end, what was assumed during the Color Riot of 1919 was just as powerfully and pervasively assumed in its aftermath in neighborhoods all over Chicago: Italians, for all their problems, were still white in the eyes of the vast majority of their neighbors.[56] As it turned out, it would take some time before many Italians fully learned this lesson or openly advertised the point. In the coming pages, I hope to explain why.

3

THE WHITE PERIL OF EUROPE

On May 26, 1924, President Calvin Coolidge signed the Johnson-Reed bill into law, severely reducing the numbers of southern and eastern Europeans permitted to migrate to the United States and excluding Japanese immigrants entirely. The bill's passage came as the culmination of a decades-long rise in anti-immigrant racialism in the United States that greeted Italians as soon as they arrived in Chicago in magazines, in newspapers, in government reports, on the job, and in their neighborhoods. But ascendant anti-immigrant racialism leading to restriction and exclusion is only part of the story.[1] A diverse set of alternative voices—from liberal intellectuals and scientists to "new" immigrants themselves—had existed for years and continued to contest racialist notions and dogma. This chapter explores some of the complex contours of this debate on "new" European immigration as it was fought out both nationally and in Chicago between the end of World War I and the passage of the Immigration Act of 1924. Because many of these debates took place at the national level, this chapter, more than others, will focus as much on events and people outside as inside Chicago.

Anti-immigrant racialism and restriction marked southern Italians (and northerners too on occasion) as racial undesirables, who were, according to men like Madison Grant and Lothrop Stoddard, as well as to their many allies in magazines, newspapers, and grassroots organizations, a biological, cultural, political, and economic menace to the American nation. Such convictions were particularly strong in Chicago, where the city's two major newspapers absorbed and disseminated them enthusiastically, and the Ku Klux Klan formed a vibrant set of local chapters. Rising racialism, however, never challenged Italians' whiteness in any consequential way. According to virtually all racialists at both the national and local Chicago levels, if Italians were a national peril, they were a "white peril" just the same.

Italians approached matters differently. Despite the many assaults against them, Italians continued to avoid identifying themselves as white in racialism and restriction debates. Instead, Italians mobilized themselves as Italians and refuted racialists by stressing the wonders of *la razza italiana*, not those of *la razza bianca*. Also, in part because restriction targeted *all* Italians—not just those from the South—Italians tended to downplay North-South differences in these battles. As a consequence, restriction and racialism may have helped unify Chicago's Italian communities by convincing northerners and southerners—not to mention Sicilians, Tuscans, Neapolitans, and Calabrians—that they all shared something in common: their *Italianita'*.

The Rise of Scientific
Anti-Immigrant Racialism

The Immigration Act of 1924 grew directly out of a scientific assault on "new" immigrants led by a group of "old" American intellectuals and academics such as Madison Grant, Lothrop Stoddard, Clinton Stoddard Burr, William McDougall, Henry Pratt Fairchild, and Henry Fairfield Osborn. In a mass of books and articles published in both scholarly and popular venues, in speeches given at organizational dinners and societies, and in testimonies before Congress, these men constructed a relatively coherent set of ideas that constituted the core of postwar scientific anti-immigrant racialism. While they may have ignored Italians by name on occasion, their theories always had profound implications for Italians' racialization and colorization in the United States and in Chicago.

Most fundamentally, these anti-immigrant racialists agreed that, in the words of sociologist Henry Pratt Fairchild, race is an immutable "biological reality" that goes much further than environment, culture, or education in determining a human being's disposition, behavior, and abilities.[2] Drawing on the works of nineteenth-century European racialist ideologues like Arthur Count de Gobineau and Houston Stewart Chamberlain, these men viewed race as *the* central determinant in the history of humankind; for millennia civilizations had risen and fallen based primarily on their peoples' germ plasm and heredity. To "gentleman zoologist" Madison Grant, for instance, the whole purpose of writing his highly influential book, *The Passing of the Great Race*, was "to rouse his fellow Americans to the overwhelming importance of race," for it "lies at the base of all manifestations of modern society, just as it has done throughout the unrecorded eons of the past." Paleontologist Henry Fairfield Osborn agreed that "race has played a far larger part than either language or nationality in moulding the destinies of men; [and] race implies heredity and heredity implies all the moral, social and intellectual characteristics and traits which are the springs of politics and government."[3]

If races were crucial motors of history, they were also motors with fundamentally unequal parts. Despite restrictionists' constant claims to the contrary, racialists were not closet egalitarians concerned more with difference than inequality.[4] The belief that some races were superior to others stood at the heart of their analyses and explained, in part, their apocalyptic fears of the "new" immigration. As Madison Grant stated clearly in *The Passing of the Great Race*, "to admit the unchangeable differentiation of race in its modern scientific meaning is to admit inevitably the existence of superiority in one race and inferiority in another." Harvard professor William McDougall, perhaps the most eminent psychologist of his time, made essentially the same point as Grant, if a bit more subtly: "races differ in intellectual stature, just as they differ in physical stature."[5]

With millions of "new" immigrants "swamping" America's shores, particularly in northeastern cities where many racialists lived, they quickly became the prime targets of racialist theories. Borrowing the taxonomy of anthropologist William Ripley, many racialists divided Europeans into three races—Nordic, Alpine, and Mediterranean—and ranked each according to the quality of its germ plasm. Atop this hierarchy was the undisputed hero of all racialists, the Nordics.[6] Some racialists expressed their admiration for this race of "supermen" unabashedly. In *The Passing of the Great Race*, for instance, Grant viewed the history of modern civilization and the glorious rise of the Nordic race as one and the same: "The Nordics are, all over the world, a race of soldiers, sailors, adventurers and explorers but above all, of rulers, organizers and aristocrats."[7] More subdued believers in Nordic supremacy existed as well. Yale sociologist Maurice R. Davie, for example, criticized Grant's more vitriolic race arguments, but still argued that "the average of Nordics is higher than the average of Alpines and Mediterraneans. . . . [Nordics] are more akin to the native American stock. They represent a lesser problem of Americanization. They seem, on the average, to be a better physical type." IQ tests that the U.S. army administered to soldiers during World War I, as well as other intelligence studies, reached the same conclusion: Nordics, or "old" Americans, were vastly superior in intellectual endowments to all other races.[8]

Nordic supremacy theories, of course, were often indistinguishable from related notions about Mediterranean and Alpine—or "new" immigrant/southeastern European—inferiority.[9] These European races were condemned for their putative degeneracy, mongrelized nature, and general physical, moral, and mental inadequacies. Physician Arthur Sweeney, in an essay on "new" immigrant intelligence, made the point most dramatically: "It is time to awaken to the necessity of protecting this country from the influx of the worthless. Unless we do so we shall degenerate to the level of the Slav and Latin races, with their illiteracy, ignorance and consequent degradation. . . . We have no place in this country for the 'man with the hoe,' stained with the earth he digs, and guided by a mind scarcely superior to the ox, whose brother he is."[10]

At times, racialists harshly critiqued Italians—especially southerners—

more specifically.[11] As Henry Pratt Fairchild explained in his book, *Immigration*, "the southern Italians belong to the Mediterranean . . . race, are shorter in stature and more swarthy, and on the whole much inferior in intelligence to their northern compatriots. . . . Unfortunately from our point of view, the great majority of our Italian immigrants belong to the southern branch." Similarly, Henry Fairfield Osborn, in a letter to the editor of the *New York Times* in 1924, scoffed at anti-restrictionists who confused race and nationality and called for the open immigration of "South Italians because Italy gave us Columbus." To Osborn, if Columbus and his compatriots from the *Mezzogiorno* shared a common nationality, their racial differences could not have been more pronounced. After all, while southern Italians belonged to the Mediterranean race, many northern Italians like Columbus—along with Galileo, Raphael, da Vinci, Giotto, Donatello, Boticelli, and Petrarch—were "clearly of Nordic ancestry."[12]

Not all racialists made these careful distinctions and, as a result, some included northerners in their blanket condemnations of Italians. In a dissertation completed in 1925, Clifford Kirkpatrick surveyed the growing literature on immigration and intelligence and compared these findings with his own work based on "certain New England groups." With some restraint, he concluded: "the total evidence, with certain exceptions, is unfavorable to the 'new Immigration,' especially the Italians, so that the effect of immigration on American intelligence might be viewed with some concern. . . . An opportunity to select immigrants from a group of Englishmen making application for immigration would probably be more profitable than an opportunity to select immigrants from an equal number of Italians." Kirkpatrick's findings coincided with Army IQ tests, on which Italians performed disastrously.[13]

Taken together, whether one spoke about physical stature, intellectual endowments, social customs, or other hereditary characteristics, one thing was certain to racialists: southern Italians (and sometimes northern ones as well) were racially inferior to the Nordic, "the white man par excellence." Interestingly, this racialist assault on Italians and other "new" immigrants stopped well short of questioning their color status as whites. It seems that most racialists—even as they did their best to emphasize *racial* difference—took the whiteness of "new" European immigrants for granted. As Henry Pratt Fairchild explained casually in his book *Immigration*, "the new immigration is made up from people of a very different racial stock, representing the Slavic and Mediterranean branches of the Caucasian race." Madison Grant included southern and eastern Europeans within the white/Caucasian category, even while questioning its overall usefulness: "The term 'Caucasian race' has ceased to have any meaning except where it is used, in the United States, to contrast white populations with Negroes or Indians or in the Old World with Mongols.

It is, however, a convenient term to include the three European subspecies [Nordic, Alpine, and Mediterranean] when considered as divisions of one of the primary branches or species of mankind."[14] Racialists, then, like many other Americans, made an important distinction between race and color—even if they failed to use these exact terms.

The racialist who distinguished most explicitly between race and color was Lothrop Stoddard in *The Rising Tide of Color*. An ardent Nordic supremacist and loyal disciple of Grant, Stoddard believed deeply in the inherent inequalities of the European races. Speaking of these groups, he argued that "migrations of lower human types like those which have worked such havoc in the United States must be rigorously curtailed. Such migrations upset standards, sterilize better stocks, increase low types, and compromise national futures more than war, revolutions, or native deterioration." Still, it was what he called the "color question"—not the "new" immigrant race question—that concerned him most and would be the "key-note of twentieth century world-politics." The "rising tide" of colored immigration and power, declared Stoddard, would forever jeopardize white world supremacy and, in turn, human beings' inexorable march from the "dank jungles of savagery to [the] glorious heights" of civilization. And in combating this crisis, white racial differences were critical. Still, when compared to the dangers of the "World of Color," even the most degenerate "new" immigrant seemed a blessing to Stoddard. "This extended discussion of the evil effects of even the white immigration," wrote Stoddard, "has, in my opinion, been necessary in order to get a proper perspective for viewing the problem of color immigration."

> When we see the damage wrought in America, for example, by the coming of persons who, after all, belong mostly to branches of the white race and who nearly all possess the basic ideals of white civilization, we can grasp the incalculably greater damage which would be wrought by the coming of persons wholly alien of blood and possessed of idealistic and cultural backgrounds absolutely different from ours. If the white immigrants can gravely disorder the national life, it is not too much to say that the colored immigrant would doom it to certain death.[15]

Scientific racialists, then, placed Italians (and other "new" European immigrants) in an ambiguous social position. After devoting years of research and writing to "demonstrating" the racial inferiority of southern and eastern Europeans, they still viewed these groups as white. The message seemed to be that "new" European immigrants were inferior—but not *that* inferior. For all their dangerous inadequacies, they still occupied a place within the "superior" *color* division of mankind, even if they were relegated to an "inferior" *racial* branch.

Scientific Racialism Comes
to Chicago

In the end, these were the scientific theories of an elite group of intellectuals isolated in the ivory towers of academia or the stuffy social circles of upper-class "old" America (or both). Alone, these racialists could not have marshaled the political support to pass the Immigration Act of 1924 nor could they have made a very large impact on everyday Chicagoans. The turbulent social world of post-World War I America made such ideas compelling to many Chicagoans, as crime, labor unrest, radicalism, and economic recessions all came to be associated to some extent with "new" immigrants.[16] Equally important, several key institutions (or sets of them) brought the academic ruminations of Grant and Stoddard, McDougall and Osborn, to a good part of everyday Chicago.

One such set of institutions was mass-circulation magazines like the *Saturday Evening Post, Literary Digest, World's Work, Current Opinion,* and *Collier's.* With varying degrees of intensity, frequency, and zeal, these magazines featured anti-"new" immigrant diatribes, often heavily influenced by, echoing the central tenets of, or written directly by scientific racialists. Reaching millions of Americans weekly and presumably a large number of Chicagoans too, these magazines ran articles with titles like "Close the Gates!," "Melting Pot or Dumping Ground," "Fewer and Better or None," "Keep on Guarding the Gates," "The Immigration Peril," "Slow Poison," and "Keep America 'White'!"[17]

The most prominent and influential of these proracialist magazines was the *Saturday Evening Post.* With a circulation of over two million, this magazine was in a unique position to spread the gospel of Grant (et al.) to millions of Chicagoans. In countless articles, primarily through the caustic writings of Kenneth Roberts and the guest submissions of men like Lothrop Stoddard, the magazine faithfully reproduced the key points of anti-immigrant racialism. They did so by repeating incessantly a common story of America's rise and potential fall. Prior to the start of the "new" immigration around 1880, the *Saturday Evening Post* told its readers, America was "a nation of Nordics" and thus filled with people who "possess . . . to a marked degree the ability to govern themselves and to govern others; and from their ranks have been recruited the world's voluntary explorers, pioneers, soldiers, sailors and adventurers."[18] In the late nineteenth century, however, a deluge of southern and eastern European immigrants—alternately scorned as "slow poison," "the scum of Europe," "foreign mush," "good-for-nothing mongrels," or "parasite races"—suddenly swamped America. These people "half ruined" and "slum-Europeanized" the country, and only immediate and severe restriction against them would save it from further decline and degeneration. As one *Saturday Evening Post* editorial put it, we need "a law that will keep out the people who are changing America into an annex of Southeastern Europe—a law that will give

America a chance to digest the millions of unassimilated, unwelcome and unwanted aliens that rest so heavily in her."[19]

In addition to this common parable, the magazine, again following the lead of scientific racialists, mercilessly maligned southern Italians. "The south Italians of to-day," explained Kenneth Roberts, "[are a] people almost as different from the north Italians of Nordic descent as an alligator pear is different from an alligator—people incapable of self-government and totally devoid of initiative and creative ability. Unrestricted immigration made a mongrel race of the south Italians. . . . Unrestricted immigration will inevitably and absolutely do the same thing to Americans." Similarly, Roberts opened another article on the perils of "new" immigration by discussing, first, how "Northern Italians are different in their temperament, stature and general appearance from Southern Italians." He then pointed out that "the inhabitants of Rome . . . are highly indignant whenever they are placed in the Southern Italian category." "These facts," insisted Roberts, "which are familiar to every traveler in Italy and to every student of Italian history" were distressingly relevant because they demonstrated that "people from certain sections of Europe are hopelessly inferior in physique, manner of thought and ability to people of other sections of Europe." This reality, argued Roberts, made immigration restriction a matter of life and death for America.[20]

Daily newspapers, particularly the *Chicago Daily News* and the *Chicago Tribune*, also did their part to bring the themes of scientific racialism to many Chicagoans. Throughout the early 1920s in frequent editorials on immigration, the former newspaper was less restrictionist and counseled against rash decision-making based more on panic and prejudice than reason and research. In early 1924, for instance, in the midst of heated congressional debates about restriction, the *Chicago Daily News* calmly opined: "Better the re-enactment or extension of the present law for a year or two than the adoption of a crude, ill-considered and flagrantly discriminatory measure certain to breed friction and ill will."[21] On occasion, the *Chicago Daily News* seemed almost a throwback to an earlier, more optimistic era when melting pots melted, immigrants brought gifts to their adopted land, and a new and improved American race was in the making. In one editorial, the newspaper argued that, despite widespread panic and alarm, the country still had room for immigrants willing to become American and work hard.[22]

Such opinions were exceptions to the rule, however. In countless editorials on immigration, while stopping short of overt scientific racialism, the *Chicago Daily News* still favored restriction legislation that would carefully maintain the racial status quo in America (that is, the proportions of Nordics, Alpines, and Mediterraneans).[23] Furthermore, it maintained that while some immigrants had been "culturally and racially valuable" to the United States, "by far the larger number has been completely inadjustable to the conditions of American citizenship." Most important, the *Daily News* often published syndicated articles, many of which were saturated with the scientific racialism of the day. In one series, Ole Hanson, former mayor of Seattle, wrote an article provocatively entitled, "White Peril Menace to American People," in which he concluded: "from reports I have received from Germany, the Balkans and Italy, I have become convinced that the Yellow Peril of Asia is not as great a menace as the White Peril of Europe. . . . Few people really understand that unrestricted immigration from Europe for ten years would change the entire living standards and ideals of our people and perhaps make it an untruth for an American to say: 'My country is the best country on the face of the earth.'"[24] The paper ran another series of articles by Secretary of Labor James J. Davis with essentially the same message. Heavily influenced by the rising eugenics movement, and in particular by the work of Harry Laughlin, one of the most prominent eugenicists of the day, Hanson warned that the "racial stocks represented in our immigration very definitely decline as we review the history of migrations from other lands. There is a steady running down hill." In the end, Davis explained America's immigration problems by classifying newcomers. Initially, the nation received immigrants of the "beaver type," who "built America because it was their nature to build." Later America became the dumping ground of the "new" immigrants, who were more akin to the "rat type," who "undermine and destroy because it is their nature to destroy."[25]

While the *Chicago Daily News* certainly helped to spread the word of scientific racialism, the *Chicago Tribune* seemed at times an official organ of the movement.[26] This newspaper was bent on severely restricting immigration—even excluding certain groups for a time—and it advertised these opinions openly. In editorial after editorial and in many a political cartoon,[27] the *Chicago Tribune* advanced more or less the same set of points: the United States needs to "watch the strains which it takes into its blood and to make certain that it preserves and does not change its stock"; the "American house is full up to the present and . . . cannot afford to allow great blocks of unassimilated aliens to be planted in this country to the detriment of American institutions"; Europeans from the north and west are infinitely more desirable than those from the south and east; the "rising tide of aliens" or the "invading hordes" were making the country "the dumping ground of Europe"; and only selective and restrictive immigration legislation would "keep the United States American" and would avert "national suicide."[28]

Chicagoans also became familiar with scientific racialism through local grassroots movements like the Ku Klux Klan. Immediately after World War I, the Klan experienced a remarkable revival throughout the country and in the Midwest, in particular. In Chicago, "naturalized" members numbered between forty thousand and eighty thousand and established over twenty neighborhood chapters.[29] Despite fierce opposition—the City Council passed anti-Klan resolutions and attempted to fire municipal employees with Klan connections; the American Unity League published a weekly newspaper that revealed the names, addresses, and occupations of Klansmen and women; and various formal and informal groups staged violent attacks on Klan property and headquarters—the Klan still flourished in Chicago in the early 1920s. It held numerous massive outdoor rallies, in which it initiated thousands of new members; it sponsored frequent dances, lectures, and cookouts; it visited countless churches to make donations and recruit new members; and it published a popular weekly, *Dawn,* which was "one of the most influential of the Invisible Empire's many periodicals."[30]

And through it all, the Klan warned Chicagoans that "the influx of foreign immigration" "threatened to crush out the Anglo-Saxon civilization." In numerous articles in *Dawn,* the Klan denounced the "mongrel hordes" from southern Europe and called for immediate and severe immigration restriction. In one article entitled, "Awake America!," Klansman Edward Young Clarke mimicked the views of Stoddard and Grant in stating that "science has proven to us conclusively that environment does not influence the physical inheritance of man, and that his racial psychology and mental tendencies are unchangeable." As a result, America must close the gates to "new" immigration or face "impending racial chaos" and certain "mongrelization."[31]

That many Chicagoans absorbed anti-immigrant racialism is reflected not only by the Klan's popularity but also by the rhetoric of countless men and women who shared their views with their local dailies through letters to the editor. In 1921 and 1924, as Congress wrestled with restriction, countless Chicagoans wrote to their local newspapers, calling for restriction and defending their views with racialist arguments. In one letter responding to the proimmigration sentiments of an Italian American, the writer argued that America was "made by the northern European races" and that "we want foreigners of racial stock that can be assimilated, foreigners of the races whose governments and institutions are akin to ours and who become real American citizens. Thousands of years of evolution cannot be changed by any quick magic formula." Another letter writer noted anxiously that "the U.S. has ceased to be a 'melting pot'; it is only a 'mixing pot' [and] the scum is running over and extinguishing the flames of pure Americanism burning underneath. Why should we not discriminate between immigrants? Some are more desirable than others. Some cannot be assimilated."[32]

Alternative Voices

By the mid-1920s, scientific anti-immigrant racialism enjoyed power and prominence throughout the United States and Chicago, but there were always dissenters. A diverse lot of liberal intellectuals, scientists, and "new" immigrants themselves, at both the national and local Chicago levels, struggled throughout these years to contest racialist doctrine and to provide their own alternative vision of race and immigration. At the national level, no one intellectual or scientist did more than Franz Boas to challenge and dispute scientific racialism. Starting around the turn of the century with a number of scholarly essays and with his ground-breaking study, *The Mind of Primitive Man*, Boas sought to discredit essentialist notions of race and to replace them with culture as the key determinant of human behavior.[33] As scientific racialism grew in intensity and power in the postwar years, so too did Boas's attacks upon it. In a bevy of articles and scathing book reviews, Boas declared that the works of Stoddard, Grant, Osborn and others were nothing more than "unscientific" and "vicious propaganda"; that races were far too mixed and variable to make their categorizations meaningful or to justify Nordics' boasts about their racial purity; that germ plasm and heredity were largely irrelevant in comparison to social conditions and cultural environment in determining the history and abilities of a people; and, finally, that "nobody has ever given satisfactory proof of an inherent inequality of races."[34]

Not all challenges to scientific racialists necessarily questioned their understandings of race. Philosopher Horace Kallen, for instance, believed that certain unique characteristics lay within the blood and hereditary make-up of people, such that "different races responding to the same stimuli are still different, and no environmental influence subtle as thought and overwhelming as a tank can ever remold them into an indifferent sameness."[35] These similarities between Kallen and racialism aside, however, he posed no small challenge to Grant and his ilk, by viewing racial differences with pleasure and optimism rather than, in the case of many racialists, with fear and revulsion. In 1924, at the height of congressional restriction debates and racialist calls for a more homogeneous America, Kallen wrote that "race, in its setting, is at best what individualizes the common heritage, imparting to it presence, personality and force. It is what an instrument is to the music of a symphony. The latter is an inert abstraction, black marks on a paper, the mere possibility of sound. It can come to actuality and loveliness only by virtue of the instrument that incarnates it." To Kallen, the thought of imposing some form of racial and cultural uniformity upon America would be criminal and catastrophic. He offered cultural pluralism as an alternative to the racialists' "Kultur Klux Klan" sweeping across America:

> As in an orchestra every type of instrument has its specific *timbre* and *tonality*, founded in its substance and form; as every type has its appropriate theme and melody in the whole symphony, so in society, each ethnic group may be the natural instrument, its temper and culture may be its theme and melody and the harmony and dissonances and discords of them all may make the symphony of civilization.[36]

A good deal of anti-racialist resistance occurred at the local level in Chicago as well, some of which had national repercussions. The Chicago

School of Sociology, for instance, worked in tandem with Boas to challenge popular racialist notions. Eminent scholars like William I. Thomas and Robert Park explored issues of culture, environment, and social conditions rather than heredity and "inborn and ineradicable traits." As Thomas noted in *Old World Traits Transplanted*, "it is easier to explain why the Jew is in the needle trades, is not a farmer, and is intelligent, on the ground of circumstances . . . than on the ground of inborn abilities."[37] Meanwhile, other Chicago institutions voiced their opposition to racialism and restriction as well. In early 1924, while the Chicago City Council passed a resolution denouncing the Johnson-Reed bill as "discriminatory, unfair, [and] un-American," the Chicago Commons settlement house spearheaded a petition drive against the legislation.[38]

At the local level, the most vocal and active anti-racialist response came from "new" immigrants themselves. This was particularly the case with Chicago Italians, who were deeply offended by theories positing their inferiority and by racialists' drives, on these grounds, to reduce dramatically their immigration to the United States.[39] There was a great deal of organized opposition to restriction and racialism through different Chicago community institutions. The local consulate, working in concert with the Italian embassy in Washington, drafted a resolution opposing the Johnson-Reed bill. The city's two main Italian-language newspapers, *L'Italia* and *La Tribuna Italiana Transatlantica*, featured innumerable articles and editorials denouncing restriction and racialism and organized a letter-writing campaign directed at the U.S. Congress. In 1924, various local organizations formed a coalition—the Chicago Committee of American Citizens of Italian Extraction (CCACIE)—to defeat restriction legislation. The group submitted a brief to the Senate and House Immigration Committees, in which it expressed its outrage at being branded an "inferior race." Some Italians also responded in less genteel ways. In July 1924, for instance, Italians helped burn down a KKK "Klantauqua" tent in Chicago Heights.[40]

Ideologically, Italians' most common response to racialism and restriction legislation was a direct and unabashed defense of "la razza." On the whole, they did not shy away from the deeply racialist language of Grant and Stoddard or from subjects like blood and heredity. Nor did they contest, like Boas and others, the specifics of racialist taxonomies that divided Europeans into the Alpine, Nordic, and Mediterranean groups.[41] They differed from the racialists on only one essential argument: that Italians were an inferior race. In countless articles, speeches, books, and letters to politicians, Italians spoke with pride and confidence about their motherland's and their race's unparalleled contributions to civilization over the centuries and about their unquestionable racial fitness and desirability. As the CCACIE stated clearly in their letter to the Senate Immigration Committee in 1924: "The Johnson Bill virtually admits that the Nordic race is superior to the Italian. We ask in what respect? What are the greatest attributes of civilization? What country has contributed more than Italy to the arts, science and literature?" The Order of the Sons of Italy in America (OSIA) advanced an identical argument in its letter to Representative Albert Johnson, chairman of the House Committee on Immigration, the leading congressional anti-immigrant racialist of his time, and a co-sponsor of the Immigration Act of 1924. To restrict Italian immigration for fear of "race deterioration," argued OSIA, was ludicrous. "From Rome down though the succeeding ages the physical vigor and strong mentality of the Italians has remained intact. . . . Sober, thrifty and industrious, sound in mind and body, he [the Italian] constitutes an unimpeachable racial factor in the formation of the American race of the future."[42]

L'Italia and *La Tribuna Italiana Transatlantica* made similar arguments in their defense of the Italian race. In one article, published by both papers in 1924, readers were told, under the subtitle, "The Potency of Heredity," that "men of intelligence know Italy's history. . . . The south European nations go back thousands of years—a long period during which the Northerners were barbarians—the ancestors of the 'Nordic'." In another article, detailing the innumerable aesthetic gifts Italians had bestowed upon America, columnist Luigi Barzini challenged America to "demolish in haste the imposing structures embodying the inspiration of Italian art . . . empty the art galleries and the museums . . . shut down the exhibitions so that Nordic 'purity' may no longer be contaminated by Mediterranean thought." If America were to do all this, argued Barzini, if it were to impose a restriction on the migration of Italian culture as well as people, it "would be living to-day in an apotheosis of ugliness."[43]

A similar Italian racial defense came in several books written by Italians within a few years of the passage of immigration restriction. Chicagoan Giovanni Schiavo, a Sicilian-American writer and popular historian, wrote *The Italians in Chicago*, in which he sought "to convince our well-intentioned Americans that the Italians of Chicago are not unworthy of the glorious traditions of their race." In his opening chapter entitled, "The Race of Columbus," Schiavo assured his readers that the "Italian civilization has never faded out" and that "time alone will show to the incredulous and the obstinate that the Italians represent just as important a factor in the progress of this nation as the members of all the Nordic races." After all, "ever since the days of Sicily's glorious civilization nearly three thousand years ago, down to our own times, the Italians have been teachers to the world and often masters to its destinies."[44]

Race, Color, and the Debate over "New" Immigration

Debates about the "new" immigration took place primarily in magazines, books, newspapers, and the halls of universities and the federal government. How might they have shaped and reflected the racialization and col-

orization of Chicago Italians, those like Schiavo who were intimately connected with the debate, as well as everyday Italians who most likely were
not—a seamstress working on the Near West Side, a street-sweeper living
in Armour Square, or a fruit peddler from Little Sicily?

These debates must have affected many Italians' racial self-understandings. While many racialists were careful to distinguish between Nordic
northern Italians and the Mediterraneans of the *Mezzogiorno*, the Immigration Act of 1924 did not recognize these distinctions and, instead, imposed one quota on all Italians. In part as a result, Italians, in their defense
against restriction and racialism, also rarely discussed North-South distinctions. Institutions like OSIA, *L'Italia*, and the Italian Chicago Chamber
of Commerce, as well as individuals like Schiavo, spoke reverently of the
glorious "race of Columbus," which did not appear to have any racial divisions within it. These debates, then, must have helped to build a more
salient and unified Italian identity, one in which race and nation were
coterminous (one Italian race = one Italian nation), not contradictory (two
[North-South] Italian races = one Italian nation). In their battles against
the Klan, Grant, the *Chicago Tribune*, and restriction legislation, many Sicilians, Tuscans, Neapolitans, and Venetians no doubt became Italians.[45]

Debates over restriction and racialism also offered powerful color lessons. While scientific racialists included "inferior" Italians among the
white races, not all racialist sympathizers in newspapers and magazines
were so convinced. In one article from April 1923 entitled "Keep America
'White'!," *Current Opinion* criticized the Immigration Act of 1921 as being
too permissive regarding southern and eastern Europeans. "Though successful in shutting off a large part of the turgid stream of undesirable and
unassimilable human 'offscourings' from southern and eastern Europe,"
wrote the magazine, "this measure did not go far enough. . . . If the tall,
big-boned, blue-eyed, old-fashioned 'white' American is not to be bred out
entirely by little dark peoples, Uncle Sam must not simply continue the
temporary quota law in operation, but must make its provisions much
more stringent." Similarly, one *Dawn* article from 1923 warned frantically
that Americans' "intermingling with the mongrel hordes threatens the
wholesale ruin of the white race." A character in Sinclair Lewis's popular
novel, *Babbitt* (1922), no doubt spoke for many Americans, when he remarked, "another thing we got to do . . . is keep these damn foreigners
out of the country. Thank the lord we're putting a limit on immigration.
These Dagoes and Hunkies have got to learn that this is a white man's
country, and they ain't wanted here."[46]

Yet even among racialist sympathizers, a group utterly convinced of the
racial inferiority of the "new" immigrants, such challenges to Italian
whiteness were less serious and frequent than one might expect. Much
more typical was the article in the *Chicago Daily News* cited earlier, entitled
"White Peril a Menace to the American People," in which "new" immigrants were considered racially undesirable—indeed dangerously so—and

yet white just the same.[47] This point is best exemplified when one compares the debate surrounding Japanese exclusion with that regarding southeastern European immigration. Throughout early 1924, Congress deliberated not only on the precise quotas for European groups but also on whether or not to exclude the Japanese entirely.[48] The latter issue, even in places like Chicago, where Asian immigration was negligible, often dominated discussions of restriction and exclusion. For instance, from the middle of April 1924, when Congress put its finishing touches on restriction legislation, to late May 1924, when Coolidge signed the Johnson-Reed bill into law, coverage of Japanese exclusion far overshadowed that of "new" European immigrant restriction in every major Chicago newspaper.[49]

While many racialists scorned both the Japanese and "new" European immigrants as menacing racial undesirables, they talked about the former in significantly different terms. In 1924, one *Chicago Tribune* editorial argued, for instance, that

> the question of the clauses concerning Japanese immigration to the United States now before congress has resolved itself to whether the Japanese shall be excluded on the same basis as half the population of the world—in Asia—or admitted on the same basis as European white immigrants. . . . The question is whether California and the entire Pacific coast shall be protected as a region of white Americans or shall eventually become an Asiatic outpost and colony.

The *Tribune*, though never stating it outright, implied that they favored a white protectorate. One letter writer to the *Chicago Herald Examiner* put the point most succinctly: "We want to preserve our dear America for the white race and not be overrun by orientals."[50] These arguments, to be sure, sound almost identical to those advanced in the "Keep America 'White'" essay cited above. The important point, however, is that this essay was an exception; these examples about the Japanese from Chicago dailies most certainly were not. The final outcome of the immigration debates demonstrates this point best: while "new" European immigrants, branded as racial inferiors, were severely reduced in numbers, the Japanese, branded as racial *and* color inferiors, were excluded altogether.

Ironically, some of the most prominent anti-racialists further confirmed this general race and color scheme that assumed Italian whiteness. Franz Boas worked tirelessly to discredit the scientific underpinnings of race and racial difference and yet even he, it seems, distinguished to some extent between race and color. Take the following statement from 1925, for example:

> We have the right to speak of hereditary racial traits only when all the individuals of a race partake of the same characteristics. Comparing Swedes and Central Africans, we may say that blond or brunette wavy hair, light eyes, and light complexion are hereditary Swedish traits, and

that black frizzy hair, dark eyes, and dark pigmentation are hereditary Negro traits. When, on the other hand, a trait is so variable that it may occur in several racial groups, we can no longer speak of racial heredity. If among 1000 Swedes and 1000 north Italians we find a number of individuals who cannot with certainty be assigned to either group, then we can no longer speak of racially determined characteristics of these individuals because they may belong to either group. These are the actual conditions found all over Europe.

While stressing the variability within and across races and the importance of culture, these points seem to have applied more to Europeans than to other peoples. In the end, racial heredity *could* be a reliable way of differentiating between human beings—just not those from Europe. As Boas wrote in 1924, for example, "if we should try to select the third of humanity that is best developed, in regard to intellect and will power, we should find representatives of all races in this group . . . Europeans . . . East Asiatic Types . . . as well as American Indians, Polynesians, and African negroes." This quotation reveals the essential limitation in his thinking and the implications this thinking had on Italians' color status. If biological notions of race were useless in separating Nordics from, say, Alpines, they were still helpful in drawing color lines between whites ("Europeans"), yellows ("East Asiatic types"), reds ("American Indians"), browns ("Polynesians"), and blacks ("African negroes"). And this sort of thinking, whether deliberate or not, divided the world's peoples in such a way as to validate Italians' whiteness.[51]

Much the same could be said about Park's work. It is true that his famous theories on "race" conflicts and the "race relations cycle" were an intellectual framework that crossed the color line and applied to a variety of social groups from African Americans and Asians to European immigrants of all kinds. But Park, like Boas, drew distinctions between certain groups and others that coincided with the color line. For instance, Park consistently argued that Asians and African Americans were, for the most part, different from European immigrants because the latter two groups were "not the right color" and were forced to wear a "racial uniform." In this way, Park, like Boas, contributed to the creation of a "monolithic whiteness" among so many racially distinct Italians, Armenians, Hebrews, and the like.[52]

As for Horace Kallen, he longed for a world in which different races with their innate and acquired differences could live together in a "new and happy form of associative harmony." But harmony had its limits: cultural pluralism was a "whites"/Europeans-only enterprise.[53] In his famous 1915 essay "Democracy versus the Melting Pot," through cultural pluralism "'American civilization' may come to mean the perfection of the cooperative harmonies of '*European* civilization.'" Similarly, in his 1924 essay "'Americanization' and the Cultural Prospect," Kallen added that, "if then cultural history and the American present are any index, the cultural prospect has been enriched, not depleted by the immigration, settlement, and self-maintenance in communities of the peoples of all Europe upon the North American continent." Several pages before this quotation, Kallen admitted quietly that "I do not discuss the influence of the Negro. This is at once too considerable and too recondite in its process for casual mention. It requires separate analysis."[54] In the end, Kallen shared one other similarity with the racialists, whom he tried so hard to discredit: all could agree that the "new" European immigrants were white, and that for all the racial differences within this category, membership still had—and should have—its privileges.

Chicago Italians had their own particular take on these color matters. Faced with intensifying racialist attacks against them, some sought protection by claiming whiteness and denigrating nonwhiteness. In one editorial appearing in *L'Italia* in June 1924, for instance, the paper ridiculed popular notions about Italian inferiority and boasted that they along with the other "peoples of the Mediterranean . . . had created the civilization of the white race." In another editorial on efforts through restriction to keep the Nordic stock pure, *L'Italia* commented that such efforts had "been tried before, but . . . [they do] not appear to have succeeded anywhere except in China. . . . The Chinese have made themselves a race apart, and mixture with other races now would be impossible, with or without immigration laws. Who would be a Chinese?"[55]

Claims to whiteness and differentiation from nonwhiteness never constituted the entire story, however. For one, Chicago Italians just as often identified with people of "color"—particularly the excluded Japanese and Chinese—as differentiated themselves from them. One *L'Italia* editorial, for instance, criticized the United States for excluding Asian immigrants and argued that the "increasing numbers of Japanese and Chinese have been a magnificent service to the Republic." In another article appearing a month earlier, the paper, again objecting to Asian exclusion, praised the "intellectual power of Asia," which helped found the "religions of the world."[56] Even when Italian-language newspapers denigrated groups of "color," it was rarely a simple instance of "othering." In one article in *La Tribuna*, for example, the newspaper blasted restrictionists for favoring "the mixed races of Mexico and South America" over southern and eastern Europeans, but also insisted that "in California, the Mexican population is far more of a local problem than the few law-abiding and less competing Japanese." In another article a week later, the paper knew no color line in disparaging "other" groups: "If the restriction were aimed at protecting the race, why the preference for African blacks? If they aim at establishing the various degrees of a people's civilization, why are the Poles put so much above the Italians?"[57]

Furthermore, while Chicago Italians addressed color issues and claimed whiteness only very rarely, when they did so, the meaning of these acts was never entirely clear. In the same *L'Italia* editorial that credited the Mediterranean peoples with developing "white civilization," the newspaper scorned racialists for their "absurd phobia" of the "races of the brown type"—to which Italians belonged. *L'Italia* thought this fear came from Americans' fatuous favoritism of people with the "characteristics of the Anglo-Saxon race"—"white skin, clear eyes, blonde hair."[58] In the end, Italians' racial defense willingly embraced essentialized and biologized notions of race; it rarely (if ever) included, however, a demand to be accepted as white or to be distinguished from "nonwhites."

4

RACE, COLOR, AND CRIME

On the night of February 22, 1926 and then again several nights later, agents from the Commissioner General of Immigration's office, the U.S. Department of Justice, the Chicago Police Department, and the Cook County Sheriff's and State's Attorney's offices raided—often without warrant—restaurants, coffeehouses, barber shops, pool rooms, soft drink parlors, club headquarters, and homes. In search of deportable "alien gangsters," agents seem to have found what they were looking for. Over two hundred people were apprehended, some of whom were detained for days without adequate food, sleeping accommodations, or heat. Of those people apprehended and detained, a few were Mexicans and Greeks, but the majority were Italians.[1]

If federal and local agents sought "alien gangsters," it was really Sicilians whom they wanted most. After all, the raids came in the midst of what the *Chicago Tribune* called "the reign of terror in Chicago produced by gangs of Sicilian gunmen." Newspapers printed bold, sensationalistic headlines like "Sicilian Gang Kills Again," "Shotguns Kill Wrong Man in Sicilian Feud," "Sicilian Slain, Two Shot in Feudists' War," and "Feudists Slay Sicilian Ally of Genna Gang." A week before the deportation drive, the *Chicago Tribune* predicted prophetically that "there will be something doing when Uncle Sam reaches his long arm into the Melting Pot and begins fishing out the Italian gangsters for scrutiny."[2]

In the end, only a handful of Italians were deported, but this entire episode dramatizes the extent to which many Chicagoans had come to see Italians as a major menace. Indeed, it was in these Prohibition years (1920–1933) of Al Capone, Johnny Torrio, the Aiello and Genna Brothers, and many others, that in the words of Horace Cayton and St. Clair Drake, "gangsters replaced Negroes in the civic consciousness as Social Problem No. 1." It was in these years that the vice president of the United States, Charles Dawes (a native of Evanston, a Chicago suburb), pleaded with the

Senate to "rescue Chicago from a reign of lawlessness" brought about by "a colony of unnaturalized persons, hostile to our institutions and laws, who have formed a supergovernment of their own—feudists, Black Handers, members of the Mafia—who levy tribute upon citizens and enforce collection by terrorizing, kidnappings, and assassinations." It was in these years that the president of the Chicago Crime Commission stated openly that "the real Americans are not gangsters. Recent immigrants and the first generation of Jews and Italians are the chief offenders, with the Jews furnishing the brains and the Italians the brawn." And it was in these years that Chicago's main newspaper, the *Tribune*, constantly condemned "alien murderers" from Sicily as *the* scourge of the city.[3]

In the 1920s, criminalization raised serious and lasting questions about Italians' racial desirability as Italians, yet never positioned them as non-white in any sustained or systematic way. If many Chicagoans in these years came to see Italians more and more as murderous and menacing mobsters, they were still (implicitly) white mobsters. As for Italians' views and actions on the matter, they avoided asserting a white identity and generally preferred trumpeting the glories of and refuting the attacks against the Italian race. If most Italians arrived in Chicago with little sense of their belonging to an Italian racial/national community, constant criminalization, like immigration restriction and neighborhood relations, helped change this in the 1920s.

Italians and Crime in the Early Years

Crystallizing around the infamous murder of Police Chief David Hennessy in New Orleans in 1890, ideas about Italians' innate criminality enjoyed wide currency throughout the United States during the late nineteenth and early twentieth centuries. Responding to the Hennessy killing, the *New York Times* fumed: "These sneaking and cowardly Sicilians, the descendants of bandits and assassins, who had transported to this country the lawless passions, the cut-throat practices, the oath-bound societies of their native country, are to us a pest without mitigation." Around the same time, the *Baltimore News* noted: "the disposition to assassinate in revenge for a fancied wrong is a marked trait in the character of this impulsive and inexorable [Italian] race." In his popular book *The Old World in the New* (1914), prominent sociologist Edward Ross lent scientific legitimacy to many of these views, arguing that "for all the great majority of the Italian immigrants are peaceable and industrious, no other element matches them in propensity for personal violence. In homicide, rape, blackmail, and kidnapping they lead the foreign born." This criminal instinct, according to Ross, was rooted in Italians'—particularly southern Italians'—"primitive stage of civilization." Summarizing (and powerfully validating) these views, the U.S. Immigration Commission concluded succinctly in its monumental Dillingham report (1911) that "certain kinds of criminality are inherent in the Italian race."[4]

In the years following the New Orleans lynchings, Italians' reputation for brutal criminality in Chicago only grew. Part of this reputation came directly from the "facts" of the day. Some Italians *were* active in crime, particularly violent crime in these early years. According to Chicago police arrest records on personal violence offenses between 1905 and 1908, Italians ranked first among all nationalities in homicides; second in abduction, kidnapping, and rape; and third in violent assault. Regarding violent offenses against public policy, Italians were arrested at almost twice the rate of any other nationality group in Chicago. Of course, arrest rates should not be viewed as objective proof of the extent of Italians' criminality. Indeed, Italians' very reputation as dangerous, stiletto-wielding hoodlums no doubt affected police officers' views and treatment of them. Still, that Italians could rank so high in violent crime, when they constituted less than 6 percent of Chicago's foreign-born population, indicates that the connection between Italians and crime was not wholly a newspaper invention.[5]

Newspapers did, however, exaggerate the connection. Between 1904 and 1912, for instance, the *Chicago Record-Herald* published fifty-three articles about Italians, nearly 80 percent of which dealt with crime of some sort—generally violent crime. Typical headlines were "Cascone Confesses Six Murders," "Italian Murders," "Italian Nuns Murdered," and "Italians Cause Shooting Panic." In 1915, reviewing Italian neighborhood violence, the paper wrote that "five persons were shot in May alone. In 1911, the dead numbered forty; in 1912, thirty-three; in 1913, thirty-one; in 1914, forty-two."[6] Similarly, the *Chicago Tribune* never tired of describing the gory details of Italian violent crime or of ruminating on the criminalistic tendencies of Italians. One article from 1910 noted that "cattle stealing, like other forms of lawlessness, prevails in Sicily because the general character of the people in all ranks of society is such as to produce crime." A year later the paper, in a front-page story about an attempted murder of an Italian around "Death Corner" on the Near North Side, printed a list of the "34 unsolved murders of Italians in 14 months in Chicago."[7]

This constant criminalizing campaign forced Italians to respond. In 1910, one man complained in a letter to the *Chicago Record-Herald* that "every time a mysterious crime is committed anywhere near an Italian settlement the papers in large letters attribute such crime to the Italians or to the so-called Black Hand, just as though only Italians were capable of committing crimes . . . of the most atrocious kinds. Such an attitude on the part of the papers brings all Italians into ill repute, causes hatred, and may possibly stir up race warfare in certain districts." In an article published in the *City Club Bulletin* in 1912, prominent Italian-American attorney and politician, Bernard Barasa, also objected to the local press's treatment of Italians: "Whenever there is a mystery in this city—somebody has been killed and nobody knows who did it—oh it's the Black hand, say the newspapers in great big black headlines. When they say Black hand that means Italians, of course, nobody else."[8]

Despite these protests, Italian-language newspapers were often just as guilty of sensationalizing Italian lawlessness and drawing implicit connections between their *connazionali* and crime. Although papers like *L'Italia* avoided deterministic racial explanations for crime, often preferring to blame poor law enforcement for the problems, they still frequently published lurid stories of Italian crime that tended to belie these arguments. In 1910, for instance, while *L'Italia* published a front-page story on how statistics proved Italians' low rates of delinquency, in virtually every issue that year the paper featured prominent front-page stories with huge headlines like "Feroce Omicidio fra Italiani" (Ferocious Homicide Among Italians); "Furente di Gelosia, Uccide il Marito" (Raging with Jealousy, Kills Husband); "Un Padre di Sette Figli Ucciso sotto gli Occhi della Moglie" (A Father of Seven Children Killed before His Wife's Eyes); "Altri Due Fatti di Sangue Turbano il West Side" (Another Two Acts of Blood Disturb West Side); "Due Assasini in Tre Giorni al North Side" (Two Assassinations in Three Days on the North Side); "Bambina di Sei Anni Sgozzata da un Bruto" (Six-year-old Child Has Neck Cut by Brute). The next year the paper ran an article on "Crimes in the Italian Colony" and stated: "Day after day, week after week, more and more crimes are being committed, the perpetrators of which are invariably Italians. . . . Naturally, these frequent crimes give a bad impression of the Italian colony to other nationalities. . . . We must do something to prevent these crimes."[9]

Thanks mainly to the reporting of Chicago's English- and Italian-language newspapers, then, "to be an Italian in Chicago was to be suspect as a member of the Black Hand or Mafia, a red-handed murderer, bomb-thrower, and extortionist." Indeed, by 1919, the connection between Italians and crime had become so intimate in the minds of many Chicagoans that a Department of Public Welfare report felt the need to refute the "popular fallacy" that Italians "possess in some way a *natural* faculty for getting into trouble."[10] With the passage of Prohibition, such "fallacies" would only multiply.

Italian Organized Crime in the Era of Prohibition

Prohibition did not create organized crime *de novo* nor did it spawn the massive "crime wave" thought to have engulfed many American cities in the 1920s. Led by men like "Big Jim" Colosimo and Mont Tennes and centering on gambling and prostitution, organized crime—at least in Chicago—predated Prohibition (which took effect in January 1920) by several decades.[11] Regardless, Chicagoans and their various institutions believed that crime was on the rise in a most menacing and meteoric way and that Italians were largely to blame for this rise. In many ways Italians represented an easy scapegoat for perceived crime increases. Italians had long been portrayed and perceived as violent and lawless hoodlums, who inhabited places like "Death Corner," formed secret criminal organizations like the Black Hand and the Mafia, and killed, extorted, abducted, and maimed at alarming rates. Equally important is that perception and reality did overlap some when it came to Italians' organized crime activity. At both the leadership and underling levels, of course, organized crime was as diverse as Chicago itself with solid representation among groups like Jews, Germans, Poles, Irish, and native-born Americans. But with leaders like Jim Colosimo, the Genna and Aiello brothers, Vincent Drucci, Johnny Torrio, Al Capone, and others, Italians represented a sizable and visible portion of Chicago's underworld during the Prohibition Era. Indeed, when in 1930 the Chicago Crime Commission first published its list of the city's twenty-eight biggest public enemies, the top eight were all Italian.[12]

A series of stories occurring at different times during the Prohibition Era dramatized the role of Italians in organized crime. Perhaps the most important of these was what Chicago-based criminologist John Landesco termed the "royal succession" of (southern) Italian underworld kings from Colosimo to Torrio to Capone. The latter two men came as close as anyone to ruling organized crime in Chicago during the Prohibition Era. Both men came from New York to Chicago, Torrio at the behest of Colosimo in 1909 and Capone at the behest of Torrio around a decade later. Upon arrival in Chicago, Torrio fast became Colosimo's most prized lieutenant, helping him to run a vast crime ring of brothels, gambling houses, and saloons. When Colosimo was murdered in May 1920 just as Prohibition was taking effect, Torrio moved quickly into the bootlegging business. Known as a "calm, poised, efficient businessman," Torrio built strong alliances with political leaders in Chicago and its suburbs, created a system of cooperation between various gangs by dividing the city into spheres of influence, and generally systematized the manufacture and distribution of alcohol in much of the city. As a result, by 1924, Torrio had become the undisputed "overlord" of the underworld.[13]

Soon territorial squabbles between gangsters like the Genna brothers and Dion O'Banion, as well as the election of tough-on-crime mayoral candidate William Dever in 1923, threatened to destroy Torrio's intricate network of bootlegging, gambling, and prostitution. After narrowly escaping an assassination attempt in January 1925, Torrio was sent to jail for nine months for his arrest during a brewery raid. Immediately upon release in the fall of 1925, fearing his life and rich from gangland profits, Torrio fled from Chicago and was thought to have never returned.

Torrio's hand-picked successor was Al Capone, who began his Chicago organized crime career in the late 1910s as a bodyguard for "Big Jim" Colosimo. After Colosimo's death, Capone rose quickly within the ranks of

Torrio's syndicate and had become second in charge by 1922. When Dever's election in 1923 forced Torrio to move his illicit activities to Chicago's western suburbs, Capone headed these operations in Cicero. When Torrio left Chicago in 1925, anarchy and violence initially reigned— between the fall of 1923 and the fall of 1926, 375 gang members were killed, 215 in battles with themselves, 160 in battles with police.[14] But Capone eventually replaced his mentor as *the* dominant figure in Chicago organized crime, by ruthlessly eliminating enemies, building alliances with the city's political leaders, and expanding Torrio's operations into new fields like racketeering and into new locales like Chicago Heights. In time, Capone became much more than a Chicago crime leader; he became an icon of the Prohibition Era—"Big Al," "Scarface Al"—"the most talked-about and written-about man in the world." By 1929, the *New York Times* remarked that "probably no private citizen in American life has ever had so much publicity in so short a period of time as . . . Capone." He was the subject of books, movies, plays, pulp fiction magazine stories, biographies, psychological analyses, and newspaper exposés.[15]

Torrio's and Capone's ascendancy and rule in the 1920s, though the best known, did not single-handedly draw attention to Italians and organized crime. There were also the vicious West Side "Beer Wars" between the Genna and O'Banion gangs during the mid-1920s, which led to the deportation drive of 1926. Over the course of several weeks, the local press ran front-page stories, declaring that "almost 1000 murders in Chicago in the last twenty years are blamed by police on Sicilians," a group of people responsible for "Black Hand. Mafia. Camorra. Murder. Bombs. Extortion. Terror." In addition, it printed front-page cartoons demonizing "alien gangsters"; ran editorials imploring the federal government to "deport the gangsters" since "Chicago and other American cities have been the scenes of scores of murders by Sicilian assassins"; and chronicled on its front-page almost daily the killing of one Italian after another.[16] The deportation drive, which largely targeted Sicilians, came as the logical culmination of weeks-long hysterical crime coverage by Chicago's press that painted Sicilians as public enemies number one.

Two and a half years later, in the summer of 1928, a string of events brought the local press to a fever pitch again. First, on September 7, 1928, came the murder of Antonio Lombardo, a close associate of Capone and an important underworld leader. The killing appeared to be a result of an ongoing battle between different Italian criminal factions over control of the Italo-American National Union and may have also been an act of revenge for the murder of New York crime chief Frank Uale several months earlier by Capone's men. A week later, in what was thought to be a related incident, newspapers reported the kidnapping of a small Italian boy, William Ranieri, on the Near West Side. These events together set off another vocal press campaign against Sicilians that lasted for several weeks. The *Chicago Tribune*, along with Assistant State's Attorney Samuel Hoffman and United States Secretary of Labor James Davis, called for the deportation of alien criminals. In an editorial discussing the "lessons of the Ranieri case," the *Tribune* complained: "a Sicilian community is deliberately an alien island in American life, made up of aliens who have no wish to become a part of American life, who stubbornly resist its influence, and do not intend to be assimilated into American citizenship. It is preposterous that such aliens have been given . . . the privileges of citizenship, the right to vote and hold office." The paper also published a short retrospective on the New Orleans lynching of eleven Italians in 1891, in which it noted approvingly that crime rates decreased significantly after the event; the point was that Chicagoans might learn something from Southerners' extreme form of crime prevention.[17]

Taken together, these stories about Capone, Torrio, Lombardo, the "Beer Wars," and the Ranieri kidnapping all sent Chicagoans the same message: Italians—and particularly Sicilians—were a criminally inclined, dangerous, sinister lot. That this message was well received is evident in many ways. Numerous everyday Chicagoans came to deeply resent Italians and "their" criminal tendencies. While many admired Capone and turned out to cheer him on during his trial, many others despised him. As one anonymous letter-writer in 1932 fumed to the Chicago Crime Commission: "Why isn't someone big enough to put a gun to the head of that dirty Italian Capone?" Another Chicagoan writing to the *Tribune*, the Chicago Crime Commission, and Judge Wilkerson (who presided over Capone's trial for tax evasion) called Capone a "rotten crook (*Italian* leader of the U.S.)" and implored the local authorities to "hang some more crooks in Cook County, or execute them with electricity, or drown them." During Capone's trial in 1931, his defense attorney, Michael Ahern, was careful to ask all prospective jurors if they harbored any "race prejudice" against Italians. Similarly, in the mid-1920s while William Dever was mayor of Chicago, he received numerous complaints from constituents about lawless "dagoes" in their neighborhood or about a certain "dago grocery store" where "they sell it like you were buying bread." Meanwhile, at the height of gang battles on the Near North Side and in the wake of the Lombardo murder, Father Luigi Giambastiani received an anonymous letter stating that "Americans of the United States in general and Chicago in particular are getting very sick and tired of the continual bulldozing and predatory acts of Italians here." The letter concluded with this not-so-subtle threat: "Americans have a habit of taking law into their own hands which regular law enforcing bodies fail to enforce."[18]

These sorts of antagonistic feelings and criminalized stereotypes had their everyday consequences for many Italians. In attempting to find neighborhood people jobs in late 1928, for instance, the Chicago Commons ran into problems when the prospective employee was Italian. One employer asked this of a Commons worker about an Italian applicant: "How do you know that this young man is not a member of some Italian gang?

Can you give assurance that he is not?" Numerous Italians from all over Chicagoland recalled in oral interviews that by the 1920s and early 1930s, many Chicagoans assumed that they had criminal connections. One man, who came of age during the Prohibition Era in Forest Park, a western suburb of Chicago, recalled: "A lot of times if you told people you were Italian, they'd look upon you and right away they thought you were a gangster." Speaking about her high school classmates in the late 1920s and early 1930s, a woman from Chicago Heights remembered that "they sort of connected everybody that was Italian with that [gangster] type of people." A man from the Near North Side noted similarly that during the Prohibition Era and for some time after it "Americans stereotyped Italians as bein' all Capones." One report on juvenile delinquency put it well: "During the late twenties and early thirties . . . Italian and hoodlum became almost synonymous [sic] in the public's mind."[19]

Race, Color, and Crime

Italians—particularly Sicilians—were subjected to constant condemnation in the local press, pulp fiction magazine stories, popular books, and movies; a deportation drive in 1926 (and again in 1930);[20] and steady questioning from their neighbors, co-workers, employers, and even connazionali on some occasions (as we will see) about their potential ties to organized crime and their supposed lawless inclinations.

But it should first be stressed that Chicago institutions and individuals did not uniformly denounce gangsters. At times, some newspapers, pulps, books, and movies could offer quite flattering portrayals of criminals. This was particularly the case with Al Capone. If newspapers were often unrelenting in their attacks against Italian criminals, many reserved an occasional soft spot for the "Big Fellow." The following headlines were not wholly atypical for Chicago's dailies in the late 1920s and early 1930s: "Al Capone Host to Schoolmates of his Son"; "Capone Gives out Soda Pop"; "Al Capone Feeds 3,000 Jobless Daily; Fan Mail Grows."[21] Similarly, popular books and pulps could betray a likable and admirable side to Capone. One pulp noted that Capone "is not the ordinary run of gangster, but a shrewd, brainy, quick thinking, cool tempered man. He is known to be very generous and is at all times helping someone." Another pulp opened this way: "Who's that big healthy-looking fellow with the grin and the blue-eyes. . . . That's Al, who's way, way up in the bucks. He made a lot of dough and he carved a place in history for himself when he was making it. Sure! General Grant and George Washington and Robert E. Lee are in the schoolbooks. Why not Al? He has ducked more bullets than Grant heard at Vicksburg. They've been shooting at Al for ten years!"[22]

Many Chicagoans (among other Americans) also secretly or openly admired Al Capone, whom, according to one biographer, was the subject of a "sort of hero worship." In 1930, some fifty citizens of Monticello, Iowa chose Capone as a write-in candidate for town mayor, while students at Medill School of Journalism in Chicago picked him as one of the ten "most outstanding personages in the world." The following year while Capone was on trial for tax evasion charges, the *Chicago American* noted: "Chicago's attitude toward the trial is a curious one. Half the town is watching the proceedings nervously, with a heavy feeling that it is time that something were done, and a sick hope that the jury will convict him. . . . The other half still looks on him as a sort of amiable pirate, and besides . . . Capone caters to a demand, and efficiently too." During the trial while Capone was detained at the Cook County Jail, one detective in charge of monitoring in-coming mail noted that the crime boss received fifty to seventy-five letters a day from all over the world. Newspapers often suggested that women in particular had a fondness for Capone. The *Chicago Times*, having remarked on the large number of admiring women on hand at Capone's trial, quoted Mrs. Beele Williamson as saying: "you know I think Mr. Capone is just a wonderful looking man. I suppose I shouldn't say so, but my heart goes out to him." At another Capone public appearance, the *Chicago Evening American* observed two girls in the crowd with "eyes wide and shining" muttering adoringly, "gee, ain't he swell."[23]

Some Chicagoans readily defended all Italians—not just the gangster celebrities like Capone—from racialized attacks. The *Chicago Daily News*, for instance, published a letter during the deportation drive of 1926 from one Mary C. Brennan, who hoped that the campaign to rid Chicago of a few undesirable Sicilians would not damage the good name of all Italians. Several years later the same paper published an editorial, titled "Worthy Italian-American Neighbors," by Chicago Commons head resident and renowned reformer Graham Taylor. Having lived among Italians on the Near Northwest Side for decades, Taylor felt compelled to support his neighbors since "a very small minority are causing the great majority of them to be cruelly misunderstood and unjustly judged." Similarly, during the deportation hysteria of 1926, local Superior Judge Michael L. McKinley declared: "it is begging the question to say that Sicilians such as the so-called Genna gangsters are responsible for corrupt conditions surrounding the enforcement of law and order. Justice is throttled and crime created not by any desperate gang of criminals, but because the pay of politics is at the throat of law enforcement everywhere." Italians also received occasional support from fellow immigrant groups, the local Catholic Church, and left-wing community activists. Joseph Miller, a writer for several labor publications, stated at an Italian protest meeting against the deportation drive that "the newspapers and politicians are to blame for attributing the criminal situation in Chicago upon the Italian people. . . . There is more crime committed by the Irish, Swedes, and Poles than by Italians."[24]

Also supporting Italians, if somewhat less directly, was a group of local sociologists and criminologists, who worked tirelessly in these years to demonstrate that criminality had its roots in environmental or social—not racial—characteristics. All connected in some way or at some time to the Chicago School of Sociology, Clifford Shaw, John Landesco, Ernest Burgess, Henry McKay, and others studied and wrote extensively about organized crime and juvenile delinquency in these years. They all worked, as well, for the Illinois Association for Criminal Justice during the 1920s, helping to write different portions of that institution's monumental *Illinois Crime Survey*, published in 1929. While all these men studied different aspects of urban crime, they adhered to one general assumption that guided their work: social conditions, not racial traits, produced criminals. As John Landesco concluded in his classic, *Organized Crime in Chicago*, "the gangster is a product of his surroundings in the same way in which a good citizen is a product of his environment. The good citizen has grown up in an atmosphere of obedience to law and respect for it. The gangster has lived his life in a region of lawbreaking, of graft, and of 'fixing.' That is the reason why the good citizen and the gangster have never been able to understand each other. They have been reared in two different worlds."[25]

Such a view must have been music to the ears of many Sicilians and other Italians, who were not oblivious to the ways in which criminalization and racialization worked in tandem. Both the type and quantity of crime coverage marked Italians unmistakably as racially distinct and problematic in a variety of ways. First, the mere appearance of Italians' constant criminal activity strongly suggested, even if it was rarely stated, that they were somehow *hereditarily drawn* to crime. This sort of subtle racialization was most apparent in the *Tribune*'s ongoing campaign of anti-Sicilian commentary and criminalization. The paper rarely spoke explicitly about heredity and inferior blood, always preferring to discuss Italians' or Sicilians' putatively problematic Old World customs, traditions, and history. Still, the paper emphasized Sicilian and Italian criminality so unrelentingly that, to many of its readers, these undesirable traits must have seemed immutable and, thus, rooted in something more constant than customs and culture—something like heredity. Sometimes the paper made outright statements to this effect. When little William Ranieri was kidnapped, his father was loath to involve the police, a "custom," the *Tribune* informed its readers, that was "inborn in Sicilians and some Italians." Most of the time, however, the paper simply hinted at heredity. In one editorial from 1928, the paper concluded that Sicily "does not produce good citizen material for this republic" and that therefore such people ought to be excluded from immigrating to the United States. After all, argued the *Tribune*, "in regard to Orientals, we have adopted a rigid exclusion on the ground that they are unassimilable, but it is to be doubted if they are less assimilable than the people of the typical Little Sicily of our cities. . . . To assimilate them [Sicilians] into American life is difficult if not impossible." In an editorial appearing in the wake of the Lombardo murder, the paper wrote: "No one can read the list of names of the dead gangsters without being impressed with their alien character. Most of them are Sicilians, children of a land notorious for its feuds for centuries. They come here with a tradition of banditry and private vengeance. Even their countrymen who seek to earn an honest living here are so steeped in the customs of their native land that they refuse to give testimony even against murderers."[26] Again, while "customs" and "traditions" are emphasized, one had to wonder why they seemed so resistant to change over "centuries" of time and an ocean of space. To these sorts of questions, race seemed like an obvious answer.

Second, crime stories also marked Italians as racially distinct and problematic by continually stressing their dark skin. In describing the tight police security at Antonio Lombardo's funeral, the *Tribune* wrote that "Chicago policemen rubbed against dark skinned mourners seeking the feel of a pistol." When reporting on the murder of gang chieftain Dion O'Banion in November 1924, the *Chicago Daily News* described the assailants as "swarthy" and thus "probably Italians." Conversely, in a story about the attempted assassination of Johnny Torrio a few months later in January 1925, the *Chicago Herald Examiner* noted that, according to one eyewitness, the assailant had a "light complexion" and was therefore most likely "not an Italian." Similarly, Al Capone was constantly portrayed in books, magazine articles, pulps, and movies as having a "dark" or "swarthy" complexion. When he appeared in court in 1929 in Philadelphia on charges of having concealed a weapon, the *Chicago Daily News* noticed that his "face, which is rather dark, assumed a dull reddish hue."[27] No one emphasized Italians' dark features more than popular writer and former newsman Walter Burns. In his book, *The One-Way Ride*, Johnny Torrio was "a slight, dapper, dark young man"; gunmen John Scalise and Albert Anselmi had "dark faces"; the Genna brothers were "swarthy, black haired, black eyed, looked not unlike Arabs, and probably had in their ancestral strain a strong dash of Saracenic [North African] blood"; Giuseppe Neroni was "a tall, dark, gaunt man with falcon eyes"; Orazio Tropea was "lean, swarthy, with a cruel face and black, wintry eyes"; and Felipe Gnolfo had "a twilight complexion, dark enough to suggest night, and cold, hard, black eyes that slanted like a Chinaman's."[28]

Finally, many commentators further racialized Italian criminals by describing them as savage—and sometimes simian—beasts more akin to animals than human beings. Mass culture's descriptions of Capone perfectly exemplify this point, which, for all its hero-worship, could be quite extreme and explicit on this point. Biographer Fred Pasley admitted that, his virtues aside, Capone was still a "Neapolitan by birth and Neanderthal by instinct. . . . 'Gorilla Man'—the flat nose; the thick, pedulous lips; the big bullet head, squatting, rather than sitting, on the lumpy neck; the scar on the left cheek, along the protuberant jawbone; and the great shaggy black eyebrows—hairy battlements, once seen, not forgotten, lending the harsh, swarthy visage a terrifying aspect." The *Chicago American* painted a similar picture: "Obese, pudgy, oily, Al Capone, the king of the rackets, not only is a repulsive creature but looks it. He rose from the water rats of Brooklyn; he never lost the slimy taint of his origin." "Thick lips, bushy brows, greedy eyes, fat hands—Capone! . . . Over the bodies of murdered men and ruined women he rose to rule." Under his fingerprints the newspaper ran the caption, "The Mark of the Beast!," and called the Capone era in Chicago the "Apex of Savagery." In a radio address given in February 1931, Henry Barrett Chamberlin, operating director of the Chicago Crime Commission, called Capone "the most dangerous, the most resourceful, the most cruel, the most menacing, the most conscienceless of any criminal in modern times"; he was, in short, "the lone gorilla of gangland."[29]

Of course, Capone was not the only Italian gangster to be described in these ways. Fred Pasley called one Capone associate a "savage wop," and the *Chicago Tribune* ran front-page headlines about Italian kidnappers threatening to behead children and stories about how only select community leaders could keep Sicilians "from murdering each other." Walter Burns painted Colosimo as "jungle bred" and a rich man who lived "on a scale of barbaric magnificence"; he likened Italian assassins to "jungle beasts watching a trail" and spoke of Sicilians as if they were a separate species entirely. In describing the mysteries of one gang murder in the late 1920s, Burns wrote: "None but Sicilians were capable of such a charmingly courteous atrocity. This unique crime was the work of artists in murderous stagecraft and adepts [sic] in the finesse of treachery. . . . The psychologist able to fathom the Sicilian soul could solve the mystery of life and death as if it were a kindergarten exercise. One wonders if God understands Sicilians."[30]

All this talk about simian and swarthy savages suggests that Prohibition-Era criminalizing discourse and action challenged Italians' whiteness. The *Tribune*, as we have seen, called for an "Oriental-like" exclusion of Sicilian immigrants, while popular writers likened Italian gangsters to "Chinamen" and speculated openly about their Saracenic blood. However, these challenges never led to any sustained or systematic positioning of Italians as nonwhite. For all the racialized and colorized criminalization targeted at Italians by newspapers, pulps, the Chicago Police Department, the U.S. Immigration Service, and the Chicago Crime Commission, the federal government never followed the *Tribune*'s advice and excluded Sicilians from immigrating to the United States; nor did it revoke Italians' right to naturalize as "free white persons"; nor did it recategorize Italians as nonwhite in the census (as it did with Mexicans in 1930). Meanwhile, in Chicago, Italians' criminal reputation caused some problems at the workplace and in neighborhoods. Still, as the *Chicago Defender* bitterly pointed out in 1928, even the most notorious Italian gangsters, unlike the most upstanding and law-abiding African Americans, were "privileged to live wherever they choose to purchase homes . . . and every community is open to them." In the late 1920s, when the Park Manor Improvement Association organized against "undesirables," no neighbors gave the Capones any trouble; indeed, Al's mom, Theresa, signed the restrictive covenant for her son. This episode seems to have been typical for the time: Italians may have been seen as horrifyingly violent, lawless, treacherous, depraved, and immoral; but they were still white.[31]

Italians Respond

Throughout the Prohibition Era many Italians were acutely aware of how criminalization marked them as "wild beasts in human semblance" and portended grave racial (and perhaps color) consequences. As one Chicago Italian-language newspaper argued passionately in 1925, "the publicity given such material in certain papers creates the impression that the Italians are knife-wielders, thieves, delinquents, and generally depraved. The American newspapers seem to be trying to outdo each other to pin anything detrimental on the Italian race." Another Italian businessman accused the *Chicago Tribune* of "inciting hatred among races" through its treatment of Sicilians. And many Italians believed they understood the reasons for this unfair treatment: the Italo-American National Union—always at the center of criminal accusations—called it "false, unfounded, and deplorable race prejudice"; *La Tribuna Italiana Transatlantica* simply called it "race hatred."[32]

Whatever its name, many Italians felt overwhelmed by a never-ending criminalization campaign that, like immigration restriction legislation, marked them as racially inferior. How did Italians respond? Perhaps surprisingly, men and women appear to have responded in similar ways, despite the fact that organized crime was largely a masculine world in terms of both popular representations and reality. To be sure, many women were actively involved in the illicit home production of alcohol, upon which the city's entire bootlegging industry depended. One Italian man from Pullman called his Aunt Emilia "Queen of the Stills" for the ways in which she transformed her home into a small alky-cooking compound.[33] These points notwithstanding, the Chicago Crime Commission listed only men as public enemies; the local and federal authorities during the deportation drive of 1926 apprehended only men; the *Tribune*'s editorial cartoons demonizing "Sicilian gangsters" featured only men; and many popular books, movies, pulps, and newspapers spoke only of male gangsters and continually stressed their masculine traits—their aggressiveness, toughness, strength, and virility.[34] If much of organized crime was racialized as Italian, it was just as surely gendered as masculine. Regardless, limited evidence suggests that Italian women objected just as strongly as men to Italian (male) criminalization and fought against it just as doggedly. After all it was their husbands, fathers, sons, and brothers who were apprehended in dragnet sweeps in their neighborhoods and denied jobs because of their assumed connections to crime. Unsurprisingly, then, nearly as many women as men, in oral interviews, recalled bitterly the popular equation of gangster and Italian in these years; and in 1929, the Chicago Italian Woman's Club, a group of *prominenti's* wives, strongly objected to a Frank Loesch speech in which he, according to the group, "condemn[ed] a whole nation for the crimes of a few."[35]

These gender similarities notwithstanding, general responses to criminalization were as varied as the Italian "community" itself. Some Italians admired the power, wealth, style, and swagger of their gangster *connazionali* and appreciated their occasional acts of charity. Having grown up on the Near West Side in the Prohibition Era, Anthony Sorrentino, who later became active in juvenile delinquency prevention and treatment, recalled that "this was the height of the roaring twenties era when youthful gangs were rifling high and mighty—the most famous of which was the '42 gang'—a daring, fearless lot, at open warfare with the police and wider society. . . . These young men along with the older men in 'organized crime' were the heroes of our day." One Italian from Chicago Heights recalled Capone's visit in the mid-1920s: "I was in the saloon and Mr. Capone came in there, and he got a root beer for me. He seemed like a very nice, affable fellow." This same man also recalled Capone attending a local wedding celebration around the same time, at which "he had a handful of money, and he passed out bills to the old ladies." Some Italians went so far as to view gangsters as proof positive of their group's overall value and worth. One young, female hoodlum bragged during the Prohibition Era: "the Italians are great people. Not like the Jews, Irish, or Germans. The Wops are the greatest people. Look who we got. Al Capone, the world's biggest bootlegger; Jack McGurn [Vincenzo Demora], the best machine-gunner of the town; Marino the best daring boy of '42.' Then we got the best bomb makers and bomb throwers."[36]

Of course, not all Italians were so enthralled with criminals; many scorned them and supported the local and federal governments' efforts to apprehend these "scourges" of their race.[37] Newspapers continued to reproach their criminal *connazionali* on occasion. After a murder on the Near North Side in 1919, for instance, *L'Italia* commented sarcastically that "these deeds which continue to be committed so barbarously can do no more than 'augment' the sympathy of the Americans for the Italians, and we hope that they will be committed with more frequency since it will save us the expense of paying the return fare to Italy, because the authorities will surely be moved to send back to Italy free of charge all of us Italians, the good as well as the bad." Similarly, during the deportation drive of 1926, it is true that several key community institutions like *L'Italia* and the local Italian consulate vigorously opposed the effort, calling it a slur on the Sicilian people. But the community was divided on this point. Alessandro Mastro-Valerio, editor and publisher of *La Tribuna Italiana Transatlantica*, supported the drive since "those killers and lawless bootleggers are casting a stigma on our race's good name and it is high time it should be stopped." One Vincent Cristofano, in a letter to the *Chicago Tribune*, also applauded the drive and assured the authorities that "the best Italians are with you and urge you to keep up the good fight." Another letter writer of Sicilian ancestry agreed with Cristofano, declaring that "lowdown imported Sicilians" must be banned and banished from the United States.[38] Finally, by the late 1920s, the Italian consulate became increasingly active in combating *connazionali* crime. While continuing to defend their compatriots against unfair press treatment, the consulate supported alien deportation efforts as well as the local prosecution of Italians by having the consul general, Giuseppe Castruccio, sit in court next to the judge presiding over the Ranieri kidnapping case.[39]

Other Italian defense strategies against criminalization were the contradictory projects of nation/race building and nation/race differentiation. If Italians bore the brunt of criminalization campaigns in the Prohibition Era, it was really Sicilians who garnered the most negative attention. This led some Italians to avoid any association with Sicilians and to stress the differences between nation (one Italy) and race (many Italians: Sicilians and non-Sicilians, North and South Italians, etc.). At the height of anti-Sicilian hysteria during the deportation drive of February 1926, one man, describing himself as Italian and "not Sicilian," wrote a letter to the *Chicago Tribune*. After exhaustively listing the major problems with Sicily and Sicilians—race mixture, illiteracy, brigandage, the Mafia, and a hatred of all government—the writer concluded that "America has certainly received more than its share of the products of this barbarism." Evidently, the employment of discourses about Italian/Sicilian barbarism and savagery was not limited to non-Italians alone.[40]

But not all Italians chose differentiation. For more Italians, criminalizing attacks encouraged them to build a stronger and more unified community, in which (one Italian) race and (one Italian) nation were coterminous. As usual, this effort was often spearheaded by middle-class-led fraternal orders and newspapers and primarily involved the glorification of the Italian race/nation and the denial or deemphasis of community differences. While the English-language press demonized Sicilians and attempted to draw qualitative distinctions between them and other Italians, newspapers like *L'Italia*, *La Tribuna Italiana Transatlantica*, and *Vita Nuova* spoke only of "la nostra razza/nazionalita' italiana"—of which Sicilians were a part—and its many virtues. In one article appearing in March 1928, *L'Italia* spoke of the "desire to defend our nationality . . . [and] to demonstrate that the 200,000 Italians of Chicago represent an honest and laborious community." Similarly, speaking about its mission as a newspaper, *Vita Nuova* noted in 1925 "the Italo-American press should . . . desist from printing stories of misdeeds and, rather, concentrate on publishing articles relating the doings of the many Italians who are truly honoring their race and adopted country. . . . We of *Vita Nuova* wish to diffuse the truth that for every delinquent Italian there are hundreds who are law-abiding, and for every misdeed committed by an Italian there are thousands of good deeds performed by others of the race." Organizations like the Italo-American National Union attempted to perform a similar service to that of newspapers. It refuted notions about Italian-Sicilian differences, arguing repeatedly that Sicily was a critical part of the Italian nation and changing its name from the Unione Siciliana to make this point and to welcome non-Sicilians as members. It also lauded Italians, "in whose veins flows the blood of that ancient and noble [Roman] civilization."[41]

Finally, Italians defended themselves against racialized criminalization by arguing, along with scholars like Ernest Burgess and Clifford Shaw, that one's environment—not one's race—explained criminality and that it was the American or Chicago environment, in particular, that produced Italian crime. Giovanni Schiavo concluded his book, *The Italians in Chicago*, by arguing that crimes "are the product of environment rather than nationality"—particularly the American environment, in which criminals enjoy "relative immunity guaranteed by lax local conditions and by the evident collusion between politicians and criminals."[42] Italian-language newspapers like *L'Italia* and *La Tribuna Italiana Transatlantica* continuously attacked the local police, judges, and politicians, as well as the Prohibition law, for turning Chicago into a veritable "Porcopolis" (literally, "Pig City").[43] The Italian consul general in Chicago, Signor Lopoldo Zunini, asked pointedly at the height of deportation hysteria in February 1926: "If the Sicilians and Italians are responsible for this criminal situation, why aren't they responsible for similar situations at home? Crime does not exist there on the scale it does here. And it is because the measures against crime in Italy are stern. . . . I believe that politicians who want votes of the good and bad regardless are in a large measure responsible for the criminal situation here." Even many in the Italian left agreed in part with the arguments of their traditional enemies, the *prominenti*, by focusing on the systemic roots of crime: to those at *Il Lavoratore*, the Italian organ of the Communist Workers' Party of America, Chicago and its rampant crime and corruption represented the quintessence of "civilta' capitalista!"[44]

What do these varied responses tell us about Italians' race and color identity at the time? For some Italians, Sicilians, particularly when they were demonized as criminals, were either not "real" Italians or a racially inferior subgroup of them. However, the bulk of the Italian community seems to have rejected such efforts in favor of a more inclusive race/nation building project. As during immigration restriction debates, Italians, particularly the well positioned *prominenti*, were working harder to transcend regional and town divisions in their "communities" and to forge a more salient Italian identity among their *connazionali*. Regarding color, because it was rarely questioned in any direct or ultimately consequential way, Italians, as in the immigration restriction debates, refrained from asserting a white identity when it came to issues of crime and criminalization. To Italians, as well as to non-Italians, color issues never seemed entirely relevant to discussions about organized crime.

Just as the passage of Prohibition did not create organized crime, the law's repeal in 1933 did not end it. Nor did it end the harsh criminalization and racialization of Italians. Criminal stereotypes continued to haunt Italians well into the World War II years and beyond. Newspapers often remained at the forefront of the attack, by publishing front-page stories on how Capone's men—all Italians—still ruled Chicago's underworld ten years after the St. Valentine's Day Massacre; by continuing to sensationalize and place undue stress on Italian crime; and by featuring columns by men like Westbrook Pegler, who became an archenemy of many Italians for his scathing critiques of "gangster culture in America," something for which no other group but Italians could take credit. After all, argued Pegler in 1938, "no Swede, Irishman, German or Jew ever bore the name of Tucillo, De Laurento, Tough Tony Califiori, Lucky Luciano, Cheeks Luciano, Montana, Mangano, Cosmano, Curozzo, Pepe or Johnny Genaro, James Belcastro, Rocco Fanelli, Danny Vallo, Alterie, Aiello, Nitti, Natti, Campagna, Canelli, Rio, Piazza, Camera, Ceaquinta, Catanda, Maggio, Maltese, Pisano, Gambina or Vincenzo Demora."

Italians remained vigilant in their counterattack against criminalization. One *L'Italia* editorial from 1938 castigated American newspapers for branding "all Italians as master criminals" and for engineering a "seemingly concerted and paid campaign of racial hatred" against them.[45] In the end, while this continuing criminalization never seriously threatened Italians' claims to whiteness, it remained the most prominent way in which Chicagoans (among other Americans) marked Italians as undesirable—whether this undesirability was seen in "racial" terms in the 1920s or in "nationality" and "ethnic" terms during World War II and beyond.

5

MAYORAL RACES,
MAYORAL COLORS

On April 2, 1927, only days before Chicago's mayoral election between William Hale Thompson and William Dever, *La Tribuna Italiana Transatlantica* weighed in on the contest. Openly expounding on the "Negro Question and Thompson," it noted bitterly that Thompson, by courting African-American support, was making Chicago "the Paradise Land of the negroes" and a living hell for "bianchi" (whites)—especially the Italians among them. According to the paper, African Americans were invading Italian neighborhoods, depreciating property values, stealing jobs, and giving rise to a "promiscuity of races" and a new generation of "cioccolattini" (little chocolate-colored people), who were "neither whites nor blacks but 'fifty and fifty.'"[1] While not necessarily typical of Italian views on politics or color at the time, *La Tribuna*'s article does accurately reflect the central role color had come to play in Chicago's mayoral campaigns of the late 1920s and early 1930s. And while race—or at least Italian race—was not mentioned in this article, it too was a part of these campaigns.

This chapter focuses on three campaigns involving Republican "Big Bill" Thompson—the Thompson versus Dever mayoral contest of 1927, the Thompson versus Judge John H. Lyle Republican primary of 1931, and the Thompson versus Anton Cermak mayoral race of the same year. All are particularly important because they occurred just as large numbers of Italians were becoming citizens and voters and because race and color issues were central components of these campaigns, probably more so than at any other time in Chicago history.

Mayoral politics offers another perspective on Chicago Italians' anomalous social position as racial outsiders and color insiders. In certain campaigns, candidates and political parties used crime wave anxieties to mobilize voters; and Italians—often implicitly, but sometimes explicitly too—were the racialized embodiment of these anxieties. At the same time, these campaigns hardly disqualified Italians from claiming the wages of white-ness in the political arena. Indeed, in 1927, when the Democratic Party at-tempted to mobilize whites as whites against "Thompson and his negroes," Italians were certainly among those voters targeted. And yet Italians seem, by and large, to have ignored such appeals, voting alongside African Ameri-cans and sharing many of the same electoral habits, partisan allegiances, and political heroes. Italians mobilized themselves electorally far more often around *Italianita'* than whiteness, a pattern that both reflected and con-tributed to the former's growing power.

Electoral Politics in the Early Years

Prior to the 1920s and 1930s, race and color issues played a minor, though not entirely insignificant, role in Chicago electoral politics. Color crept into mayoral politics as soon as African Americans started migrating in large numbers to Chicago. From the very start of his first term in office in 1915, Mayor "Big Bill" Thompson openly courted African-American voters by, among other means, distributing a small fraction of civil service jobs and political appointments to them.[2] It did not take long for Thompson oppo-nents to condemn these practices as preferential treatment for African Americans and to label City Hall derisively "Uncle Tom's Cabin." Barely six months into his first term, aldermen found stuffed in their City Hall mail-boxes a mock playbill announcing the coming of a "Grand Performance! Mayor Thompson as Uncle Tom." Meanwhile, the *Chicago Tribune* openly reported that Thompson's generous hiring policies with regard to African Americans were "supplanting white men." By the 1919 mayoral election, according to one report, "all the prejudice tom-toms were sounding furi-ously."[3]

When Thompson won reelection, color tensions only mounted. One Democratic newspaper announced in a massive headline: "NEGROES ELECT BIG BILL." Meanwhile, "the white people of Chicago" according to one citi-zen, "greatly resented" the growing political importance of African Ameri-cans and "the way in which the colored voter put Mayor Thompson in of-fice again in this last election." Equally infuriating was the way the "colored people freely talk of their power over the whites through their hold over 'Big Bill' Thompson—their equality with the whites."[4] In the end, however, African Americans were still too small a percentage of the electorate to become too big a political issue in the early 1920s. Then in 1923, when Thompson failed to run for reelection because of internal divi-sions within the local Republican Party, color issues in local politics faded from view.

The same could not be said for race, however, at least with regard to Ital-ians and their own intracommunity forms of political mobilization. Throughout these early years, Italian-language newspapers and fraternal orders used passionate appeals to the Italian race and nation to get their compatriots to the polls and to vote in particular ways. *L'Italia*, for instance, while always fiercely Republican, never allowed partisan issues to interfere with supporting "la nostra razza." It reminded its readers repeatedly in these years that "it is the duty of every Italian patriot to give the preference to the Italian candidates not paying attention to what party they belong [*sic*]." Similarly, fraternal orders like the Alleanza Riciglianese called on Italian voters to flock to the polls and put their *patria* before their partisanship. As President Vito Mescia urged the membership during World War I, "we have more Italian candidates on the Republican and Democratic ticket—Every one deserves our support—It is our duty to show our solidarity in order to assure the victory of the Italian candidates. Our generous nation [Italy] is contributing, in this World War, the blood of her best sons and many other sacrifices. It is our duty to protect her interest."[5]

Italian-American community institutions also used explicit racial and national appeals in an attempt to get particular candidates elected. Certainly, the best example of this was in 1923 when many Chicago Italians' golden child, Bernard Barasa, ran in the Republican mayoral primary. Throughout his campaign, *L'Italia* made innumerable appeals to "honor the race" by voting for "un fratello di sangue" (a blood brother).[6] And race appeals were not always reserved for Italian candidates. Several years earlier, *L'Italia* endorsed Judge Crowe for State's Attorney's office, despite the fact that Barasa—"a member of our race"—had supported his opponent, because Crowe had "married a woman of our race" and because his opponent David Matchett "has nothing in common with our race and is completely indifferent to our desires."[7]

These racial and national appeals appear to have resonated with some Italians, at least the fraction of those who were voting in these early years. Italians supported Barasa, for instance, overwhelmingly in the primary, and lost all interest in the election after he was trounced. One Italian laborer, according to two political scientists, "said that his candidate lost in the election and that he did not care to vote for anyone else. He declared that he wanted a candidate of his own race before he would vote." In his book on Italian Chicago published in the late 1920s, Giovanni Schiavo found a similar attachment among many Italians to candidates of their own race/nation: "It cannot be denied . . . that most Italians will vote for an Italian on the Democratic or Republican tickets." Always interested in portraying Italians as ideal candidates for American citizenship, Schiavo was sure to add that these Italian voting tendencies were quickly disappearing: "With the recognition of the Italian vote, the descendants of the Italians will merge the interests of their race with the interests of the community at large, and will not vote for a man of their own race simply because he happens to be one of their own." It is revealing, however, that as late as the 1920s, this transition in Italian voting patterns, according to Schiavo, had not yet occurred.[8]

Regardless of how prominent race and color issues might have been to elections in these early years, however, they could not have had too powerful an impact on the mass of Chicago Italians. The simple fact was that not enough of them were seriously involved in electoral politics yet. Many Italians were not yet American citizens. As late as 1924, only about 35 percent of Italian men and women in Chicago were naturalized, and in some neighborhoods these numbers were even lower.[9] But even among naturalized Italians or Italian Americans, many failed either to register or to vote. This appears to have been particularly a problem with Italian women. Having canvassed certain heavily Italian communities in the mid-1920s, political scientists Harold Gosnell and Charles Merriam found that "less than one-half of the adult female *citizens* were registered." And nonregistering and nonvoting plagued Chicago at large. At the time of Chicago's 1923 mayoral election, only 64 percent of eligible voters registered, and only 52 percent actually voted.[10]

Many reasons explain Italians' general failure to vote. When Gosnell and Merriam asked 315 American citizens of Italian birth why they had not voted in Chicago's 1923 mayoral election, they received a range of responses: some said they were too sick to vote (13 percent); some feared "loss of business or wages" (6.3 percent); some were disgusted with politics in general or with their own party (8.2 percent); some were not in town to vote (5.1 percent); some did not believe in women voting (5.1 percent). Still by far the largest reason for not voting was "general indifference," a response given by just under one-third of all Italian respondents. As one young Italian woman from the Near West Side remarked, "taxes and rents are high. The alley has not been cleaned twice in the summer and the children have no place to play but in the streets and alleys. It does no good to vote. You are always told to see someone else and nothing is done." Similarly, Sam Reda from the Near North Side told an interviewer at the same time that he "does not care especially to vote, for candidates promise so much before they are elected and then they fulfill none of [their promises]."[11]

It is not hard to understand why many Italians were so disillusioned with, and thus indifferent about, local electoral politics. For one, Chicago's ward system throughout this time period offered Italians minimal ward-level representation. Because of the way local politicians drew up ward boundaries, Italians were small voting minorities throughout the city. The one exception to this rule was on the heavily Italian Near West Side, where, after a series of ferocious battles between local Irish and Italian politicians, the Irish redrew ward boundaries to divide and dilute Italians' growing electoral strength. As a result, it was not until the election of Albert Prignano in the Near West Side's Twentieth Ward in 1927 that Italians had a compatriot alderman.[12] And there are other examples of Italians' significant underrepresentation in Chicago politics. Their political appointments at all levels of city and county government—from precinct captains to mayoral cabinet posts—were well under their county- and citywide proportions.[13] Rampant voter fraud in their neighborhoods must also have disillusioned many Italians. Of those wards with the most frequent cases of voter fraud, as well as "election murders, kidnappings, sluggings, and terrorizings," many were heavily Italian.[14] Finally, voting, as political scientists have recently theorized, is not only about individual-level actions but also about the "strategic mobilization" decisions of politicians, parties, interest groups, and the like. And it appears that in some Italian neighborhoods, these sorts of institutions and actors never completely committed themselves to getting new Italian voters to the polls or to naturalizing and registering the foreign-born among them. Among Italians on the Near West Side in the mid-1920s, for instance, Gosnell found that precinct captains were often far more interested in padding registration lists than in "trying to interest all their constituents in voting."[15]

By the late 1920s and early 1930s, however, many Chicago Italians' orientation toward local electoral politics—particularly voting—began to change. This was part of a much larger movement on the part of "new" European immigrants and ethnics to the registration booths and polling places in these years. Between 1920 and 1936, voter turnout in presidential elections more than doubled in Chicago, and much of this new turnout came from newly "immunized" immigrant groups like Italians.[16] Several factors explain Italians' new interest in voting. Increasing numbers of Italians became eligible to vote in these years as naturalization rates increased steadily in the 1920s and early 1930s and as growing numbers of second-generation Italians came of age.[17] Between 1920 and 1930 in the heavily Italian neighborhood around Chicago Commons, for example, the numbers of the naturalized foreign-born increased from 22 percent to 48.3 percent, thus doubling the proportion of the neighborhood's adult population eligible to vote.[18]

As a result, in part, of these demographic changes, local politicians and parties became more interested in mobilizing Italians. This change in priorities is most evident by looking at party appointments and the composition of party slates. Between 1918 and 1931, the average total number of Italians on Republican and Democratic Party slates was just over one person; by 1932, this number had jumped to six. Italians' representation among ward committeemen also increased dramatically in these years. Between 1918 and 1928, Italians had no more than one ward committeeman; by 1930, they had two; and by 1932, they had five. Four years later, Car-men Vacco was Democratic ward committeeman for the Twentieth Ward, while Daniel Serritella, William Pacelli, William Parillo, James Vignola, and Joseph Porcaro all were Republican ward committeemen for the First, Twentieth, Twenty-Fifth, Twenty-Sixth, and Twenty-Eighth Wards, respectively.[19]

Italians' rising electoral participation in the late 1920s and 1930s also came in response to an increasingly active state that shaped many Italians' lives in more profound ways everyday. This new activism could be repressive—as in the case of 1920s policies like Prohibition, immigration restriction, and repeated deportation drives—and/or benevolent—as in the case of 1930s New Deal relief, social insurance, home loans, jobs, and union protection.[20] Regardless of which, as the state impinged ever more on their everyday lives, Italians no doubt became more determined to shape its policies and actions. That this was the case is not just evidenced by increasing voter turnout. On the issue of housing, for instance, various Chicago Italians' routinely sent personal letters and petitions to President Roosevelt, Harold Ickes of the Public Works Administration (PWA), Senator J. Hamilton Lewis, among other public figures, to have a say in state policy and actions in their neighborhoods. When news broke that the federal government was considering building public housing projects in the 1930s on the Near North Side, Italian women like Josephine Scimeca and Ann Dovichi immediately wrote FDR and Ickes to offer their opinions on the project. Several years later on the Near West Side, Italian merchants and property owners sent numerous petitions to Washington, urging the federal government to go ahead with their local pubic housing plans, which, they hoped, would revitalize the neighborhood.[21]

"Shall the White People Continue to Rule Chicago?": The Mayoral Election of 1927

Just as Italians were becoming more involved in electoral politics, race and color came to the fore as central issues in this arena. This was particularly the case in the 1927 mayoral contest of William Dever and "Big Bill" Thompson. Debates raged during the election as to who was most to blame for the injection of these issues into the campaign. Thompson and his camp regularly accused Dever of stirring up "racial passion and prejudice for the purpose of . . . creating a hatred between whites and Negroes," while Dever and his crew made similar counteraccusations and newspapers and other partisans debated the issue hotly.[22] Regardless, by early April 1927, all could agree that race and color—particularly color—were at the very heart of the mayoral contest. What were once subtle innuendoes became central campaign slogans and mobilizing strategies. As the *Chicago Tribune* stated on election eve, "to the end, the colored question was exploited not only openly but almost flamboyantly." The *Chicago Herald Examiner* wrote that the campaign brought "the largest torrent of appeals to race and religious prejudice ever known in Chicago's history."[23]

Despite their many denials, Democrats largely initiated the color campaign. An undated memo written by Dever campaign strategists makes this point eminently clear. In what was called the "general outlines of the campaign," the memo stated that the only line of attack that would put Thompson on the defensive would be creating fear in the minds of the voters as to the consequences of another Thompson administration. But that fear must touch the average voter more intimately than, for instance, the city's credit, increased taxes, or the school board would. Or in other words Mr. Dever must appear in the role of a Knight Errant who will save the citizens from a very real peril that even the most illiterate can understand.

At the top of this list of potential "perils" was "the colored Voters." The memo noted that "Mr. Thompson in his primary campaign has promised the colored voters that if elected he would afford them facilities to spread out. If skillfully used this could be made into an issue that would make the South Side Voters sit up and take notice." After all, according to the memo, "the white neighbors [of African Americans] resent their invasion not only because they object to their presence, but worse because they fear that it will cause their property to depreciate." The Democrats should "capitalize [on] this fear."[24]

And capitalize they did—in any number of forms and venues. While Dever often tried to avoid color issues in his public appearances, all of his campaign speakers made it central fare for their stump speeches and comments for public consumption. Local Democratic Party leader George Brennan set the tone for the campaign when, only days after the primary victories of Thompson and Dever, he predicted that the latter would be reelected mayor because "I cannot believe that the people of Chicago will . . . turn the city over to be ruled by the Black Belt." Later in the campaign on the eve of the election, Brennan was even more blunt in his predictions: "Dever will be reelected mayor by a majority greater than he received four year ago for the reason that this is a white man's town."[25] Other speakers were equally forthright regarding color issues. State Representative from the South Side Michael Igoe placed the question—"shall the white people continue to rule Chicago?"—at the center of many of his stump speeches for Dever. Former State's Attorney Maclay Hoyne toured the city blaming the Color Riot of 1919 on Thompson's unwillingness to check African-American lawlessness. Along with Dever aide Raymond Robins, Hoyne also assailed Thompson for "talking America first, but acting Africa First." Finally, commissioner of Public Works under Dever, A. A. Sprague, used color appeals to scare working-class whites into the Democratic fold. On the Near North Side, he announced that if Thompson were to win, "all the crapshooting, undesirable colored men from the southern cities would migrate to Chicago. . . . It seems to me the laboring man should realize what a big influx of colored men would mean to him."[26]

And the Democratic color campaign extended well beyond speeches. In early March, just as the campaign was heating up, Dever police squads raided the Black Belt, shutting down businesses and arresting scores of people. While African-American leaders, Thompson, and other Republicans denounced the action as a deliberate attempt on the part of Democrats to "terrorize and intimidate colored voters," Democrats and police officials claimed the raids were necessary to bring some law and order to South Side African-American neighborhoods and to protect the law-abiding African-American citizens there.[27] However, these latter statements revealed that, if nothing else, fomenting white color consciousness and resentment against African Americans and Thompson was as much a motivating factor for the raids as anything else. Police Chief Collins used provocative color images and language in defending the raids. Initially, he stated that since Thompson's nomination, "white people did not dare stand on the sidewalks for fear that they would be elbowed off" and that "an orgy of lawlessness has been promoted in the colored wards that has never before been approached." "The trouble is," opined Collins publicly, "that some colored people think Oscar DePriest [prominent African-American politician] is mayor and the town is wide open."[28] Over time his remarks became even more inflammatory. By late March, a week or so before the election, Collins defended the raids by recounting stories of African-American men taking drunk "white" girls off to South Side vice resorts and by calling the Black Belt a "disgrace to civilization"; "it requires constant police activity to keep this part of the district in any semblance of decency."[29]

Democrats pushed these same color-coded messages in other ways. Throughout the city they hung posters proclaiming: "Is the Negro or the White Man to Rule Chicago?" or "Negroes First—William Hale Thompson for Mayor." They distributed handbills with, on one side, a cartoon of Thompson ignoring a "white" child and kissing a "black" one, and, on the other, the America First/Africa First slogan. According to the Thompson campaign, they "imported a number of gangs of colored men from other cities and are sending them, pretending to be drunken, to ride in street cars, jostling passengers and trying to provoke quarrels."[30] Democrats sent out a forged Thompson letter to thousands of African Americans asking them to meet him personally at his Loop headquarters on April 1. While Democrats "chortled" at the hoax as nothing more than a harmless "April fool joke," Thompson denounced the scheme as an attempt to "flood the loop with Negroes wearing Thompson badges to create race hatred."[31] Democrats took out ads in local newspapers in which one South Side man is quoted as saying that "it's all right for a man to hold up his trousers with a black belt, but that's no way to try to hold up a city." Another advertisement contained provocative news clippings from Chicago papers on Collins's stories about "Negroes and white girls," on Thompson's infamous kissing of an African-American child at a South Side rally, and on Maclay Hoyne's frequent blaming of Thompson for the Color Riot of 1919.[32] Democrats even placed calliopes playing "Bye, Bye Blackbird!" on the backs of trucks that they drove nonstop throughout the Loop area during the latter stages of the campaign.[33]

Democrats were not alone in injecting color into the campaign. Newspapers like the *Chicago Daily News* and *Chicago Tribune*, despite their constant decrying of color-conscious campaigning, repeatedly printed articles on how all African-American voters blindly supported "Big Bill," how thousands more from the South were poised to swamp the city in the event of Thompson's victory, and, less frequently, how "white" girls and "Negroes" cavorted openly on the South Side (in part, because of Thompson's lax law enforcement in the Black Belt).[34] Similarly, many trade unions did their part to spread the Democrats' color messages. Dennis Lane, secretary-treasurer of the Amalgamated Meat Cutters and Butcher Workmen of North America, stated in a speech at a campaign event that Thompson was to blame for his union's defeat in their strike of 1921, since he had made Chicago a "haven" for African-American strikebreakers. The Dever for Mayor Trades Union Committee charged the Thompson administration with importing "more than 70,000 non-union Negroes . . . most of them for the purposes of breaking the strike of the stockyards workers." It also took out newspaper ads that featured cartoon images of Thompson, a hoodlum type, and a sambo-like African American all attempting to roll a "graft and corruption" boulder onto railroad tracks in order to derail Dever's "Prosperity Special."[35]

Similarly, ward level politicians attempted to bring color themes to bear on their own local races. In an aldermanic contest in the South Side Fifth Ward, Joseph Artman distributed campaign flyers, warning "white voters" to be "ON GUARD!" "If you want NIGGERS kept out of Hyde Park High School; If you want Jackson Park Beach maintained for WHITE PEOPLE; Then vote for Joseph M. Artman the 100 per cent WHITE candidate for Alderman of the Fifth Ward." The flyer ended with this command: "Defeat Cusack the NIGGER-LOVER!" Even independent, good government reform types occasionally played a role in pushing color issues. The Peoples Dever for Mayor Committee, whose membership included people like Jane Addams, Harold Ickes, and Graham Taylor, took out an ad on election eve in a local Austin paper, in which they made coded color appeals to white homeowners, whose neighborhood was getting closer every day to an expanding West Side African-American community. The ad stated: "We in Austin are blessed with homes in a beautiful neighborhood. We want to protect them and our families in them. We must be continually watching to see that no harmful influences invade them." Within the context of this campaign, there can be little doubt about whom exactly the ad had in mind.[36]

How did Republicans respond to this relentless color campaign? Many in Thompson's camp well understood the potential dangers of dividing "white" and "black" along partisan lines. As Thompson supporter and bailiff of the Municipal Court, Bernard Snow, stated, "if the Democrats are able to create a division of the white men and the black men, there will be no Republican Party in the future. . . . Nothing is more dangerous than this racial issue."[37] In response, Republicans attempted to clarify Thompson's stance as being in favor of equal rights for all, not just for African Americans. They also constantly accused Dever and the Democrats of raising the "question of color" in the campaign and of trying to start another color riot in Chicago. Finally, they criticized Dever's inconsistent treatment of African Americans. One Thompson handbill showed a picture of Dever from 1923 with some African-American supporters stating: "Double-Faced Dever—He Would Strike Down Those Who Helped Raise Him Up." In 1923, "Dever begged the support of the negroes, dined with them, catered to them—and carried the Second Ward by a 4,500 majority." Four years later, "because the Colored Citizens would not vote for him again, he threw a thousand of them in jail without just cause, introduced the un-American race issue in the campaign, and pursues campaign tactics which imperil the lives of innocent persons because of the possibility of a race riot."[38]

Thompson also had his allies on these points. While the *Daily News* and the *Tribune* never missed an opportunity to trash him, the Hearst papers—the *Chicago American* and *Chicago Herald-Examiner*—defended him and consistently blamed the "Democratic spellbinders" for their "scandalous effort . . . to inject the racial question into the campaign," which over time was "thoroughly understood and resented by all liberty-loving, honest Chicagoans." On election eve, the *Chicago American* pointedly asked: "Do the Brennan-Dever Democrats, who dragged the race question into the campaign . . . expect to pursue their tactics to a point that will produce a race riot?"[39]

Many African Americans also attacked Thompson's enemies. When Collins defended the South Side police raids by alleging African-American impudence on city sidewalks, African-American leaders like A. L. Foster of the Urban League dismissed his statements as "manifestly political propaganda" and nothing more. At the same time, African-American Aldermen Louis Anderson and Robert Jackson demanded investigations into the police raids and in a City Council resolution assailed the police actions as "hard boiled" "Cossack" measures, leading to the arrest of hundreds of innocent people, who were "beaten, kicked and otherwise maltreated."[40] State Senator Adelbert Roberts introduced a similar resolution on the floor of the state legislature in Springfield. The *Chicago Defender*, too, condemned Democratic campaign tactics. Several days after the election, the paper reflected: "If ever there was a campaign conducted along the most deadly lines, if ever attempts were made to arouse man's baser passions, if ever unscrupulous lies were broadcast to align man against his fellow man, these things were done in the campaign just closed." Such was "the filth that Brennan and his gang injected into the campaign."[41]

Some African Americans, however, saw Thompson, not Dever, as the true enemy of "the Race." Just days before the election, key African-American South Side political figure and close ally of Governor Len Small,

Edward Wright, lambasted Thompson as the real instigator of color hatreds during the campaign. At an African-American political rally on April 3, he declared: "William Hale Thompson was the first man to talk of a possible riot and thereby implant a germ in people's brains that can grow and grow until real trouble results."[42]

And, indeed, Wright had a point. Thompson was never entirely innocent himself of exploiting color issues. No doubt his far-fetched campaign promises and rhetoric to African Americans often did little to downplay color in the campaign. Prior to one of his speeches, a perceptive African American called a Thompson aide and asked that he not "put it on too strong this afternoon. Whenever the race issue is accentuated in a campaign we lose." His vitriolic attacks on his opponents—such as his dismissal of the Peoples Dever for Mayor Committee as nothing more than a "group of lily-white gentlemen"—helped little in downplaying color as well.[43] More damaging was his subtle (and sometimes not so subtle) endorsement of the color line and color inequality. For instance, when Thompson repeatedly denounced Democratic-disseminated cartoons of him kissing an African-American child as "vile," it was never exactly clear why he felt this way. Was it that Thompson agreed with the Democrats that the very act of "whites" and "Negroes" kissing was utterly disgraceful? This was likely the point since at several speeches Thompson stated: "if I were nasty and much like they I suppose I might have one of my boys draw a cartoon of Dever kissing a Chinaman."[44] Thompson's point must have been clear to all who attended these speeches: "Chinamen" and "Negroes" were different sorts of people, whom no self-respecting "white" person would ever kiss.

Many Italians were actively involved in this election campaign. Some were avid Dever supporters, who willingly accepted and disseminated his color messages. The most blatant example of this was the "Negro Question and Thompson" editorial in the *La Tribuna Italiana Transatlantica*, but other examples exist. Italian-American leaders like attorney Stephen Malato formed the Italian Committee for Mayor Dever, which gave speeches throughout Chicago's many Little Italies, took out ads in Italian-language newspapers, and wrote campaign literature for Dever in Italian. One pamphlet featured a long list of reasons why Italians should support Dever, ending with this one: "if you do not want your compatriots to lose their position and be replaced by blacks, vote for the faithful and loyal friend of the Italians, WILLIAM E. DEVER." Some Italian unionists, like Joseph Seppi of the Pressmen's Union, joined the Dever for Mayor Trades Union Committee, which criticized Thompson for supporting "undesirable" labor. Finally, some Italians worked with local Democrats to spread the word about "Thompson and his Negroes." On March 26, Joseph Bazzario and Charles Labato, who both lived and worked in Lincoln Park and owed their jobs to local Democrats, crisscrossed their neighborhood "with paste brushes, pails, and posters." According to the county commissioner who spotted them, "one man would daub a telephone post with paste and the other would slap on a poster reading: 'Negroes First—William Hale Thompson for Mayor'."[45]

Not all Italians were anti-"Negro" devoted Deverites, however. Thompson had important friends among Italian *prominenti*—most notably, Bernard Barasa and Oscar Durante—who enthusiastically supported his candidacy and defended his record on numerous issues, including color. A week before the election, *L'Italia* declared that "in eight years of Thompson's mayoralty, he has demonstrated equality toward all nationalities without preference to any one."[46] Even *La Tribuna* made this point forcefully in a March 26 article, likely paid for by the Thompson campaign or the Italian Committee for Thompson. It assailed the Democrats for "seeking to inject into the campaign race hatred. Doing this demonstrates that they do not hold dear the principles promulgated in the Declaration of Independence and reaffirmed by Lincoln in the Civil War. The idea that if Thompson wins the Italian jobs will be given to blacks is a vulgar falsehood." Thompson, the article concluded, "was mayor for eight years and proved [during this time] his impartiality toward all nationalities."[47]

Despite the fact that many Italians still did not vote in these years and that electoral corruption pervaded many of their neighborhoods, the best evidence regarding everyday Italians' views is vote totals. The best estimate is that 51 percent of Italians voted for Thompson and roughly 46 percent for Dever.[48] What role color considerations played in Italians' decisions at the polls is hard to say, since they cared deeply about other campaign issues besides color such as Prohibition, crime, and law enforcement. Noteworthy, nonetheless, is that those neighborhoods closest to African-American areas were not necessarily more supportive of Dever. While Armour Square, the one large Italian neighborhood bordering the Black Belt, did vote overwhelmingly for Dever (71–28 percent), all other Italian neighborhoods in close proximity to African-American areas supported Thompson—sometimes by large margins. Most surprising is the Near North Side, where, despite deteriorating relations between Italians and African Americans, Thompson received 70 percent of the vote.[49]

Less central than color issues, European race issues were still present in the 1927 mayoral campaign. After all, it came only a year after massive anti-Sicilian hysteria led to a deportation drive and the arrests of over one hundred Italians. Indeed, these were also the years of Capone, Torrio, the Genna brothers, and others. Given this context, any talk of crime during the campaign must have brought to many Chicagoans' minds images of criminally inclined and racially depraved Italian gangsters. And the 1927 campaign—with its heavy emphasis on Prohibition issues—certainly contained its share of comments on crime. Indeed, both candidates blamed the other for the "reign of lawlessness" in Chicago. On numerous occasions, Thompson and his many campaign speakers denounced Dever for being the "hoodlum candidate," whose lax law enforcement policies had given rise to an "orgy of crime" in Chicago.[50] The Dever campaign, meanwhile, made "Decency versus Hoodlumism" a central campaign slogan. On March 31, for example, five thousand Dever supporters marched through Chicago's Loop area with a massive banner reading "Dever for Decency." Dever also declared that "as Mayor of Chicago I fought a gang of organized gunmen and cut-throats who tried to get by with murder by calling themselves bootleggers. These fellows were robbers and killers."[51] Democratic leader George Brennan also rarely missed an opportunity to exploit crime as a campaign issue. At its inception, he stated provocatively that "not all supporters of Thompson are hoodlums, but every hoodlum is supporting Thompson," and later predicted: "the people of Chicago will [not] repudiate honest and efficient government and turn the city over to be ruled by the black belt, the gunman, and the hoodlums."[52]

Sometimes, though rarely, these discussions of crime referred to Italians more directly. At a crime prevention conference held early in the campaign, Dever "attributed a large part of Chicago crime to 'large villages,' one on the west [side] in part, which permit corrupt government and harbor bootleggers and murderers who prey upon Chicago." Dever added that "I have quietly appealed to these communities to sit in with us and help enforce the laws, but complete cooperation has been lacking." Given that Chicagoans had railed for years against Italians' "crime-infested" Near West Side neighborhood, there can be no question as to what community Dever had in mind. He also blamed the crime wave in Chicago on groups like Italians, who were strongly opposed to Prohibition.[53] At a time when Italians' criminality was thought to be somehow racially determined, Dever's talk of crime—no matter how subtle and how loosely associated with Italians—must have helped further substantiate popular connections between Italians, race, and crime.

Race was part of the campaign in another way. For years, Italian leaders and organizations used race/nation appeals to mobilize voters and the 1927 mayoral race was no exception. The Italian campaign committees for both Dever and Thompson published campaign literature and took out numerous ads in Chicago's Italian-language papers, in which they appealed to "i nostri connazionali" to vote one way or another. In one ad, the Dever camp stated that "the Italians of Chicago must not forget how much [Dever] has done for our nationality, and how many Italians are respected and in excellent municipal posts" because of him. Another pamphlet written and distributed by the Italian Committee for Mayor Dever noted that these appointments were a "great honor to our race." The Thompson camp made similar appeals. In one open letter from Bernard Barasa to *connazionali* published in *La Tribuna*, Barasa provided a long list of Thompson's accomplishments as mayor and concluded that he is a "proven friend of our nationality."[54]

"Dagoes" and "Bohunks": The Republican Mayoral Primary and Election of 1931

In many ways the 1931 Republican primary and mayoral race were the mirror images of the campaign in 1927. Whereas in 1927, color was central and race tangential, in 1931, color receded to the background and race emerged as an important issue in the campaign. Chicago's 1931 mayoral election is well known, particularly because it marked the beginning of local Democratic Party hegemony, which has lasted to this day. It is also well known for Thompson's colossal campaign blunder of making the "bohunk" background of Democratic candidate, Anton Cermak, a political issue. But European race issues found their way into the campaign in other ways, especially through discussions of crime.

This was particularly the case during the Republican primary in February 1931, thanks mainly to candidate Judge John H. Lyle. Borrowing from Dever's earlier campaign slogans and tactics, Lyle attempted to capitalize on Thompson's oft-discussed gangster connections and soft-on-crime reputation. As Lyle declared on February 2, he was running for mayor to defeat the "gangsters, hoodlums, and racketeers who have fed, fattened, and thrived under Thompsonism."[55] His campaign slogan was "Lyle or Lawlessness" and, as the campaign wore on, he increasingly made Capone, rather than Thompson, his primary opponent. In speech after speech, Lyle declared: "the fight in this campaign is to determine whether Lyle or Capone shall occupy City Hall, for Thompson is merely Capone's proxy."[56] Unlike Dever, Lyle also willingly spelled out the racial implications of these points. In one speech to a church group in Morgan Park, Lyle promised: "If I get elected mayor . . . we will start in the first ward and run the Dagoes out of the south end of it. You don't like that word? . . . There is one race that has more killers in it than any other. . . . I will say it again. We will run the Dagoes out of the south end of that ward."[57]

Lyle received help on his anti-crime and anti-Italian messages, particularly from the *Chicago Tribune*, always a big believer in both projects and an enthusiastic supporter of the judge. Though it never made statements as direct or provocative as did Lyle, the *Tribune* still made constant connections between Italian criminals, Thompson, and Chicago lawlessness. Toward the end of the primary campaign, this newspaper published numerous photos and articles associating Italians—criminals like Capone and "Dago" Lawrence Mangano or politicians like Daniel Serritella, who was purported to have close Capone connections—with Thompson's administration and campaign. In one article, the paper called these three men the "Thompson trio" and for weeks ran numerous political cartoons railing against the Capone-Thompson alliance. In one such cartoon, "your city" was locked down by the twin evils of Thompson and Capone. In another,

Al Capone was pictured speaking on the phone from his palatial estate in Miami Beach: "Hello, Chicago! This is Miami Beach—Al Capone speaking! Say, I want you to line up all the boys against this guy Lyle. He's dangerous. Don't spare expense or anything—You know what I mean. I want results!"[58] Finally, in the last days of the primary campaign, the *Tribune* helpfully summarized its views on Chicago politics and crime in the following sensationalistic front-page headlines: "Lyle or Gang; Up to Voters" and "Rout Gang: Vote Plea Today."[59]

Other candidates in the primary made similar points—though never as frequently or as bluntly. Even Thompson, considered by many Italians to be a great champion of their "race," made mention of Italian criminality in his responses to that "nutty Judge" Lyle. In one speech early in the campaign, Thompson spoke out against "gangsters and assassins," declaring that "when the Prohibition laws are changed, those fellows can go back to Sicily and make their money kidnapping people into the mountains for ransom." On other occasions, Thompson dismissed Capone as "not my child but Lyle's" and opined that Chicago crime was the result of Prohibition laws that attracted "crooks . . . from other countries." Again, given the context of this speech, it is not hard to imagine which countries Thompson and his audiences had in mind.[60]

In the end, Thompson beat Lyle handily (approximately 296,000 votes to 228,000 votes), and there is every reason to believe that Italians contributed to this outcome.[61] In the weeks leading up to the primary, both Italian-language newspapers ignored Thompson's questionable statements on Sicilians, yet publicized Lyle's anti-Italian commentaries and excoriated him for his "denigration of the Italian element." Similarly, at a pro-Thompson Italian-American rally that drew some four thousand people, a long list of Italian speakers, from Barasa and Durante to Serritella and Alderman William Pacelli, offered nothing but "parole di fuoco" (words of fire) for Judge Lyle. These speakers also denounced the *Tribune* for being Chicago's "italophobic newspaper par excellence."[62]

When Thompson won the primary and Lyle ended his candidacy, race and crime issues hardly disappeared from the campaign. The *Tribune* made sure of this. One week before the election it ran a huge, front-page headline—"Capone Police Rule Exposed"—and it continued to publish crime-related political cartoons. One featured a despondent Chicago Republican Party elephant sighing "If Only I Can Get Rid of It All." "All" is a series of cans tied to the elephant's tail labeled "THOMPSON DOMINATION," "BALLYHOO," "WASTE," "CRIME," and "CAPONEISM."[63] And Anton Cermak, Democratic mayoral candidate and the Bohemian-American chairman of the Cook County Democratic Organization (CCDO), though hardly vocal about the matter, still managed to connect Thompson and Capone. He did this most powerfully through his involvement in the last-minute indictment of Daniel Serritella for allegedly masterminding, as city sealer, a short-weighting scheme throughout Chicago. His highly publicized arrest only further substantiated the month-long charges of the *Tribune* and Lyle that Italian criminals were, through their Thompson ties, deeply infecting Chicago's body politic. And many Chicagoans must have seen this infecting, at least implicitly, as a consequence of Italians' sinister racial predilections.[64]

Race made its way into the campaign in one other way—through Thompson's repeated barbs about Cermak's Bohemian background. Some of Thompson's more memorable taunts were "Tony, Tony, where's your pushcart at? Can you imagine a World's Fair Mayor with a name like that?"; and "I won't take a back seat from that Bohunk—Chairmock, Chermack or whatever his name is." Harking back to an earlier era, Thompson published campaign pamphlets calling for 100 percent Americanism and showing Cermak's typical supporters as a group of Bohemians, Germans, Swedes, Poles, and Irish.[65]

These campaign tactics drew immediate outrage. Cermak responded that "we couldn't all come over on the Mayflower—or maybe the boat would have sunk. But I got here as soon as I could, and I never wanted to go back, because to me it is a great privilege to be an American citizen."[66] Cermak's allies attacked Thompson more forcefully. Days before the election, one politician denounced Thompson for his "prejudice, intolerance, and bigotry" and stated: "Americans are Americans whether they are naturalized or native, Americans by choice or by birth, whether born in the rugged highlands of Scotland . . . or sunny Italy." The editors and publishers of fifty-eight local foreign-language newspapers came together to oppose Thompson and his attempts to stir up "racial and religious strife." And the *Tribune* continued to publish their anti-Thompson editorials and cartoons. In one front-page example of the latter, Thompson is seen using "appeals to race prejudice" to write his own political obituary.[67] In the end, Cermak's best response to Thompson's anti-immigrant race appeals was doing what he had always done as chairman of the CCDO: appoint people of all backgrounds to political posts. Indeed, the year he ran for mayor, there were electoral races for five other offices and his hand-picked candidates were a Czech, Italian, Irish, German, and Pole. Thus, while Thompson openly advertised anti-immigrant views, Cermak made "multiethnicity . . . the new guiding principle of the Democratic Party."[68]

How did African Americans fit into this new Democratic "multiethnic" framework and what role did color play in the 1931 mayoral election? First, Cermak quickly scrapped the Brennan strategy of trying to make color and partisan lines neatly correspond and instead made an effort to attract African-American voters into the Democratic fold. For several years before the election, Cermak had attempted, with some success, to build a Democratic base of support in the Black Belt. In 1930, when he became CCDO chairman after Brennan's death, his first party slate included an African American along with assorted European Americans.[69] Once the campaign got started, Cermak stumped some in the Black Belt, denounced race/color bigotry (of which he claimed to have been a victim), and widely distributed campaign literature to African Americans. One booklet, entitled "An Appeal to Reason," noted in its foreword that its sole purpose was to "make more Democrats among Negroes and to keep them in the party." A Cermak poster stated: "Stand by the Man whose Humanity Has Known No Color Line! Vote for A. J. Cermak."[70]

Thompson made his customary appeals to African Americans and in the process tried to paint Cermak and the Democrats as unreformed bigots and to preserve color as a campaign issue. In one stump speech Thompson noted that Cermak "calls himself the 'Master Executive' . . . you Negroes know what a master is?" Meanwhile, Republican flyers stated boldly: "Don't Bring the South to Chicago! Don't Start Lynchings in Chicago! Vote the Straight Republican Ticket!" Certain African-American speakers also spoke out for Thompson in stump speeches, highlighting color issues in the process. At one South Side rally, an African-American woman proclaimed: "What is Thompsonism? It's the Negro in the Mayor's Office. . . . He has given us recognition that no other man has given us. We want every vote of every Negro in Chicago to be cast for Thompson. So we can walk in the World's Fair Grounds without asking the man at the gate if we can go in the front way or the back."[71]

The most blatant injection of color into the campaign came from a circular, distributed throughout the city just days before the election, for which neither candidate was willing to take credit. It stated:

WAKE UP TO THE MENACE OF THOMPSON AND HIS NEGROES. VOTE FOR CERMAK AND HIS WHOLE DEMOCRATIC TICKET. THINK OF IT! . . . IF THOMPSON IS ELECTED Negroes Will want Work as Motormen and Conductors on Elevated and Streetcar Lines. IF THOMPSON IS ELECTED Negroes will Compete with White Men for Jobs in Building the Subway. IF THOMPSON IS ELECTED Thousands of Negroes will get Jobs that otherwise go to White Men.

The Democrats blamed the Republicans for the circular and Thompsonites swiftly counterattacked. According to the *Chicago Defender*, "the regular Second ward Republican organization had 5,000 of these circulars printed with the wording above telling the voters to 'read what the Democrats are distributing in the wards where no Negroes reside'." Regardless of which party was responsible for the flyer, this was the best example of color-coded continuity between the 1927 and 1931 mayoral contests.[72]

How did Italians involve themselves in and respond to the 1931 mayoral race? Estimates of Italian voting in this election suggest that Italians split their votes more or less evenly between Cermak and Thompson.[73] Cermak must have alienated some Italians by making crime an issue and by indicting Serritella, a popular local politician among many Italians.[74] At the same time, Cermak, as chairman of the CCDO, had long worked diligently to build up his base of support among Italian Americans. As Paul Colianni, a key Italian American in the CCDO and Sanitary District trustee, stated on the eve of the mayoral election, "one of his [Cermak's] finest traits has been his fairness to every race, and his recognition of all our citizens in the matter of public offices." Thus, by the time of the election, Cermak could count on a wide range of influential *prominenti* to mobilize Italians in his favor. Indeed, these *prominenti* had formed the Italian-American Regular Democratic Organization, which had as members former Alderman Albert Prignano, Municipal Judges Francis Allegretti and Francis Borelli, and Italo-American National Union leader Constantino Vilitello.[75]

Thompson could count important supporters within Italian-American communities, as well. He was, as both *L'Italia* and *La Tribuna* never tired of repeating, "a proven friend of Italians," who had appointed them to important municipal posts and had helped to make the Italian language a subject of study in Chicago high schools. But Thompson had liabilities, as well, which Cermak's allies in Italian-American communities did their best to highlight and exploit. One ad for Cermak, which appeared in *La Tribuna* and was paid for by the Italian-American Regular Democratic Organization, assailed Thompson for his racialist insults of Cermak because "his name sounds foreign and not anglo-saxon. . . . [We Italian Americans] feel all the force of the insult given to Cermak and protest against this grand injustice. The cause of the immigrant CERMAK is our cause."[76]

Regardless of Italians' particular views on this election, the two contests involving Thompson, Lyle, and Cermak must have powerfully shaped their consciousness as Italians. Indeed, as in 1927, both Democratic and Republican Italians relied heavily upon *Italianita'* to mobilize *connazionali* for particular candidates. Every newspaper article, ad, and pamphlet in favor of Thompson spoke of "il Simpaticone Tommasone" as helping "il nostro elemento," "la nostra nazionalita'," "la nostra communita'," and "la nostra razza" (our element, our nationality, our community, our race). And the same was true for Cermak. One ad announced: "Why Italians Must Vote for Cermak" and his campaign literature made numerous appeals to "gli elettori italiani" (the Italian voters) and "i nostri connazionali."[77]

While color was not as central a part of this campaign as it had been four years earlier, Italian-language papers on several occasions spoke openly of Thompson's popularity among both Italians and African Americans. Indeed, even *La Tribuna* (which, in direct contrast to 1927, endorsed Thompson enthusiastically, in part, because he supported the progress of all people regardless of "religion, nationality, race, or color") reveled in the prediction among certain African-American leaders that "the negroes will be faithful to Thompson." In the political realm, then, at least as far as the 1931 mayoral election is concerned, many Italians were not overly concerned about differentiating themselves from the "colored races."[78]

Mayoral Races, Mayoral Colors

Mayoral campaigns throughout the 1920s and 1930s—but especially those in 1927 and 1931—were, if nothing else, large-scale attempts on the part of political parties, newspapers, local political groups, trade unions, and so forth to get Italians (among other people) to identify and, based in part on these identifications, to vote in certain ways.[79] From early in the twentieth century through the 1927 and 1931 mayoral contests and beyond, every attempt to mobilize Italian voters was done, at least in part, through an appeal to the Italian nation/race. Thus, in 1923, when Bernard Barasa ran in the Republican mayoral primary, *L'Italia* encouraged its readers to vote by arguing that the judge's victory would "honor the [Italian] race"; similarly, in the mayoral battles of 1927 and 1931, both Democrats and Republicans worked tirelessly through newspaper ads, pamphlets, community organizations, banquets, and speeches to portray their candidates as the "true" friends of the Italian people and the "true" supporters of *Italianita'*. This focus on *Italianita'* in the electoral arena continued in the 1930s. In one essay around election time in March 1932, for instance, the Order of the Sons of Italy reminded its membership that "it is the duty of all Italian-American voters to draw attention to themselves as a group regardless of party affiliation . . . [and to support] unconditionally . . . all candidates of Italian birth or origin." Italian voters, argued OSIA, must "maintain, for the honor of the country and race which gave them birth, a spirit of Italianism."[80]

Just as political parties and various Italian-American community institutions pushed *Italianita'* at election time, the Democratic Party—most blatantly and relentlessly during Chicago's 1927 mayoral campaign—pushed whiteness. Indeed, the Democratic Party's central campaign strategy when it came to color was to divide Chicago neatly into "whites" and "Negroes" and then to assign each group to one major party. The Democrats openly and repeatedly claimed to be the "true" representative of "whites," when Brennan predicted Dever's victory because Chicago's a "white man's town"; when Michael Igoe declared that the battle between Dever and Thompson was really about whether the "white people" will "continue to rule Chicago"; or when newspaper ads denounced Thompson for not knowing the "difference between black and white." And some Italian community institutions helped disseminate these messages, as when *La Tribuna* railed against the influx of "neri" in Chicago and the catastrophic effects this was having on "bianchi" throughout the city. This color-conscious mobilization strategy further demonstrates the security of Italian whiteness in these years. Indeed, during an election when Democrats openly divided the city into "whites" and "Negroes" and only appealed to the former, Italians were a key constituency within this "whites"-only electoral coalition, with their own Dever for Mayor Committee and close ties with the Democratic Party.[81]

The story is a bit more complicated, however, when one takes Italians' own views and perspectives into account. Indeed, some Italians—thanks in part to the Democrats' campaigning strategies—learned to identify as whites in these years. No doubt, of the roughly 46 percent of Italian Americans who voted for Dever in 1927, a fraction of them did so to protect "white rule" in Chicago. Still, more evidence from electoral politics suggests that Italians' white identity remained underdeveloped. For one, Italians did not flock to the polls to vote for Dever and white supremacy in 1927. Instead, Thompson received just over half the Italian vote and did well even in neighborhoods with serious color tensions. Perhaps more conclusively, many Italians willingly voted alongside African Americans throughout these years. Indeed, in the 1931 election of Anton Cermak, of all race/color groups in Chicago, only Italians and African Americans continued to support Thompson in significant numbers.[82] Furthermore, some Italians never seemed overly concerned about belonging to the same party as African Americans, even when the Democrats furiously fought to paint that party as "Negro" through and through. Indeed, Italian-language newspapers openly advertised the point that Italians and African Americans held similar party affiliations, and on one occasion, *L'Italia* held up African Americans as a model for Italian political organization and behavior. The electoral realm in the 1920s and early 1930s, then, seems to confirm the general picture of Italians' white consciousness in these years: opportunities for growth, but underdeveloped just the same.[83]

6

FASCISM, EMPIRE, AND WAR

On October 3, 1935, dispensing with the formalities of war declarations and violating international law and a number of treaties, Italy invaded Ethiopia, the last-remaining independent African nation. At first, bad weather, rough terrain, economic sanctions from the League of Nations, and Ethiopian resistance frustrated Italian imperial designs. By May 1936, however, after sparing no expense and employing the most ruthless of weapons and military tactics, Italy proudly proclaimed itself victor of "the greatest colonial war known to history."[1] By this point, Italian troops had occupied the capitol of Addis Ababa, driven Emperor Haile Sellassie and his royal family into exile, and made Ethiopia the new crown jewel of Mussolini's revived Roman empire.

The war was not limited to the high, dusty, desert plains of Ethiopia. Thousands of miles west across the Atlantic in scores of American cities, a diverse cast of characters—African Americans and Italian Americans, fascists and anti-fascists, elite and everyday folk, the Italian state and American mass culture—also battled over the meaning, merits, and outcome of the Italian-Ethiopian War and its implications for different social groups' claims to power and prestige in America. Many Americans and various institutions agreed that the war was a color battle between "whites" and "Negroes" and that Italians, despite some undesirable qualities, belonged to the former. Many Chicago Italians, however, approached matters differently. Having been raised for years on nationalist rhetoric emanating from the fascist state and a powerful network of community institutions like the Catholic Church, newspapers, and mutual aid societies, they rallied around *la razza* and spoke seldom about color.

"Deep Grow the (Fascist) Roots"

Chicago Italians' response to war in Ethiopia is directly related to the powerful fascist presence in their communities beginning in the 1920s.

Concerned with the steady emigration of young, healthy citizens and their potential "denationalization" abroad, Mussolini, beginning in the early 1920s, worked to strengthen ties between emigrant outposts and the *madrepatria* (motherland). To this end, the Italian state, with the help of loyal emigrants, established *fasci* or small emigrant organizations in cities and towns across North America. These organizations, often led by community *prominenti* but controlled abroad by the Italian state, boasted thousands of members by the end of the decade and became an important fascist tool for self-promotion and propaganda. In Chicago in the early 1920s, a local Italian lawyer and ardent fascist sympathizer, Mario Lauro, helped found the *Fascio Italiano del Chicago.*[2] In 1929, however, unfavorable press condemned these *fasci* and their parent organization—the Fascist League of North America—for being the backbone of "Mussolini's American Empire" and forced them to dissolve.[3]

Yet these events did not leave fascists bereft of significant influence within Italian-American communities. Easily assuming some of the *fasci*'s earlier functions and steadily growing in importance were Italian consular offices and agents. In Chicago during the 1920s and 1930s, consul generals like Mario Carosi and Giuseppe Castruccio became ubiquitous figures within Italian-American neighborhoods, writing letters to local papers defending the name of Italians; fighting successfully to build a monument honoring Columbus in Chicago's Grant Park; attending and giving speeches at community events from club dinners and dances to communions, graduations, and baptisms; and establishing Italian language and culture schools for second-generation immigrants.[4] Most important, consuls, with control over Italian government employment contracts and funds, also forged close ties with key Italian-American community institutions in Chicago—particularly the Catholic Church, Italian-language newspapers, neighborhood (often parochial) schools, and powerful fraternal orders like the Italo-American National Union (IANU), the Chicago Italian Chamber of Commerce (CICC), and the Order of the Sons of Italy (OSIA). These institutions, in turn, became faithful purveyors of fascist propaganda about trains running on time, a Bolshevist threat denied, the genius of Mussolini, and the inexorable rise of the "New Italy." *Vita Nuova*, an Italian-language weekly in Chicago, spoke for all these institutions when it stated glowingly in 1928: "There is the Italy of Mussolini; beautiful, prosperous, robust, filled with energy and filled with faith in itself, that securely treads the path to a future filled with glory."[5]

Several reasons explain these institutions' enthusiastic embrace of fascism. First, as noted, institutions received vital financial support from the Italian state in exchange for a fascist-friendly orientation and agenda. Second, Italian-American institutions were not alone in their philo-fascism. For much of the 1920s and early 1930s, a wide range of Americans, and many Chicagoans among them, also adored Mussolini.[6] Third, many Italians, deeply scarred by restriction, racialism, and criminalization, drew great pride from the rise of the "New Italy," from Mussolini, and from the widespread popularity of both in America. Long relying on past glories to defend themselves, many Italians were overjoyed to have contemporary events serve the same purpose.[7] Finally, Italian-American community institutions took to fascism so readily because their leaders shared so many of the same goals as Mussolini. *Prominenti* had long been interested in building a more unified Italian community—one free, in particular, of North/ South distinctions and *campanalismo*. Over time this project only became more explicit. One article in Chicago's IANU newsletter implored its readers in 1927: "Be united and abolish that false rhetoric. We are no longer Tuscans, Lombardos, Sicilians, Emilians, Abruzians, Sardinians, Calabrians, etc. We must remember that 10,000,000 Italians scattered throughout the world, and 45,000,000 Italians in Italy are proud of their Italian origin and ready to act as one man for the prestige of the Motherland and the Italian name in foreign countries." Similarly, *L'Italia* and *La Tribuna Italiana Transatlantica* continued to publish weekly articles on the glories of "la nostra razza," on "l'orgoglio della razza" (the pride of the race), or on "La Patria!," which "every Italian holds near to his heart." This race/nation building project was, of course, similar to that of Mussolini and the fascists, who wanted desperately for Italians of the world to unite. As such, the multitude of consular activities all had one primary ideological objective: in the words of Consul General Castruccio, to make known to Italians born abroad "the Patria of their parents, its past greatness, its present and future glories."[8] Therefore, the fascist agenda, nationalist to the core, corresponded perfectly with that of Chicago's *prominenti* and the key community institutions they led.

Given fascism's powerful hold on the institutional foundations of Italian Chicago and many Americans' support for Mussolini, it is no surprise that many Italian Americans soon boarded the profascist bandwagon. In his 1928 book, *The Italians in Chicago*, Giovanni Schiavo noted that "since the advent to power of Mussolini, the 'patriotism' of the Italians has been fanned to an extent probably never reached before." Similarly, the *Chicago Evening Post* observed a year later that "many Italians of Chicago have manifested a love for the fatherland they have never shown before. . . . They see in Mussolini the savior of Italy, and they admire him for what he has done for the good of their race." Evidence from oral histories tends to confirm these assessments. As one Italian-American man from the Chicago suburb of Forest Park recalled, "I know my Dad and all the other Italian friends would sit hours at night talking about Mussolini, what a wonderful man he was, what good he did for Italy." Teresa De Falco had similar recollections from her childhood on the Near West Side: "everyone was real proud of being a fascist"—even if, as she admitted later, many people were a bit hazy on what this exactly meant.[9]

Not all Italians, however, shared Mrs. De Falco's fascist pride. Italian anti-fascists represented a minority of their compatriots, but they were vocal and active in Chicago throughout the 1920s and 1930s. The most consistent anti-fascist critique came from the Italian left, particularly their press and local organizations like the International Workers Order, the Socialist Party of America, and the Communist Party. The local Italian socialist paper, *La Parola Proletaria*, lambasted community fascists on a weekly basis and in 1923 challenged them to an open debate. The Italian communist and syndicalist papers were equally condemnatory. Organizations also sprang up to combat the rising influence of fascism. On the South Side in the 1930s, for instance, the Centro Operaio di Roseland "became an anti-fascist headquarters, uniting workers under the influence of Socialists, Communists, and Anarcho-syndicalists." At the same time, another "group of professional anti-Fascist terrorists" emerged, which concentrated on "breaking up Fascist organization meetings and camps." In addition, anti-fascists often sent letters to Chicago's English-language papers to denounce Mussolini. In 1935, for instance, one Aldo Spero, in a letter to the *Tribune*, asserted that Il Duce has "'civilized' forty million people by instituting a government by force, violence, assassination, castor-oil, and years of prison imposed on everyone who disagreed with him." With tensions mounting between anti-fascists and fascists in these years, violent clashes erupted occasionally on the streets of different Chicago Italian neighborhoods.[10] Still, it was hardly a fair fight. Fascists enjoyed all the resources and support of the Italian state and the vigorous backing of many key institutions both within and without Italian-American communities. Moreover, many anti-fascists faced repression in America as socialists and communists, to say nothing of Italian consular surveillance and ostracism within certain bourgeois Italian-American circles.[11]

On the eve of war in Ethiopia, then, fascists occupied a highly advantageous position in Chicago, best exemplified by the city's rousing reception of Italo Balbo in 1933. That summer during the Century of Progress Exposition, fascist General Italo Balbo led a squadron of planes on a record-setting transatlantic flight from Rome to Chicago and received on arrival a hero's welcome from tens of thousands of ecstatic well-wishers. The *Chicago American* wrote: "Chicago, quick to admire courage and initiative, has taken the Italian visitors to its heart. . . . [They have] thrilled and inspired America and brought pride to the heart of every Italian. The world goes forward through the achievements of such intrepid, scientific men, marking new heights, new records and a surpassing demonstration of the friendship of one nation for another." The *Chicago Daily Times* was equally adoring: "Mark Anthony and Cicero survive as well as Caesar and Agrippa in Mussolini's revived and reunited Italy. Gen. Balbo is an eloquent evangel as well as a happy warrior of the skies, a man with a message. He flew here not to put over a mere aviation stunt, but to bring the story of the new Italy and its meaning. Gen. Balbo and his countrymen can well be proud of his new laurels." In the end, so impressed by Balbo, the city named an important street in downtown Chicago after him.[12]

Many Italians were equally thrilled with the achievements of their countrymen. The Order of the Sons of Italy held a posh dinner and reception for Balbo and the "migliore elemento della colonia" (the better element of the colony) and honored the fascist flyer by naming a new fraternal lodge after him. Italian-language newspapers hailed Balbo as the "Modern Columbus," who along with his boss, Il Duce, was bringing long-overdue prestige and praise to their motherland.[13] And many years later, scores of Italians recalled heading down to the lakefront to catch a glimpse of Balbo and to share in the exhilaration of his (and their nation/race's) achievement. One Italian-American woman from the Near West Side remembers the day as "a beautiful and joyous occasion" when Italians, bedecked in fascist buttons and singing fascist songs, finally "had something to be proud of." Emilio Leonardi, an Italian janitor from the same neighborhood, had almost an identical memory: "Oh yes a lot of people came— flags, much joy and happiness. . . . It was a big [sic] for the Italians."[14] Anti-fascists, to be sure, attended many of these celebrations as well—if only in an attempt to squash them. At Balbo's landing, for instance, anti-fascists did some flying of their own—to drop anti-Mussolini and anti-Balbo literature on crowds from above.[15] Still, as was often the case, the fascists carried the day. Many Italians (among other Chicagoans) came increasingly to support Balbo, Mussolini, and the "glorious" "New Italy" for which they both stood.

War

When war broke out between Italy and Ethiopia in the fall of 1935, the Italian-American communities of Chicago were well primed for hearty and organized support and did their part to aid the *madrepatria*.[16] The Italian-language newspapers hailed the war as the noblest of Italian undertakings, reported dutifully on all of Italy's "stunning victories," solicited donations for the war effort, regularly printed speeches of Mussolini and Consul General Carosi, and rebuked Americans who criticized Italy's actions.[17] Fraternal orders raised money for Italian troops from their members and spoke and wrote about the wonders of the war at dinners, at lodge meetings, and in their monthly publications.[18] The Catholic Church in Chicago, and particularly many of its Italian priests and parishes, served a similar role as the fraternal orders. Although some priests abstained, many raised funds for the war effort, added their authoritative voices to the chorus of prowar cheers, and christened many war-related ceremonies and celebrations.[19] Finally, Italian neighborhood movie theaters faithfully and repeatedly presented fascist propaganda films hailing Il Duce as the heroic "man of courage," while Italian-language radio stations broadcast Mussolini's speeches daily to thousands of his *connazionali* in Chicago.[20]

No doubt influenced heavily by this powerful network of prowar and profascist community institutions, many Italians rallied around their motherland, Mussolini, and their compatriots fighting in east Africa. Perhaps the most dramatic example of this was the donation made by thousands of Italian-American women of their gold wedding rings in Chicago (among other places) to aid the war effort. The *Chicago Daily News* reported in the spring of 1936, that at a community celebration for the war nearly three thousand Italian women were "remarried" with new steel rings sent by Mussolini and that seventy-five thousand Italians from a variety of organizations were on hand for the ceremonies. Similarly, one Italian-American woman from the Near West Side recalls as a child that "one of our finest local doctors . . . went to Ethiopia to help the Italian army as a doctor" and that the neighborhood staged a huge parade to celebrate his "heroic" return. But support went beyond these public events. At her house in Cicero, seamstress Velia Pancelli hosted a private party for her fellow Italian-American co-workers in May of 1936 to celebrate the "victory" over Ethiopia. The observation of one settlement house worker living in the Grand Avenue community no doubt held true for a good part of Italian Chicago: "The neighborhood is overwhelmingly pro-Mussolini and looks upon anyone who does not approve of the Ethiopian venture as not worthy of being an Italian."[21]

Civilizing Missions, Race, Nation, and Color

In supporting the war effort, Italians mobilized a whole set of ideas about civilization and civilizing missions that were common throughout Europe during the "Age of Imperialism."[22] And while these ideas had various meanings that changed over space and time, in the context of the Italian-Ethiopian War, they signified (at the very least) two related points: that Ethiopians were a "barbarous" people in need of civilizing and that Italy, the "mother of all civilization," was in a unique position to provide the "service." Such ideas were around to some degree in the late nineteenth century during Italy's initial imperialistic forays in Africa, but they grew ever more prominent (not coincidentally) as Mussolini in the early- to mid-1930s looked to expand his new Roman empire into Abyssinia. When war came in the fall of 1935, the fascist propaganda machine had made Italy's civilizing mission "a major theme, summoning other civilised peoples to stand together with Italy against cannibals and slave-owners who were a threat to European superiority." Fascists even produced postcards as propaganda, many of which were no doubt sent from Italy to friends and family in the United States. In one series, a young Italian boy is shown teaching his Ethiopian counterparts valuable lessons about hygiene, work, and discipline. In another series, an Italian nurse gives an Ethiopian a vaccination; the caption below, a Mussolini quotation, speaks of how civilization is triumphing over barbarism.[23]

Unsurprisingly, Italian Americans, in their attempts to understand and justify Italy's actions in the Ethiopian War, made great use of these civilizing mission ideas. Chicago's two most popular Italian-language dailies in the 1930s—*L'Italia* and *Il Progresso Italo-Americano*—wrote constantly in their coverage of the war of both Ethiopian "savages, barbarians, and slave-owners" and Italy's noble "l'opera di civilizazzione" (civilizing work). In one typical article, entitled "The Future Will Prove Italy's Noble Intentions," *Il Progresso* argued that "history demonstrates that owing to her lack of spiritual resources, Abyssinia has not progressed on the road to civilization. . . . Everything would seem to point to Italy as the most suited among the European powers to undertake the task . . . of civilizing Abyssinia."[24] Many of Chicago's *prominenti* towed an identical ideological line. The wartime addresses of George Spatuzza, a Sicilian-American lawyer, the Grand Venerable of the Illinois Grand Lodge of the OSIA for many years, and an active member of IANU and CICC, exemplify this point well. In speech after speech, Spatuzza hailed Italy's war with Ethiopia as the most noble of "missions to mankind" to bring light to the "darkest regions of Ethiopia." At Chicago's Italian-Ethiopian War victory banquet in May 1936, Spatuzza called Italy's "triumph" "the victory of the Age—the victory of mankind—the victory of civilization." After all, Ethiopia "for centuries had been the haven for slave holders and a living hell for their human chattel." Thankfully, according to Spatuzza, "destiny ha[d] called upon Italy . . . to civilize" Ethiopia; and with the help of Mussolini—the "greatest humanitarian—the greatest statesman of all times"—this is precisely what Italy—"the greatest contributor to civilization"—would do.[25]

To what extent the masses of everyday Italian Americans accepted such ideas is difficult to say. Anti-fascists, for one, rejected this lofty propaganda outright. In articles throughout the war in a number of different newspapers, left-wing anti-fascists scoffed at Mussolini's attempts to pass conquest off as civilizing work. They also ridiculed fascists for their (mis)understandings of who was and was not civilized. The Industrial Workers of the World (IWW) newspaper *Il Proletario* remarked in 1935: "If being 'primitive' means avoiding the pestilence of speculation and of capitalistic profit and the pestilence of politics which now afflicts the white world," than perhaps primitivism is something to defend not destroy.[26] As for the less left-wing-inclined Italian Americans, the pervasiveness of civilizing mission ideas had its effects. One Italian-American man born on the Near West Side recalled his father's frequent and proud remarks about "what wonders they [Italians] did in Ethiopia." Similarly, in a letter to the *Chicago Defender* in 1936, Benedict Agosto from the Italian Grand Avenue community assured the paper's largely African-American readership that Mussolini, like Lincoln many decades before, would free all (in this case, Ethiopian) slaves, "bringing forth Christianity and a new civilization." To this day, some older

Chicago Italians, who were alive during the war, continue to insist that Mussolini deserved (and deserves) more credit for all the schools, roads, and hospitals he supposedly built in Ethiopia. In the end, it seems highly probable that Vincent Frazzetta, a factory worker from Bridgeport, Connecticut, spoke for many of his compatriots in Chicago when he stated: "What Mussolini done in Ethiopia, I think he done a good thing because that country belonged to him, and he want to make the people there civilized like they should be. He is making schools for these people and he is making them like Christians. . . . Some day Mussolini will fix them up, and maybe they get to be like people someday, and not like animals."[27]

Frazzetta's remarks highlight the ways in which ideas about civilization touched on many other issues—from being Christian or heathen to being human or animal. They touched on issues of race and color as well. For decades prior to the Italian-Ethiopian War, as historian Gail Bederman has shown, "civilization" was a deeply racialized concept: a group's inborn characteristics, it was thought, determined largely the level of civilization it could achieve.[28] The thoughts of many Chicago Italians fit well into this ideological tradition. In all their talk about savagery and civilization, Chicago's Italians clearly viewed themselves as racially superior to the "backward" Ethiopians. To be sure, Italians did not always express these convictions in the most condemnatory of ways. As in other colonial situations in other parts of the world, notions about the friendly natives utterly grateful for the colonizer's boundless generosity did appear in Italian-language newspapers and consul speeches.[29] Also, their decisive and humiliating loss to the Ethiopians at the Battle of Adowa in 1896 forced many Italians to show respect to their erstwhile opponents. Still, an implicit or explicit air of superiority pervaded virtually all Italian-American discussions about their civilizing mission. Long scarred by restriction, racialism, and criminalistic stereotyping, all of which branded *them* as undesirable and inferior, some Italians no doubt responded by claiming Ethiopian backwardness and Italian civilization, believing that the more barbaric Ethiopians appeared, the more civilized and desirable their own people would become in the eyes of Americans.[30]

That self-promotion through differentiation and denigration (the act of "othering") was the general idea is best exemplified by the outrage Italians expressed when these methods backfired. One angry editorial in *L'Italia* demanded that the *Chicago Tribune* "respect what is dearest to us—the dignity of our race which is inferior to none. And, above all we ask these newspapers not to present to the public unfounded or unconfirmed facts, reports and rumors which have the tendency of placing the Italians in the worst light so they appear to be the savages, instead of the Abyssinians."[31]

This "othering"—as well as Italians' general belief in their superiority over Ethiopians—was not, however, a simple move of denigrating blackness to claim whiteness. For one thing, many Italian Americans did not view Ethiopians as "true Negroes." Echoing a common belief at the time, many Italian Americans argued (as *L'Italia* did on several occasions) that their adversaries in east Africa were really a fusion of diverse "stocks"— "Abyssinians," "Arabs," "Semites," "Pygmies," "Negroes," "Somalians," and so on. Furthermore, Italian Americans spoke seldom about color or their color status, even if fascists in Italy sometimes did.[32] One fascist paper from Italy, for instance, claimed that "the white nations of Europe should abandon their long suffering toleration towards" Ethiopia, which is a "gander to the white race."[33] And these ideas traveled to America by way of (among other routes) Mussolini's speeches, which newspapers printed, Italian-language radio stations broadcast, and Fascist Party organs distributed internationally. *The Italian Echo* of Providence, Rhode Island, for instance, parroted the color ideas of Il Duce and other Italian fascists when it remarked in July of 1935 that "if we condemn Italy, we are condemning White Man's Civilization and branding it as unworthy of perpetuation."[34] Chicago Italian Americans, however, had little use for color discourse, appearing to have felt much more comfortable touting their superiority as Italians rather than as whites. When the Italian-American community came together to celebrate their "glorious victory" over Ethiopia, it was the Italian race—not the white one—that received all the credit. When George Spatuzza lauded in speech after speech the glories of *la razza italiana* and the great contributions it would make to backward Ethiopia, he spoke not at all of *la razza bianca* (or *la razza nera* for that matter). And when fascist *prominente* Dr. Emanuele Nicola excoriated the *Chicago Tribune* for "their violent hatred and spiteful, obdurate hostility . . . against the Italians," he defended his people not by claiming membership in the white race, but by extolling the Italian one, which "had reached the highest stage of justice when your [the *Tribune*'s] forefathers groped in damp caves."[35]

This focus on race and nation as opposed to color should come as little surprise. From Mussolini's march on Rome up through the war, fascists worked tirelessly to mobilize Italians as Italians. If fascists spoke at times about defending "white civilization," this was nothing in comparison to their efforts to rally Italians (at home and abroad) around the twin pillars of *la patria* and *la razza*. And these efforts, as we have seen, were plenty visible throughout Chicago during the war. Our Lady of Pompeii, an Italian Catholic church on the Near West Side, urged its parishioners to pray "for the Patria, for its inevitable destiny, for our people in arms, for our soldiers. . . . We implore from the heart of the Mother and the Son for the prompt conclusion of a victorious peace that renders the Patria greater and more glorious. One is not an Italian who does not help the Patria in the grave moments."[36] Indeed, because of this repeated and powerful emphasis on *Italianita'*—understood as both a racial and national identity—color issues and identities never received much attention from Chicago's Italian Americans.

This was not the case for all Italian Americans, however, particularly many left-wing anti-fascists. Steeped in a long tradition of anti-imperialist and anti-colonialist thought within the Communist Party, the Socialist Party, and syndicalist circles, left-wing anti-fascists were the one Italian group that consistently framed the Italian-Ethiopian affair as a color (and class) conflict between full-fledged (working-class) "blacks" and full-fledged (capitalist) "whites." In one editorial entitled "the Stench of [white] Civilization," *Il Proletario* argued in November 1935 that Italy, as an integral part of "il mondo bianco" (the white world), had no right invading Ethiopia, a country vastly more advanced than Italy or any other capitalist European nation. As the paper opined, "a sincere critique of white 'civilization' would be a true revelation. We would uncover, if the truth were known, that in Ethiopia there is less hunger, less unemployment, less economic disadvantages than in Italy or in any of the countries of power who view Ethiopia as 'primitive.'" Such views were well received by leftists—Italians and otherwise. Within Chicago's mainstream Italian-American communities, however, they were often ridiculed and reviled. As one anti-fascist from Chicago later recalled: "those few who raised their voices in opposition to Fascism and Mussolini were smeared as 'Reds' and labeled enemies of the Italian people."[37]

"Hands Off Ethiopia": African Americans and the War

Italians were hardly the only group in America concerned about the Italian-Ethiopian War and determined to shape its meaning and outcome. Also touched deeply by the events were scores of African Americans furious with Mussolini for his attack on independent Ethiopia, which many viewed as a sacred homeland. To be sure, African Americans, like Italian Americans, were not all in agreement on the matter. Internationally acclaimed performer Josephine Baker, married to one Pepito Abbatino, openly supported the Italian cause. And *L'Italia* reveled in reporting about Chicago African Americans who sympathized with Italy. Still, such instances were very rare; evidence suggests that the vast majority of African Americans sided with Ethiopia. Playwright Lorraine Hansberry, for example, only a child in Chicago during the war, later vividly recalled "newsreels of the Ethiopian war and the feeling of outrage in our Negro community. Fighters in spears and our people in a passion over it; my mother attacking the Pope blessing Italian troops going off to slay Ethiopians." Horace Cayton and St. Clair Drake made a similar observation in their classic *Black Metropolis*: "When the Italian legions invaded Ethiopia, the barbershops and street-corners of the [Chicago] Black Belt buzzed with indignation."[38]

This indignation found expression in a wide variety of actions among African Americans across the country. There were, for instance, well-documented marches, street disturbances, and anti-Italian boycotts in Harlem and behind-the-scenes lobbying by groups such as the NAACP in

Washington.[39] A great deal of activism also took place in Chicago, where African-American churches, lodges, clubs, the Urban League, the Communist Party, the Chicago Federation of Labor, and even some Italian antifascist groups helped organize groups like the Joint Committee for the Defense of Ethiopia, the Negro World Alliance, and the Society for the Aid of Ethiopia. These groups held marches and petition drives to "stop Mussolini's robber war" and collected relief funds for besieged "brothers" and "sisters" abroad.[40] The Joint Committee also organized a demonstration outside the Italian consulate, in which two women in sweatshirts bearing the slogan, "Hands Off Ethiopia," chained themselves in protest to a lamppost. Protest took place at the individual level as well: scores of people wrote letters to the *Chicago Defender*, condemning Mussolini as the "meddlesome coward nemesis" and volunteering to fight for Ethiopia; one Chicago man, a leader in a Back-to-Ethiopia organization, "burned an American flag to symbolize the surrender of allegiance to the United States and the assumption of allegiance to Ethiopia"; and the "Brown Condor," John C. Robinson, an aviator from the South Side, journeyed to Ethiopia at the outset of hostilities to serve as a special air courier for Haile Sellassie.[41]

Many African Americans, then, like many Italian Americans, grasped early the importance of the war in Ethiopia for their communities and committed themselves to aiding their "racial kin" in any way possible. But they had their own way of understanding and discussing the war. Many African Americans—particularly public intellectuals—challenged Italians' claims to have a monopoly on civilization. Ethiopia was one of the earliest "outposts of Christianity" and for centuries a dynamic hub of African civilization. As one article in the *Chicago Defender* put it, "for more years than Italy has existed, Ethiopia has maintained and developed a civilization! . . . [And] Ethiopia, as all history will show, is the oldest Christian nation in the world!"[42] Moreover, Italian civilization, as a number of African-American public intellectuals pointed out, was in reality coldblooded conquest, not charity. If fascism were to come to America, warned David Pierce in the NAACP's organ, *The Crisis*, "violence and murder will necessarily be an integral part of the installation ceremonies." An editorial in the *Chicago Defender* put the matter most clearly, if perhaps a bit optimistically: the world, in time, will see past the Italians' civilizing charade and vilify and punish Mussolini for the gangster he is.[43]

Significantly, however, in their condemnation of Italian civilization, African Americans confirmed—rather than questioned—Italian whiteness. Whereas most Italians ignored color, many African Americans stressed it, insisting that, if nothing else, the Italian-Ethiopian War was a color crisis between common adversaries—the colonizing and the colonized, "whites" and "colored peoples." Many African Americans came to these conclusions by way of several interrelated points: First, they agreed and insisted that Ethiopians *were* bonafide "Blacks" and not, as some Italians and other people suggested, a mixed "non-Negroid" people or a darker, distant relative of the "white race." As W. E. B. Du Bois asserted categorically in 1935, "Ethiopia is Negro. Look at the pictures of Abyssinians now widely current. They are as Negroid as American Negroes. If there is a black race they belong to it." And judging by the solidarity many everyday African Americans felt with Ethiopians, Du Bois's point seems to have had a popular base of support.[44] Second, if Ethiopians were "Black/Negro," Italians were just as surely "white." Making this point most powerfully was the young writer, Langston Hughes, in a poem written during the Ethiopian War and entitled "White Man": "Sure I know you! You're a White Man. I'm a Negro. . . . You enjoy Rome—and *take* Ethiopia. White Man! White Man!" One letter titled "White Man's Civilization" published in the *Chicago Defender* several years after the war, presented as typical of this civilization the following facts: "Italian army invades Ethiopia, homes are looted and burned, women attacked and prisoners tortured."[45] Finally, in part because they placed Ethiopians and Italians into well-defined color categories, many African Americans understood the war not as some isolated skirmish between the Italian and Ethiopian races—as many Italians seemed to see it—but as a global conflict between the "colored" and "white" worlds. In the most diverse of media—speeches, essays, poems, shouts on the street, group position papers, and letters to the editor—African Americans of many political persuasions vigorously advanced this understanding. Moderate sociologist George Edmund Haynes, writing in *The Christian Century* about the effects of the war, warned Americans that "perhaps at no other time in history has the question of the relation of whites to blacks moved with such rapidity towards a crisis." And more left-wing African-American thinkers agreed. Du Bois, writing in *Foreign Affairs* argued that whether Ethiopia or Italy prevailed, the coming color crisis between "the white world" and "the whole colored world—India, China and Japan, Africa in Africa and in America, and all the South Seas and Indian South America"—was inevitable. "Italy has forced the world into a position," wrote Du Bois, "where, whether or not she wins, race hate will increase. . . . Black men and brown men have been aroused like never before."[46] Indeed, these very condemnations were just as often directed at "whites" or "Europeans" as they were at Italians— terms African Americans, or at least many of their newspapers and public intellectuals, seemed to use more or less interchangeably.

To be sure, not all African Americans saw the war in precisely these terms. James Ford, an important African-American communist leader, for instance, argued that "to raise the cry of 'all Negroes' against 'all whites' is to play into the hands of Mussolini's campaign of race hatred." Such cries, according to Ford, also made little sense because the Italian-Ethiopian War had given rise not only to a global color crisis, as Du Bois, Haynes, and so many other African Americans suspected, but also to its opposite—cross-color, working-class alliances: "The struggle of the Ethiopian people," proclaimed Ford in a speech in Madison Square Garden during the war, "has aroused a bond of sympathy among millions of toilers, black, white, yellow, and brown, throughout the world." Still, even Ford's analysis, as this second quotation suggests, was not opposed to that of other African Americans when it came to color conceptions and classifications. When discussing the need to unite Italian Americans and African Americans in a "joint struggle" against fascist imperialism, Ford reverted back to traditional ideas about "blacks," "whites," and so on.[47]

Fitting the war into a "white"-"colored" rubric that made sense to them and comported well with their experiences in the United States, then, many African Americans—whether Communists or middle-class moderates, whether discussing civilization or the coming color crisis—could all agree on one thing: Italians belonged to the "white race." Ironically, African Americans insisted more on Italian whiteness than did Italians themselves.

"White Peril" Redux: "Other" Americans and the War

Italian Americans and African Americans were most directly touched by the war in Ethiopia and had the greatest stake in its outcome. But other Americans and some of their key institutions like newspapers and magazines also followed the events closely and offered a variety of opinions. To start, Italian fascists had their friends in America, who willingly supported their contentions about who was and was not civilized. The Hearst-owned *Chicago Herald Examiner*, for instance, regularly ran reports during the war of Ethiopia's "savage" attacks upon Italian troops and wrote approvingly at the onset of hostilities that "Mussolini plans to send soldiers, and later, colonists to Ethiopian regions that for thousands of years have been given over to barbarism as complete as that which reigned in this country while the Indians owned it. . . . Italy is only carrying on the slow, inevitable process of time, planning to replace barbarism with civilization." Even *Chicago Daily News* columnist Westbrook Pegler, long despised by Italian Americans for his vicious barbs against them, conceded that "Italians . . . do have a mission to carry the light—perhaps the torchlight—of civilization to the primitive brothers of a backward country."[48]

But there was just as much suspicion of, as support for, Italy's so-called civilizing mission. In fact, in Chicago there seems to have been a good deal more of the former, where both the *Chicago Tribune* and the *Chicago Daily News* (Pegler's comments notwithstanding) roundly condemned Italian aggression in Ethiopia and ridiculed Italy's claims to be defending and extending civilization. One *Tribune* editorial cartoon showed Italian planes dive-bombing an Ethiopian town, destroying homes, and massacring innocent civilians. The sardonic caption read: "Bringing civilization to Ethiopia." Similarly, *Daily News* editorials consistently branded Italy as a blatant aggressor in the Ethiopian crisis who had nothing to teach Ethiopia or any other country about civilization. The day after Italy first invaded Ethiopia, the *News* noted caustically:

> It is not surprising that, fed for thirteen years on a perverted philosophy of history and of national greatness . . . the people of Italy rally blindly behind their magnetic dictator in this hour of destiny. The people of Germany did the same in 1914. So did the people of France in the mad days of Napoleon and his feeble imitator, Napoleon III. All paid dearly for their misplaced trust. Will fate deal more kindly with the people of Italy, who yesterday undertook to rewrite history and redraw national boundaries in blood and destruction?[49]

These views extended well beyond the Chicago press. Several books and a wide variety of magazines—liberal and conservative, high-brow and middle-brow, religious and secular—also raised serious doubts about Italy's ability, much less desire, to civilize another country. In one *Collier's* article, for instance, W. B. Courtney scolded Italians for their propensity to "go native," fraternize too freely with the "native girls," and do nothing to "raise" the level of civilization in Ethiopia. "The Italian," Courtney wrote disgustedly, " . . . does not lift native cultures; he accommodates himself to them. . . . [T]he Italian is content to work back to back with the native—to eat and live as he does, and provide him no example of betterment." To liberal weeklies like the *Nation* and the *New Republic*, that Italy failed to "civilize" Ethiopia was hardly a surprise; after all, its war against Ethiopia was much less about civilizing work than "burglary," "murder," "imperialist aggression," and "mad adventure." President Franklin Roosevelt put the matter most clearly in a letter to U.S. Ambassador to Italy Breckinridge Long in late 1935. Discussing the gathering of war clouds over Ethiopia and other parts of the world, Roosevelt wrote: "What a commentary this whole situation is on what we like to think of as modern and excellent civilization."[50]

If many Americans had serious doubts about Italians' ability and desire to civilize, they too harbored questions about Italians' race and color. For one, the many discussions about Italians' own brand of barbarism, along with their uncanny willingness and ability to "go native," must have raised doubts about Italians' proper race/color status. In the *Chicago Tribune's* many editorial cartoons condemning Italian aggression in Ethiopia, the paper often portrayed Mussolini as ape-like and once as an organ grinder's monkey. That the racial/color point of such treatment was clear is best exemplified by Italians' outraged responses to the *Chicago Tribune*. *L'Italia* demanded on one occasion that the paper "respect what is dearest to us—the dignity of our race which is inferior to none." On other occasions, Italians wrote letters admonishing the paper for its "prejudice against my [Italian] race" or for its "morbose [sic] Italophobia . . . and unfounded hatred for a great and glorious people."[51]

In the end, these occasional and often implicit questions about Italians' race and color status notwithstanding, many mainstream "white" American commentators of diverse political orientations agreed with their African-American counterparts and viewed the Italian-Ethiopian War first and foremost as a color conflict between European "whites" and African "coloreds." In this formulation, Italians were always white. Lothrop Stoddard noted in November of 1935, for instance, that the "racial factor" stood at the heart of the east African war, which ominously "aroused men of color" against Italians and other "white" Europeans throughout Asia and Africa. In the *Nation*, pacifist Oswald Garrison Villard warned similarly that the longer the conflict carried on in Ethiopia between "white" Italians and "black" Africans, the greater the color tensions would become around the world. Boake Carter agreed in his popular account of the war *Black Shirt Black Skin*: Italians' "aspirations plunge them headlong not only to self-destruction—but into something more disturbing, more menacing— the explosive problem of—color. The teeming millions which from Africa's population are ruled by a comparative handful of whites. Mussolini's intention to wage war on a black race has set the fires of race differences and dislike glowing again, as they have not glowed for decades."[52]

And what if Italy were to lose this conflict? Harvard anthropologist Carleton Coon predicted in the *Atlantic Monthly* that "the tenuous prestige of white men in all of Negroid Africa will sink to so low a level that black men will no longer come running with newly shined boots or whiskey and soda at the snap of a finger." Nathaniel Peffer, a left-wing journalist and vigorous critic of "white" imperialism, offered predictions quite a bit more foreboding for the "white world": "If . . . Italy should fail, the enemy will not be the single western empire that has conquered, but the West as West, white as white, one white nation indistinguishable from another, since all recognize neither law nor morals when dealing with the nonwhite. In headline moods we used to talk of Yellow Peril. It was a chimera, and as a rallying cry it proved to be hollow. The cry of the White Peril may be more convincing."[53]

Italians did "win" the war, however, successfully annexing Ethiopia and inheriting a serious problem of anti-colonial resistance for years. And if, as some commentators thought, a loss would have damaged "white" and Italian prestige, the opposite may have been true in "victory." To be sure, Italian aggression in Ethiopia provoked widespread and vigorous criticism in the United States, some of which was racialized and colorized. Nevertheless, Italy's "success" in the war no doubt further cemented its claim to be a major world power—and, at least implicitly, a major "white" power—even if a wide range of Americans (among others) objected to Italy's means of achieving this status. In the end, the war and its outcome may have raised questions about Italians' good faith and judgment when it came to treaties, international law, and world peace; but they did not, by and large, raise questions about their whiteness. Almost all American commentators on the war—from W. E. B. Du Bois and Lothrop Stoddard to the *Chicago Tribune* and the *Chicago Defender*—could agree on this point.

Despite this apparent unanimity, however, Chicago's Italian Americans remained largely silent on issues of color. In conflict with an enemy considered by many to be "black" or "colored," Italian Americans rarely openly asserted their (supposed) whiteness, denigrated Ethiopians for their (supposed) blackness, or understood the war in color terms at all. *Italianita'* and not whiteness was Italians' social identity of choice within the context of the Italian-Ethiopian War, a fact that makes eminent sense. Both the fascist state and powerful Italian-American community organizations worked tirelessly throughout these years to build a more unified Italy and Italian diaspora. If many Italian immigrants had little concern for or conception of Italy when they first arrived in Chicago, then times had certainly changed by the 1930s. At the end of the Italian-Ethiopian War, tens of thousands of Chicago Italians identified strongly with and cared deeply about *la patria* and *la razza italiana*.[54]

Yet two key developments in relation to the war no doubt affected Chicago Italians' self-understandings, particularly regarding color. Most obviously, the "unanimity" discussed above regarding Italians' whiteness must not have been lost on Italians. Equally important, immediately following the war, Italy undertook an extensive empire-building project which, through the dissemination of fascist doctrine and the implementation of fascist law, drew the strictest of color lines between ruler and ruled, "white/Aryan" Italians and "black" Ethiopians. These policies, which Chicago's Italian-language newspapers followed closely and approvingly, no doubt further established in Italians' minds the importance of the color line and Italians' "proper" position along it.[55] Both developments must have increased Italians' awareness of the color line and "their" whiteness.

7

RADICALISM, UNIONISM, AND THE DEPRESSION

In the summer of 1932, with the United States facing its most severe depression ever, a destitute and desperate Nick Colletta left Chicago for Detroit in search of work. By late July, Mr. Colletta, having had little luck, wrote to the Chicago Commons settlement staff: "I haven't any hope to take work now, because in every place there is worst business. And about the future there is pessimist [*sic*]. I don't know what I shall do. . . . I will continue to fight for the life until I can't fight, and when I shall see that it is impossible and in vain to fight, I shall decide what I should do. . . . Now life seems to me strange and hard. It seems that the moral of the humanity goes down." Many working-class Chicagoans shared Colletta's despair. Over 40 percent of the city's workforce was unemployed and even those with jobs faced severe problems. Employers all over the city drastically reduced the hours and incomes of their workers, pushing millions of Chicagoans to the brink of starvation, into the streets, or both. With over two hundred Chicago families facing evictions weekly in the summer of 1931, "Hoovervilles" sprouted up at the eastern end of Randolph Street and in Grant Park, both in the Loop area.[1]

These events hit Italians—the vast majority of whom were working class and struggling financially even before the crash—particularly hard.[2] Speaking of the nearby Italian community, the Chicago Commons reported in 1932 that the Depression

> has left in its wake discouraged and disheartened men and women, constantly fearful that relief funds will cease; panicky when grocery orders are delayed or cut down; faced with continual irritation from landlords unpaid for many months and themselves struggling to exist; going without clothing, bedding and housing supplies; using candles and oil lamps for light, and trying to heat a four-room apartment with a small garbage burner which also serves as a cook stove.

Every Italian neighborhood in Chicago had high relief rates. On the Near West Side, for instance, 44 percent of the population was on relief in 1934. And such conditions were demoralizing indeed. Occasionally, *L'Italia* reported the suicide of a destitute and disheartened Italian.[3]

But suicide was only one relatively rare way Italians responded to the Depression. Other Italians naturalized and voted regularly for the first time, joining the ever-expanding New Deal coalition; others continued to look to mutual aid societies like the Italo-American National Union (IANU) and the Order of the Sons of Italy (OSIA), both of which survived the Depression intact; others placed their faith in their bosses and welfare capitalist measures; still others chose to escape the problems of their everyday lives through a giddy celebration of fascist imperialism and conquest. Many Italians pursued several of these strategies at once. This chapter explores two other prominent public responses to the Depression: Italians' involvement in left-wing political movements like those connected to the Communist and Socialist Parties and, most important, in the organized labor movements of the Congress of Industrial Organizations (CIO) and the American Federation of Labor (AFL).[4]

Italians' left-wing radical and organized labor experiences played a critical role in their race and color formation in Chicago. On the one hand, working, organizing, and marching with the most cosmopolitan of groups, Italians ventured out of the parochial worlds of *campanalismo* and *Italianita'* and into movements like those of organized labor that often (but not always) worked to build bridges between workers of diverse race and color classifications. On the other hand, much both inside and outside these movements helped to sustain an Italian identity for many *paesani*. As a result, on the issue of race/nation, a compromise was reached: Italians were becoming Italian Americans (a process that only intensified during the World War II years). Regarding color, little compromise was needed. Whether Italians' Depression-era experiences consisted of organizing the unemployed with the Communist Party or joining an AFL or CIO local, each of these movements, actions, and institutions further consolidated Italians' hold on whiteness, nurturing, in the process, their color consciousness.

Movements on the Left

With the capitalist system appearing to implode worldwide, the Depression was a boon for left-wing ideas and movements. And widespread philo-fascism notwithstanding, they deeply touched many Chicago Italians, some of whom had long traditions of anarcho-syndicalist, communist, and socialist activism.[5] Most generally, some Chicago Italians were active in both the Socialist and Communist Parties. As for the former, the most devoted community was no doubt the Tuscan settlement around Twenty-fourth Street and Oakley on the West Side. For decades prior to the Depression, this neighborhood supported a vocal and sizable socialist population, which met regularly as members of the left-wing Lavagnini Club, organized and led annual May Day parades, staged anti-capitalist and anti-clerical dramatic productions, and participated in union drives mainly in the garment industry with the Amalgamated Clothing Workers of America (ACWA). With the coming of the Depression, socialists became even more active, participating in the Farm Equipment Workers' Organizing Committee's (FEWOC) drives to organize workers (many of whom were neighborhood Italians) both at International Harvester's nearby Tractor Works and McCormick Works in the late 1930s and early 1940s. They were also very active in ACWA's Local 270, in which socialists like Louis Chiostra were leaders.[6] Italians constituted only a small fraction of Chicago's Communist Party (CP). According to party records, a mere fifty-four Chicago Italians belonged to the Party in 1931, just under 3 percent of total city membership. Still, as membership swelled during the Popular Front from 683 in 1930 to a peak of 5,750 eight years later, no doubt more Italians joined. Furthermore, there were several very prominent Italian communists active in these years, particularly in the CIO. People like Ernie De Maio, regional director of the United Electrical and Radio Workers of America (UE), and the Steel Workers Organizing Committee's (SWOC) Mario Manzardo, Anthony Cassano, Max Luna, and Peter Calacci, all were either active CP members at different points in their lives or closely aligned with the ideas and activities of the party.[7]

Larger numbers of Italians came into contact with the CP and the Socialist Party (SP) less through active membership and more through the joining of movements and organizations closely affiliated with these groups. Besides unions, there were the movements of the unemployed in Chicago and the International Workers Order (IWO). By the early 1930s, it had become increasingly clear that government and private agencies were wholly unprepared to deal with the magnitude of the Depression. As a result, both the SP and CP built hundreds of local organizations nationwide—Unemployed Councils (UC) for the latter and Workers' Committees on Unemployment (WCU) for the former—to fight for adequate public relief provisions and an end to rent evictions. These movements were particularly strong in Chicago and some Italians were involved. Philip Martino, for instance, was chairman of the UC in Humboldt Park in the early 1930s, and other Italians like Vito Russo, Giuseppe Bruno, Vincent Bianco, Sam Concialdi, and Gino Alessandro started an Italian local of the Chicago Workers' Committee in the Grand Avenue area of the Near Northwest Side. In the fall of 1932, when both the WCUs and UCs staged a joint demonstration in Chicago, an Italian radical, Dino Renzi, was on hand to give a speech in Italian. Despite conflicts and little cooperation, the UCs and WCUs served a very important purpose by organizing rallies all over the city, moving evicted families back into their homes, encouraging banks to lend monies for relief when state funds were not forthcoming, and demanding a more active and efficient relief program from the local, state, and federal governments. In 1936, when these two organizations eventually merged into the Workers Alliance of America, Italians became active in its local branch, the Illinois Workers Alliance.[8]

As for the IWO, this was a fraternal benefit association established in 1930 by Jewish Communists and other pro-Soviet leftists, who broke from the socialist-controlled Workmen's Circle, another left-wing mutual aid society based in New York. The Order first provided sickness, disability, and death benefits to its members, but expanded quickly in the 1930s to include a network of lodges, schools, and summer camps, many of which sponsored a wide range of recreational, educational, and cultural activities, ranging from brass bands and boxing to lectures and drama. In addition, the IWO was closely connected to radical left-wing politics, particularly the CP, which furnished most of the Order's leadership and deeply informed its ideological and political orientation. An IWO pamphlet in Italian from 1931 declared: "The IWO recognizes that the only enemies of the workers are the capitalists and their servants. . . . If you are workers, and you recognize that you are being exploited, bled, impoverished, brutalized by the intense exploitation of the classes of bosses . . . your place should be in the IWO."

By offering insurance benefits cheaply and efficiently to all people regardless of race or color and creating a vibrant left-wing political culture, the IWO became the fastest growing fraternal benefit society in America, expanding from 3,000 to 165,000 members between 1930 and 1940.[9] While more Italians were active in mainstream, *prominenti*-led organizations like OSIA and IANU, the IWO did have significant Italian participation. In 1933, the city had nineteen Italian lodges and 640 Italian members; five years later, the number of lodges dropped to fifteen but membership increased to nine hundred. And lodges were located in most of Chicago's key Italian communities such as West Englewood, the Near Northwest Side, the Near West Side, Kensington, Twenty-fourth Street and Oakley, and Humboldt Park.[10]

Organized Labor

While all these movements and actions were important, far greater numbers of Italians turned to the CIO and AFL for an antidote to their worst Depression-era problems. There was nothing inevitable about this choice, as the 1920s were trying times for organized labor. Deeply disturbed by the intense labor militancy that swept across the United States during World War I and its immediate aftermath, employers struck back at unionization efforts through a fierce and organized open shop movement, as well as through welfare capitalist measures like wage incentives, vacation plans, stock options, insurance benefits, and recreational and social programs. In these years, the federal government aided big business by using troops and court injunctions to break up strikes, and through Supreme Court decisions like the one in 1922 that ruled that a striking union, like a trust, could be prosecuted for illegal restraint of trade. The results of these various actions were disastrous for organized labor. Labor militancy declined dramatically as union membership nationally dropped from five million in 1920 to three million by the time of the crash, a mere one-tenth of the nation's industrial workforce. Once vigorous unions like the United Mine Workers lost 80 percent of its membership in the decade.[11] In Chicago, key sectors of the workforce—most significantly packing and steel—remained completely unorganized and other relatively strong unions like the International Ladies' Garment Workers' Union (ILGWU) steadily shrank in membership from 6,195 in 1919 to being "all but eliminated" in the city a decade later. Although some Chicago unions like those in printing, the building trades, the garment industry, and baking showed signs of revival in 1929, the awesome severity of the Depression quickly shattered these unions' renewed hopes.[12]

In the 1930s, however, organized labor's fortunes changed quickly, thanks to New Deal legislation like the Wagner Act, to unions' creative new strategies to attract workers and overcome working-class fragmentation, and to workers themselves, many of whom united across race and color lines and used workplace and electoral activism to build and protect unions. This was particularly the case with the CIO, which first emerged in 1935 as a splinter group within the AFL to organize industrial workers. By the fall of 1938, it had become officially independent from, and a rival to, its parent organization. These factors together produced impressive results: union membership nationwide, which stood just below three million in 1933, soared to ten million by 1940 and fifteen million by the end of World War II. In Chicago, in particular, unions witnessed astonishing gains, where by 1945, the CIO had successfully organized large segments of steel, packing, electrical, farm equipment, and auto workers. Among steelworkers alone, membership in the United Steelworkers of America's (USWA) District 31, encompassing the Chicago-Calumet region, skyrocketed from eighteen thousand in 1940 to nearly one hundred thousand a mere five years later. Meanwhile, the AFL enjoyed significant growth as well, despite the fact that it lost large numbers of workers to the CIO.[13]

Because little information on the national or racial composition of organized labor in these years exists, it is difficult to determine in which locals and to what extent Italians were active. Still, culling information from various sources—AFL and CIO newspapers, the Chicago Federation of Labor (CFL) voting lists, oral histories, several union archival collections, and lists of union and local officers from the time—reveals several things. First, Italians served as officers in countless AFL and CIO locals in these years, meaning presumably that other Italians were active in many of these same locals. Italians were officers in the widest range of AFL trade-unions such as the Journeyman's Barbers' Union, Local 548, the Chicago Federation of Musicians, Local 10, the Hod Carriers, Building, and Common Laborers' Union, the Terrazo Workers' Union, Local 41, the ILGWU, Photographers and Photo Finishers, Local 17880, Plasterers and Cement Casters, Local 301, Race Track Employees, Local 620, and the Macaroni Workers Union, Local 465.[14] An equally large number of Italians belonged to a diverse set of CIO locals. Though the largest number of Italians were active in nearly two dozen USWA locals in and around Chicago, they belonged as well to key locals in ACWA, UE, United Farm Equipment and Metal Workers Union (FE), and the United Auto Workers (UAW). In fact, the only major CIO union in which Italians constituted a negligible element was the United Packinghouse Workers of America (UPWA), since historically few Italians worked at Chicago's many meat-packing plants.[15]

Italians were not simply rank-and-file union members or local officers. By the Depression and war years, they had come to occupy real positions of leadership within both the CIO and AFL beyond the local level. This was particularly the case with the CIO, where Italians like Nicholas Fontecchio and then Joe Germano ran USWA's District 31 (which represented 10 percent of USWA workers nationwide) from its inception well into the 1970s. At the subdistrict levels of USWA, Italians like Raymond Sarocco were also prominent leaders. In addition, Ernie De Maio was district director of UE, Paul M. Russo held a similar position for the UAW, and Frank Annunzio became Illinois Director of Political Action USA-CIO just after the war.[16] In the AFL, there were powerful local union leaders like James C. Petrillo ("the Mussolini of Music") and James V. Moreschi, both of whom in time became presidents of their Internationals—the American Federation of Musicians and the Hod Carriers Union, respectively. These men's success aside, however, Italians were never as well represented in the local AFL power structure, the CFL, as they were in that of the CIO. Over the course of the 1930s and World War II years, Italians never had more than one person serving as a CFL officer or committee member (roughly sixty-four people total), and oftentimes they had none.[17]

While the names mentioned to this point are all male, Italian women were also active in unions, particularly during World War II, when more and more women entered the paid workforce to fill the void created by departing male soldiers and to meet the ever-rising demand of booming wartime production. Italian women, like their male counterparts, joined both AFL and CIO unions and served as local officers. In 1944, for instance, at Diamond Wire and Cable Co. in Chicago Heights, USWA Local 3167 won bargaining rights in a National Labor Relations Board election, thanks mainly to a number of Italian women active in the local—Matilda Granucci, president; Estella Camelli, financial secretary; and Margaret Fiorenza, Josephine Azzrello, and Regina Concetti, all negotiating committee members. In addition, Italian women like Anna Lagaglia, Mary Violante, Florence De Pasquale, Theresa Amelio, Edith Sinari, Lorraine Donota, Ester Albertini, Rose Bruno, and many others also served as officers in various UE, USWA, and ACWA locals. Italian women also served on CIO women's auxiliaries, particularly for the USWA where Marie Rondelli, for example, was president of Acme Steel's organization in the late 1930s. Some Italian women held leadership positions and belonged to AFL trade unions, as well. Lydia Comastro of the ILGWU and Geraldine Calzaretta of the International Brotherhood of Electrical Workers both served on their respective unions' executive boards during the war, while at the same time Edna Romano served as a central committee member for the Belt Workers Union.[18]

Unionism and Radicalism, Race and Color

A complicated racial story emerges from Italians' diverse experiences in unions and left-wing politics. In the CIO, these were the years, as historian Lizabeth Cohen has noted, of an ascendant and powerful "culture of unity," when unions walked the fine line between celebrating racial/national identities and forging working-class solidarity. On the one hand, the CIO recognized that it was critical to organize all workers regardless of race and that, for these organizing efforts to be successful, it would have to take workers' racial/national identities seriously. As a result, the CIO chose a group of organizers representing the diversity of Chicago's workforce (SWOC's organizers, for instance, read like a list of future United Nations delegates: Wisniewski, Pecovich, Sarocco, Ingersoll, Krzywonos, Hansen, Gold, Johnson); it staged events that celebrated "Old World" traits (SWOC Local 1010 in East Chicago, for instance, organized "language days," which added "colorful European peasant garb to more standard picket-line attire"); it distributed leaflets, made signs, and prepared speeches in a variety of languages; and, during organizing drives, it solicited the help of national organizations like the IWO and other fraternal orders like the Societa' Filmonia Bel' Italia in Roseland.[19]

On the other hand, for the CIO really to succeed, it needed its members to see past these racial and national differences and to unite as workers.[20] To this end, the CIO avoided "language locals" (where different racial/nationality groups had their own locals) and, instead, made them as diverse as their group of organizers. The CIO also made efforts to mix their workers outside the workplace in a wide variety of social and recreational activities such as dances, picnics, bowling and softball leagues, and summer camps. FE's West Pullman Local 107, for instance, sponsored a bowling team with members named Lulkowski, Lange, Stanky, Wilson, Churilla, and Paghero.[21] These CIO efforts paid dividends. Strikes, which in the past had aggravated racial divisions, seemed to have had, in the main, the opposite effect in the 1930s. One student of a USWA local in East Chicago noted that when workers decided in May 1937 to strike against Inland Steel, they took to the streets in a spontaneous celebration of their own working-class version of *e pluribus unum*: "In broken English and foreign tongues literally thousands of Harborites discussed the CIO strike in the streets, Turkish coffeehouses, and bars of the working district." In the end, the workers were "participants in a real social movement or crusade to better their lot. They were together with all of their national and racial differences submerged." One steelworker from the time echoed this assessment: Because of the union, workers "are drawn closer together on the job. . . . Through union activity the men get to know each other so that now the tendency is greater association together, instead of, as in the past, association with rigid national groups."[22]

The AFL—or more particularly its local institution, the CFL—was similar to the CIO in extolling and fighting for racial/national unity—at least when it came to the European races and nations. Long before the CIO was established, the CFL mixed workers together in locals with little regard to (European) race and by encouraging workers to socialize off the job by sponsoring recreational and social activities for its members. Typical was the diverse bowling team of the Laundry and Dye House Chauffeurs Union, Local 712; in 1930, its members included Nicodemus, Danielson, Guzybowski, Quigley, Kieckerman, Apato, Radloff, and Lacoco.[23] In addition, the CFL, particularly during World War II, trumpeted the wonders of European racial pluralism by sponsoring radio programs on its station, WCFL, entitled "Americans All, Immigrants All." These programs sought "to promote attitudes of good feeling among races and especially toward those laboring masses of differing backgrounds who made America great," by featuring numerous articles in its newspaper, *Federation News*, attacking "race prejudice" against European alien groups as "mostly absurd," and by sponsoring enormous "Americanism Day" rallies, in which on one occasion seventy thousand people of the most diverse European backgrounds packed Soldier Field to listen to speeches, marvel at parades, and enjoy a circus program.[24]

Taken together, Italians engaged in a number of cosmopolitan experiences in these years, many of which forced Italians beyond the parochialisms of *Italianita'* and *campanalismo*. Still, this point should not be exaggerated. Indeed, some of these experiences could just as surely reinforce as undermine these more "traditional" outlooks and identities. In the AFL, for instance, for well into the World War II years, some locals like those in the Hod Carriers Union were still heavily Italian. In addition, throughout the 1930s, the *Federation News* attacked Mussolini mercilessly (calling him on one occasion a "Wop dictator"), which could only have enraged many philo-fascist Italians, frustrated CFL attempts to build working-class solidarity between Italians and other groups, and heightened Italians' awareness of their *Italianita'*.[25] Meanwhile in the CIO, racial unity was at times more of a goal than a reality. In 1937, for instance, one student of the ACWA noted: "The union has had to deal with the disrupting influence of race differences [probably between Jews, Poles, Bohemians, and Italians— the main groups in the union] on numerous occasions." Similarly, one machinist and FE member at the McCormick plant (where many Italians worked) recalled that in the 1940s and 1950s there was "a lot of expressed prejudice between ethnic groups" at the plant.[26] And of course, the CIO's own inclusive organizing techniques could backfire. There was no telling whether CIO foreign language pamphlets, speeches, and signs would, for some workers, heighten their racial consciousness to the detriment of the union and working-class solidarity. Finally, left-wing organizing, while bringing diverse groups together in common struggle and championing a "universal" class identity over racial and national "particularities," still did much to reinforce Italians' identity as Italians, since almost all left-wing groups still organized along "language" lines. Both Italian anarchists and socialists belonged to Italian branches of national organizations and read Italian newspapers. Similarly, well into the 1930s and 1940s, the CP organized its foreign-born membership (half of the party in Chicago in 1931) into "language departments," one of which was Italian. The IWO, though national leadership often fought the trend, was widely (though not exclusively) broken up into language lodges itself, so that, again, Italians organized and socialized mainly with each other.[27]

In the end, as Italians combated the Depression in the most racially diverse of unions, unemployed movements, and so on, they did not lose their connection to *la razza italiana*. Certainly, international events like the rise of fascism and the Italian-Ethiopian War went a long way in ensuring this but so too did certain characteristics of the labor and radical movements themselves. At the same time, in the long run, an American working-class identity was also on the rise. Therefore, Italians most likely made a compromise regarding their race/nation identity: they became Italian Americans.[28]

A general story about color also emerges from the diverse particularities of left-wing politics and unionism. From the Left, the CIO, and even some AFL locals, Italians learned quite a bit about color tolerance and understanding. And the CIO and CP went well beyond these goals and attempted to dismantle some aspects of the workplace color structure. Still, one piece of the color structure that no one attempted to change was Italians' position within it. Each left-wing and union movement, in its own way and with varying degrees of intentionality and enthusiasm, helped to consolidate Italian whiteness.

To be sure, communists, socialists, and anarchists adhered, at least officially, to positions of color equality and wished, at least in theory, to talk more about class divisions than color ones. The CP exemplifies this point best with its tireless efforts to organize across the color line. In 1931, while African Americans made up only 6.9 percent of Chicago's population, they comprised nearly one-quarter of the city's CP membership, a higher proportion than in any other American city at the time. Similarly, according to one estimate from 1934 of the UC's and WCU's composition, while the latter's leadership and membership were a mere 6 percent and 5 percent African-American respectively, the former's were a whopping 21 percent and 25 percent. Indeed, not only did African Americans comprise a significant portion of the CP rank and file, but they also occupied key leadership positions from top to bottom of the party's local and national structures.[29] And to the extent that the CP constantly pushed an international working-class identity and sought to deconstruct the color line in unions and workers' social circles, it helped its members—Italians among them—to envision a world beyond color designations such as "white," "Negro," "Oriental," and so forth.

CP rhetoric, however, militated hard against such visions. In scores of Popular Front speeches, slogans, banners, newspaper articles, position papers, and parade floats, communists spoke incessantly about "Negroes" and "whites" and their need to "Unite and Fight." Though a noble pursuit, the CP, by discursively dividing the social world into these two categories, made a powerful statement to Italians and other European Americans about "their" whiteness. The CP did not create these categories, of course. Indeed, the "Negro"/"white" divide—always prevalent in the United States—only grew more so by the 1930s and 1940s, as many Americans—after immigration restriction, the horrors of the Holocaust, and the increased northern migration of African Americans—lost interest in delineating racial differences between European groups and concerned themselves more with solving the "American [color] dilemma." Also, the CP spoke about "whites" and "Negroes" because these categories meant a great deal to Chicagoans, whose lives and resources—their education, housing, jobs, unions, social circles, and so on—were always deeply structured by color. Thus, while one could hardly fault the CP for organizing workers along these lines, this strategy still assigned all Europeans to the white side of the color divide and, as such, encouraged its members—Italians among them—to identify in these ways.[30]

Italians' experiences with the CIO, a good number of whose locals were led by party members and fellow-travelers, were varied indeed, but in the end seem similar to those with the CP. Often the CIO was also committed to organizing all groups regardless of color; it encouraged "colored" workers to assume leadership positions in their locals, to become stewards, and to serve on grievance committees; it made unity across the color line a repeated and central part of its operating ideology; it often made its social activities like dances, picnics, and bowling teams open to all and encouraged social interaction between unionists of all backgrounds; and finally, it fought frequently for the rights and equal treatment of its "colored" union members in word and deed. What all these actions meant was that the CIO—like the CP—made a genuine effort to dismantle some of the very workplace systems or structures that manufactured and reinforced color difference on a daily basis—most notably segregated washrooms and cafeterias and a deeply colorized job structure that reserved the foremen and skilled positions for "whites" only and the unskilled, least desirable, and most dangerous positions for "others."[31] Although their level of commitment surely varied, all major CIO unions in Chicago, with any "colored" presence to speak of, were waging these battles.

And numerous Italians were involved, as the steel industry demonstrates particularly well. Between the time of the SWOC's first organizing drive and the end of World War II (by which time the SWOC had changed its name to the USWA), many locals emerged with large numbers of Italians and African Americans and in some cases Mexicans as well. Some examples were 1033 at Republic Steel, 1135 at Chicago Malleable Casting, 1178 at Wisconsin Steel, 1834 at Pullman Standard Car Manufacturing, 2490 Acme Steel, 2674 Western Foundry Company, 1133 General American Transportation Corporation, and 1546 Perfection Gear Company.[32] In many of these locals, the SWOC/USWA fought hard to build unity across the color line by having organizers in the mills speak constantly to workers about the superficiality of color differences and by fully "integrating" all locals' membership, leadership, and social and recreational activities. These efforts, according to many workers and observers at the time, had powerful effects. One African-American steelworker stated in 1937: "I'll tell you what the CIO has done. Before everyone used to make remarks about, 'That dirty Jew,' 'that stinkin' black bastard,' 'that low-life Bohunk,' but you know I never hear that stuff anymore." A "white" steelworker agreed: "I think the CIO will get us away from thinking so much about color." Speaking of the SWOC in general in 1939, two African-American sociologists concluded dramatically: "The effect of working together for a common goal, of facing a common enemy, and of day by day cooperation in union affairs has been to draw white and Negro workers together to an extent perhaps never before equaled in this country."[33]

Italians were certainly involved in this "drawing together." Local 1033 of Republic Steel, for instance, which had numerous Italian officers in it, spearheaded a walkout and strike in 1937 that led not only to the bloody Memorial Day Massacre (in which ten unarmed workers were murdered—two of whom were Italian and one of whom was African American) but also to an impressive display of color unity. As Horace Cayton and St. Clair Drake put it in *Black Metropolis*, "The Republic Steel Strike demonstrated that in a time of crisis white workers would not only struggle side by side with Negroes, but would also follow them as leaders and honor them as martyrs." Demonstrating the point, Local 1033 forced Republic Steel to abolish its segregated washrooms at the plant. In another USWA/SWOC local in 1937, one African-American steelworker related the following story: "On June 11, my wife's birthday, the white women of the East Side gave her a surprise party at a white woman's house. It was a fine party.

Italian-American and African-American workers at the Inland Steel Plant in Chicago Heights, 1941. Italian-American Collection, Department of Special Collections, The Richard J. Daley Library, University of Illinois at Chicago.

. . . There were so many flowers, I thought someone had died. They called me to come over and we didn't know what it was all about. The party was at the home of Joe Petronio. He's an Italian. He's financial secretary of the union."[34]

Italians' color experiences in steel may not have been unique. At the Buick Plant in Melrose Park, where the UAW Local 6 represented many African Americans and Italians, one government official reported in 1943 that "foremen and petty bosses are continually amazed at the good relationship of whites and Negroes."[35] Similarly, UE locals like 1114, 1150, and others—whose membership and leadership included large numbers of both African Americans and Italians—held integrated dances, sponsored color-integrated bowling teams, spoke out vigorously against color discrimination at the workplace, hosted the Negro People's Theater at one meeting, nominated African-American as well as European-American women for "Personality Girl of the Local" contests, and made various efforts at the workplace to secure equal opportunities in the hiring and promotion of African Americans. Finally, FE too had integrated locals like 101 at Tractor Works that Italians and African Americans (among others) jointly led and that published a newspaper regularly denouncing color discrimination. Taken together, for the Italians active in the CIO in these years—especially those active in integrated and progressive locals—these experiences must have been powerful. From working, socializing, organizing, and striking with fellow unionists of all "colors," Italians learned a great deal about color tolerance and understanding. It is also possible that some Italians' color consciousness decreased in these years, as the CIO attempted to do "away with this color question."[36]

But the CIO experience—as was the case with race—was never all about unity, tolerance, and understanding. For one, there was always a sector of the CIO that never quite accepted the official CIO line of unity and tolerance, the "interracial" mixing at dances, or the vigorous pursuit of color equality at the workplace. One Italian president of a steelworkers' women's auxiliary had this to say about integrated social events in 1937:

> As my husband and I have said to each other, you give them [African Americans] a foot and they'll take a yard. If you ask them to your dances, they'll come and they won't just dance with each other, but some of them will try to dance with white people. If they do, the white women will just stop going to dances. There's something about colored men that just makes you afraid. . . . I know that Negroes are workers and I suppose that they really are human, but there's just something about that black skin.

Similarly, at the International Harvester Plant in Melrose Park, which the UAW had organized and where many Italians worked, several observers noted immediately after World War II that "some of the white workers did not want to mix socially with the Negroes, though they usually supported the idea of equal rights on the job. Because of the color issue the local had had much less success with dances than with picnics."[37]

The most explosive issues did not necessarily involve socializing; often the promotion of an African American into a supervisory role previously closed to her or him could set off the most serious problems. Indeed, the World War II years witnessed the outbreak of several hate strikes at CIO plants in the Chicago area. In 1944, at Pullman's shipbuilding division on the Far South Side, over one thousand "white" workers initiated a wildcat strike when management appointed Barney Morgan, an African American, to lead an "integrated" group of pipe-fitters. The strikers, half of whom were members of USWA Local 2928, refused to follow USWA District Director Joe Germano's orders to return to work and, in fact, booed him off the stage when Germano denounced the strikers as having no justifiable grievance. In the end, the strike failed when neither the union nor management was willing to consider the strikers' demands. Still, this hate strike—as well as other ones in the Chicago area at Studebaker's plant in 1942, American Steel Foundries in 1943, and at Youngstown Sheet and Tube and Allied Steel Casting both in 1944—demonstrates the extent to which the CIO's "social revolution" on color remained incomplete (at best) by the war years.[38]

And color tensions and divisions did not always percolate from the bottom up. Whether it was because of "white" rank-and-file resistance, their own problematic views on color, or other factors (e.g., competition from other unions), the CIO local leadership was at times less than vigorous in their battles for color equality. The leadership of Local 108 at International Harvester's McCormick Works (which had a significant number of Italians in it), for example, could be both progressive on color issues and restrained by the "political realities of the shop." With fierce competition from the UAW for control over the plant, the local leadership claimed it could only go so far on color issues without alienating large numbers of "white" workers and potentially losing plant control to their rival union. Thus, the leadership—unlike that of more progressive Chicago unions like the UPWA—avoided speaking out against those color privileges most prized by many "white" workers—their segregated neighborhoods and their seniority and promotion advantages.[39] Local leadership sent the wrong color signals to the rank and file in another way as well: many CIO newspapers, for all their pluralist and progressive rhetoric, continually represented workers, the labor movement, and the CIO as white and male. USWA's weekly publication, *Steel Labor*, for instance, offers countless examples of this. These repeated visual representations spoke volumes about what CIO leadership thought a "real" worker was, and who was most responsible for union activism and thus most entitled to the full benefits of collective bargaining.[40]

Much like the CP, moreover, the CIO often reproduced the color line discursively. The CIO—when it spoke about color—spoke only about "Negroes" and "whites" and, in some cases, Mexicans. For instance, at a USWA convention in 1940, union leadership pledged to fight for the "unity of Negro and white union members," while in the *Chicago Defender's* Victory Parade in 1942, the CIO featured a float on which a call for "Negro" and "white" unity was emblazoned and behind which "Negro and white CIO members" marched "in a demonstration of solidarity."[41] As with the CP, CIO locals, in speaking about "Negroes" and "whites," assigned Italians to the latter category and thus encouraged them to think in these terms.

Finally, there were certain workplace color lessons that CIO leaders (among others), regardless of how committed and vigilant, simply could not control. Indeed, on the job, the "boss"—whether a foreman, a superintendent, or owners themselves—still controlled a lot; the process of color-making was no exception to this rule. In certain cases, as noted, CIO unionists worked to eliminate deeply colorized job structures, hiring policies, washrooms, and cafeterias. Even when these efforts proved successful, however, there was no telling how deeply something like a segregated washroom, in existence for decades, shaped workers' color identities. When Hedges Manufacturing Company, located in the heart of Italians' Armour Square neighborhood, posted a sign in 1942 that read "Girls Wanted: Whites Only," it requires little imagination to guess what this sign must have meant both to the Italian "girls" who ended up working at this plant, as well as to their *connazionali* who saw the sign daily. Indeed, the boss—as much as anything the CIO did or did not do—played a crucial role in the formation of "white" workers'—Italians among them—color consciousness.[42]

Taken together, the CIO—sometimes with help from the boss—affirmed Italian whiteness. This was, to be sure, always mitigated seriously by the CIO's impressive and pervasive ideas and actions concerning color unity and equality. However, a crucial part of the CIO experience—from hate strikes to "Negro/white" rhetoric—led to (and, in the case of the former, resulted from) an increased white color consciousness for groups like Italians; this would prove deeply problematic for the CIO's "culture of unity" in the postwar years.

If the CIO seems to have unwittingly increased the white consciousness of Italians, the AFL taught a similar lesson, despite the fact that it too could be progressive on color issues at times. Throughout the Depression some AFL unions had large numbers of African-American members, several African-American leaders, and not a few integrated locals. And with the coming of World War II, the massive transformation of Chicago's workforce, the increased competition from the CIO, and the ongoing pressure exerted by African Americans both inside and outside the union, some AFL locals began to reform the ways it traditionally approached and treated workers of "color" by actively organizing them and defending their rights and dignity on the job.[43] In the summer of 1940, for instance, the Laundry and Dye House Drivers and Chauffeurs Union, 712, a local in which Italians were active as leaders and rank-and-file members, successfully performed a work stoppage to force their employer to reinstate an African American who had been unfairly discharged.[44] In addition to such actions, the CFL's newspaper—*Federation News*—and its radio station—WCFL—increasingly broadened its conception of pluralism to include "colored" groups; wrote and broadcast repeatedly about the need for Southern states to abolish the poll tax and for the U.S. Congress to pass anti-lynching legislation; called regularly for equal rights for all in housing, education, and jobs; and, in the case of the *News*, added in 1942 a weekly column—"Color in the News"—written by a local African-American unionist.[45]

But there were severe limits to the AFL's fight for color equality. Well into the World War II years there remained many AFL unions that either excluded African Americans and other "colored" people outright or, through a variety of measures, made it exceedingly difficult or impossible for them to join. For example, the International Association of Machinists required all new members to pledge that they would nominate "only white persons" as future members while stereotypers (an apt name in this case), printers, electrotypers, and other printing trade unions ran mandatory apprentice schools that barred African Americans. Because of such measures, many AFL locals in Chicago—among them the United Association of Plumbers and Steamfitters, the Milk Wagon Drivers Union, Local 753, the Pattern Makers Association, the International Bridge and Iron Workers, the Photo Engravers Union, the Franklin Union no. 4 of the Printing Pressman and Assistant's Union, and some forty electrical workers unions—had no African-American members throughout these years. An equally large number of locals admitted only the tiniest fraction of "colored" members. Italians were members and leaders of some of these unions, including Sam Cardamone, vice president of the Franklin Union no. 4 in 1944; M. J. Ballestro, secretary of the Machinists Union Local 134 in the late 1920s; Adolf Corazzo, secretary of the Electrical Workers of America Local 214 in 1934; and Mr. Giannoni, an officer for the Stereotypers Union no. 4 in 1939.[46]

Certainly, the most dramatic story involving Italian AFL unionists' exclusion of "colored" workers came in the summer of 1930. On the morning of September 16, several hundred unemployed African Americans, angered by their systematic exclusion from the Tracklayers Union (which was, at the time, extending the city's traction lines through the Black Belt and other parts of the city), marched en masse to Fifty-first Street and South Parkway, where a gang of Italians were laying track. The African Americans seized the Italians' tools and refused to allow them to continue working until the union abolished their color bar and hired African Americans on the project. The protest was a success. Afterward, local politicians and Chicago Rapid Transit Line officials negotiated a settlement, in which the latter began hiring African-American workers immediately on traction projects throughout the city. Following a meeting between the officers of the Italian Tracklayer's Union and local ward committeeman Daniel Serritella, the former agreed to admit African Americans into the union.[47]

This happy story of integration was hardly typical, however. Even during World War II, the CFL and its many locals continued to send mixed signals (at best) to "colored" workers. Certain locals continued stubbornly to resist color integration, while others played the "color card" in attempts to beat out the CIO in National Labor Relations Board elections. In the winter of 1942, for instance, the AFL's Mattress and Bedding Workers Union attempted to win "white" workers to their side by telling them that only "Negroes" joined the CIO. Also, at the leadership level, the CFL—especially in comparison to the CIO—remained extremely timid on color issues, never willing either to move beyond educational and voluntary measures to root out color inequality or to challenge the autonomy of locals that continued to discriminate against "colored" workers. Thus, as many CIO locals fought hard to organize "colored" workers and partially restructure the colorized workplace, the CFL simply called for schools, colleges, and churches to redouble their efforts to teach color tolerance.[48] Finally, the *Federation News*, its rising wartime pluralist rhetoric notwithstanding, continued throughout these years to publish offensive and demeaning cartoons of sambo-like African-American characters and, similar to the CIO, to feature visual representations of workers and the labor movement that were always white and male. One issue featured a drawing of an overweight woman with enormous lips and the blackest of skin accompanied by the following help-the-war-effort poem:

> A cheerful old mammy named Hannah,
> Who'd lived eighty years in Savannah,
> Said—"Sho'nuff, I'll buy
> defense bonds, 'cause I
> Am in love with the Star Spangled Bannah!"[49]

The color lessons Italian AFL members learned at the workplace and union hall were not simple and certainly varied from one local to the next. Certainly, some Italians, especially those in color-integrated and progressive locals, might have become less conscious or more tolerant of color differences or both. The opposite, however, was most likely the case. From "old mammy" iconography to countless all-"white" locals, Chicago Italians active in the AFL must have learned the same lesson, albeit more directly and forcefully, that their CIO, socialist, and communist *connazionali* had: they belonged to the "white race," and membership had its privileges.

8

THE COLOR OF HOUSING

In the fall of 1942, many Near North Side Chicagoans had reason to rejoice. Long considered one of the city's worst slums, the neighborhood now boasted the Frances Cabrini Homes, a new, state-of-the-art housing project, with sunny apartments and modern kitchens. Not everyone was so excited, however. Initially, thinking the Homes would revitalize the crumbling neighborhood, Father Luigi Giambastiani, long-time pastor of the nearby St. Philip Benizi Church, had grown increasingly bitter about the project in these months. In a letter to the Chicago Housing Authority, he explained why: "The cohabitation or quasi-cohabitation of Negro and White hurts the feelings and traditions of the White people of this community. . . . You know neither you, nor I, would cherish the idea of living next door to a neighbor from whom nature, tradition and culture have segregated us. By this cohabitation, the Negroes might be uplifted but the Whites, by the very laws of environment feel that they will be lowered."[1]

By the early 1940s, both Giambastiani's aversion to living with "Negroes" and his heightened color consciousness were not uncommon among many Chicago Italians. Having long avoided asserting "their" whiteness openly, many Italians' self-understandings regarding color began to change in these years, a change most apparent in the realm of housing, where color battles were fierce and source material is rich. As quality homes grew more and more scarce and as "colored" groups increasingly breached neighborhood boundaries, some Italians fled old neighborhoods fast undergoing color succession; others stayed behind and fought numerous battles mainly with African Americans in neighborhoods like the Near West Side, the Near North Side, and the Near Northwest Side. In all these experiences, Italians learned powerful lessons about color and, for the first time, began to mobilize and demand rights and privileges as whites. This newfound affinity for whiteness did not dissolve older race/nation identifications nor did these identifications fade, as many Italians moved from older neighborhoods to more Americanized outlying areas. *Italianita* still had its many adherents, but it was whiteness that was really on the rise.

On the Move

While many Italians had been moving from one neighborhood to the next from the moment they arrived in Chicago, residential mobility increased significantly in the 1930s and 1940s. During these two decades, older Italian communities like the Near North Side, the Near Northwest Side, the Near West Side, Armour Square, Pullman, Bridgeport, and the Near South Side all lost an average of more than half of their Italian foreign-born populations or a total of over twenty thousand people. Meanwhile, this same population increased by 53 percent in West Garfield Park, 23 percent in Humboldt Park, 28 percent in Austin, and 15 percent in Portage Park. Even older outlying communities like Chicago Heights and Melrose Park lost around 30 percent or nearly three thousand of their Italian foreign-born populations during this same period. Certainly, a good deal of these drops were due to natural decreases. After all, Chicago's foreign-born Italian population lost almost twenty thousand people from 1930 to 1950, without much suburban out-migration occurring. Given this fact, that certain neighborhoods experienced significant increases in their foreign-born Italians, indicates that a great deal of in-migration had occurred.[2]

Why did many Italians move? First and most obviously, many moved to improve their living conditions. In the older neighborhoods, housing was much more likely to be in disrepair, overcrowded, old, and without some increasingly common household amenities like a private toilet and central heating. Of the older neighborhoods listed above, in 1940, an average of 14 percent of the buildings were in need of major repair and nearly 70 percent had been built prior to 1899. In the newer neighborhoods to which Italians were migrating, half as many buildings were in need of major repair and less than a third dated back to 1899. Indeed, during the war when the Chicago Commons surveyed its Italian neighbors, many of those who wished to leave the neighborhood wanted better housing, a yard, or a place for their children to play.[3]

Italians also moved to purchase a home in an area where it was affordable and seemed like a safe investment. Both at the time and since, many observers have commented on the dogged desire of "new" European immigrants to own their homes, and Italians, in the main, conformed to this generalization. By 1940, nearly 40 percent of all Chicago foreign-born Italians owned their home; this percentage, while slightly below that of several other immigrant groups, was nearly twice that of "native-born whites" (21.7 percent). And the 1940s was certainly the time to buy. While housing prices in Chicago rose just over 50 percent, income increased at almost three times that rate. More important, after the passage of the National Housing Act in 1934, the newly formed Federal Housing Administration (FHA), by insuring lending institutions against loss, encouraged these institutions to offer attractive home loans with low down payments, low interest rates, and long terms. These loans revolutionized the private housing market in the United States often making it cheaper to buy than to rent. And buy many Americans did. In Chicago between 1939 and 1949, owner-occupied homes increased almost 60 percent from 371,908 to 583,000.[4] And it was in outlying, newer residential areas, where FHA loans were easiest to secure. Italians wishing to move to these areas and buy homes, then, were greatly encouraged by New Deal housing policies. Whereas communities like the Near North Side, the Near Northwest Side, and the Near West Side had Italian home ownership rates between 25 and 30 percent in 1940, most newer neighborhoods had significantly higher rates like 45 percent in Humboldt Park, 53 percent in West Garfield Park, 61 percent in Austin, and 66 percent in Portage Park.[5]

Finally, many Italians moved when their older neighborhoods began to "change"—that is, when even the smallest number of African Americans (and in some cases, though much more rarely, Mexican Americans) entered these areas. During World War I and throughout the 1920s, African Americans had flocked to Chicago in record numbers. This in-migration, though slowed considerably by the Depression, continued during the 1930s and exploded during the prosperous war years, when an estimated sixty thousand African Americans arrived.[6] This massive in-migration strained African-American communities, which, because of restrictive covenants, discriminatory lending and real estate practices, and grassroots neighborhood resistance, had always been the most overcrowded, dirty, and dilapidated in the city. As one confidential Metropolitan Housing Council (MHC) report put it in 1943, "The Negro district, prevented from expanding by restrictions on all sides, housing an already overlarge population in 1940, and housing that population in deteriorated, inadequate, indecent accommodations, *is today bursting at the seams.*"[7]

Faced with this impossible situation, many African Americans increasingly crossed color boundaries, often settling with large numbers of Italians in neighborhoods such as the Near North, Near West, and Near Northwest Sides. Disturbed by these population shifts, many Italians moved fast. One woman from the Near North Side recalled that in the 1930s "the blacks started moving in there and we had to get out, because it—I don't know—it smelled so." Similarly, an Italian man from the West Side remembered that "the reason we got out of there [was that] it was getting black. Understand? It was getting black." An Italian woman from Armour Square put it most succinctly: she moved from the neighborhood in 1944 because "the Black people that were . . . in that neighborhood were very bad."[8] Given these attitudes, it can hardly be coincidental that virtually every area into which large numbers of Italians moved in the 1930s and 1940s—places like Austin, Humboldt Park, Lincoln Park, and West Garfield Park—had minuscule African-American populations or none at all. In the words of one Italian, these communities were "just concentrated white," and Italians were seeking these neighborhoods out more and more by the 1930s and 1940s.[9]

Staying Put and "Fighting Back"

Not all Italians so readily yielded to demographic shifts or willingly abandoned old neighborhoods for the comfort, collateral, and color-homogeneity of outlying areas. In the Near North, Near West, and Near Northwest Sides—still the most populous Italian neighborhoods in 1940—many Italians resented and fiercely resisted African Americans' arrival and presence there. This chapter will first examine these stories and then turn to the larger race/color lessons Italians learned in a range of new and old, lily-"white" and "integrated" neighborhoods. The focus will be on Italian–African-American relations, since the former never seemed too concerned about other groups—"colored" or otherwise.[10] On the Near North and Near West Sides, the story revolves around the local public housing projects that were built in these years and quickly became key sites of color conflict. In this conflict, certain institutions and organizations—the Chicago Urban League, the *Chicago Defender*, the Public Works Administration (PWA), the United States Housing Authority (USHA), and the Chicago Housing Authority (CHA)—powerfully shaped Italians' color lessons and experiences and, thus, receive extensive attention in the pages that follow.

The Jane Addams Houses

The Near West Side was not simply the largest and best known of all Italian neighborhoods in Chicago, it was also one of the city's poorest and most run-down. During the Depression, 44 percent of its population was on relief, and as late as 1940, nearly a quarter was still unemployed. Three-quarters of the neighborhood's homes and apartments had been built in the nineteenth century and almost a fifth were in need of major repair. When the Home Owners Loan Corporation (HOLC) examined this neighborhood in 1940, it gave the Near West Side its worst rating (D) and noted that "the future of this blighted neighborhood is hopeless. . . . The entire area is just as bad, if not worse, than the large colored blighted area where Chicago's three hundred odd thousand colored people live. . . . [The neighborhood] is becoming, increasingly, a serious problem and a menace." Given these severe conditions, it is no surprise that when the Housing Division of the PWA decided to build fifty test public housing projects all across the country in 1936, the Near West Side was one of the three sites chosen in Chicago.[11]

Backed by Jane Addams and federal funds made available under the Emergency Relief Appropriation Act of 1935, the Housing Division first broke ground on the project in November 1935 and completed it in the summer of 1937. While progress was rapid, problems plagued the project from the start, the most intractable of which was related to color.[12] The PWA's other two test projects in Chicago—the Trumbull Park and Julia Lathrop Homes on the Far South Side and North Side, respectively—were built in neighborhoods with negligible "colored" populations. Therefore, the CHA strictly followed its neighborhood composition rule—that stipulated that the tenant composition of projects must closely match that of the project's neighborhood or site prior to demolition—and openly excluded all African Americans from living in these projects.[13] Some concern about housing Mexicans at Trumbull Park also developed, but in the end they were accepted, if only in the smallest of numbers (3 of 562 tenants or 0.53 percent).[14] The Jane Addams Houses (JAH) were a different story entirely. Of the 145 families displaced in the building of the homes, 30 were African American. Furthermore, the PWA's own twenty-six block canvas of the neighborhood around 1935 counted the following cosmopolitan group of families: 2,264 Italian, 88 African American, 108 Mexican, 87 Irish, 35 Russian, 15 Polish, 13 English, and so on. This canvas clearly avoided the neighborhood just south of Roosevelt Road, which was heavily African American at this time. These demographic realities forced the CHA to confront color on the West Side—or, more particularly—African-American tenancy. Although Mexicans were underrepresented at the JAH from a "neighborhood composition" standpoint, I have found no evidence that this was by design or that the CHA was ever that concerned about Mexican tenancy.[15]

African-American tenancy was a different matter, which developed into three separate though interrelated issues in these years. First was the simple issue of inclusion. When the CHA gained control over the JAH in 1937, it was by no means clear that it would admit African Americans as tenants. For one, the Chicago Urban League had been urging PWA administrator, Harold Ickes, for months—and ultimately in vain—to commit publicly to a nondiscriminatory tenant-selection policy. The CHA was even less responsive to African Americans' needs.[16] One government official later noted that "when the Jane Addams Housing Project was about to open the question was discussed among the leaders of the Authority as to whether it would be wise to permit Negroes to live in the project. . . . I heard officials say it would be a dangerous thing." The JAH management office manifested such attitudes daily by sending informational flyers only to white neighborhood residents and discouraging those African Americans that visited their office from applying for apartments. The office often advised these prospective tenants to consider the South Side project "for colored people," later called Ida B. Wells, which was being built at the time.[17]

Many African-American individuals and organizations, finding this

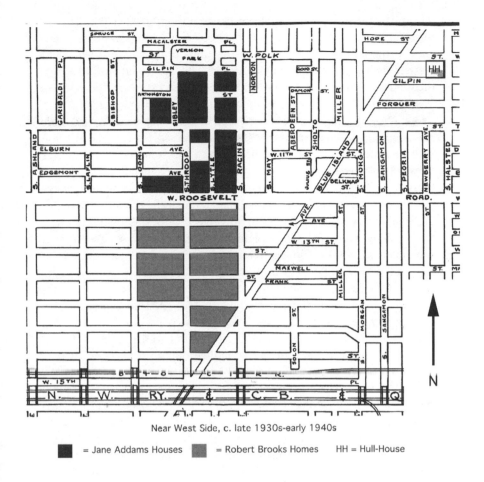

Near West Side, c. late 1930s–early 1940s

■ = Jane Addams Houses ■ = Robert Brooks Homes HH = Hull-House

mistreatment wholly unacceptable, mobilized a powerful protest movement against CHA's policies at the JAH: local churches educated their con-
gregants on the issues and sent protest letters to Mayor Kelly; organizations like the NAACP, the Chicago and Northern District Association of
Colored Women, the Chicago Council of Negro Organizations, the Citizens'
Committee on Housing, and the Communist Party's Chicago Council of the
National Negro Council, all spearheaded a citywide petition drive; and individual African Americans attended meetings at local YMCAs and wrote
letters to politicians to air their many grievances with the CHA. In one letter to President Roosevelt in 1938, a neighborhood man admonished FDR
for the JAH's exclusion of African Americans because "God made them a
few shades darker than a clean snow ball."[18]

These protests paid immediate dividends. In September 1937, the federal
government dispatched Dewey Jones of the Department of the Interior to
investigate African Americans' complaints and to attempt to find a solu-

tion to the tenant selection problem. Several months later, the CHA resolved at their regular meeting that "colored families be accepted for tenancy in the Jane Addams Houses in the same proportion as they are at present represented in the neighborhood." By March of 1938, the first three African-American families moved into the JAH with the promise from the CHA that twenty-five more would be accepted shortly.[19]

But once African Americans' inclusion in the project was secured, their precise numbers became a second issue. As promised, the CHA did increase African Americans' numbers to thirty by 1940, but this remained far below their "proportion as they are presently represented in the neighborhood." The CHA fudged on this point by adhering to a loose and murky definition of "neighborhood," sometimes calling it the project's surrounding area (and being very selective in how they defined this area), and other times calling it the JAH site prior to demolition. In either case, African Americans were grossly underrepresented. According to a survey done by Horace Cayton and Estelle Scott in January 1938, if the JAH were at the center of a circle with a one-mile radius, this circle's area would encompass 77,336 people, 17.6 percent of whom were African American. According to these numbers, African Americans were entitled to roughly 175 apartments in the JAH—17 percent of 1,027—not 30. The CHA's notion of "neighborhood" was limited indeed—limited only to the largely "white" area north of the Roosevelt Road color boundary.[20]

Even more problematic, however, was the simple fact that the CHA seems not to have held any other group to such severe quotas. Poles, for instance, while only 0.5 percent of the neighborhood according to the PWA's 1935 survey, occupied over 3 percent of the JAH apartments or six times more than their rightful allotment. Conversely, evidence abounds that the CHA, despite numerous resolutions and public statements decrying "racial discrimination," carefully limited African Americans' numbers at the project. As Elizabeth Wood, the executive secretary of the CHA, openly stated in 1940: "We have kept down and will keep down the number of Negro families, on the basis that the site before clearance had only twenty-five Negro families on it." In the end, because of community activism, the JAH increased the number of African-American families to a peak of roughly sixty during the war (which was then reduced to approximately forty until the early 1950s).[21] Never during this time, however, did the CHA assign African Americans their fair share of apartments at the JAH.

In these years, the CHA never fully color-integrated the project either. This was the third and most volatile of color issues facing the Housing Authority. By the late 1930s, many African-American activists could feel proud of their accomplishments. They were still vastly underrepresented at the JAH, but they successfully resisted the efforts of some members in the CHA to exclude them outright from the project. In early 1938, however, as the first African Americans were moving in, a deeply disturbing discovery was made: these families were permitted to choose apartments in only one building. Despite resolutions and public statements to the contrary, the CHA was openly following Jim Crow tenant-placement policies. As Elizabeth Wood later admitted, the CHA "did not want to place Negro families in white buildings." It appears, as well, that the leaders of the USHA tacitly approved this policy. When Chicago Urban League Secretary A. L. Foster wrote Robert C. Weaver of the USHA to ask whether his agency had authorized color segregation at the JAH, Weaver replied that "in matters of this type the USHA accepts the actions of the local authorities."[22] Once again, African-American organizations and individuals, through public protest, were able to force concessions out of the CHA. Robert Taylor, a local African-American housing specialist, was appointed to the Authority in 1939 and he, along with other sympathetic CHA members, passed a resolution in August of that year that ended the most blatant forms of color segregation at the JAH.[23]

At this point a new set of actors entered the fray—"white" tenants. With Taylor's resolution passing, the CHA attempted to "integrate" one building that had previously been reserved for "whites" only. On the night of August 8, the day after Maurice Haynes, his wife, and their three-month-old son Maurice Jr. moved into their apartment, small-scale rioting broke out as angry "whites" hurled a brick through a window in the Haynes apartment, narrowly missing the baby. The following night a group of "white" tenants met and drafted an ultimatum for Ira Hulbert, manager of the JAH: uphold color segregation or they would move out. Now stating that "it is absolutely essential to adopt the most liberal attitude possible and uphold it with the most patriotic talk that can be summoned up," the CHA refused to concede anything to the rioters, and in time tensions subsided. The CHA, however, never fully abandoned its policies of segregation. Well into the World War II years, the CHA maintained only two to three "mixed" buildings and refrained from placing "white" tenants in the "original Negro buildings." In 1942, the CHA finished an entirely new housing project just south of the JAH and the Roosevelt Road color boundary—the Robert Brooks Homes—which were ostensibly for African Americans. These points help explain why "white" rioting was short lasting and why, in its aftermath, there was "nearly perfect acceptance" of African Americans at the JAH.[24] Brooks housed "Negroes"; Addams housed "whites."

Throughout these years Italians represented around 40 percent of all JAH tenants. The CHA's color segregation polices and their initial attempts to exclude African Americans from the project, then, must have made quite an impression on Italians. It is equally likely that many Italians were active in the rioting in 1939, as well as in the more organized, "white" tenant movement—short-lived as it was—to maintain the project's color line. Evidence of this point exists beyond numbers alone. When the project first opened, a local newspaper interviewed several Italians about their thoughts on their new home. One Nick Di Giovanni stated that "I live in

An Italian-American family, the Purciarellos, in front of their apartment at the Jane Addams Houses, c. 1940. Italian-American Collection, Department of Special Collections, The Richard J. Daley Library, University of Illinois at Chicago.

them and I like it. They will help to improve the community with new faces and a better class of people. Undesirables, though, should be kept out." Neighbor Frank Esposito agreed: "The Housing Project is a good thing. It will help the neighborhood. Undesirables should not be allowed."[25] That these tenants made these remarks just as the CHA was introducing African Americans into the project suggests strongly whom exactly they found "undesirable." Events outside the project on the Near West Side also offer a clue as to how Italians responded to "integrated" living at the JAH. As Donald Fumarolo recalled many years later, while Italians and Mexicans fought a great deal in the neighborhood, African Americans were not even permitted there: "Black people didn't go in that neighborhood [Italians' area of the Near West Side]. They didn't walk around Taylor Street." Similarly, one graduate student studying the area in the late 1940s and early 1950s noted that African Americans' "growth northward [across Roosevelt Road] has been blocked by the persistence and resistance of the Italian community," and that "the attempts of Negroes to use public facilities [here] . . . still meet with violence."[26]

The Frances Cabrini Homes

During the late 1930s and early 1940s, the Near North Side had a similar public housing history to that of the Near West Side, as it too was among the most blighted neighborhoods in all the city. The HOLC graded the area D, noting: "The section has no future and . . . is definitely blighted. . . . Housing accommodations are, in most cases, little more than minimum shelter" and "streets are dirty and alleys are strewn with refuse."[27] For these reasons, the PWA had chosen the Near North Side as one of its first public housing sites in Chicago in 1934. However, land acquisition problems as well as opposition from property owners associations doomed plans from the start and two years later, the PWA abandoned the project altogether. In the early 1940s, however, the CHA revived the "Blackhawk Project," started clearance of the area and then construction immediately, and began moving tenants in by late 1942. The new project was called the Frances Cabrini Homes.[28]

From their recent battles on the Near West Side, the CHA seemed to learn something about segregation and racial composition rules. On the Near North Side, it faced a much more color-integrated neighborhood without a prominent color boundary like Roosevelt Road and it, therefore, did not segregate Cabrini along color lines or enforce its racial composition rule as discriminatorily: African Americans were deemed 20 percent of the neighborhood and were thus allotted 117 of the 583 apartments. CHA policies, however, remained problematic in ways. It was entirely unfair, for in-

The Frances Cabrini Homes, c. 1942. Italian-American Collection, Department of Special Collections, The Richard J. Daley Library, University of Illinois at Chicago.

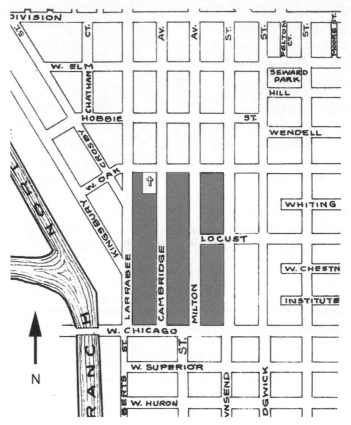

Frances Cabrini Homes, Near North Side, c. early 1940s

✝ = St. Philip Benizi Church
■ = Frances Cabrini Homes

stance, that it restricted African Americans alone to an apartment quota and carefully followed these set limits, even when scores of qualified African Americans desperately needed housing and many "white" apartments lay vacant. Indeed, in 1944, when the CHA scrambled to fill its many "white" vacancies, Elizabeth Wood noted in a CHA memo that "we have upwards of 250 Negro applicants already declared eligible for the Frances Cabrini Homes, who cannot be accepted for tenancy until present Negro families in the project move out."[29] This said, the CHA did offer African Americans a much larger percentage of apartments at Cabrini than at Addams and was becoming more active in enforcing and defending color integration.

Indeed, the best proof that this new commitment to color integration was real was the opposition it drew from local "white" residents. Members of the Near North Side Property Owners' Association (NNSPOA), utilizing connections they had in powerful institutions like the MHC, urged the CHA to institute "reasonable segregation which would preserve the character and values of the neighborhoods on the north side." They wished to confine African-American tenants to only those buildings on "Larrabee Street, as close to Chicago Avenue as possible."[30] They were, in the end, unsuccessful.

By far the most vocal and active opponents of CHA color integration were local Italians, the vast majority of whom were not members of the NNSPOA.[31] Neighborhood leaders made public statements and met with city and CHA officials in attempts to affect policy decisions. The most important and outspoken of these leaders was Father Luigi Giambastiani. Always feeling his church was threatened by local population shifts, Giambastiani had been active for years in Italians' efforts to keep African Americans out of "Little Sicily," including his leadership in the 1935 eviction drive of 4,700 African Americans. The pastor increased his activism in the early 1940s, becoming a bitter opponent of the CHA's attempts to color-integrate Cabrini. But it was not always so. Throughout the planning and construction phases of the project, Giambastiani and the CHA—particularly Elizabeth Wood—were in close and friendly contact. Indeed, it was Giambastiani who encouraged the CHA to name the project after Mother Cabrini (the Italian-born founder of the Missionary Sisters of the Sacred Heart and the first American to be canonized) and who gave the invocation at the project's dedication ceremonies on August 29, 1942. On that day, Giambastiani proclaimed optimistically: "With the help of thy grace we salute today these humble homes as the token of rebirth of the neighborhood . . . as the beginning of a national awakening towards the cherished goal of a new life, new ideals, new order of things, new society where, we hope and pray, that true justice, security of life, and universal love will reign forever supreme and unchallenged."[32]

These high hopes did not last long. Hardly a month later, Giambastiani wrote Elizabeth Wood, deeply distressed: "This letter has been in mind since the Dedication of our beloved project," admitted the pastor. "You will agree with me that the dedication was not the social success we all expected: the program was fine, the elite was there, the organization was well represented, but the people, my people, the people of this old Community was conspicuous only for his [sic] absence." The reason for this, explained Giambastiani, was the CHA's insistence on putting African Americans "on the same level and house to house with the White people: this is being resented by all and I must add, in order to be candid with you, that I don't like it either." Significantly, Giambastiani expressed these views (though toned down some) in public statements, as well as in private letters. The pastor told the *Chicago Defender* in 1943, for instance, that "separation of the two groups ["whites" and "Negroes"] . . . is the only practical road to community brotherhood. Negroes have the Ida B. Wells project. Why do they want to come into this project where they are not wanted?"[33]

Italians' opposition to integration and African Americans in general extended beyond rhetoric and beyond Father Giambastiani. Italians and African Americans had been struggling in this neighborhood since the mid-1920s, and these struggles only intensified over time. Even before the project opened, tensions were rife. In 1941, a group of young men calling themselves the "Black Hand Gang" (given the name, these boys were most likely Italian) terrorized their African-American neighbors by beating and even shooting people and preventing them from using neighborhood recreational facilities.[34] When the project came and the CHA made it a point to integrate, these problems only worsened. Commentators at the time and since have tried to explain these problems by pointing to the changing status of the Cabrini project after Pearl Harbor from public housing to war housing, a switch that left the 380 Italians displaced by the project with little hope of returning home. What this explanation ignores is that the only other people to suffer seriously from this displacement were African Americans, who constituted a quarter of those displaced (135 total).[35] Thus, the change in the project's status, if anything, should have brought Italians and African Americans closer together since they shared a common plight. It did not. Italians grew only more hostile toward African Americans when the CHA "announced that Negroes would be returned to the project in the same percentage that existed before."[36] Having tried for decades to rid "their" neighborhood of African Americans, many Italians must have considered the construction of Cabrini the final solution. When it became clear that this would not be the case, many Italians rebelled.

While some Italians left at this point, many others decided to stay, organize, and fight. Some "white" residents led a petition drive to force the CHA to adopt segregation policies at Cabrini. As Elizabeth Wood noted, "We have been repeatedly told that families would move in [to Cabrini] if the Negroes were segregated, but they would not if they are not segregated." Others enrolled their children in St. Philip Benizi's "all-white" parochial school. Still others reverted to violence in the form of regular fights in the neighborhood, culminating in a riot on the night of April 13, 1943 between three hundred "Negroes and whites" sparked by the firing of several shots into an African American's apartment. At this time, the *Chicago Defender* warned that "the Francis [*sic*] Cabrini project can easily become another Sojourner Truth incident," referring to "race rioting" at a Detroit federal housing project the previous summer, which led to over one hundred arrests and scores of injuries. The MHC agreed with this ominous assessment. In a confidential report written in May 1943, it noted that around the time of the riot "many of those who were informed about the situation [at Cabrini] became gravely concerned with the possible repetition in Chicago of the shameful housing riot in Detroit."[37] As a result of these fears, the city stationed a heavier police guard at Cabrini than at any other housing project in Chicago, and the FBI, the Office of War Information, and numerous community organizations closely monitored community color relations.

In the end, serious violence was narrowly averted but potentially explosive tensions remained. The CHA constantly struggled to find enough "whites" willing to live in the project and thus, as early as 1943, began accepting African Americans slightly over their initial quota. By the 1950s, as more and more Italians were leaving the neighborhood, the project became increasingly African American; in 1954, it was half "white" and half African American; by the early 1960s, "whites" had dropped below 10 percent. One CHA publication from 1951 described postwar neighborhood relations between Italians and African Americans thus: "Many of the Sicilians remaining in the area are older people maintaining homes in which they have lived for more than a generation. While they resent what they feel is an 'invasion' of their neighborhood by the Negroes, they have apparently resigned themselves to the situation, but remain aloof from the newcomers in social contacts. . . . Despite expressed verbal hostility between them, however, there is seldom any open conflict."[38]

The Near Northwest Side

As serious color tensions rocked the Near North Side, hardly a mile southwest across the northern branch of the Chicago River a similarly explosive situation was fast developing in the Italian neighborhood around the Chicago Commons. Unlike the Near North and Near West Sides, this neighborhood, though seriously blighted in its own right, never received a public housing project and was, therefore, less affected by outside institutions like the CHA, the PWA, and USHA.[39] Like these other communities, however, many Italians' fierce resistance to living with African Americans led directly to neighborhood organizing and severe violence, as color succession hit the neighborhood hard beginning in 1943 and 1944.

Violence was hardly inevitable, as Italians and African Americans had coexisted peacefully in the area for years. Just south across Grand Avenue, a large African-American community had developed since World War I and by 1940 numbered close to twelve thousand. Neighborhood hostility between Italians and African Americans was rare in the 1920s and 1930s, and some friendliness extended into the early 1940s. The Chicago Commons continued to sponsor a camp in New Buffalo, Michigan for neighborhood kids, which was moderately color-integrated and seems to have drawn no serious protest from Italians. There were, moreover, several instances of intergroup socializing, as when the Common's Italian Mothers Club visited a similar group of African Americans at the Ida B. Wells Homes in 1940–1941 and enjoyed themselves immensely. Another Commons club at the same time invited an African-American choral group to the settlement house to perform and to offer recitations on singing. As one Commons worker noted at the time, the event was a great success: "Both groups were somewhat shy and inclined to sit by themselves at first . . . but after the Negro group had sung and given recitations, appreciation and interest increased rapidly, and after refreshments and some social games, several of the old colored ladies were discovered in the girls' lavatory with one of the Italian members of the Commons' Club, dancing and having a wonderful time."[40]

These happy stories aside, there were reasons to be cautious about Italian–African-American relations. For one, some of the former harbored strongly negative views of the latter. In early 1942, for instance, when a group of Italian boys met at Chicago Commons, African Americans became the main topic of what became a bitter and hateful discussion. As one Commons worker later reported it, "Some of the popular ideas [were]: 'Ninety percent of the negroes are syphylletic.' 'Negroes should keep their place which is shining shoes and cleaning toilets. The South is right the way they treat them down dere.' 'Niggers smell.'" Furthermore, these two groups still did not interact very often and this trend continued into the early 1940s. Although many Italians and African Americans lived close to one another just north and south of Grand Avenue, respectively, very little boundary crossing seems to have occurred. As one Italian-American woman from the neighborhood later recalled: "We never had an occasion to mix in with them [African Americans]. . . . They minded their own business and we minded ours." Lack of conflict in these years, therefore, must be credited at least in part to scrupulous boundary maintenance by both groups.[41]

Indeed, it was the crossing of this very boundary in late 1943 that set off the most explosive color tensions. In 1940, the small neighborhood around the Chicago Commons had a total of sixteen African-American residents, or 0.7 percent of the area's total population. By 1945, African Americans' numbers had risen dramatically to 605, representing around 20 percent of the neighborhood.[42] Such a drastic color transformation drew immediate reaction from local Italians. Some decided to flee the old neighborhood at once. When African-American in-migration first began in late 1943, one local Italian woman became so distressed that "when her husband came home they talked things over, were quite convinced there would be [more] move-ins, made plans to move, and within a week they had left." Other Italians fought neighborhood "colored infiltration" by organizing both a petition drive to appeal to local politicians and a Property Owners League that sought to buy up all available homes in the neighborhood in order to exclude African Americans from renting or buying them. Indeed, at the League's first meeting, four hundred people showed up, "swamping the organizers." "In fact," reported one Commons staff member, "it was said that they [League organizers] could not take the $5 initiation fee from all who desired to enroll the first night because of lack of time and personnel." Meanwhile, many local Italian shop owners initially refused to serve

African-American customers, and Italian parents carefully instructed their children on the finer points of color exclusion. At the Commons, when staff members met with a parent whose son had been causing color problems at the house, the father responded that he had told his son to "fight the niggers," and that if such behavior caused a color riot, all the better. The father boasted defiantly that "he'd start 10 riots, made no difference to him."[43]

While a riot never occurred, violent acts most certainly did; they were, in fact, Italians' most powerful and common response to African-American in-migration. In January 1944, when a group of African-American families moved into a building around the corner from the Commons, neighborhood "whites" immediately ransacked it by breaking windows and attempting to set it ablaze. Several months later in the middle of March, when more African Americans attempted to rent local apartments, violence was even more widespread and destructive. Four fires were set in one building in one week alone, one of which destroyed two apartments completely. Covering the story, the *Chicago Defender* ran a front-page headline— "Burn Homes to Oust Tenants: Scores Threatened in White Community"— and reported that "vandalism and arson, intimidation and threats of murder, this week produced a wave of terror that harassed new colored tenants of West Side buildings and made them a target for attacks by whites who resented their 'intrusion' into the neighborhood." The newspaper also noted that vandals had fired shots and thrown bricks into African-American apartments and threatened and accosted African Americans on the streets. Indeed, tensions were so serious that the city assigned twenty-four-hour police units to the neighborhood. Also, the Commons staff was in constant contact with the Chicago Urban League and the Mayor's Committee on Race Relations (a new organization established after the Detroit Race Riot to prevent a similar event from occurring in Chicago) and managed to set up a conference between these organizations and several local Italian businessmen in an attempt to reduce color tensions in the area.[44]

Although tensions ebbed and flowed, they never wholly dissipated and, if anything, intensified after the war. Late 1947 was a particularly troubling time when, at the nearby Wells High School in September, some six hundred students and a sprinkling of adults struck because there were "so many negroes in our school." Several young Italians—Natale Bavaro, John Pignotelli, and Paul de Franko—were the alleged leaders of the strike. A month later, the Commons area witnessed its most fatal arson attack of all when ten African Americans died and many more were injured in a massive fire at 940 W. Ohio Street. That night was deeply symbolic of neighborhood color relations. As Lea Taylor later recalled, "the Italian neighbors had lined up opposite the fire on Ohio Street and the Negro families were on Sangamon or Morgan Street, for even in disaster there was no integration."[45]

Race and Housing

Italians' diverse range of housing experiences—from the violence on the Near Northwest Side to the flight to "white concentrated" suburbs—powerfully shaped and reflected their racialization and colorization. First, by the early 1940s, these processes were becoming one and the same, a trend that was particularly evident in the housing realm. Take the "racial composition" rule, for example. In much of the 1920s and 1930s, this might have required housing projects to admit the correct proportion of Poles, Jews, Irish, Italians, Bohemians, and Swedes. However, as we have seen with the JAH and Cabrini projects, these never became the most controversial racial issues—indeed, they never seem to have become *racial issues at all*. Instead, whenever the CHA spoke of and acted on its need to maintain the racial make-up of a particular community, they almost always meant a community's color make-up or, more precisely, its "Negro"/white" proportions. Their applications made this eminently clear, in which they asked prospective tenants to list their race and nationality and offered the following acceptable answers: "Race: White, Negro, Mexican, Japanese, Chinese. Nationality: Native-born Italian; Foreign-born Italian." Despite their apparent interest here in "races" beyond "Negroes," the CHA never seemed overly concerned about these groups. At the JAH, for instance, Japanese, Filipino, and Mexican families together represented only a slightly smaller number than that of African Americans, and yet they were never discussed when it came to composition or integration issues.[46]

This melding of race and color bespoke an unmistakable declining significance of European race and a rising salience of Americanness. While the steady growth of an Italian-American second-generation had much to do with these changes, housing experiences—especially during the war years—were crucial too. Though never as simple as the Chicago School had predicted with its concentric circles and "zones of city growth," Italians' abandonment of their traditional communities did, on the one hand, remove them in some cases from Italian stores, people, neighborhood organizations, churches, and so forth and, on the other hand, bring them into closer, everyday contact with more native-born Americans.[47] In many cases, these changes made Americanness less foreign and *Italianita'* less powerful. Father Giambastiani's words about the Near North Side were equally applicable to other older Italian communities: "Many of the people, as they have been able to afford it, have moved farther north, especially the young people who marry. They . . . bring up their families more nearly according to the standards which they learned at school. They read newspapers in English, eat food which is no longer strictly Italian and show in many other ways that the old colony is disappearing." In addition to migration, the often closely-related act of home ownership could also have a powerful effect on Italians' sense of Americanness. In 1936, Edith Abbott wrote of one Italian, who felt he "belonged" to the United States more after he had purchased his home.[48]

These Americanization processes were at work for many of the Italians who decided to stay in the old neighborhoods as well. Indeed, the very cosmopolitan experience of living in public housing projects could break down European racial barriers and encourage Italians to associate and identify more with Americans. As one *Chicago Daily News* article from May 1942 put it, "Residents of Chicago's housing projects, especially the children, are discovering America. The discovery is being made not only where the tenants are chiefly native stock but also and particularly in the most cosmopolitan projects." And, of course, the very housing battles discussed in this chapter—ones pitting "whites" of various European backgrounds against "Negroes"—could only have further increased the commonalties among European Americans and decreased the salience of *Italianita'*. Indeed, as we saw in the Chicago Color Riot of 1919 and many times since, few things united European Americans like anti-African-American mobilizing. As one observer on the Near North Side noted around 1940, "remnants of these old settlers [Irish, German, and Scandinavian] still live in the community and make common cause with the Italian against the latest invader of the neighborhood, the Negro." And these "common causes" could lead to Americanization. One Near West Side youth gang, for instance, some of whose leaders were Italian and whose main activity was starting "fights with niggers and stuff like that," called itself the All-American Raiders.[49]

One should not exaggerate, however, the power of Americanization nor the declining significance of European race. There was still much in Italians' community experiences that strengthened their *Italianita'*. This was the case even if, by the 1940s, more and more Italians were fast fleeing to outlying areas. For one, Italians often transported their traditional racial/national institutions—particularly mutual aid organizations like the Order of the Sons of Italy and the Italo-American National Union—to their new communities. Lakeview had a Betterment Club of Italians that remained so faithful to Old World ways that it excluded southern Italians until the early 1940s. Furthermore, in places where Italians were less successful at transplanting their traditional institutions, simple Americanization processes did not always occur, in part, because Italians often returned to the "old neighborhood" for shopping, church, and *feste*. Lawrence Spallitta, who moved north from the Near North Side in the 1920s, recalled returning every Wednesday for his catechism classes at St. Philip Benizi.[50]

Just as important, the resistance many Italians faced as they moved out "among the Americans" could retard Americanization and increase the salience of an Italian identity. Teresa De Falco's family, for instance, left the Near West Side in the 1930s for the quieter, tree-lined streets of Austin. But this experience—of moving from the most populated Italian community in Chicago to one with few Italians—ironically led to the strengthening, not weakening, of an Italian identity. De Falco recalled that it was in Austin where "we started to feel that we were Italians. . . . We knew we were not welcome. . . . My kids felt it. It was all Irish there and we were the only Italians. . . . We were ostracized." Similarly, when Joachim Martorano and his family left the Near North Side in the 1940s for a Swedish-Irish neighborhood north of there, he recalled becoming much more conscious and ashamed of his Italianness since his neighbors resented his family being on the block, and many of his classmates were noticeably different from him in character, habits, dress, and complexion.[51]

Powerful state and private institutions—particularly the real estate industry and the federal government—also helped to sustain these negative quasi-racialized views of Italians. Chicago realtors for decades had been warning prospective buyers about the potentially adverse effects an influx of "low class" (often southern) Italians could have on property values. In his classic and highly influential text, *One Hundred Years of Land Values in Chicago*, Homer Hoyt reproduced a list made by a West Side realtor that ranked "races and nationalities with respect to their beneficial effect upon land values." Southern Italians were eighth on this list of ten groups, just above African Americans and Mexican Americans.[52]

And Hoyt's hierarchy became commonly accepted by scores of realtors across the country and, most important, by the federal government. The HOLC appraised neighborhoods all across America in the 1930s and rated them A–D according to their "desirability . . . from a residential viewpoint." Lower ratings—C or D—could be given for various reasons, but the presence or the potential future infiltration of an "undesirable" population ensured a poor grade. HOLC's appraisals and ratings in Chicago were unequivocal when they came to (often "low-class") Italians; virtually all of their neighborhoods received a C or D grade and more often the latter. In the HOLC survey report on Chicago in its section on "Racial concentrations," it had this to say about Italian communities, generally: "Vandalism is rife in these sections. There is a high rate of crime and delinquency, and lending agencies shy away from these areas generally." Describing the heavily Italian Greater Grand Crossing community in 1940, the HOLC rated it a D, stating that it has a "very poor grade population: gangsters, vandals, and in general dangerous elements." Even Austin, which seemed to have many of the characteristics of a better neighborhood, still received C and D grades because it was being "adversely affected by the marked infiltration of low class Italians and Sicilians."[53]

The racial story on housing is not a simple one. On the one hand, older understandings of European races as well as the salience of *Italianita'* hardly disappeared in these years, as Italians continued to face resistance from their new neighbors in their new communities and as Italians transplanted their "traditional" racial/national institutions into these same communities. On the other hand, for many Italians these years brought the declining significance of *Italianita'* and European racial distinctions, especially as second-generation Italian Americans came of age; as the "white"/"Negro" divide assumed unprecedented attention; and as Italians increasingly moved into more Americanized outlying areas and into cosmopolitan inner-city housing projects. If older notions of race were slowly fading, *Italianita'*—fast becoming an "ethnic" or "national" consciousness—remained strong.

Color and Housing

This fading of older racial notions served only to further consolidate Italian whiteness. This was particularly the case in the realm of housing and neighborhoods, though the exact process of "consolidation" may have differed depending on whether Italians "stayed put" in older (often more working-class) neighborhoods or migrated to newer (slightly more middle-class) ones in these years.

Regarding the latter, as migrants moved farther from inner city areas, they came into contact with ever more color-conscious communities, rife with lessons about the importance and precise location of the color line. A crucial purveyor of these lessons was the real estate industry. While many real estate agents harbored serious doubts about some Italians' residential desirability, as Hoyt's hierarchy revealed, he was quick to add that "the classification . . . applies only to members of the races mentioned who are living in [immigrant] colonies at standards below those to which most Americans are accustomed"; Americanized and/or middle-class Italians were hardly a concern. The same was not true for African Americans (and in some cases Mexicans and Asians), who were undesirable in the eyes of realtors regardless. After all, as Hoyt declared authoritatively, "the influx of negroes into a district in Chicago usually causes its property values to decline." And such views were hardly particular to Hoyt alone. Instead, they represented the core of the real estate industry's race/color creed and were repeated ad nauseam in countless realty textbooks, manuals, conferences, courses, and state examinations. Between 1924 and 1950, the National Association of Real Estate Brokers' (NAREB) code of ethics forbid any of its members from "introducing into a neighborhood . . . any race or nationality . . . whose presence will clearly be detrimental to property values."[54]

This race/color creed had a profound impact on Chicago's realtors. Deeply committed to the creed, the Chicago Real Estate Board (CREB) voted unanimously in 1921 to expel any member who rented or sold property on a "white" block to African Americans. By the late 1920s, the CREB drafted a model restrictive covenant (that targeted *only* African Americans) and spearheaded a city-wide campaign to encourage neighborhoods to adopt and enforce these agreements. The CREB, historian Thomas Philpott found, "sent speakers across the city to stir up interest in restriction. . . .

They made the rounds of YMCAs, churches, women's clubs, PTAs, Kiwanis clubs, chambers of commerce, and property owners' associations, sounding the alarm: Black organizations were conspiring 'to settle a negro family in every block in the city' and make Chicago a 'mecca' of racial mongrelization." Realtors did not mellow over time. Having conducted an exhaustive survey of Chicago's "real estate men" in the 1950s, sociologist Rose Helper found that the vast majority "believe that the cultural level of most Negroes is still far beneath that of the white people, that white people are opposed to having Negroes as neighbors, and that property values go down and the area declines physically and socially when Negroes enter." As such, 80 percent of "white" Chicago realtors refused to sell property to African Americans in "white" areas.[55]

Equally important for color lessons, and often closely affiliated with the real estate industry, were neighborhood improvement associations. Some of these organizations dated back to the turn of the century and had dealt mainly with issues of neighborhood beautification. With the increasing migration of African Americans into Chicago during and after World War I, their numbers multiplied rapidly and they concerned themselves more and more with the exclusion of "colored" groups from the neighborhood, especially African Americans. Though estimates vary, Thomas Philpott found over 175 active "white" improvement associations in Chicago in 1930; by 1950, this number had grown to over two hundred, and many local groups were joining ward- and city-level federations to bolster their political power.[56] In an attempt to keep their neighborhoods lily-"white," these organizations lobbied city councils for zone restrictions, threatened to boycott realtors willing to sell to African Americans, and collected money to buy up property that remained vacant for too long or to buy out African Americans in the area in an attempt to rid the neighborhood of "undesirables." By far their most effective weapon, however, was the restrictive covenant—a mutual agreement among property owners not to sell or rent to particular people over a given period of time. While the target of these covenants varied to some degree from one location to another, in Chicago, African Americans unquestionably bore the brunt of restriction. In their survey of 215 covenants on Chicago's South Side in 1944, sociologists Herman Long and Charles Johnson found that all but 1.4 percent of these agreements targeted African Americans *exclusively*. While estimates vary greatly, by World War II, covenants covered no less than 40 percent of Chicago's residential neighborhoods.[57]

These improvement associations, and the restrictive covenants they fought for and implemented, were important to Italians' color learning process in several obvious ways. First, if some realtors viewed Italians as undesirable on occasion, improvement associations did not. Instead, they often encouraged Italians to join their "white" clubs and sign their restrictive covenants. Although information on membership is scarce, Italians did join these organizations and, in some cases, even became leaders. Victor Curto was instrumental in keeping the Uptown section of Chicago "99 44/100% white"; Ralph Finitzo helped organize the Southwest Neighborhood Council (a wardwide federation of neighborhood groups); and Louis Dinnocenzo was the vocal and controversial leader of the South Deering Improvement Association during the months-long grassroots campaign in the 1950s to keep the Trumbull Park Homes all "white."[58] These groups, often through their drives to implement restrictive covenants, developed among their members a "segregation consciousness" by publishing newspapers, holding frequent mass meetings, and engineering membership drives, in which block captains went door to door to recruit new neighbors to the prorestriction side. One set of sociologists called these groups and their covenant campaigns a veritable "social movement" replete with "slogans and propaganda." Their color lessons, as a result, were powerful.[59]

In the end, perhaps the most powerful color lessons in housing came from the federal government. The 1930s and beyond witnessed an unprecedented rise in state involvement in private home appraisals and mortgages. In entering this new field, the federal government had some options: It could assume a democratic approach and reject all loans where discrimination or segregation was practiced; it could assume a passive approach and allow the courts and private enterprise to deal with the sticky color issues in real estate; or it could follow a discriminatory approach and openly support and mandate color discrimination and segregation.[60] The state, particularly the FHA, chose the final option. Deeply influenced by real estate interests and hiring key figures within the industry like Blalock and Hoyt to help shape policy, the FHA from the very beginning of its operations institutionalized many of the key color assumptions and practices of the private real estate industry: namely, that the influx of "colored" groups was detrimental to property values and, thus, that color homogeneity, protected by restrictive covenants, was the hallmark of a desirable neighborhood. To be sure, the state was more subtle than many realtors. It never spoke directly about particular groups like African Americans and instead warned obliquely that "if a neighborhood is to retain its stability it is necessary that properties shall continue to be occupied by the same social and racial classes." Similarly, its support for restrictive covenants was only cryptically connected to color. The FHA's Underwriting Manual recommended covenants for the "prohibition of the occupancy of properties except by the race for which they are intended."[61]

Still, if the FHA's wording was subtle, its actions were not. Appraising all loans based on the highly problematic A–D rating system described above, all-"white" outlying areas and suburbs received thousands of loans, while neighborhoods with any "colored" population, or threat of it, received almost no support. According to one 1940 study of Chicago, the FHA made less than 1 percent of its loans to inner-city areas (3 of 374). Even more insidious, the private lending and real estate industries faithfully followed the FHA and its appraisal and lending practices. The FHA's discriminatory polices, then, fast became the norm in real estate transactions nationwide. The results were staggering. As Kenneth Jackson has shown, "the main beneficiary of the $119 billion in FHA mortgage insurance issued in the first four decades of FHA operation was ["white"] suburbia." Figures in the private real estate industry must have been equally disparate.[62]

Taken together, the significance of various institutions' actions—the real estate industry, improvement associations, restrictive covenants, and the state—was not simply that migrant Italians learned more and more about the color line and where they stood in relation to it. Of perhaps greater significance was a point that came less directly and sank in only over time. Because of the policies of these various institutions, the areas to which more and more Italians were moving were "white" protectorates, "safely" sealed off from "adverse influences" like "colored" folks. Thus, to the extent that place plays a powerful role in shaping group identity, Italians' new all-"white" neighborhoods must have increased the salience of "their" whiteness immeasurably.[63]

Italians who eschewed or could not afford migration to these newer neighborhoods were privy to their own set of color lessons, some of which were not too dissimilar to those just described. Property owners associations, with Italian members, emerged on the Near North and Near Northwest Sides during African Americans' in-migration, and some fought successfully for restrictive covenants. In 1939 on the Near North Side, in leasing two apartments to two Italian families, the Olivet Community Center made it clear that the neighborhood was restricted against "negroes."[64] In addition, realtors in these neighborhoods passed information on to "white" clients about "inharmonious residential mixing," declining property values, and the like. Thus, when Italians complained on the Near Northwest Side about African Americans' supposedly disastrous effects on property values, they no doubt received this argument in part from local realtors, who had been stressing this point publicly and privately for decades. Other color lessons were more particular to these older neighborhoods. Most important was public housing, where the federal government and the CHA worked together to segregate "whites" from "Negroes" at the JAH, to limit the latter's numbers at places like Cabrini and Addams, and to exclude them altogether at other projects like Bridgeport, Lawndale, Trumbull Park, and Julia Lathrop (all of which must have had Italian tenants) well into the 1950s.[65]

Regardless of whether Italians lived in their polychromatic old neighborhoods or in their monochromatic newer ones, then, many key housing experiences and institutions strongly reinforced Italian whiteness. Equally clear was the many concrete benefits Italians received from this arrangement. While large areas of Chicago were effectively off-limits to African Americans and in some cases other "colored" groups, regardless of their financial or class status, Italians were free to move anywhere they could afford and often received extensive private and public support in the form of FHA loans to do so. While some people in outlying areas like Austin and Belmont-Cragin were unfriendly toward and resentful of their new Italian neighbors, they never started riots or established "improvement" organizations to restrict them from their neighborhoods. This level of collective action was reserved for "colored" groups—not for "white" Italians.

This whiteness conferred enormous advantage in the public housing market as well. On the Near West Side at a time when quality housing was exceedingly scarce, particularly in poorer neighborhoods, the CHA openly and severely limited African Americans' numbers at the JAH and in turn increased the number of apartments available to "white" tenants. With over 40 percent of these apartments going to Italians, it was they who benefited most from CHA's color policies. Taken together, Italians' color lessons in housing—coming from the CHA, the USHA, the FHA, improvement associations, realtors, and their own actions in various neighborhoods—taught them that they were white and that this whiteness was not some meaningless social category, but something that carried considerable power and provided them with innumerable resources.

Identifying as White

By the early 1940s, many Italians began taking these lessons to heart and openly identifying and making demands as whites. This point is particularly evident on the Near Northwest Side, where source material is richest. In the mid-1940s, at the height of neighborhood tensions between Italians and African-American newcomers, numerous Commons' reports documented an increasing white consciousness among their Italian neighbors. In handwritten notes from 1944, for instance, Lea Taylor jotted down the following fears Italians had of "Negroes": "property values deteriorate; sell now; they'll move next to us . . . they use razors; they are immoral; fear of incidents; fear of the unknown; police protection to Negroes; what about whites?" And it appears that a healthy cross-section of the Italian community shared these views, particularly the last one: six young women, in January 1946, "burst into the [Commons] office with their aprons on to demand a cooking class for white girls only"; a year earlier a local Italian businessman, Mr. Gatto, ran into Lea Taylor on the street and was "wild about the Negroes" and howling passionately about "we whites"; in 1947, a grandmother pleaded with a Commons worker: "Can't you get these Negroes out of here? . . . . They should not live with white people"; and local residents posted "white tenants only" signs on vacant neighborhood buildings to prevent African Americans from moving in.[66]

Father Luigi Giambastiani provides perhaps the best example of a rising white consciousness among Italians in these years. Prior to the 1940s in his many public statements and essays in defense of Italians, he mentioned whites rarely. In 1922, for instance, in an article that appeared in his church's monthly bulletin, he focused on race, but not color: "It is true that some idealists dream of an American millennium when all races will be fused into one new American race," wrote Giambastiani, "but in the meantime it is good that each one think of his own. . . . Italians go to the Italian church. . . . The Italian Church ought to be not only a symbol of glory for you, but a symbol of union, of faith, and of race." In the late 1920s, when gang violence engulfed "Little Sicily" and federal authorities threatened to deport many "Sicilian gunmen," Giambastiani defended Italians by highlighting their virtues as Italians, not as whites. He told the *Chicago Tribune* in 1928: "It is unjust and foolish to call the Italians a people of criminals. . . . the law we have, our very constitution, find their origin in the Italian people." Most revealing, even in his neighborhood battles against incoming African Americans in the mid-1930s, he shied away from explicit talk about whiteness. In 1935, the *Chicago Defender* quoted him as saying: "The Italians resented the invasion of the neighborhood by the colored people, since the neighborhood always belonged to them."[67]

By the mid-1940s Giambastiani's language had changed dramatically, as Italians became "whites" and race became color. Throughout the tumultuous early years of the Cabrini project, when tensions between Italians and African Americans were at their height, Giambastiani wrote regularly to Elizabeth Wood and unabashedly showcased his new race/color thinking. In what appears to have been a rough draft of a letter to Wood in the early 1940s, Giambastiani wrote bitterly:

> I know you champion the cause of the colored people because you, like a good Christian and American, feel it to be your duty to side with the "under-dog"; but perhaps I could submit to your attention the possibility that today the white people at St. Philip are the under-dog—what about my people being afraid to walk the streets of the neighborhood where they were born and raised—what about hundreds of thousands of dollars of church property being in danger of being occupied day and night—what about our people deprived of their "freedom of religion" to come and worship in the church where they were baptized? As a priest . . . I cannot harbor any ill feeling toward any minority or majority, race or creed different from mine, but I refuse to be unjust and unkind to the white people for the sake of the newly come Negroes.

In another letter to Wood written in the fall of 1943, the pastor returned to his underdog theme, denouncing the CHA for attracting "Negro children from all around with the result that White children are kept away from St. Philip School and Church and its premises. It is evidently the case that in order to be fair to the Negroes, one has to become unfair and unjust to the White." Significantly, Giambastiani also shared his color-conscious views publicly. In 1943, he told the *Chicago Defender* that strict color segregation "is the only practical road to community brotherhood. . . . The colored families do not wish to live with the white families. They know that the true course to harmony and good will is through an amicable separate distribution."[68]

Not all Italians, of course, sympathized with *connazionali* like Giambastiani or shared his strong white consciousness. Alternative forms of self-identification always existed as did alternative race/color projects and ideologies. On the Near Northwest Side, when a group of local businessmen met at the Commons in early 1946 to discuss the "race situation," Mr. Cinquini insisted that it was against the law and the bill of rights to exclude African Americans from the neighborhood, while Mr. Cousetti warned that "if Negroes are discriminated against, a time may come when Italians or Jews may be discriminated against." When the Commons' Mother's Club met to discuss whether to include African Americans as members, many women were against the idea. One woman argued, for instance, that "I don't think we are ready for it; I wouldn't want to sit next to them." But not all women agreed. One mother asked pointedly that if "our children play together in the nursery, why should we hesitate to invite them into our club?" Another woman added: "there is no reason in America why we can't invite them in; that's what we are fighting for." One Italian woman's article in a Near West Side newspaper in 1940 illustrates nicely the alternative forms of self-understanding available to Italians at the time. In her column, "A Woman's View," Florence Giovangelo (later Florence Scala, who still lives on the Near West Side and has been active in community politics for years) wrote the following about her and her cosmopolitan neighbors' plight: "We're a few mothers. As for us, we're tired of being penniless and half-clothed. We're tired of scrimping and living in filthy crowded tenements. . . . We're the Negro mothers from Blue Island Avenue, and we're the Italian mothers; we're the Greek mothers and we're the Mexican mothers." For Giovangelo, and some of her *connazionali*, identifications based on gender, class, nation, and circumstance could still transcend those based on whiteness.[69]

In the end, these Italians were exceptions. More common were the experiences in older neighborhoods, where Italians fiercely defended their "white" communities, and in newer ones, where Italians fled in search of "concentrated white" havens. In both cases, Italians' color consciousness was on the rise. Older racial/national identifications did not simply fade as a result, because much in Italians' daily lives—in places as diverse as Pullman and Portage Park, Cabrini and Kensington—continued to sustain a vigorous *Italianita'*. Still, whether it was the CHA, neighborhood improvement associations, state institutions like the FHA and the USHA, restrictive covenants, the real estate industry, or an increasing number of *connazionali* themselves, all could agree that Italians were white. Whiteness was becoming, for the first time, a central part of Italians' public self-understanding.

CONCLUSION

"There is no such thing as a white community in Chicago."
Mayor Martin H. Kennelly, August 21, 1950

For decades, Italian Americans of all generations would have agreed with Mayor Kennelly's assertion. Indeed, from the late nineteenth century through the interwar years and despite the views and actions of a wide variety of individuals and institutions—such as the state, labor unions, employers, the Communist Party, anti-immigrant racialists, restrictive covenants, newspapers, and various neighbors and co-workers —many Italian Americans consistently avoided much talk of color. When identifying publicly, they did so in any number of ways—depending on the time and context as Italians, South and North Italians, Sicilians, Luccese, Americans, Italian Americans, workers, women and men, Catholics, and so forth—but hardly ever as whites.

Things changed around World War II for a variety of reasons. Italian Americans' rising wartime white consciousness owed a great deal to their decades-long accumulation of knowledge about Chicago's color line and their privileged position in relation to it. For Italian Americans of all generations this knowledge could have grown out of their earliest Chicago experiences, as well as the Color Riot of 1919, neighborhood relations in its aftermath, immigration restriction battles of the early 1920s, criminalization campaigns and local electoral politics in the late 1920s and early 1930s, the Italian-Ethiopian War, union experiences, left-wing politics, and struggles over housing in the late 1930s and early 1940s. As a result, Italian Americans—particularly those of the growing second generation—were well primed to identify as whites; non-Italians had been seeing and treating them as such for years.[1]

Numerous wartime color lessons were equally crucial in encouraging Italian Americans to identify publicly as whites. First, the war further Americanized Italians of all generations, classes, and political persuasions. Thousands of young men and some women marched off to serve abroad, while on the home front, thousands more did their part to win the war.[2] In September 1942, some sixty societies, clubs, fraternal orders, and trade unions came together to form the Italian-American Victory Council, which held mass "win-the-war" and "Italian-American Day" rallies, spon-

172

sored radio programs, and published a monthly newsletter to mobilize Italian Americans behind the war effort. In addition, other Italian-American organizations and individuals donated money to the Red Cross, bought war bonds, sponsored "spaghetti nights" for servicemen, and became block captains for civilian defense.[3] Thanks in part to these efforts, the war years often brought about a more widespread acceptance of Italians as full-fledged Americans.[4] This occurred at the national level in the form of pleasantly plural pop culture platoons, which always seemed to include an Italian American, or in novels like Sinclair Lewis's *Cass Timberlaine*, in which one character remarks: "the new America is not made up of British stock and Irish and Scotch, but of the Italians and Poles and Icelanders and Finns and Hungarians and Slovaks." And to appreciate this fact was to "speak the American language."[5] This acceptance was also well apparent at the local level. Chicago's City Hall always invited Italian Americans to take part in their massive "I Am an American Day" celebrations at Soldier Field, and every major city newspaper widely praised "Chicago's Army of Italian Folk"—who "have been assimilated and Americanized to a large degree"—for going all "out to win the war."[6]

How Americanization affected Italian Americans' white identities is not a simple question. On the one hand, the very meaning of Americanness seemed to expand some in the war years, becoming an idea to which, theoretically, all race/color groups could subscribe. At the national level, for example, the Office of War Information produced propaganda films like *War Comes to America* (1943) that hailed "the English," "the Pole," "the Negro," "the Italian," "the Mexican," and others for having "built this country." The *New York Times Magazine* published a two-page spread entitled, "They're All Americans," featuring photographs of a "Japanese American," "Chinese American," "American Negro," "Italian American," among others.[7] In Chicago, Italian Americans learned similar lessons from celebrations like "Pan-American Week" at the Chicago Commons and "I Am an American Days" at the citywide level, all of which had the widest variety of groups participating.[8] On the other hand, long-standing connections between whiteness and Americanness powerfully persisted during the war. As historian Gary Gerstle has argued, the war invigorated "the idea that America was, first and foremost, a white nation" through pop culture's lily-white representations of U.S. soldiers, the internment of tens of thousands of Japanese and Japanese Americans, riots and hate strikes at workplaces, in neighborhoods, and on army bases, and the segregation of the armed forces.[9]

It appears that these latter experiences and lessons, often more powerful and prevalent in Chicago, played a crucial role in developing Italian Americans' white consciousness. The thousands of Chicago's Italian Americans serving abroad almost always did so in all-"white" units. On the home front, faced with the migration of tens of thousands of African Americans and their ever-increasing determination to democratize the U.S. race/color order, Italian Americans participated in hate strikes at steel plants on the South Side, rioting and arson on the Near North, Near West, and Near Northwest Sides, and out-migration to "white havens" across the city. Meantime, as the federal government forcefully relocated approximately 110,000 Nisei and Issei on the West Coast, claiming that their "racial affinities" for Japan jeopardized national security, it paid relatively scant attention to Italian "enemy aliens" (to say nothing of Italian Americans), despite their large numbers, their well-known and long-standing sympathy for Mussolini, and government wartime reports that called Chicago's Italian community a "hotbed of surly fascism."[10] Only a handful of Chicago Italians were interned and as early as Columbus Day, 1942, Attorney General Francis Biddle announced that the U.S. government would no longer classify Italian noncitizens as "enemy aliens." By the fall of 1943, after Mussolini had been deposed and executed and Italy signed a preliminary armistice with the Allies, many Italian Americans breathed a sigh of relief and must have wondered how they escaped this perilous period so unscathed. Numerous valid explanations existed—the political power of Italian Americans, their large numbers that made mass internment logistically improbable, even their reputations as harmless buffoons—but their whiteness and Americanness were also crucial.[11] This point must have become increasingly clear to many Italian Americans during the war.

Wartime shifts in race/color discourse taught a similar set of lessons. The war years witnessed the increasing collapse of race and color categories. Exemplifying this point well at the national level is the U.S. naturalization application, which from the turn of the century asked immigrants to provide both their race and color and expected different answers for each. For example, Italians were often listed as southern or northern Italian for race and white for color. By the beginning of World War II, however, Italians, as well as many other groups like Armenians, Yugoslavians, Greeks, English, Syrians, and Mexicans, began offering the same answer for the race and color questions: white. This change reflected a shift in government directives. As one Department of Justice official instructed an Immigration and Naturalization Director in New York in 1941, "Your inquiry as to whether declarations or petitions filed by admittedly white persons should describe them as of the white race instead of Irish, Flemish, German, etc. race, as heretofore, is answered in the affirmative." By the early 1940s, in order to avoid any further confusion, the government revised its forms entirely, making it no longer possible for "admittedly white" applicants to fill in the race question with answers like "Irish," "Hebrew," or "South Italian"; now the only acceptable answer was "white."[12]

In Chicago, this same melding of race and color categories was occurring. The Mayor's Committee on Race (later Human) Relations, for instance, which was established in 1943 and which in an earlier period might have concerned itself with Sicilian-Swedish strife on the Near North Side, now concentrated mostly on "colored"-"white" affairs (particularly those between "Negroes" and "whites"). Similarly, just after the war, the Chicago Federation of Settlements noted approvingly that many neighborhood centers were sponsoring a "Neighbors Around the World" Project, in which "as the various racial groups were studied, [kids] colored in the sections of the map where those people lived. Four major groups were used, Indian or red race, Sino-Japanese or yellow, Indonesian or brown, African and American Negro or black."[13] Chicago Italians also learned to collapse race and color from reading *L'Italia*. Reproducing over the course of several weeks excerpts from Ruth Benedict's bestseller, *The Races of Mankind*, the paper translated Benedict's key arguments into Italian: that no races are pure and that all races are equal, but also that "le tre razze primarie del mondo sono: La Caucasica, La Mongolica, e la Negroide. Gli Ariani, gli Ebrei, gli Italiani, non sono razze." (The three primary races of the world are: the Caucasoid, the Mongoloid, and the Negroid. The Aryans, the Jews, the Italians are not races). Some unions with significant Italian membership reprinted the exact excerpts in their newspapers. This simplifying of race/color discourse encouraged Italian Americans to see themselves *racially* as white. With races like "Italian" fast becoming "ethnic" or "nationality" groups (indeed, the term "il nostro gruppo etnico" began appearing in *L'Italia* during the war), many Italian Americans must have felt they had little other choice.[14]

Finally, Italian Americans' "choice" to identify as white also happened to be eminently beneficial to them, particularly in the war years. For decades, whether it was battles over immigration restriction, neighborhood succession, deportation drives, criminalization campaigns, or the Italian-Ethiopian War, Italian Americans' most often defended themselves and made claims on the institutions that shaped their lives by identifying and mobilizing as Italians. More specifically, they often argued that their virtues as members of the glorious Italian race should allow them to, say, immigrate freely to the United States, escape the criminalizing attacks of certain Chicago newspapers, and bask in the glory of their "civilizing mission" in Ethiopia. These claims became decidedly less effective in late 1941, when Italy and the United States declared war on one another. No matter how much other Americans were coming to accept them, Italian Americans could not flaunt an Italian racial/national identity without appearing gratuitously seditious—a dangerous thing indeed when the state was interning Japanese Americans by the tens of thousands and passing legislation like the Smith Act in 1940, which made it easier to deport aliens with even the most innocent of fascist ties.[15] In search of a new wartime political identity, Italian Americans, especially within the context of local struggles with "Negroes," increasingly chose whiteness.

Whiteness also chose Italian Americans. For decades, a wide range of individuals and institutions deeply racialized Italian immigrants and their children—criminalizing them mercilessly, restricting them from immigrating to the United States in large numbers, ostracizing them in various neighborhoods, and denying them jobs on occasion—but they never challenged Italian whiteness in any sustained or systematic way. And this color status made an immense difference in every Chicago Italian's life—whether they realized it or not, whether they identified as white or not. Whiteness was what, in historian Matthew Jacobson's apt phrase, "opened the Golden Door" for so many Italian (and other European) immigrants and what kept it open for decades to come.[16] It alone made some things possible—such as the ability to immigrate to the United States and naturalize as citizens—and other things immeasurably easier, such as buying a home, finding a job, joining a union, and attending a quality school. European immigration historians have often talked about the "Old World" resources migrants brought with them to help make it in the "New." Whiteness, often ignored by these historians, was the most critical resource of all.

This point would not have been news to all Chicago Italians. In the early years when some Italians willingly joined the Color Riot of 1919 on the "white" side, others abstained and identified openly with the riot's African-American victims. Later, in the 1920s and 1930s, when color relations soured in various Chicago neighborhoods and many Italians resisted the "colored" influx at all cost, others lived closely and harmoniously with African Americans, Asian Americans, and Mexican Americans, befriending and struggling alongside them in unions, movements for the unemployed, and marches against fascism. And by World War II, as many Italians became more assertive of "their" whiteness and more insistent on maintaining community color boundaries, other Italians like Florence Giovangelo worked to mobilize the "penniless and half-clothed" mothers of all backgrounds on the Near West Side. Similarly, some Italians understood the power of color and the "wages of whiteness." As Municipal Judge, George L. Quilici, noted at the Mayor's Conference on Home Front Unity in Chicago in 1945:

> [Chicago Italians] were, like the Negroes, people who had no urbanization, did not know the customs and usages of the city; they were people without resources, with no schooling; and they were people who found themselves truly amongst strangers, amongst people of very different culture. The reason they have been able to succeed and to overcome the discriminations, to gain an economic foothold, to improve their level of education, and to become considerably integrated into the community, is that *opportunity was given them for which there was no color barrier*. I would differ with anyone who believes the color barrier to be the sole factor, but certainly we must confront it realistically and realize that it is a prime factor.[17]

A prime factor indeed—in the history of Italian Americans and all Americans. My hope is that this book, in its own small way, helps us to better understand yesterday's color barriers and the roots of some still with us today.

NOTES

RULOHP Roosevelt University Labor Oral History Project
SPBPP St. Philip Benizi Parish Papers, Our Lady of Sorrows Basilica
Archives
UC University of Chicago Special Collections
UIC University of Illinois at Chicago Special Collections
USWA United Steelworkers of America Papers, CHS

Introduction

1. *CD*, January 24, 1942, p. 14.

2. *CD*, September 27, 1924, pt. 2, p. 12. For similar arguments about African Americans and European immigrants, see *CD*, November 29, 1924, pt. 2, p. 14; *CD*, December 6, 1924, pt. 1, p. 14; *CD*, February 18, 1933, p. 14; *CD*, February 25, 1933, p. 14.

3. House Committee, *Hearings Relative to the Further Restriction of Immigration*, 1912, pp. 77–78; *CT*, August 19, 1910, p. 9.

4. For some particularly penetrating critiques of the "idealist" theorization of race, see Bonilla-Silva, "Rethinking Racism," pp. 465–469; Wellman, *Portraits of White Racism*, pp. 27–62.

5. Bonilla-Silva, "Rethinking Racism," pp. 469–470. For earlier work in this vein, see especially Blumer, "Reflections on Theory of Race Relations," pp. 3–21; Blalock, *Toward a Theory of Minority Group Relations*; Blalock, *Race and Ethnic Relations*; Schermerhorn, *Comparative Ethnic Relations*; Shibutani and Kwan, *Ethnic Stratification*.

6. For a particularly helpful recent discussion of race/ethnicity differences, see Jenkins, *Rethinking Ethnicity: Arguments and Explorations*, pp. 74–87; pp. 81, 74–75 (quotations).

7. In his recent, incisive book, *The Color of Race in America*, Matthew Pratt Guterl alludes to a race/color distinction similar to my own. For instance, he argues that during and after the Great War, American intellectuals, mass culture, and the polity became ever more concerned with "race-as-color"— or what I am simply calling "color." The only difference between our conceptual schemes is that Guterl seems to stress skin color as the key determinant of "race-as-color" categorization. See Guterl, *The Color of Race in America*, esp. pp. 5, 155, 188. Matthew Jacobson also occasionally hints at a race/color distinction. See Jacobson, *Whiteness of a Different Color*, pp. 6, 95, 129, 275.

8. In contrast to the title of David Richards's recent book, then, I argue that the interwar years witnessed the "ethnicizing" of a racial identity rather than the other way around. See Richards, *Italian American*. On the collapse of race and color, see Jacobson, *Whiteness of a Different Color* and Guterl, *The Color of Race in America*. Both works, while proposing a slightly different periodization and using different concepts than I do here, are nonetheless excellent examinations of the mid-twentieth-century shift in race/color discourse.

9. For a small sample of the superb historical work on the social construction of race in the United States, see the following books and articles: Almaguer, *Racial Fault Lines*; Baker, *From Savage to Negro*; Bederman, *Manliness and Civilization*; Brattain, *The Politics of Whiteness*; Foley, *The White Scourge*; Gordon, *The Great Arizona Orphan Abduction*; Hale, *Making Whiteness*; Haney Lopez, *White by Law*; Jacobson, *Whiteness of a Different Color*; Lewis, "To Turn as on a Pivot," pp. 765–785; McGreevy, *Parish Boundaries*; Roediger, *The Wages of White-*

ness; Savage, *Broadcasting Freedom*; Shah, *Contagious Divides*; Sugrue, *The Origins of the Urban Crisis*; Yu, *Thinking Orientals*.

10. Prior to the 1990s, very few studies of European immigrants to the United States dealt with race at all. Some notable exceptions to this rule are Lieberson, *A Piece of the Pie*; Philpott, *The Slum and the Ghetto*; and Zunz, *The Changing Face of Inequality*. For recent work that has stressed the centrality of race in European-American immigration history, see Orsi, "The Religious Boundaries of an Inbetween People," p. 335; Jacobson, *Whiteness of a Different Color*; Sánchez, "Race, Nation, and Culture in Recent Immigration Studies," pp. 66–84; and much of the whiteness scholarship cited in note 11 below.

11. The recent literature on whiteness is extensive. For some representative books and articles on U.S. history, see Roediger, *The Wages of Whiteness*; Roediger, *Toward the Abolition of Whiteness*; Barrett and Roediger, "Inbetween Peoples," pp. 3–44; Saxton, *The Rise and Fall of the White Republic*; Allen, *The Invention of the White Race*; Allen, *The Origin of Racial Oppression in Anglo-America*; Lott, *Love and Theft*; Ignatiev, *How the Irish Became White*; Morrison, *Playing in the Dark*; Rogin, *Blackface, White Noise*; Hale, *Making Whiteness*.

12. See Gerstle, "Liberty, Coercion, and the Making of Americans," p. 552; Gerstle, "Working-Class Racism," 38; Gerstle, "Race and the Myth of the Liberal Consensus," pp. 584–585; Roediger, *Toward the Abolition of Whiteness*, p. 184; Roediger, *The Wages of Whiteness*, p. 134; Barrett and Roediger, "Inbetween Peoples," pp. 4, 10, 33; Brodkin, *How Jews Became White Folks*; Sacks, "How Did the Jews Become White Folks," p. 78; Nelson, *Divided We Stand*, pp. xxxiv, 24–25, 44; Sugrue, *The Origins of the Urban Crisis*, pp. 234, 240; Peck, *Reinventing Free Labor*, pp. 2, 11; Waldron, "'Lynch Law Must Go!,'" pp. 56, 68. Some scholars of Italian Americans, in some cases anticipating the whiteness scholarship, have also suggested that Italians were at times something other than fully white in the United States. See, for example: Orsi, "The Religious Boundaries of an Inbetween People," pp. 313–319; Vecoli, "Are Italians Just White Folks?," pp. 149–161; DeConde, *Half Bitter, Half Sweet*, p. 102; Cinel, "Italians in the South," p. 14; Richards, *Italian American*, pp. 172, 185.

13. Bonnett, "Who Was White?" p. 1045; Cleaver, "The Antidemocratic Power of Whiteness," p. 160; Warren and Twine, "White Americans, The New Minority?" pp. 202–206; Hyde, "The Meaning of Whiteness," pp. 87–95; Prashad, *The Karma of Brown Folk*, p. 159; Waters, *Black Identities*, p. 340; Roy, *Making Societies*, pp. 96–98; Feagin, *Racist America*, pp. 31, 211–212; and Hayden, *Irish On The Inside*. Many historians, who do not work on European immigrants specifically, have also accepted the inbetweeness argument. See, for example: Gordon, *The Great Arizona Orphan Abduction*, pp. 12, 19; Escobar, *Race, Police, and the Making of a Political Identity*, p. 7; Foley, *The White Scourge*, p. 6; Glickman, "The 'Ism' That Won the Century," p. 36.

14. By "sustained" I mean color challenges that are not isolated incidents, but rather occur over a prolonged period of time. By "systematic" I mean color challenges that become entrenched in institutions such as the U.S. census, law, residential patterns, restrictive covenants, hiring policies, union membership rules, dating and marriage customs, and so forth.

15. Matthew Jacobson makes this same point in *Whiteness of a Different Color*, p. 6. For scholars who are more in line with my "white on arrival" argument, see Lipsitz, "The Possessive Investment in Whiteness," p. 370; Frank, "White Working-Class Women and the Race Question," p. 82; Arnesen,

"Whiteness and the Historians' Imagination," pp. 3–32; Kolchin, "Whiteness Studies," pp. 154–173.

16. The following are Italians' foreign-born population figures for 1890, 1900, 1910, and 1920, respectively: New York (including Brooklyn in 1890): 49,514; 145,433; 340,770; 390,832. Philadelphia: 6,799; 17,830; 45,308; 63,723. Chicago: 5,685; 16,008; 45,169; 59,215. See Bureau of the Census, *Population* (1910), pp. 854, 856; Bureau of the Census, *Population* (1920), p. 758. Despite Italians' large numbers in Chicago, they remain woefully understudied. There is only one published, book-length, scholarly study of Chicago's Italians—Nelli, *The Italians in Chicago.*

17. CCRR, *The Negro in Chicago*; Frazier, *The Negro Family in Chicago*; Gosnell, *Negro Politicians*; Drake and Cayton, *Black Metropolis*; Cohen, *Making a New Deal*; Grossman, *Land of Hope*; Hirsch, *Making the Second Ghetto*; Philpott, *The Slum and the Ghetto*; Spear, *Black Chicago*; Tuttle, *Race Riot.*

18. See the following IAC interviews: Avignone, p. 11; Mariani, pp. 34–36; Giuliano, p. 90; Kowalski, p. 62; Bruno, pp. 80–81; (Mattioni) Arrow, p. 3; Sabella, p. 31; Loguidice, p. 18; Muzzacavallo, pp. 42, 54. Having done extensive fieldwork among Near West Side Italians in the 1960s, sociologist Gerald Suttles argued similarly that since "the Negroes are the biggest recipients of public aid and housing. . . . [t]he Italians are loath to admit that they were once in the same position." See Suttles, *The Social Order of the Slum*, p. 101 n. 5.

19. Gatewood, "Strangers and the Southern Eden," p. 10. For more on the South, see chap. 1. For evidence of Italians' (initially) friendly relations with "colored" groups in Chicago, see chaps. 1 and 2.

Chapter 1

1. For population figures, see Philpott, *The Slum and the Ghetto*, pp. 6–7. On the early history and growth of Chicago, see Cronon, *Nature's Metropolis*; Mayer and Wade, *Chicago.*

2. Burgess and Newcomb, *Census Data of the City of Chicago, 1920*, p. 21; Beck, "The Italian in Chicago," p. 7.

3. Gabaccia, *Italy's Many Diasporas*, p. 1.

4. Numerous explanations have been given for Italian emigration, but virtually all have stressed the primary importance of economic factors. On Chicago Italians, in particular, see Nelli, *The Italians in Chicago*, pp. 3, 15; Vecoli, "Chicago's Italians prior to World War I," pp. 81–91; Candeloro, "Chicago's Italians," pp. 229–230; Schiavo, *The Italians in Chicago*, p. 21; Mastro-Valerio, "Remarks upon the Italian Colony in Chicago," p. 131. See also the following IAC interviews: Cosentino, pp. 2–3; DiMucci, p. 7; Catrambone, p. 2; Lizzo, p. 11; Licata, p. 2; Bertucci, p. 1; Muzzarelli, p. 7; Amella, p. 2.

5. Mastro-Valerio, "Remarks upon the Italian Colony in Chicago," p. 131. On return migration, see Cinel, *From Italy to San Francisco*, p. 1; Cinel, *The National Integration of Return Migration, 1870–1929*, especially pp. 96–121; Gabaccia, "Is Everywhere Nowhere?" p. 1131; Gabaccia, *Militants and Migrants*, pp. 155–163; Gabaccia, *Italy's Many Diasporas*, pp. 7, 72–73; and the following interviews from the IAC: Cosentino, pp. 2–3; Cassano, pp. 2–7; Provenzano, p. 3; Zoppetti, p. 22; Morandin, pp. 2–3. Return migration was common among many different immigrant groups from Europe, Asia, and Latin America. On this point, see Morawska, "The Sociology and Historiography of Immigration," p. 195.

6. See the following IAC interviews: Mazzei, pp. 7–8; Lazzaretti, p. 2; Inter-

landi, p. 3; Dal Cason, p. 1; Spallitta, p. 1; Pandolfi, p. 2; DeMarco, p. 1; Bruno, p. 1; Occhipinti, p. 8; Amella, p. 1; Bacci, pp. 51–52; Baldacci, p. 7; Provenzano, p. 3; Zoppetti, pp. 1–2; DeStefano, p. 1.

7. Virtually every Chicago Italian interviewed, who spoke about the migration process, mentioned or stressed the importance of family or *paesani* (or both) in planning and making their trip to the United States. For further evidence of this point in Chicago, see Vecoli, "Chicago's Italians prior to World War I," pp. 86, 91; Vecoli, "The Formation," p. 407; Candeloro, "Chicago's Italians," p. 229; Schiavo, *The Italians in Chicago*, p. 21.

8. The following discussion of Italian settlements in Chicago, as my footnotes will indicate, owes much to Rudolph Vecoli's indispensable essay, "The Formation."

9. On the Genovese settlement, see Vecoli, "The Formation," pp. 6–7; Nelli, *The Italians in Chicago*, pp. 22–24.

10. Norton, "Chicago Housing Conditions, VII," p. 531. On Polk Depot, see Vecoli, "The Formation of Chicago's 'Little Italies,'" pp. 7–8; Vecoli, "Chicago's Italians prior to World War I," pp. 138–141; Nelli, *The Italians in Chicago*, pp. 23–24.

11. U.S. Department of Commerce, Bureau of the Census, *Population* (1910), v. 2, pp. 512–514; Burgess and Newcomb, *Census Data of the City of Chicago, 1920*.

12. Walker, "Chicago Housing Conditions, X," p. 290; Hunter, *Tenement Conditions in Chicago*, pp. 196–199.

13. On the strong regional and town loyalties on the Near West Side, see Vecoli, "The Formation," p. 10; Vecoli, "Chicago's Italians prior to World War I," p. 153; Interview with Panico, p. 10, IAC. On the great heterogeneity of the Hull-House district, see Burgess and Newcomb, *Census Data of the City of Chicago, 1920*; Hunter, *Tenement Conditions in Chicago*, p. 184; Gaetano DeFilippis, "Social Life in an Immigrant Community," student paper [1930], p. 16, BUR, Box 130, Folder 2.

14. The 1910 figure is based on the combined populations of wards 1 and 4. For the 1918 number, see Beck, "The Italian in Chicago," p. 7. On these Italians' occupations, see Candeloro, "Chicago's Italians," p. 231; Vecoli, "The Formation," pp. 10–11; and the following IAC interviews: Lizzo, pp. 1, 7; Tellerino, pp. 5, 28; Clementi, p. 4.

15. Vecoli, "The Formation," p. 11. On Italians' neighbors and the diversity of the neighborhood, see Burgess and Newcomb, *Census Data of the City of Chicago, 1920*; LCRC, v. 4, pt. 1, "Armour Square and Near South Side," and v. 6, pt. 2, "West Englewood," documents 9b, 9g, 9h; Abbott, *The Tenements of Chicago*, p. 113. For more general information on the Italians of these neighborhoods, see the various issues of "By Archer Road" (the publication of the Francis Clark Settlement in the Armour Square area), CHS.

16. On migration to this neighborhood from the sugar parishes of Louisiana, see Interview with Lagattuta, pp. 1–3, IAC; Zorbaugh, *The Gold Coast and the Slum*, p. 165; Vecoli, "The Formation," p. 12.

17. On *campanalismo*, see Zorbaugh, *The Gold Coast and the Slum*, p. 164; Interview with Lagattuta, p. 32, IAC; Interview with Penio, p. 20, IAC; Interview with Rafaelli, p. 22, IAC; LCRC, v. 3, pt. 2, "History of the Lower North Side Community," documents 27, 32; Raymond Sayler, "Interview with Father Louis of St. Philip's Church," typed transcript, n.d. but c. 1928, BUR, Box 135, Folder 6; Vivien Palmer, "Study of the Development of Chicago's Northside,"

typed report prepared for the United Charities of Chicago, December 1932, p. 72, CHS.

18. *Black Hand* was a term used frequently in the early part of the twentieth century to refer to "extortion by letters containing threats." More specifically, the term almost exclusively referred to *Italian* extortionists. For more on the Black Hand, see chap. 4, especially n. 7.

19. On Little Sicily's bloody reputation, see Norton, "Chicago Housing Conditions, VII," p. 510; Zorbaugh, *The Gold Coast and the Slum*, p. 171; Palmer, "Study of the Development of Chicago's Northside," p. 73. For examples of the frequent newspaper articles on crime on the Near North Side, see: *CRH*, December 19, 1909, p. 10; *CRH*, April 25, 1910, p. 8; *CT*, March 17, 1911, p. 1; *CT*, June 13, 1915, p. 8; *CT*, June 12, 1915, p. 1; *LIT*, July 16, 1910, p. 1; *LIT*, April 30, 1910, p. 1; *LIT*, March 18, 1911, p. 1; *LIT*, February 4, 1917, p. 1; *LIT*, November 18, 1905, p. 1; *LIT*, January 22, 1907, p. 1; *LIT*, February 8, 1908, p. 1. On the inmigration of African Americans, see especially [H.N. Robinson], "The Negro in the Lower North District," typed report for the Chicago Urban League, [1925], Martin Bickham Papers, Box 237, Folder 2, UIC. On Italians' varied group of neighbors to the east, see Zorbaugh, *The Gold Coast and the Slum*, pp. 1–16.

20. For information on the demographics of this Near Northwest Side community, see various reports in the CC, Box 5, Folder "Annual and Other Reports, 1908–1928"; Burgess and Newcomb, *Census Data of the City of Chicago, 1920*; Beck "The Italian in Chicago," pp. 5–6; Reports of the U.S. Immigration Commission, *Immigrants in the Cities*, v. 26, pp. 256–257; Interview with Interlandi, p. 15, IAC; Interview with DeStefano, p. 2, IAC. On the work of these Italian immigrants, see "Report of the Work of Chicago Commons for the Year ending September 30, 1916," typed report; and "Industries of the Seventeenth Ward," typed report, 1914; both in the CC, Box 5, Folder "Annual and Other Reports, 1908–1928"; and the following IAC interviews: DiMucci, pp. 11–17; Tonietto, pp. 2–6, 25; Argenzio, p. 46. On Italians in the Chicago Commons area more generally, see "The Lower Northwest Side," typed study, n.d., but c. 1928, CC, Box 23, Folder 9. For Graham Taylor's quotation, see his *Pioneering on Social Frontiers*, p. 194.

21. This population figure is for ward 33, which included the Greater Grand Crossing and Burnside Italian communities.

22. On this area in these early years, see Vecoli, "The Formation," pp. 13–14; Nelli, *The Italians in Chicago*, pp. 46–47; and the IAC interviews with Avignone, Dal Cason, Dalle Molle, and Baio.

23. On Chicago Heights in these early years, see Candeloro, "Suburban Italians," pp. 239–268; Vecoli, "The Formation," pp. 14–15; Nelli, *The Italians in Chicago*, p. 50. See also the IAC interviews with Pandolfi, Tieri, and Bruno.

24. On Melrose Park, see Vecoli, "The Formation," pp. 15–16; and Interview with Bonevolenta, IAC.

25. Interview with Tarabori, p. 25, IAC. For information on this neighborhood, see U.S. Immigration Commission, *Immigrants in the Cities*, v. 26, p. 255; Vecoli, "The Formation," p. 13; Nelli, *The Italians in Chicago*, p. 46; and the IAC interviews with Mirabella, Fantozzi, Gentile, and Valiani.

26. Nelli, *The Italians in Chicago*, p. 25. For a similar argument, see also Philpott, *The Slum and the Ghetto*, pp. 67, 133–138; and Vecoli, "The Formation," p. 17. On the rare blocks that were 90 percent or more Italian, see Beck, "The Italian in Chicago," p. 6; Norton, "Chicago Housing Conditions, VII," pp. 511, 531.

27. On Chicago "Italians'" general lack of a national consciousness in these early years, see Nelli, *The Italians in Chicago*, p. 5; Nelli, "The Role of the 'Colonial Press,'"p. 81; Vecoli, "Chicago's Italians prior to World War I," p. 116; Vecoli, "*Contadini* in Chicago," p. 406; Campisi, "The Adjustment of the Italian Americans to the War Crisis," p. 92; D'Agostino, "Missionaries in Babylon," p. 134. On *campanalismo*, see discussions on neighborhoods above, as well as Puzzo, "The Italians in Chicago, 1890–1930," p. 12; and the following IAC interviews: Avignone, pp. 9, 14, 17–18; Pandolfi, p. 9; Kowalski, pp. 7–8; Panico, p. 10; and Fantozzi, p. 14.

28. On immigration and return migration, see note 5. On residential mobility in Chicago, see Nelli, *The Italians in Chicago*, pp. 21–54; Candeloro, "Chicago's Italians," p. 231. On seasonal labor migration, see Vecoli, "Chicago's Italians prior to World War I," pp. 108–110; Vecoli, "*Contadini* in Chicago," pp. 410–411; and the following IAC interviews: Moreschi, pp. 7–8; DiMucci, p. 16; Mariani, pp. 7–9; DeMarco, pp. 1–2; Parise, p. 3.

29. Dino Cinel, *The National Integration*, p. 11. On peasant opposition to "unification," see ibid., pp. 11–14, 31; Verdicchio, *Bound by Distance*, pp. 24–25; Galasso, *Il Mezzogiorno nella Storia d'Italia*.

30. Cinel, *The National Integration*, pp. 3, 11–44; Lumley and Morris, *The New History of the Italian South*; Schneider, *Italy's 'Southern Question'*; Bruno Bongiovanni, "The Question of the South" and "Anthology of the Problem of the South," in Pirovano, *Modern Italy*, v. 1, pp. 89–98; and v. 2, pp. 41–61, respectively; Seton-Watson, *Italy from Liberalism to Fascism, 1870–1925*, pp. 306–324.

31. Northern Italians were by no means the only ones to subscribe to these anti-*meridionali* ideas. Indeed, Sergi and Niceforo were themselves southern Italians.

32. Covello, *The Social Background of the Italo-American School Child*, p. 25. On the anti-*meridionali* racialism in Italy, see, in addition to Covello, Gibson, "Biology or Environment?" in Schneider, *Italy's 'Southern Question,'* pp. 99–115; and Dickie, "Stereotypes of the Italian South, 1860–1900," and Gribaudi, "Images of the South," both in Lumley and Morris, *The New History of the Italian South*, pp. 114–141 and pp. 83–98, respectively; Verdicchio, *Bound by Distance*, pp. 21–29; Cinel, *The National Integration*, pp. 14, 28, 31, 67, 90, 232; Smith, "Regionalism," in Tannenbaum and Noether, *Modern Italy*, pp. 128, 135–137; Bertellini, "Southern Crossings," pp. 42–82, 348–363; Dickie, *Darkest Italy*; Battacchi, *Meridionali e Settentrionale nella Struttura del Pregiudizio Etnico in Italia*; and Teti, *La Razza Maledetta*.

33. Dickie, "Stereotypes of the Italian South," p. 135; Gribaudi, "Images of the South," p. 96.

34. I use the term *racialism* to mean a coherent set of ideas about race. For more on this term, see chap. 3, n. 1.

35. On *meridionalisti*'s occasional racialist assumptions, see Verdicchio, *Bound by Distance*, p. 30. On Italy's emigration statistics, see Provana del Sabbione, "Condizioni della Emigrazione nel. R. Distretto Consolare in Chicago," pp. 26–27; and Covello, *The Social Background of the Italo-American School Child*, p. 29.

36. For the thinking behind this early racial classification scheme, see Report submitted to T. V. Powderly, Commissioner General of Immigration, by Edward F. McSweeney, J. S. Rogers, Richard Campbell, and Victor Safford, June 26, 1898, RG 85, Entry no. 9, Box 143, File 52,729-9, NAI. On page 3, the Re-

port states: "Under the head of races, Italy is divided into Northern Italian and Southern Italian. Northern Italian includes the natives of the following 'regioni': Tuscany, Emilia, Liguria, Venice, Lombardy, and Piedmont; also the people in other countries whose native tongue is Italian. Southern Italian includes the natives of the remaining 'regioni' of Italy and Sicily and Sardinia."

37. Reports of the U.S. Immigration Commission, *Dictionary of Races and Peoples*, pp. 81, 82. For further distinctions between northern and southern Italians in the Dillingham Commission, see Reports of the U.S. Immigration Commission, *Bituminous Coal Mining*, v. 6, pt. 1, pp. 590, 652; *Iron and Steel Manufacturing*, v. 9, pt. 2, pp. 10, 192, 205; *Clothing Manufacturing*, v. 11, pt. 6, p. 431; *Slaughtering and Meat Packing*, v. 13, pt. 11, p. 431; *Immigrants in Cities*, v. 26, pp. 249–341.

38. Ross, *The Old World in the New*, pp. 95–119; "To Keep Out Southern Italians," *The World's Work* 28 (August 1914): 378–379.

39. *CT*, August 19, 1910, p. 9. For other examples of Dorsey's racialist attacks on *meridionali*, see the following *CT* columns: April 15, 1910, p. 8; April 22, 1910, p. 6; April 30, 1910, p. 8; May 2, 1910, p. 8; May 11, 1910, p. 10; June 2, 1910, p. 10; June 4, 1910, p. 8; June 7, 1910, p. 8; June 25, 1910, p. 10; June 29, 1910, p. 10; July 4, 1910, p. 8; July 20, 1910, p. 8; August 11, 1910, p. 8; August 18, 1910, p. 8. On the *CT*'s long history of racialist assaults on southern Italians, see Vecoli, "Chicago's Italians prior to World War I," pp. 401–407. From the quotations above, it is clear that Dorsey's racialized language regarding Italians was also gendered. For excellent work on the overlapping discourses of race and gender in the United States at this time, see Bederman, *Manliness and Civilization* and Newman, *White Women's Rights*.

40. *CDN*, May 25, 1891, quoted in Vecoli, "Chicago's Italians prior to World War I," p. 403.

41. For articles in the *CRH* that ridiculed Italians, see June 14, 1910, p. 2 and October 30, 1907, p. 1. The *CRH*, like all Chicago newspapers, also focused intensely on Italian criminality. Between 1904–1911, for instance, of the fifty-three articles related to Italians listed in the newspaper's index, forty-two dealt with crimes of some kind—most frequently violent ones. And yet, as noted above, the *CRH* was generally the most complimentary of all Chicago newspapers toward Italians. For examples of this, see May 3, 1905, p. 8; August 8, 1905, p. 6; March 26, 1910, p. 7; March 12, 1906, p. 6.

42. D'Agostino, "Missionaries in Babylon," pp. 138–144.

43. Addams, *Forty Years at Hull-House*, v. 1, p. 232; LCRC, "History of the Lower North Side Community," v. 3, pt. 2, document 27a, pp. 9–10.

44. Sager, "Immigration Based Upon a Study of the Italian Women and Girls of Chicago," p. 16. For further evidence of the University of Chicago sociology's unflattering treatment of southern Italians, see Zorbaugh, *The Gold Coast and the Slum*, pp. 159–181; William J. Dempsey, "Gangs in the Calumet Park District," paper for Sociology 270, n.d., esp. p. 1, BUR, Box 148, Folder 5; Young, "A Sociological Study of a Disintegrated Neighborhood." For more on settlements, see Divers, 'The Black Hole,' pp. 5–6, 22.

45. For quotations, see *Skandinaven*, May 8, 1900, CFLPS; Zorbaugh, *The Gold Coast and the Slum*, p. 160. For further information on anti-Sicilian neighborhood tensions, see *Svenska Nyheter*, July 19, 1904, CFLPS; *LIT*, July 23, 1904, p. 1; Palmer, "Study of the Development of Chicago's Northside," p. 60; LCRC, "History of Lower North Side Community," documents 23a, 23b, 25, 61.

46. Taylor, *Pioneering on Social Frontiers*, p. 192; Lea D. Taylor, "Lea D. Tay-

lor: Her Life and Work between 1883–1968," typed transcript of autobiographical tape produced by the Training Center, National Federation of Settlements
and Neighborhood Centers, n.d., but c. 1968, p. 42, Graham Taylor Papers,
Folder "Lea Taylor," NL; Cressey, "The Succession of Cultural Groups in the
City of Chicago," p. 255; Taylor, "Lea Taylor," p. 8. See also "The Lower Northwest Side." The quasi-phonetic spelling of the Italians' comments above are
from Cressey. They may be seen as another way in which Chicago School scholars demeaned southern Italians.

47. Cressey, "The Succession of Cultural Groups," p. 256; LCRC, "East
Side," v. 6, pt. 1, document 8. Although South Italians faced more resistance to
their in-migration in these early years, North Italians shared similar experiences on occasion. For instance, when Tuscans moved into the "old" immigrant neighborhoods around Twenty-fourth Street and Oakley in the first
decade of the twentieth century, one old-time resident recalled: "For the first
couple of years, the [Italian] men had to walk around with protection on them
when they came home at night so they wouldn't get hit" by their resentful German, Irish, and Swedish neighbors. See Interview with Tarabori, p. 2, IAC.

48. Dunne, *Memoirs of Zi Pre'*, p. 32; Cressey, "The Succession of Cultural
Groups," p. 233; LCRC, "History of the Lower North Side Community," documents 19, 23.

49. The point here is that racial ideology cannot exist apart from a racial
structure that supports it, and vice-versa; ideology and structure are mutually
constituitive and depend upon each other for survival and growth. On this critical theoretical point, see Bonilla-Silva, "Rethinking Racism," pp. 465–480;
Omi and Winant, *Racial Formation in the United States*, pp. 53–76, Almaguer,
Racial Fault Lines.

50. *LIT*, June 13, 1915, p. 1; House Committee on Immigration and Naturalization, *Hearings Relative to the Further Restriction of Immigration*, 1912, pp. 77–
78; Leiserson, *Adjusting Immigrant and Industry*, pp. 71–72; Barnes, *The Longshoremen*, p. 8; Higham, *Strangers in the Land*, p. 66. See also Thwaites, *Afloat on
the Ohio*, p. 69; Gambino, *Blood of My Blood*, p. 77; Mangione and Morreale, *La
Storia*, p. 192; Vecoli, "Chicago's Italians prior to World War I," pp. 320, 322,
330–331, 419.

51. Cunningham, "The Italian, A Hindrance to White Solidarity, 1890–
1898," p. 34; Campisi, "The Adjustment of the Italian Americans to the War
Crisis," p. 83. See also Baiamonte, Jr., *Spirit of Vengeance*, p. 15; Scarpaci, "A
Tale of Selective Accommodation," pp. 38–39, 44; Carter, *Southern Legacy*,
pp. 105–112; Brandfon, "The End of Immigration to the Cotton Fields," p. 610.

52. *LIT*, October 15, 1904, p. 1; *CT*, June 11, 1915, p. 13. For further evidence
of lynchings of Italians, see *LIT*, December 21, 1907, p. 1; *LIT*, September 24,
1910, p. 1; and the following secondary sources: Baiamonte, Jr., "'Who Killa de
Chief' Revisited," pp. 117–146; Botein, "The Hennessy Case," pp. 261–279;
Haas, "Guns, Goats, and Italians," pp. 45–58; Ingalls, "Lynching and Establishment Violence in Tampa, 1858–1935," especially 626–628; Karlin, "The Italo-
American Incident of 1891," pp. 242–246; Kendall, "Who Killa de Chief,"
pp. 492–530; Rimanelli and Postman, *The 1891 New Orleans Lynching and U.S.-
Italian Relations*. On African Americans being the prime targets of lynching
violence, see Brundage, *Under Sentence of Death*, p. 2; and *LIT*, January 10, 1915,
p. 7.

53. *CT*, June 13, 1915, p. 1; *CT*, June 7, 1910, p. 8. See, also, Vecoli,
"Chicago's Italians prior to World War I, " pp. 402–407; and the following arti-

cles in the *CT*: April 14, 1910, p. 6; April 15, 1910, p. 8; April 18, 1910, p. 6; April 22, 1910, p. 6; April 30, 1910, p. 8; May 2, 1910, p. 8; May 9, 1910, p. 8; May 11, 1910, p. 10; June 2, 1910, p. 10; June 3, 1910, p. 8; July 4, 1910, p. 8; August 18, 1910, p. 8; August 19, 1910, p. 9.

54. Foerster, *The Italian Emigration of Our Times*, p. 407.

55. On the Near North Side riot, see *LIT*, October 22, 1912, p. 3. On the nationwide resistance to Johnson's attempt to marry a "white" woman, see Mumford, *Interzones*, pp. 3-18; Bederman, *Manliness and Civilization*, pp. 3-5. Fully aware of African Americans' unequal treatment on matters of intimate relations, the *CD* ran an editorial cartoon in 1924 of a white man and his wife having the following conversation: Man: "A [white woman] eloped today with Tony Raffelo, an Italian scissors grinder." Woman: "Isn't that romantic." Man: "What Th___! Frank T. Lottagold, a wealthy jeweler of this city, was married today to Hazel Smith, a Negro maid who has been in the employ of the family for several years." Woman: "DISGRACEFUL! What is society coming to? Why that is an *outrage*!!" Asians, like African Americans, were also quite restricted in their marriage options. See Ifu Chen, "Chinatown of Chicago," paper for Sociology 466, 1932, p. 14, BUR, Box 128, Folder 8. But, see note 56 as well.

56. Philpott, *The Slum and the Ghetto*, pp. 116–182; Spear, *Black Chicago*, pp. 21–33; Grossman, *Land of Hope*; Hoyt, *One Hundred Years of Land Values in Chicago*, pp. 315–319; Tuttle, *Race Riot*, pp. 159–176; Abbott, *The Tenements of Chicago*, pp. 117–126. On Asians, see *LIT*, April 30, 1910, p. 2 on a rich Chinese man, Moy Ding, who built for himself a "superb residence" in the well-to-do suburb of Hinsdale and who "has for a wife a white woman."

57. On discrimination against Italians by employers, unions, and fellow workers, see Vecoli, "Chicago's Italians prior to World War I," pp. 342–345, 350, 360, 419–424; *La Parola dei Socialisti*, January 4, 1913, CFLPS. On the far more widespread discrimination against African Americans, see Philpott, *The Slum and the Ghetto*, p. 119; Spear, *Black Chicago*, pp. 30–41; Grossman, *Land of Hope*, chaps. 7–8; Tuttle, *Race Riot*, pp. 108–130.

58. *LIT*, April 10, 1909, CFLPS, talks about a "nickel show"-owner, Louis Lang, who was on trial for refusing admittance to several Italians. Spear, *Black Chicago*, pp. 42–49; Grossman, *Land of Hope*, pp. 127–128. See also *LIT*, September 10, 1910, p. 2 on some Chicagoans' resistance to one Japanese and two Chinese students attending a local high school. On the deeply colorized/racialized nature of Chicago's dance halls, see Cressey, *Taxi Dance Halls*.

59. Around the turn of the century, scientists worldwide began to seriously question the validity of the white color category. As anthropologist, William Ripley, argued in his highly influential, *The Races of Europe* (1896), "it may smack of heresy to assert, in face of the teaching of all our textbooks on geography and history, that there is no single European white race of men; and yet that is the plain truth of the matter." Even to scholars like Ripley, however, if no monolithic white race (in the singular) existed, there were still assorted white races (in the plural), and Italians certainly belonged among these. For Ripley's quotation, see Count, *This Is Race*, p. 194. On the general assumption that Italians belonged among the white races (now plural), see Ripley, "Races in the United States," pp. 745–759; and the extended discussion of this subject in chapter 3.

60. U.S. Immigration Commission, *Dictionary of Races and Peoples*, p. 3.

61. Lord, *The Italian in America*, pp. 20, 232.

62. For naturalization applications of various Chicago Italians, see RG 21,

National Archives Great Lakes Branch, Chicago, IL. Declaration of Intention and Petition for Naturalization forms varied from the late nineteenth to the mid-twentieth centuries. However, throughout this time period, on all questions regarding "color," Italians were always "white." "Race," during these years, was a different story. Throughout virtually this entire time period, Italians were listed as North and South Italians in the "race" category. For general work on the importance of naturalization laws in the construction of racial/color categories in the United States, see Haney Lopez, *White By Law*; Jacobson, *Whiteness of a Different Color*, pp. 223–245; Henry B. Hazard, "Memorandum for Mr. Earl G. Harrison," November 5, 1942, pp. 4–26, RG 85, Accession No. 58A734, Box 726, File 55882/926, NAI.

63. For general information on changes in race/color census categories and related shifts in how enumerators were instructed to fill in such categories, see Bohme and Odom, *200 Years of United States Census Taking: Population and Housing Questions, 1790–1990*, pp. 26, 30, 36, 41, 50, 60, 69. On the power of censuses in general to construct social categories, see Anderson, *Imagined Communities*, pp. 163–170, 184–185; Ngai, "The Architecture of Race in American Immigration Law," p. 73; Clara E. Rodriguez, *Changing Race*, chap. 4.

64. *LIT* championed the Italian race/nation in virtually every issue. For some representative articles, see: January 26, 1901, p. 1; December 27, 1902, p. 1; October 31, 1903, p. 1; January 14, 1905, p. 1; April 6, 1907, p. 1; October 30, 1909, p. 1; November 3, 1912, p. 1; July 6, 1913, p. 1; September 21, 1913, p. 1; February 8, 1914, p. 1; June 13, 1915, p. 1; June 20, 1915, p. 1; June 27, 1915, p. 1; July 15, 1917, p. 2; November 18, 1917, p. 4; February 17, 1918, p. 4; June 23, 1918, p. 5. *LIT* downplayed regional and *paese* identities by ignoring them completely; by reading the Italian-language paper, one would hardly have known *campanalismo* existed. For the paper's occasional attempts to ease intra-"community" tensions, see January 27, 1912, p. 4; August 9, 1912, p. 1.

65. On Columbus Day parades, see *LIT*, October 8, 1910, p. 1; and October 15, 1910, p. 1. See, as well, *CRH*, September 9, 1903, p. 14 for a story about how three thousand Italians attended a parade to celebrate Italian unification.

66. For a recent essay on Italian immigrants' World War I experiences in the United States, see Sterba, "'More Than Ever, We Feel Proud to Be Italians,'" pp. 70–106.

67. *CT*, March 5, 1886, quoted in Vecoli, "Chicago's Italians prior to World War I," p. 402; LCRC, "History of the Lower North Side," document 29, CHS; Interview with Mirabella, p. 33, IAC.

68. *LIT*, September 2, 1899 in Bessie L. Pierce Papers, Box 167, Folder "Clubs—Italians—Societies and Festivities," CHS. For further evidence of North/South divisions in Chicago's Italian communities, see Interview with Badame, p. 2, Foreign Populations—Chicago, Box 1, Folder 3, CHS; and the following IAC interviews: Lazzaretti, p. 42; Avignone, p. 4; Dal Cason, p. 22; Roselli, pp. 43–44; Sabella, p. 14.

69. Interview with De Falco, pp. 14, 23, IAC; Interview with Pandolfi, p. 18, IAC; *LIT*, March, 14–15, 1896, in Bessie L. Pierce Papers, Box 167, Folder "Italian Nationalist Societies and Celebrations," CHS.

70. *LIT*, June 1, 1912, p. 1; *LIT*, September 23, 1911, p. 2; *LIT*, July 13, 1905, p. 1; *LIT*, October 15, 1904, p. 1; *LIT*, August 21, 1909, p. 1. See also *LIT*, June 17, 1913, p. 6 for a story about two "white" twins from Philadelphia—Antonio and Paolo Amato—who, having contracted a disease, were fast becoming "neri" (blacks).

71. *LIT*, September 19, 1903, p. 1.

72. On Italian emigration to and settlement in Africa, historian Christopher Seton-Watson notes that in 1909, 192,000 Italians lived in Africa, only five thousand of whom were in areas under Italian rule. See *Italy from Liberalism to Fascism*, p. 363 n. 2. On *meridionali*'s fighting in Africa, see ibid., pp. 380–381; Douglass, *Emigration in a South Italian Town*, p. 99; Cinel, *The National Integration*, p. 33. See, as well, Rudolph Vecoli's "The African Connection" for a discussion of the close ties between Africa and Italy. By "colored people," I mean those human beings that were generally understood as such in the United States at the time.

73. On the general isolation of villages in the *Mezzogiorno*, see Cinel, *The National Integration*, pp. 45–67. On illiteracy rates that compounded this isolation, see Seton-Watson, *Italy from Liberalism to Fascism*, pp. 79, 318.

74. U.S. Immigration Commission, *Iron and Steel Manufacturing*, v. 9, pt. 2, p. 192. On Sicilians migration from sugar parishes to the Near North Side in Chicago, see note 16. For Italian migrants' encounters with color in South America, see Gabaccia, "The 'Yellow Peril' and the 'Chinese of Europe.'"

75. Myrdal, *An American Dilemma*, p. 603; Ralph Ellison quoted in West, *Race Matters*, p. 3; Du Bois quoted in Roediger, *Black on White*, p. 199; Drake and Cayton, *Black Metropolis*, p. 57. See also Malcolm X with Alex Haley, *The Autobiography of Malcolm X*, p. 406. For an early, if brief, look at these issues, see Vecoli, "'Ethnic versus Black Metropolis,'" pp. 34–39. Of course, not all African Americans held such bleak views of immigrants and their color attitudes and behavior. On this point, see chap. 2.

76. *LIT*, December 30, 1905, p. 1; *CT*, December 25, 1905, p. 3; *LIT*, September 23, 1911, p. 2; *LIT*, May 14, 1910, p. 2. See also the following articles in *LIT*: May 6, 1905, p. 1; May 13, 1905, p. 1; July 8, 1911, p. 2; May 2, 1903, p. 1; May 11, 1901, p. 1; May 23, 1901, p. 1; July 6, 1901, p. 1; February 2, 1913, p. 2. Certainly, the worst Italian–African-American violence of these years occured several hundred miles south of Chicago in Spring Valley, Illinois. In 1895, in rioting that lasted two days, a mob of Italians and other European immigrant groups attacked a community of African Americans, injuring scores of people and leaving hundreds homeless. For more on the riot, see in the *CT*: August 5, 1895, p. 1; August 6, 1895, p. 2; August 7, 1895, p. 1; August 8, 1895, p. 1; August 9, 1895, p. 6; August 10, 1895, pp. 4, 12; in the *New York Times*: August 5, 1895, p. 6; August 6, 1895, p. 3; and Waldron, "'Lynch Law Must Go!'," pp. 50–77. See also the clippings from the African-American newspaper, the *Daily Inter-Ocean*, in the Negro in Illinois Papers, Box 27, Folder 2, Vivian G. Harsh Research Collection, Carter G. Woodson Regional Library.

77. See, for example, in *LIT* where the cause of battle was a labor dispute (May 6, 1905, p. 1; May 13, 1905, p. 1); thievery (May 14, 1910, p. 2; July 8, 1911, p. 2); and a traffic accident (May 11, 1901, p. 1). There was one instance (September 23, 1911, p. 2), in which "odio di razza" was cited. The same reason, however, was given for a battle in Utah between native-born Americans, Greeks, Italians, and Austrians (February 11, 1911, p. 1). For a similar argument that "race/color" conflict need not necessarily have meant "race/color" consciousness or hatred, see Scarpaci, "A Tale of Selective Accommodation," p. 43; Scarpaci, "Immigrants in the New South," p. 142.

78. On the English-language press, see note 41. On the Italian-language press, see in *LIT*: August 31, 1901, p. 1; September 14, 1901, p. 1; September 21,

1901, p. 1; April 12, 1902, p. 1; June 28, 1902, p. 1; August 3, 1904, p. 1; September 10, 1904, p. 1; September 17, 1904, p. 1; September 24, 1904, p. 1; January 1, 1905, p. 1; March 11, 1905, p. 1; September 22, 1905, p. 1; December 23, 1905, p. 1; September 8, 1906, p. 2; April 22, 1907, p. 1; November 2, 1907, p. 1; August 7, 1909, p. 1; February 12, 1910, p. 1; June 4, 1910, p. 1; June 18, 1910, p. 1.

79. On instances of conflict between Italians and other non-"colored" groups, see earlier discussions of this and the following articles in *LIT*: November 28, 1903, p. 1; August 12, 1905, p. 1; January 13, 1906, p. 1; June 30, 1906, p. 1; October 6, 1906, p. 1; November 10, 1906, p. 1; May 9, 1908, p. 2; March 25, 1911, p. 1. For the story of the altercation between the saloonkeeper and his patron, see *LIT*, July 6, 1901, p. 1.

80. Norton, "Chicago Housing Conditions, VII," p. 536. On the lack of conflict in neighborhoods that Italians and people of "color" shared, one should keep in mind the following statement from the CCRR: "Where amicable relations prevail and where adjustment has become fixed and acknowledged, the public hears and knows little or nothing of the relations, for there is nothing in these relations to cause comment or attention." See CCRR, "The Negro in Chicago," mimeographed draft, Housing, pt. 3, p. 1, n.d., in the Victor Lawson Papers, NL. Many people at the time and since have commented on the friendly relations (at least initially) between Italians and African Americans in the South. For evidence of this, see U.S. Immigration Commission, *Iron and Steel Manufacturing*, v. 9, pt. 2, p. 192; Scarpaci, "Immigrants in the New South," pp. 141–143; Ross, *The Old World in the New*, p. 104; Cinel, "Sicilians in the Deep South," pp. 75–76; Cunningham, "The Italian, A Hindrance to White Solidarity in Louisiana, 1890–1898," pp. 22–36; Gatewood, "Strangers and the Southern Eden," p. 10; Higham, *Strangers in the Land*, pp. 168–169; Mormino and Pozzetta, *The Immigrant World of Ybor City*, p. 263; Pozzetta, "Foreigners in Florida," p. 179; Scarpaci, "A Tale of Selective Accommodation," pp. 37–50; Shankman, *Ambivalent Friends*, p. 99; Shufelt, "Strangers in a Middle Land," pp. 36–40; Tannenbaum, *Darker Phases of the South*, p. 179; Trotter, *Coal, Class, Color*, pp. 110–111; Williams, "The People of Tangipahoa Parish," p. 106. On Italians' friendly relations with Chinese immigrants in Mississippi, see Loewen, *The Mississippi Chinese*, p. 114.

81. *LIT*, October 27, 1912, p. 1; *LIT*, September 29, 1906, p. 2; *LIT*, May 25, 1912, p. 3. For Signor Chan's advertisements, see virtually every issue of *LIT* in 1910, for instance.

82. For quotations, see *LIT*, December 8, 1906, p. 1; *LIT*, September 5, 1910, p. 1. On lynchings, *LIT* would carry stories of this form of brutality (as well as other forms perpetrated against African Americans) in a large percentage of its issues. For some examples, see: March 2, 1901, p. 1; August 3, 1901, p. 1; August 1, 1903, p. 1; December 5, 1903, p. 3; August 20, 1904, p. 1; March 12, 1904, p. 1; June 27, 1908, p. 1; June 12, 1909, p. 5; March 12, 1910, p. 6; October 21, 1911, p. 5; September 2, 1911, p. 5; July 19, 1914, p. 5; March 15, 1916, p. 7; April 16, 1916, p. 6; November 18, 1917, p. 6. For articles that were particularly condemnatory of "Civilta' Americana," see May 22, 1909, p. 5; August 19, 1911, p. 5; December 1, 1906, p. 1; November 18, 1917, p. 6; August 31, 1919, p. 1.

83. CCRR, *The Negro in Chicago*, p. 19; Addams, *Twenty Years at Hull-House*, p. 183.

Chapter 2

1. *Chicago Evening Post*, November 16, 1929.

2. On the African-American migration to Chicago during and after World War I, see Grossman, *Land of Hope*; Drake and Cayton, *Black Metropolis*, pp. 58–64; Spear, *Black Chicago*, pp. 129–146; Tuttle, *Race Riot*, pp. 74–107; CCRR, *The Negro in Chicago*, pp. 79–105.

3. CCRR, *The Negro in Chicago*, p. 1. The best study of the riot and its causes remains Tuttle's *Race Riot*.

4. *LIT*, August 3, 1919, p. 1; *LTIT*, August 2, 1919, p. 1.

5. *CT*, August 1, 1919, p. 2; *CT*, July 30, 1919, p. 4; *LTIT*, August 2, 1919, p. 1; *Il Progresso Italo-Americano*, July 31, 1919, p. 3; *LTIT*, February 18, 1922, p. 3; *Chicago Daily Journal*, July 29, 1919, p. 2; CCRR, *The Negro in Chicago*, pp. 663–664; Tuttle, *Race Riot*, p. 40.

6. CCRR, *The Negro in Chicago*, p. 585; see also *CT*, July 30, 1919, p. 2 for the same remark.

7. "Report of the Coroner's Jury on the Race Riots," RG 60, Entry no. 126, Box 4, Folder "Chicago, IL, #2," pp. 6–7, NAII. On the Lovings murder, see also *Il Progresso Italo-Americano*, July 31, 1919, p. 3; *CT*, July 30, 1919, p. 2; CCRR, *The Negro in Chicago*, pp. 7, 585, 597, 659; Tuttle, *Race Riot*, p. 49; *Congressional Record*, 66th Cong., 1st sess., 58, pt. 4: 3392–3393.

8. CCRR, *The Negro in Chicago*, pp. 113–114; Interview with Lagattuta, pp. 36–37, IAC; Interview with Loguidice, p. 2, IAC. For more on the Near North Side during the riot, see *Il Progresso Italo-Americano*, July 30, 1919, p. 3; *CT*, July 30, 1919, p. 2; Interview with Anonymous, February 10, 1999.

9. For descriptions of this area as Irish, Polish, or both, see Tuttle, *Race Riot*, pp. 35, 102–104, 167, 249; Drake and Cayton, *Black Metropolis*, p. 66; Spear, *Black Chicago*, pp. 201, 206. For a corrective to these descriptions and on Italians' large numbers west of the Black Belt, see Philpott, *The Slum and the Ghetto*, pp. 136, 375 n. 15; Pacyga, "Chicago's 1919 Race Riot: Ethnicity, Class, and Urban Violence," p. 188.

10. For a list of riot deaths, see CCRR, *The Negro in Chicago*, pp. 665–667. For the official injury list, see *CT*, July 29, 1919, p. 3 and July 30, 1919, p. 4.

11. Lea Taylor, "Lea Demarest Taylor: Her Life and Work between 1883–1968," typed transcript of autobiographical tapes produced by the National Federation of Settlements and Neighborhood Centers, p. 50, Graham Taylor Papers, NL; CCRR, *The Negro in Chicago*, p. 19. For more on the Near Northwest Side, see *CT*, August 3, 1919, p. 5.

12. For a discussion of Italians' naturalization rates and voter turnout, see chap. 5.

13. On Italians' underrepresentation in the meat-packing industry, see Sandburg, *The Chicago Race Riots, July, 1919*, p. 75; Vecoli, "Chicago's Italians prior to World War I," pp. 338–341. For Chicago color conflict in the meat-packing industry prior to the riot, see Tuttle, *Race Riot*, pp. 125–156; Barrett, *Work and Community in the Jungle*, pp. 188–239.

14. On the South Side housing battles prior to the riot, see Tuttle, *Race Riot*, pp. 156–183; Philpott, *The Slum and the Ghetto*, pp. 163–182; CCRR, *The Negro in Chicago*, pp. 113–135. On the location of Italians' neighborhoods, see chap. 1.

15. Pacyga, "Chicago's 1919 Race Riot," pp. 198–201; *LIT*, August 3, 1919, p. 1. For Pacyga's point, see also: Pacyga, "To Live Amongst Others," pp. 55–73; Pacyga, *Polish Immigrants and Industrial Chicago*, pp. 219–227.

16. On newspapers' emphasis on the "white"/"Negro" color line during the riot, see *LIT*, August 3, 1919, p. 1; *Daily Jewish Courier*, July 30, 1919, CFLPS; *LTIT*, August 2, 1919, p. 1; *Il Progresso Italo-Americano*, July 29, 1919, p. 3; *Il Progresso Italo-Americano*, July 30, 1919, p. 3; *Il Progresso Italo-Americano*, July 31, 1919, p. 3; *Il Progresso Italo-Americano*, August 1, 1919, p. 3; *CT*, July 30, 1919, p. 4; *CT*, July 29, 1919, p. 3; *Chicago Daily Journal*, July 29, 1919, p. 2; *CDN*, July 29, 1919, p. 8; *The New World*, August 1, 1919, p. 4; *CD*, August 2, 1919, p. 1.

17. LCRC, "History of the Lower North Side," v. 3, pt. 2, document 30c. For evidence that tensions remained between Sicilians and Swedes and the Irish, see LCRC, "History of the Lower North Side," v. 3, pt. 2, documents 18, 37; Raymond Sayler, "A Study of Behavior Problems of Boys in the Lower North Community," unpublished, typed paper, n.d., p. 39; Raymond Sayler, "Notes from Case Records of Junior Members," typed, n.d.; both in BUR, Box 135, Folders 4 and 5, respectively.

18. For the house-to-house canvas, see Quaintance, "Rents and Housing Conditions," pp. 44–45. On African Americans' migration to the Near North Side, see LCRC, "History of the Lower North Side," v. 3, pt. 2, documents 27, 27a, 57; [H.N. Robinson], "The Negro in the Lower North District," typed study for the Chicago Urban League, [1925], pp. 2–4, Martin L. Bickham Papers, Box 237, Folder 2, UIC. On the further migration of African Americans in the wake of a renewal of gang violence in the late 1920s, see [Raymond Sayler], "The Negro in 'Little Italy,'" typed study, October 30, 1931, p. 1, BUR, Box 135, Folder 5; Interview with Father Louis Giambastiani of St. Philip's Church by Raymond Sayler, n.d. but c. 1928, p. 2, BUR, Box 135, Folder 6; Vivien M. Palmer, "Study of the Development of Chicago's Northside," typed study for the United Charities of Chicago, December 1932, p. 73, CHS; Pasley, *Al Capone*, pp. 232–233; *LTIT*, September 22, 1928, p. 7; *CT*, September 8, 1928, p. 2; *CT*, September 9, 1928, pp. 1–2; and chap. 4.

19. CCRR, *The Negro in Chicago*, p. 607; Interview with Penio, pp. 11, 62–63, IAC. See also Interview with Rafaelli, pp. 10, 29, IAC; [H.N. Robinson], "The Negro in the Lower North District," p. 21. For more on the friendly relations between Italians and African Americans on the Near North Side, see Cressey, "The Succession of Cultural Groups," p. 249; *CD*, April 6, 1935, p. 1.

20. Quaintance, "Rent and Housing Conditions," p. 38; Zorbaugh, *The Gold Coast and the Slum*, p. 148. See also Desmond, "The Lower North Community Council," p. 72; and Abbott, *The Tenements of Chicago, 1908–1935*, p. 109.

21. [Raymond Sayler], "The Negro in 'Little Italy,'" p. 2; Sayler, "Reminiscences of an Old Resident of the Neighborhood," typed notes, n.d., n.p., BUR, Box 135, Folder 6; Sayler, "A Study of Behavior Problems," p. 42.

22. [Paul L. Schroeder], untitled typed report, October 16, 1933, Chicago Area Project Papers, Box 14, Folder 1, CHS; *CD*, May 23, 1925, p. 1; *CT*, May 28, 1925, p. 3. On the North Side Improvement Association, see *LTIT*, May 17, 1930, p. 4; *LTIT*, August 1, 1931, p. 5; Sayler, "The Negro in 'Little Italy'," p. 1; D'Agostino, "Missionaries in Babylon," p. 394.

23. Drake and Cayton, *Black Metropolis*, p. 182; Sayler, "The Negro in 'Little Italy,'" p. 2.

24. *CD*, April 6, 1935, p. 2; *CD*, May 4, 1935, p. 3. See also *CD*, May 11, 1935, pp. 1–2.

25. On African Americans, see Herman Dixon, "The Near West Side," n.d., Negro in Illinois Collection, Box 37, Folder 20, Carter G. Woodson Regional Library; on Mexicans, see Kerr, "Chicano Settlements in Chicago," p. 22. See

also Garcia, *Mexicans in the Midwest, 1900–1932*, pp. 37, 46; and Arredondo, "'What! the Mexicans, Americans?'"

26. R. D. McCleary, "General Survey of Attitudes Involved in the Formation of a Youth Council on the Near-West Side," n.d., n.p., Chicago Area Project Papers, Box 101, Folder 10, CHS; Anthony Sorrentino, "It's an Inside Job: The Story of the Near West Side Community Committee," unpublished, typed manuscript, 1952, pp. 5–6, 24, CHS. For more on anti-Italian prejudice and discrimination on the Near West Side, see Interview with Leonardi, p. 8, IAC; Interview with DeLiberto, pp. 2, 22, IAC; Interview with De Falco, p. 14, IAC; Gaetano DeFilippis, "Social Life in an Immigrant Community," p. 28, BUR, Box 130, Folder 2; Anthony Sorrentino, "Study of Non-Delinquents in a Delinquent Area," typed paper, 1941, p. 21, Anthony Sorrentino Papers, Box 2, Folder 21, CHS.

27. Addams, *Forty Years at Hull-House*, v. 2, p. 282; Manuel Bueno, "The Mexicans in Chicago," typed paper, 1924, pp. 17–18, 33, BUR, Box 187, Folder 4. For more on Italians' relatively friendly relations with Mexicans, see Kerr, "Chicano Settlements in Chicago," p. 24; Kerr, "The Chicano Experience in Chicago, 1920–1970," p. 29; Taylor, *Mexican Labor in the United States*, pp. 245–250.

28. Addams, *Forty Years at Hull-House*, v. 2, p. 283; Taylor, *Mexican Labor in the United States*, p. 221; McCleary, "General Survey Attitudes," n.p. On summer camp with healthy mixtures of Italians and Mexicans, see "Camp Report," August 28, 1931, and W. Ryland Boorman to G. H. Cross, January 14, 1931, both in Chicago Boys Club Papers, Box 47, Folder 1, CHS. On intermarriages, see the Carillo case record, 1928–1931, Madonna Center Records, Series 4, Box 1, Folder 4, Marquette University Special Collections. On church, see Jones, "Conditions Surrounding Mexicans in Chicago," p. 129. It should be noted that some Mexicans had their serious questions about Italians as well. One Mexican-American man remarked in the early 1920s: "I do not like the manners of the Italian and Polish people; they are too disrespectful towards women; they do not discriminate between good and bad, between the lady and the servant; all are women to them. They want to touch them all over, even their breasts; they are too free, and this is repulsive to me." See Bueno, "The Mexicans in Chicago," p. 22. On Italians' harassment of Filipino Americans on the Near West Side, see Posadas, "Crossed Boundaries."

29. CCRR, *The Negro in Chicago*, pp. 19, 283–284; Donald H. Seward, "The Natural Area within the City," typed paper for Sociology 264, 1930, p. 43, BUR, Box 154, Folder 4.

30. *CD*, June 13, 1925, p. 2; Interview with Cosentino, p. 27, IAC; McCleary, "General Survey of Attitudes," n.p. On Roosevelt Road being seen as an important neighborhood "dividing line," see Interview with Sorrentino, side 1. For more subtle forms of anti-African-American and anti-Mexican prejudice among Italians on the Near West Side, see Ruth Porter Boyd field notes diary, summer 1933, Chicago Area Project Papers, Box 118, Folder 3, CHS. In this diary, the author jotted down the following notes about how Italian girls teased each other on occasion: "Once some Mexicans came down the street. 'There goes your cousin . . . ' 'Huh, you mean yours.' Once some negroes drove by. 'There's your boyfriend.' There was a similar answer to this" (p. 10). See also chap. 8.

31. Abbott, *The Tenements of Chicago*, p. 116; Interview with Baio, p. 36, IAC; Interview with Lizzo, p. 4, IAC. On Wentworth being *the* color boundary

in the neighborhood, see LCRC, "History of Armour Square," v. 4, pt. 1, document 1, p. 1.

32. Jenkins, "Changes in Ethnic and Racial Representation among Professional Boxers," p. 90; *CD*, October 25, 1924, pt. 1, p. 3; *Il Lavoratore*, September 24, 1924, p. 4. See also the *CD*, August 26, 1939, p. 14.

33. The Chinese population figure is from Newcomb and Lang, *Census Data of the City of Chicago, 1934*, p. 668; the Italian figure is from Burgess and Newcomb, *Census Data of the City of Chicago, 1930*, p. 276.

34. "Economics of the Chinese Family," n.d. but c. 1933; and "Unadjusted Girl," n.d. but c. 1933, p. 1, both in BUR, Box 137, Folder 2.

35. For positive views of the Chinese, see Interview with Bertucci, p. 16, IAC; and Interview with Manella, pp. 34–35, IAC. For negative views, see Interview with Tellerino, p. 12, IAC; Interview with Clementi, pp. 23–24, IAC.

36. Interview with Sabella, p. 40, IAC; Interview with Chidichino, p. 33, IAC; L. Pacey, "Area Served by Benton House," pp. 3–4, Benton House Papers, Box 4, Folder 17, CHS. On Italians' recollections about harmonious relations with their European neighbors around Armour Square, see, for example, Interview with Manella, pp. 31–32, IAC.

37. On the geography of the Italian neighborhood on the Near Northwest Side and the movement of its population, see Burgess and Newcomb, *Census Data of the City of Chicago, 1930*; Lea Taylor, "Report of the Work of the Chicago Commons for the Year Ending September 30, 1924," 1924, CC, Box 5, Folder "Annual and Other Reports, 1908–1928." On Italians' relations with other European groups beside Poles, see, for example, Mathilde Schwerdt, "Neighborhood Report for the Month of December, 1928," 1928, p. 5, CC, Box 23a, Folder "January 1928–April 4, 1929."

38. Interview with (Mattioni) Arrow, p. 27, IAC; and Interview with Tonietto, p. 28, IAC; Taylor, "Lea Demarest Taylor," p. 65; "Erie Chapel in 1934," handwritten bound volume, 1934, p. 2, Erie Neighborhood House Papers, Box 1, Folder 2, CHS.

39. Interview with Dominic Badame, August 8, 1945, Foreign Populations—Chicago Collection, p. 2, Folder 3, CHS; Cressey, "The Succession of Cultural Groups," p. 258 [spelling from original].

40. "Near Northwest Side Survey, Diary of the Area Project Representative," November 11, 1938, p. 7, Chicago Area Project Papers, Box 108, Folder 12, CHS; Cressey, "The Succession of Cultural Groups" p. 258 [spelling from original]; "The Polish Busy Bees Clubs, Record of Activities," 1929, CC, Box 6, Folder "Clubs and Groups 1929–1933." For more evidence on Italian-Polish problems in the area, see "Report of the Work of the Chicago Commons for the Year Ending September 30, 1929," 1929, p. 11, Box 5, Folder "Annual and Other Reports, 1929–1932"; Karl Borders, "Annual Reports, Boys Department, 1928–1929," 1929, Box 6, Folder "Clubs and Groups 1929–1933," both in CC.

41. Zaloha, "A Study of the Persistence," p. 26. For evidence that Italian-Polish relations were improving, see M. Leonard and A. Caffarello, "Reports of Play Leaders on Lot and Doorstep Play," 1934, Box 6, Folder "Clubs and Groups 1935–1936"; and Mabel Cates and Lucile Brotsman, "Girls' Department Report, 1940–1941," Box 7, Folder "Clubs and Groups, 1940–1942," both in CC.

42. William J. Dempsey, "Gangs in the Calumet Park District," paper for Sociology 270, n.d., p. 8, BUR, Box 148, Folder 5; Newton I. Zemans, "South Deering," paper for Sociology 269, 1929, p. 3, BUR, Box 185, Folder 1; Interview

with Zaranti, pp. 5–6, IAC; Interview with Bonevolenta, p. 31, IAC. On anti-Italian feelings and actions in other locations, see Davis, "Housing Conditions in the District of Burnside," pp. 8–9; and the following IAC interviews: Cesario, p. 13; Giuliano, p. 75; Dalle Molle, pp. 24–25; Petri, pp. 6, 32; Zoppetti, p. 50.

43. Interview with Tieri, p. 39; Interview with Petri, p. 32; both in IAC.

44. Interview with Cesario, p. 38; Interview with Zaranti, p. 33; both in IAC.

45. *Mexico*, April 5, 1930, CFLPS; Baur, "Delinquency Among Mexican Boys in South Chicago," pp. 29, 52, 121–122. See also Garcia, "History of Chicanos in Chicago Heights," p. 296.

46. I will discuss and explain this point further in this chapter and in chap. 8. Suffice it to say here that there is an enormous sociological literature on neighborhood contact and "race relations." My argument here is not that contact, in and of itself, produces conflict. It is, instead, the context (in this case I mean Chicago's colorized social system and its microlevel neighborhood manifestations) that is critical and that teaches Italians and other groups how to treat their neighbors.

47. Cressey, "The Succession of Cultural Groups in Chicago," p. 81.

48. LCRC, "History of the Lower North Side Community," v. 3, pt. 2, document 37b, p. 1.

49. For a sampling of work on Chicago that stresses the importance of competition of one sort or another, see Radzialowski, "The Competition for Jobs and Racial Stereotypes," pp. 5–18; Spears, *Black Chicago*, chap. 11; Tuttle, *Race Riot*. For a sociologist's theorization of one version of this argument, see Bonacich, "A Theory of Ethnic Antagonism," pp. 547–559.

50. On Chicago, see Pacyga, "Chicago's 1919 Race Riot," p. 205; Addams, *Forty Years at Hull-House*, v. 2, p. 283; Cressey, "The Succession of Cultural Groups," pp. 152–153; Grossman, *Land of Hope*, p. 253; Philpott, *The Slum and the Ghetto*, p. 161; Vecoli, "'Ethnic versus Black Metropolis',"p. 238; Barrett, "Americanization from the Bottom Up," pp. 1002, 1006. For an early departure from this argument, see Hirsch, "Making the Second Ghetto," pp. 379–393.

51. See Ignatiev, *How The Irish Became White*, p. 2; Roediger, *The Wages of Whiteness*, p. 137; Nelson, *Divided We Stand*, pp. xxxiv–xl.

52. My analysis here is informed by the following work: Bonilla-Silva, "Rethinking Racism," pp. 465–480; Bonilla-Silva and Lewis, "The 'New Racism'"; Blumer, "Race Prejudice as a Sense of Group Position," pp. 3–7. On competition not being the answer, see also Roediger, *The Wages of Whiteness*, p. 147.

53. I will talk more about migration and home ownership in chap. 8. On the role of local Catholic institutions in particular, see especially Gamm, *Mass Exodus* and McGreevy, *Parish Boundaries*.

54. There were exceptions to this rule, of course. In the late 1920s, for instance, one Italian noted: "I don't want my kids to associate with the Mexicans. God made people white and black, and He meant there to be a difference." And recall that some Italians objected to Mexicans using Bowen Hall and Hull-House because they were "people of color." The point must have been that Italians were *not* this and were therefore white.

55. Colley, *Britons*, p. 5. See also, Colley, "Britishness and Otherness," pp. 309–329.

56. Cressey, "The Succession of Cultural Groups," p. 276. On restrictive covenants and neighborhood associations in Chicago, see Philpott, *The Slum and the Ghetto*, pp. 147–202; Mikva, "The Neighborhood Improvement Associa-

tion"; Washington, "A Study of Restrictive Covenants in Chicago"; Plotkin, "Deeds of Mistrust."

Chapter 3

1. I use the term *racialism* to mean a coherent set of ideas about race. *Anti-immigrant racialism* denotes, then, a set of ideas that primarily target immigrants based on notions of racial difference and inferiority. *Scientific anti-immigrant racialism* is a set of racialist ideas produced largely by social and natural scientists. I have abstained from using *nativism* because it places too much emphasis on foreignness. John Higham, for instance, defined *nativism* as being an "intense opposition to an internal minority on the ground of its foreign (i.e., 'un-American') connections." To my mind, many Americans feared and reviled Italians and other "new" immigrants less for their foreignness and more for their racialness—a whole set of qualities that, according to racialists, persisted well into the American-born generations. For this reason, I might have chosen *racism* rather than *racialism*. I prefer the latter because it can mean a wider variety of things. As historian Peggy Pascoe has recently put it, *racialism* covers "a wide range of . . . ideas from the biologically marked categories scientific racists employed to the more amorphous ideas . . . called 'romantic racialism.'" See Pascoe, "Miscegenation Law, Court Cases, and Ideologies of 'Race' in Twentieth-Century America," pp. 47–48. For the Higham quotation, see *Strangers in the Land*, p. 4. Many thanks to Terry McDonald for pointing out to me the possible limitations in the term *nativism*.

2. Fairchild, *Immigration*, p. 400. For examples of the importance of race over environment or education, see Grant, *The Passing of the Great Race*, pp. vii, xix; Burr, *America's Race Heritage*, p. 136; Stoddard, *The Rising Tide of Color*, p. 306; Roberts, *Why Europe Leaves Home*, p. 22; *New York Times*, April 18, 1924, p. 18.

3. Grant, *The Passing of the Great Race*, pp. xxviii, xxi, vii. For a discussion of the influence of de Gobineau and Chamberlain on twentieth-century U.S. racialists, see Gossett, *Race*, pp. 342–353.

4. See, for instance, *CT*, November 16, 1920, p. 8; *CT*, January 27, 1924, p. 8; *Congressional Record*, 68th cong., 1st sess., 1924, 65, pt. 6: 5467, 5673; Garis, *Immigration Restriction*, p. 237. Interestingly, Horace Kallen also argued that what frightened racialists most was not racial inequality but racial difference. See *Culture and Democracy in the United States*, p. 115.

5. Grant, *The Passing of the Great Race*, pp. xxviii–xxix; McDougall, *Is America Safe for Democracy?*, p. 67. See also Stoddard, *The Rising Tide of Color*, p. 306.

6. To be sure, racialists could alternate freely between championing Nordics and Anglo-Saxons; but these were not incompatible views. In *America's Race Heritage*, for instance, Burr argued both that "everything . . . worthwhile in America is Anglo-Saxon in origin" *and* that "within the American people the Nordic stock has always been the most important" (pp. 209, 137). Racialists seemed to believe that Anglo-Saxons were to Nordics as Nordics were to whites—the purest and most ideal form. In Henry Fairfield Osborn's words, "the Anglo-Saxon branch of the Nordic race is again showing itself to be that upon which the nation must chiefly depend for leadership, for courage, for loyalty, for unity and harmony of action, for self-sacrifice and devotion to an ideal" (Grant, *The Passing of the Great Race*, p. xi). So Anglo-Saxonism survived

and flourished well into the 1920s, but now it served as a corollary to a more general theory: Nordic supremacy.

7. Grant, *The Passing of the Great Race*, p. 228.

8. Davie, *A Constructive Immigration Policy*, p. 34. For examples of other either implicit or explicit pro-Nordic intelligence studies, see especially: Brigham, *A Study of American Intelligence*; McDougall, *Is America Safe for Democracy?*; Sweeney, "Mental Tests for Immigrants," pp. 600–612; and Kirkpatrick, *Intelligence and Immigration*.

9. The two terms—"new" immigrant and southeastern European—were used more or less interchangeably by scientific racialists. Categories like Alpine and Mediterranean were more specific racial categories, but together they roughly constituted the more general "new" immigrant/southeastern European group.

10. Sweeney, "Mental Tests for Immigrants," pp. 610–611. See also Grant, *The Passing of the Great Race*, pp. 165, 166; Burr, *America's Race Heritage*, p. 113.

11. See chap. 1.

12. Fairchild, *Immigration*, p. 140; *New York Times*, April 18, 1924, p. 18. For further references to the differences between northern and southern Italians, see Burr, *America's Race Heritage*, pp. 115–116; Grant, *The Passing of the Great Race*, 157–158.

13. Kirkpatrick, *Intelligence and Immigration*, pp. 104–107. On the work of Sweeney and Brigham, see n. 8.

14. Fairchild, *Immigration*, p. 140; Grant, *The Passing of the Great Race*, pp. 65–66. For further evidence of scientific racialists' inclusion of "new" immigrants within the white color category, see Burr, *America's Race Heritage*, pp. 5, 17; Brigham, *A Study of American Intelligence*, pp. 118–121; Huntington, *The Character of Races*, p. 5; Davie, *A Constructive Immigration Policy*, p. 7. Several studies of "new" immigration and issues of race have assumed that the flowering of post–World War I anti-immigrant racialism necessarily called into question the whiteness of "new" immigrants. My research on the subject does not support that assumption. See Barrett and Roediger, "Inbetween Peoples," p. 14; Gerstle, "Liberty, Coercion, and the Making of Americans," p. 552.

15. Stoddard, *The Rising Tide of Color*, pp. 308, 299, 267.

16. On Chicago in 1919, see especially Cohen, *Making a New Deal*, pp. 38–51.

17. Creel, "Close the Gates!," pp. 9–10; Creel, "Melting Pot or Dumping Ground," pp. 9–10; Curran, "Fewer and Better, or None," pp. 8–9; "Keep on Guarding the Gates" *Current Opinion* 74 (June 1923): 652–654; Speranza, "The Immigration Peril"; Roberts, "Slow Poison," pp. 8–9, 54, 56, 58; "Keep America 'White,'" *Current Opinion* 74 (April 1923): 399–401.

18. Roberts, *Why Europe Leaves Home*, pp. 47, 22, 47. On the *Saturday Evening Post*'s circulation, see Tebbel, *George Horace Lorimer and the Saturday Evening Post*, p. 79.

19. Roberts, "Slow Poison," p. 8; Roberts, *Why Europe Leaves Home*, p. 168; "America Last," *Saturday Evening Post* 194 (March 4, 1922): 22; Roberts, *Why Europe Leaves Home*, p. 22; Roberts, "Slow Poison," pp. 8, 58.

20. Roberts, *Why Europe Leaves Home*, p. 54; Roberts, "Slow Poison," p. 8. See also Frazer, "Our Foreign Cities: Chicago," especially p. 102.

21. *CDN*, March 1, 1924, p. 8; see also *CDN*, December 9, 1920, p. 8; *CDN*, January 7, 1921, p. 8; *CDN*, March 13, 1921, p. 8; *CDN*, April 10, 1924, p. 8.

22. *CDN*, December 4, 1920, p. 8.

23. *CDN*, December 1, 1920, p. 8; *CDN*, February 3, 1921, p. 9; *CDN*, February 8, 1921, p. 8; *CDN*, February 17, 1921, p. 8; *CDN*, February 22, 1921, p. 8.

24. *CDN*, December 1, 1920, p. 8; *CDN*, February 9, 1921, p. 7. This Hanson article was the eighth in the series.

25. *CDN*, May 22, 1924, p. 5; *CDN*, May 30, 1924, p. 5; *CDN*, May 29, 1924, p. 5; *CDN*, May 20, 1924, p. 5.

26. In one *CT* editorial, the paper wrote happily about a skating event for kids of "all races," which demonstrated that beneath the "natural marks of race" are Americans after all. See *CT*, January 22, 1924, p. 6.

27. For political cartoons regarding the "new" immigration, see *CT*, January 30, 1920, p. 8; *CT*, December 14, 1920, p. 8; *CT*, December 11, 1920, p. 8; *CT*, April 16, 1924, p. 1.

28. *CT*, November 28, 1920, p. 8; *CT*, December 6, 1920, p. 8; *CT*, January 27, 1924, pt. 1, p. 8; *CT*, April 15, 1924, p. 8; *CT*, November 19, 1920, p. 8; *CT*, March 13, 1924, p. 8; *CT*, December 2, 1920, p. 8; *CT*, December 12, 1920, pt. 2, p. 6; *CT*, February 26, 1924, p. 8; *CT*, May 13, 1921, p. 8.

29. Jackson, *The Ku Klux Klan in the City*, p. 126. On the 1920s revival of the Ku Klux Klan, see Higham, *Strangers in the Land*, pp. 286–299; Moore, "Historical Interpretations of the 1920s Klan," pp. 341–357; Moore, *Citizen Klansmen*; Lay, *The Invisible Empire in the West*; Blee, *Women of the Klan*.

30. Jackson, *The Ku Klux Klan in the City*, p. 101. On anti-Klan resistance in Chicago, see ibid., pp. 94–96, 102–115; *Dawn*, December 30, 1922, p. 6; *Dawn*, October 20, 1923, p. 5; Thurner, "The Impact of Ethnic Groups on the Democratic Party in Chicago, 1920–1928," pp. 124–125; Phillpott, *The Slum and the Ghetto*, pp. 188–190. On different Klan activities in the Chicago area, see the following *Dawn* articles: on initiation ceremonies and meetings, see: October 21, 1922, pp. 5, 11; November 4, 1922, p. 12; November 11, 1922, p. 11; May 19, 1923, p. 6; August 25, 1923, p. 4; October 27, 1923, p. 6; November 3, 1923, p. 12; on parties and banquets, see: November 11, 1922, p. 6; December 23, 1922, p. 8; July 14, 1923, p. 8; on church donations, see: November 11, 1922, p. 6; November 25, 1922, p. 9; December 23, 1922, p. 6; January 27, 1923, p. 10. On Klan activities, see also the following *CT* articles: August 16, 1921, p. 11; September 21, 1921, p. 1; August 20, 1922, p. 1; November 26, 1922, p. 3.

31. *Dawn*, December 23, 1922, p. 6; *Dawn*, November 25, 1922, p. 1. For other examples of *Dawn*'s anti-immigrant racialism, see the following articles: November 11, 1922, p. 10; January 6, 1923, p. 12; January 20, 1923, p. 11; May 5, 1923, p. 11; June 2, 1923, p. 12; July 21, 1923, p. 17; August 11, 1923, p. 7; September 8, 1923, pp. 9, 11; September 15, 1923, p. 13; October 6, 1923, pp. 5–6; November 3, 1923, pp. 9, 34–40; November 10, 1923, pp. 14–20. At the national level, see Hiram Wesley Evans, "The Menace of Modern Immigration," address delivered on Klan Day, Dallas, TX, October 24, 1923, Labadie Collection, University of Michigan Special Collections; Evans, "The Klan's Fight for Americanism," pp. 33–63. In line with recent historiography, I have found that Klan anti-immigrant rhetoric was no more strident or extreme than that in mainstream publications like the *Chicago Tribune* or the *Saturday Evening Post*. On this historiography, see the more recent works cited in n. 29.

32. *CT*, March 4, 1924, p. 8; *CT*, February 6, 1924, p. 8. See also: *CDN*, November 4, 1920, p. 9; *CDN*, January 29, 1921, p. 9; *CDN*, February 3, 1921, p. 9; *CDN*, February 2, 1921, p. 9; *CDN*, March 18, 1924, p. 9; *CDN*, March 24, 1924,

p. 9; *CT*, March 2, 1924, pt. 1, p. 8; *CT*, March 4, 1924, p. 8; *CT*, March 23, 1924, p. 1; *CT*, February 6, 1924, p. 8; *CT*, February 7, 1924, p. 8; *CT*, February 23, 1924, p. 6; *CT*, February 26, 1924, p. 8; *CHE*, May 5, 1924, p. 8.

33. For Boas's early anti-racialist work, see Boas, "Human Faculty as Determined by Race," pp. 301–327; Boas, *The Mind of Primitive Man*; Boas with Boas, "The Head Forms of Italians as Influenced by Heredity and Environment," pp. 163–188; Baker, *From Savage to Negro*.

34. For quotations, see Boas, "The Rising Tide of Color," p. 656; and Boas, "The Question of Racial Purity," p. 169. For Boas's other anti-racialist work at the time, see Boas, "What Is a Race?" pp. 89–91; Boas, "This Nordic Nonsense," pp. 502–511; *New York Times*, April 13, 1924, section 9, p. 19. For general work on Boas's fight against racialism, see Stocking, *Race, Culture, and Evolution*; Gossett, *Race*, pp. 418–430; Baker, *From Savage to Negro*.

35. Kallen, *Culture and Democracy*, pp. 178–179. For a discussion of Kallen's race thinking, see Gleason, "American Identity and Americanization," pp. 43–47.

36. Kallen, *Culture and Democracy*, pp. 180, 124–125.

37. Park and Miller, *Old World Traits Transplanted*, pp. 303, 302, 303. See also Park, *Race and Culture*, especially p. 251. My crediting above of *Old World Traits Transplanted* to W. I. Thomas is not a mistake. Having already written the bulk of the manuscript, Thomas was fired from the project just before publication for his alleged involvement in an extramarital affair. On Thomas's dismissal, see Janowitz, *W.I. Thomas on Social Organization and Social Personality*, pp. xiv–xv. For work on the role and importance of the Chicago School in undermining racialism of the early twentieth century, see Matthews, *Quest for an American Sociology*, pp. 157, 160, 163, 170, 173; Person, *Ethnic Studies at Chicago*, pp. 38, 45–46, 54, 81–82; Wacker, *Ethnicity, Pluralism, and Race*, pp. 8–9, 17–18, 22, 33. I should note here as well that Robert Park, while generally deemphasizing innate differences between groups and believing in racial equality, still contended, at least early in his career, that races possessed particular "temperaments"—"certain special traits or tendencies which rest on biological rather than cultural differences" and which "historical causes do not, it seems, adequately account for." See, for example, Park, *Race and Culture*, pp. 264–265, 280–282; also Matthews, *Quest for an American Sociology*, pp. 171–172; and Persons, *Ethnic Studies*, pp. 81–82.

38. Senate Committee on Immigration, *Hearings: Selective Immigration Legislation*, 68th Cong., 1st sess., 1924, pp. 86–88; *LIT*, February 24, 1924, p. 1; *LIT*, February 10, 1924, p. 3; *LTIT*, March 22, 1924, p. 1.

39. All Italians did not share the same views on immigration and restriction, of course. Chicago's Cairoli Gigliotti, for instance, an editor of an English-language newspaper for Italian Americans, openly expressed his support for restriction in his newspaper (several of his articles were reprinted in the Klan's newspaper *Dawn*), in a statement presented to the House Committee on Immigration and Naturalization, and in a letter to the editors of the *CT*. In the latter, Gigliotti called for a temporary cessation of all immigration until America improved its ability to weed out the "unfit." See *CT*, March 25, 1924, p. 8. For Gigliotti's articles in *Dawn*, see September 1, 1923, p. 6; September 8, 1923, pp. 9, 11; October 13, 1923, pp. 19–20; November 3, 1923, p. 14; December 15, 1923, p. 18; January 5, 1924, p. 8; February 9, 1924, p. 5. For his "unorthodox" views on immigration, Gigliotti complained of being ostracized by the Italian-American community in Chicago. See Cairoli Gigliotti to James Forgan, January 16, 1923, James Berwick Forgan Papers, CHS. For critiques of Gigliotti in

Chicago's Italian-language newspapers, see *LIT*, February 17, 1924, p. 1; *LTIT*, January 12, 1924, p. 7; *LTIT*, February 9, 1924, p. 2.

40. On the Italian Consulate, see *LTIT*, March 22, 1924, p. 1; Finkelstein, "The Johnson Act, Mussolini and Fascist Emigration Policy," pp. 38–55. Regarding Chicago's Italian-language newspapers, articles in opposition to restriction and racialism appeared in every issue and, thus, are far too numerous to cite here. For some representative examples, see *LIT*: February 27, 1921, p. 1; April 17, 1921, p. 4; October 14, 1923, p. 1; October 28, 1923, p. 1; February 10, 1924, p. 1; February 17, 1924, p. 1; March 2, 1924, p. 1; March 9, 1924, p. 1; April 6, 1924, p. 1; April 20, 1924, p. 1; May 25, 1924, p. 1; November 9, 1924, p. 1; and see *LTIT*: February 2, 1924, pp. 1–2; February 8, 1924, p. 2; February 16, 1924, p. 1; February 23, 1924, p. 3; March 15, 1924, p. 3; Mach 22, 1924, p. 1; March 29, 1924, p. 3; April 12, 1924, p. 1; April 19, 1924, p. 3; April 26, 1924, p. 1. On the Chicago Committee, see *Hearings: Selective Immigration Legislation*, pp. 117–120; *Chicago Italian Chamber of Commerce* (April 1924), pp. 1–14, CFLPS; *LIT*, March 16, 1924, p. 1. On the attack on the Klan tent in Chicago Heights, see Candeloro, "Suburban Italians," p. 262.

41. The one minor exception to this statement is that Italians would on occasion question the legitimacy of the Nordic racial category by placing *Nordic* in quotation marks or by labeling it a so-called race. That the Mediterranean race existed, however, was never questioned. For examples of Italians' skepticism about the Nordic category, see *LTIT*, June 21, 1924, p. 3; *LIT*, May 25, 1924, p. 1; House Committee on Immigration and Naturalization, *Hearings: Restriction of Immigration*, 68th Cong., 1st sess., 1924, p. 1028.

42. *Hearings: Selective Immigration Legislation*, pp. 117–120; *Hearings: Restriction of Immigration*, pp. 1164–1166.

43. *LIT*, May 25, 1924, p. 1 and *LTIT*, June 7, 1924, p.7; *LIT*, March 9, 1924, p. 1 and *LTIT*, March 15, 1924, p. 3. See also *LTIT*, March 22, 1924, p. 2; *LTIT*, April 26, 1924, p. 1; *LIT*, March 6, 1921, p. 4.

44. Schiavo, *The Italians in Chicago*, pp. 12, 15, 16, 15. For a similar argument, see also Stella, *Some Aspects of Italian Immigration*.

45. For further (if, in some cases, later) evidence of Italians' belief in a monolithic Italian race, see *LIT*, March 26, 1933, p. 8; *LIT*, March 21, 1937, p. 3; *BOSIA* (May 15, 1934): 1–4, CFLPS; *BIANU* (March 1927): 1–2, CFLPS; Cipriani, *Selected Directory of the Italians in Chicago*, pp. v–xi.

46. "Keep America 'White'!" p. 399; *Dawn*, August 25, 1923, p. 8; Lewis, *Babbitt*, p. 122.

47. *CDN*, February 9, 1921, p. 7. For further examples of the common assumption of Italians' whiteness, see notes 14 and 15 and *Congressional Record*, 68th Cong., 1st sess., 1924, 65, pt. 6: 5467–5468, 5665; *Hearings: Restriction of Immigration*, p. 915; Evans, "The Klan's Fight for Americanism," pp. 6, 19; Evans, "The Menace of Modern Immigration," p. 6; *CT*, April 15, 1924, p. 8; *CDN*, March 18, 1924, p. 9; *Dawn*, March 21, 1923, p. 13.

48. Few scholars have addressed how the 1924 Immigration Act affected Japanese immigration. For recent exceptions to this rule, see Mae Ngai's essay "The Architecture of Race in American Immigration Law," pp. 67–92; King, *Making Americans*; Gerstle, *American Crucible*, pp. 109–121.

49. For the *Chicago American*, see: April 12, 1924, p. 1; April 14, 1924, pp. 1, 16; April 15, 1924, p. 1. For the *CHE*, see: April 15, 1924, p. 1; April 16, 1924, pp. 1, 8; April 22, 1924, p. 8; April 25, 1924, p. 8; May 12, 1924, p. 8; May 25, 1924, pt. 2, p. 1; May 28, 1924, p. 8 . For the *CDN*, see: March 27, 1924, p. 8;

April 16, 1924, p. 8; April 17, 1924, p. 8; April 22, 1924, p. 8; April 30, 1924, p. 9; May 26, 1924, pp. 1, 3. For the *CT*, see April 15, 1924, p. 8; April 16, 1924, pp. 1, 8; April 17, 1924, p. 8; April 18, 1924, p. 8; April 19, 1924, p. 8; April 21, 1924, p. 8; April 23, 1924, p. 8; April 25, 1924, p. 8; April 26, 1924, p. 8; May 7, 1924, p. 8; May 9, 1924, p. 8; May 18, 1924, p. 8; May 22, 1924, p. 8; May 28, 1924, p. 8.

50. *CT*, April 15, 1924, p. 8; *CHE*, April 18, 1924, p. 6. It should be noted that, of all Asians, the Japanese were targeted in 1924 because by this point virtually all other Asians had already been excluded from the United States by virtue of the 1917 Immigration Act.

51. Boas, "This Nordic Nonsense," p. 504; *New York Times*, April 13, 1924, section 9, p. 19.

52. Park, *Race and Culture*, pp. 253, 252; Yu, *Thinking Orientals*, p. 43. The point on Park above owes much to Henry Yu's work cited above and Jacobson, *Whiteness of a Different Color*, pp. 104–106.

53. Terms like "whites" rarely appeared in Kallen's writing, but he clearly viewed the "different European stocks" as "white men," as he noted once in *Culture and Democracy*, p. 124.

54. Kallen, *Culture and Democracy*, pp. 97, 231, 226 (emphases mine). For a discussion of the eurocentrism of Kallen's cultural pluralism, see Higham, *Send These to Me*, p. 210.

55. *LIT*, June 8, 1924, p. 1; *LIT*, July 6, 1924, p. 1; and *LTIT*, July 19, 1924, p. 7.

56. *LIT*, June 8, 1924, p. 1; *LIT*, May 25, 1924, p. 1; and *LTIT*, June 7, 1924, p. 7. *LIT*'s support for Asian immigrants predated by several decades the debates on Japanese exclusion. See, for example, *LIT*, December 8, 1906, p. 1; *LIT*, November 13, 1909, p. 1; *LIT*, September 10, 1910, p. 2; *LIT*, April 23,1913, p. 1.

57. *LTIT*, June 21, 1924, p. 3; *LTIT*, July 12, 1924, p. 7.

58. *LIT*, June 8, 1924, p. 1.

Chapter 4

1. *CT*, February 13, 1926, p. 4. Deportation drives took place in several locations on the South Side of Chicago as well, in which larger numbers of Mexicans were apprehended. See, for instance, the *CHE*, March 2, 1926, p. 2.

2. For general information on the deportation drive, see Adena Miller Rich, "Chicago's Deportation Drive of 1926," unpublished typed report, n.d., Immigration Protective League Records, Box 2, Folder 21, UIC; and "An Italian Taken in the Alien Deportation Raids of February and March 1926," January 1927, typed report, Immigrant Protective League Records, Box 4, Folder 50, UIC. See also: *CT* between February 12–28, 1926; *CDN*: February 23, 1926, pp. 1–2; February 25, 1926, p. 5; and the *CHE*: February 23, 1926, pp. 1, 5; February 25, 1926, p. 2. For the headlines cited above, see *CT*: February 22, 1926, p. 1; March 8, 1926, p. 3; March 7, 1926, p. 1; February 16, 1926, p. 1. For the quotation, see *CT*, February 13, 1926, p. 4.

3. Drake and Cayton, *Black Metropolis*, p. 77; *Congressional Record*, 69th Cong., 1st sess., 67, pt. 5: 5456; Loesch quotation from Bergreen, *Capone*, p. 365. The *CT*'s constant campaign of criminalization against Sicilians will be discussed in greater detail below. For some representative editorials and editorial cartoons, see *CT*, February 12, 1926, p. 8; *CT*, February 15, 1926, p. 1; *CT*, February 16, 1926, p. 8; *CT*, February 24, 1926, p. 6; *CT*, September 10, 1928, pp. 1, 12; *CT*, September 13, 1928, p. 12; *CT*, September 18, 1928, p. 12; *CT*, November

22, 1928, p. 12. Outside of Chicago, the 1920s also witnessed the much-publicized murder trial and execution of Italian anarchists Bartolomeo Vanzetti and Nicola Sacco, which no doubt further encouraged many Chicagoans to view Italians as hopelessly criminalistic. On the Sacco-Vanzetti case, see especially Avrich, *Sacco and Vanzetti*.

4. For the *New York Times* and the *Baltimore News* quotations, see Iorizzo and Mondello, *The Italian-Americans*, p. 70; and Higham, *Strangers in the Land*, p. 90; Ross, *The Old World in the New*, pp. 106, 101; Dillingham report quotation from Nelli, "The Role of the 'Colonial' Press," p. 104.

5. Reports of the U.S. Immigration Commission, *Abstracts of the Reports of the Immigration Commission*, v. 2, pp. 198–203. On population figures for 1910, see Burgess and Newcomb, *Census Data of the City of Chicago, 1920*, p. 21.

6. For the percentage of crime articles, see the *Index to the Chicago Record-Herald*, CHS; for the headlines, see *CRH*, August 15, 1909, p. 7; *CRH*, November 13, 1905, p. 1; *CRH*, December 11, 1904, p. 1; *CRH*, March 13, 1910, p. 2. The 1915 quotation is cited in Landesco, *Organized Crime in Chicago*, p. 112.

7. *CT*, May 21, 1910, p. 10; *CT*, March 17, 1911, p. 1. For other *CT* articles on Italian crime during this time, see *CT*, June 12, 1915, p. 1; *CT*, June 13, 1915, p. 8; *CT*, May 15, 1893 in the CFLPS; *CT*, April 15, 1910, p. 8; *CT*, April 16, 1910, p. 6; *CT*, April 18, 1910, p. 6; *CT*, April 19, 1910, p. 6; *CT*, April 22, 1910, p. 6; *CT*, May 3, 1910, p. 8; *CT*, May 10, 1910, p. 8; *CT*, May 12, 1910, p. 6; *CT*, May 14, 1910, p. 6; *CT*, May 21, 1910, p. 10; *CT*, May 26, 1910, p. 8; *CT*, June 4, 1910, p. 8; *CT*, June 11, 1910, p. 10; *CT*, June 29, 1910, p. 10; *CT*, July 18, 1910, p. 6; *CT*, July 19, 1910, p. 8; *CT*, August 22, 1910, p. 10. See also the *CDN*, May 25, 1913, quoted in Landesco, *Organized Crime in Chicago*, p. 113; and *Chicago Daily Journal*, July 18, 1911, p. 8. Although many newspapers described the Black Hand as an organized society, it was simply a method of extortion through letters used by individuals or small groups of individuals. It was most prevalent in the late nineteenth and early twentieth centuries and tended to die out with the onset of the Great Depression and with the greater organization of crime in Chicago and other American cities in the 1920s. For more information on the Black Hand, see Nelli, *The Italians in Chicago*, pp. 132–140; Nelli, *The Business of Crime*, pp. 69–100; Landesco, *Organized Crime in Chicago*, pp. 108–120.

8. *CRH*, March 26, 1910, p. 7; Barasa quoted in Vecoli, "Chicago's Italians prior to World War I," p. 455. See also, *CT*, July 30, 1910, p. 4; *LIT*, October 8, 1892, p. 1; *LIT*, July 5, 1914, p. 1; *CRH*, August 1, 1911, p. 8.

9. For the article about Italians' low crime rates, see *LIT*, December 31, 1910, p. 1; for the headlines that belie this point, see *LIT*, June 18, 1910, p. 1; *LIT*, February 26, 1910, p. 1; *LIT*, July 16, 1910, p.1; *LIT*, May 7, 1910, p. 1; *LIT*, April 3, 1910, p. 1; *LIT*, April 23, 1910, p. 1. For the "Crimes in Italian Colony" editorial, see *LIT*, April 1, 1911, p. 1 (translation from the CFLPS). *LIT*'s crime articles are far too numerous to cite here. For some representative examples, see *LIT*, January 1, 1901, p. 1; *LIT*, May 10, 1902, p. 1; *LIT*, August 9, 1902, p. 1; *LIT*, March 28, 1903, p. 1; *LIT*, July 16, 1904, p. 1; *LIT*, June 23, 1906, p. 1; *LIT*, January 22, 1907, p. 1; *LIT*, February 8, 1908, p. 1; *LIT*, February 29, 1908, p. 1; *LIT*, April 25, 1908, p. 1; *LIT*, April 17, 1909, p. 1; *LIT*, February 25, 1911 p. 1; *LIT*, February 2, 1912, p. 1; *LIT*, August 10, 1913, p. 1; *LIT*, February 8, 1914, p. 1; *LIT*, May 7, 1916, p. 1; *LIT*, June 30, 1918, p. 1.

10. Vecoli, "Chicago's Italians prior to World War I," p. 455; Beck, "The Italian in Chicago," p. 28. (emphasis added).

11. On 1920s crime wave myths, see Burnham, "New Perspectives on the

Prohibition 'Experiment' of the 1920s," p. 61; Landesco, "Prohibition and Crime," pp. 120–129; Rose, *American Women and the Repeal of Prohibition*, p. 45.

12. On the CCC's public enemy list, see *CT*, April 24, 1930, pp. 1, 8 (this list was alphabetically organized). But see also: *Criminal Justice: Journal of the Chicago Crime Commission* 58 (May 1930): 1; transcript of CCC President Frank Loesch's radio address given on the NBC Radio Network and WGN, January 27, 1931; Gerhardt F. Meyne to Judge John P. McGoorty, June 4, 1931; and CCC, "Public Attacks on Public Enemies," pamphlet, n.d.; all in BUR, Box 4, Folder 9 (all of these lists were organized according to the importance of the gangster). For further evidence of Italians' important place in Chicago's organized crime world during the Prohibition Era, see William F. Ogburn and Clark Tibbits, "A Memorandum on the Nativity of Certain Criminal Classes Engaged in Organized Crime, and of Certain Criminal and Non-Criminal Groups in Chicago," July 30, 1930, Charles E. Merriam Papers, Box 102, Folder 3, UC, which found that 30 percent of Chicago's 108 underworld leaders were Italian. On Italians' involvement in crime more generally, see Jacob Horak, "Criminal Justice and the Foreign Born: Preliminary Report—Summary of the Study of Foreign Born Prisoners in the Illinois State Penitentiaries," typed study, May 1, 1930, Immigrant Protective League Records, Box 2, Folder 21, UIC, which found that Italians constituted the largest percentage of foreign-born inmates (89/532, 16.7 percent); and Quaintance, "Rents and Housing Conditions," pp. 3–5.

13. Both quotations are from Asbury, *Gem of the Prairie*, pp. 320, 321.

14. Landesco, *Organized Crime in Chicago*, p. 97.

15. Asbury, *Gem of the Prairie*, p. 364; *New York Times*, May 26, 1929, cited in Bergreen, *Capone*, p. 319. The popular and scholarly literature on Torrio's and Capone's rise and rule in Chicago is immense. In addition to the works cited above, see Landesco, *Organized Crime in Chicago*, pp. 25–26, 43, 85–95, 178–179; Sullivan, *Rattling the Cup*; Pasley, *Al Capone*; Burns, *The One-Way Ride*; Peterson, *Barbarians in our Midst*, pp. 107–111, 121–151; Allsop, *The Bootleggers and Their Era*; Kobler, *Capone*; Schoenberg, *Mr. Capone*; Nelli, *The Italians in Chicago*, pp. 149–151, 211–222; Nelli, *The Business of Crime*, pp. 163–168. Connected to Capone and Torrio were other huge crime stories such as the mysterious murder of Assistant State's Attorney William H. McSwiggin on April 27, 1926; the St. Valentine's Day Massacre in 1929, in which six gangsters and an optometrist were gunned down outside a garage on the Near North Side; and the many other assassinations of major gang leaders like Dion O'Banion in 1924, three of the Genna brothers in 1925, Hymie Weiss in 1926, and "Schemer" Drucci in 1927.

16. For quotations, see *CT*, February 12, 1926, p. 1; *CT*, February 16, 1926, p. 8; *CT*, February 12, 1926, p. 8. For the general newspaper coverage of these events and their focus on Italians and/or Sicilians, see *CT*, February 12–March 11, 1926; *CDN*, February 13, 1926, p. 8; *CDN*, February 16, 1926, p. 1; *CDN*, February 22, 1926, p. 1; *CDN*, February 23, 1926, pp. 1–2; *CDN*, February 24, 1926, p. 1; *CDN*, February 25, 1926, p. 5; *CHE*, February 13, 1926, p. 8; *CHE*, February 17, 1926, p. 8; *CHE*, February 23, 1926, pp. 1, 5; *CHE*, March 2, 1926, p. 8; *CHE*, March 3, 1926, p. 1; *CHE*, March 8, 1926, p. 1.

17. *CT*, September 25, 1928, p. 3; *CT*, September 18, 1928, p. 12; *CT*, September 21, 1928, p. 2. For the general newspaper coverage of the Lombardo murder and the Ranieri kidnapping and their focus on Italians and/or Sicilians, see *CT*, *CHE*, and *CDN*, September 8–28, 1928.

18. Anon. letter to the CCC, April 10, 1932, cited in Ruth, *Inventing the Pub-*

lic Enemy, p. 74; C. E. S. Smith to the *CT*, n.d., but c. late 1931, CCC Files, File No. 13190–4; *CDN*, October 6, 1931, Al Capone Scrapbooks, CHS; Handwritten note to William Dever, n.d.; see also Jeane Adaine to Dever, February 4, 1927; J. O'Malley to Dever, August 15, 1924; Rev. Cask to Dever, February 8, 1927; all in William E. Dever Mayoralty Papers, Box 3, Folder 26, and Box 4, Folder 29, CHS; *CT*, September 23, 1928, p. 2; and Amberg, *Madonna Center*, p. 85.

19. Mathilde Schwerdt, "Neighborhood Report for the Month of December, 1928," p. 6, CC, Box 23a, Folder "January 1928–April 4, 1929"; Interview with Bertacchi, p. 4, IAC; Interview with Kowalski, p. 46, IAC; Interview with Loguidice, p. 115, IAC; "Report on Juvenile Delinquency in the Near West Side," n.d., but c. 1946, Anthony Sorrentino Papers, Box 3, Folder 13, CHS. For further evidence of Italians feeling the effects of criminalization, see: the following IAC interviews: Faustini, p. 41; Giuliano, pp. 85–86; DeMarco, p. 29; Mirabella, p. 58; Provenzano, p. 76; Martorano, pp. 23–25. See also Bergreen, *Capone*, pp. 149-150; and Allsop, *The Bootleggers and Their Era*, p. 265.

20. On the Deportation Drive of 1930, see *CT*, June 3, 1930, p. 1.

21. *CT*, May 19, 1930; *Chicago American*, May 19, 1930; *Chicago Times*, November 20, 1930; all in CCC, Al Capone Folder 1, Al Capone Folder 1, Al Capone File 13190–1, respectively. For further evidence of newspapers' praising of Capone, see *CDN*, August 29, 1931; and *Chicago Post*, October 12, 1931, both in CCC Files, Al Capone File No. 13190–4; *CT*, July 19, 1930, p. 3; *CT*, December 5, 1930, p. 1; Hoffman, *Scarface Al and the Crime Crusaders*, pp. 7, 131; Bergreen, *Capone*, pp. 400–401.

22. Anon., *Does Crime Pay?*, p. 5; Anon., *Life of Al Capone in Pictures!*, p. 1. For more positive portrayals of Capone in pulps and books, see Enright, *Al Capone on the Spot*, pp. 16, 20; Sullivan, *Rattling the Cup*, pp. 44–45; Pasley, *Al Capone*, pp. 68–70, 86, 90; Burns, *The One-Way Ride*, p. 32. See also Ruth, *Inventing the Public Enemy*, pp. 118–143. In chap. 5, Ruth suggests that the inventors of Capone's image focused far less often on his negative traits than his positive ones—his toughness, virility, business acumen, individuality, efficiency, and generosity.

23. Pasley, *Al Capone*, p. 83; *Chicago American*, April 2, 1930, CCC Files, Al Capone Folder 2; Bergreen, *Capone*, p. 403; *Chicago American*, October 7, 1931, CCC Files, Al Capone File No. 13190–4; CCC handwritten notes, n.d., CCC Files, Al Capone File No. 13190–6; *Chicago Times*, October 8, 1931, CCC Files, Al Capone File No. 13190–4; *Chicago Evening American*, July 30, 1931, Al Capone Scrapbook. See also *Chicago Times*, November 20, 1930, CCC Files, Al Capone File No. 13190–1; *CHE*, February 26, 1931, Al Capone Scrapbook; Gerould, "Jessica and Al Capone," pp. 92–97. See also: Kobler, *Capone*, pp. 270–271, 313–319, 328; Allsop, *The Bootleggers and Their Era*, pp. 249–251, 289–294; Schoenberg, *Mr. Capone*, pp. 179, 303–304.

24. *CDN*, February 27, 1926, p. 9 (Brennan letter also reprinted in *LTIT*, March 6, 1926, p. 8); *CDN* clipping, n.d., but c. 1928, Martin Bickham Papers, Box 99, Folder 5, UIC (see reprint in *Mens Italica* [July 1928], CFLPS; and Jane Addams' similar sentiments in *CDN*, February 13, 1926, p. 1); *CDN*, February 15, 1926, p. 3; *Daily Jewish Forward*, February 18, 1926, CFLPS; *The New World*, June 5, 1925, p. 4; *CT*, February 15, 1926, p. 3.

25. Landesco, *Organized Crime in Chicago*, pp. xviii, 221. For some important works by these scholars, see Shaw, *Delinquency Areas*; Shaw, *The Jack-Roller*; Shaw and McKay, *Social Factors in Juvenile Delinquency*; Landesco, "Crime and the Failure of Institutions in Chicago's Immigrant Areas," pp. 238–248; Lan-

desco, "Life History of a Member of the Forty-Two Gang." One can follow the research of these scholars by examining the Ernest W. Burgess and John P. Landesco Papers at UC and those of Henry McKay and Clifford Shaw in the Chicago Area Project Papers at the CHS.

26. *CT*, September 15, 1928, p. 1; *CT*, November 28, 1928, p. 12; *CT*, September 10, 1928, p. 12. For other examples of biological (or quasi-biological) explanations for Italian crime, see Burns, *The One-Way Ride*, p. 123.

27. *CT*, September 12, 1928, p. 1; *CDN*, November 10, 1924, p. 1; *CHE*, January 26, 1925, CCC Files, Johnny Torrio File; *CDN*, May 17, 1929, CCC Files, Al Capone File No. 13190. For other examples of attention to Capone's "swarthy" features, see *CT*, July 19, 1930, p. 3; Enright, *Al Capone on the Spot*, p. 5.

28. Burns, *The One-Way Ride*, pp. 8, 121, 130, 132, 145, 154. See also *CT*, May 12, 1920, p. 1. On Italian characters in movies having dark complexions, see Rostow, *Born to Lose*, p. 43; Casillo, "Moments in Italian-American Cinema," p. 376.

29. Pasley, *Al Capone*, pp. 11–12; *Chicago American*, May 12, 1933, pp. 1–2; Henry Barret Chamberlin, Radio Talk over WBBM, February 11, 1931, CCC Files, Al Capone File 13190–1. For further examples of animalistic/savage/simian images of Capone, see Enright, *Al Capone on the Spot*, p. 5; Randolph, "How to Wreck Capone's Gang," p. 8; *CT*, December 6, 1927, p. 1; *Time* (September 21, 1931): 14; *New York Times*, October 8, 1931, p. 2; Hoffman, *Scarface Al and the Crime Crusaders*, pp. 131–132; Bergreen, *Capone*, pp. 402, 408. Some of these negative, racialized characteristics could be stressed in subtler ways as well. When Capone stood trial on tax evasion charges in 1931, for instance, the press made frequent comparisons between him and U.S. District Attorney and Chief Prosecutor George E. Q. Johnson. And these comparisons, pitting the "new" immigrant criminal versus the "old" American paragon of rectitude and order, invariably favored the latter. The *New York Times*, for instance, remarked that "Johnson's face is not crude like Capone's. Instead, it is distinctly gentle and gentlemanly" (June 21, 1931, p. 5). The *CT* observed similarly that "Capone's thick-featured face, the roll of flesh at the back of his neck, present a contrast to the attorney's [Johnson's] lean face, his shock of gray hair, and his general appearance of wiriness" (October 9, 1931, p. 1). In 1933, the magazine *The Real Detective* took these contrasts furthest in their article on Johnson— "The Man Who Broke Chicago's Gang Rule." In this piece, Johnson was portrayed as the perfect picture of ("old") American masculine virtue: "He has the sturdy, pioneering and fearless blood of rugged, Swedish pioneer stock. He was raised under the beating rays of an Iowa sun. Farm toil gave strength to his muscles and to his soul. Godliness was his credo from childhood. Always he has followed the hard road of work and right living and it has led him to success and accomplishment." Seen as Johnson's total antithesis, Capone was of "new" immigrant stock, who had made his fortunes not through "work and right living" but through corruption, violence, and reckless lawlessness. See Editor, "The Man Who Broke Chicago's Gang Rule," pp. 33–34.

30. Pasley, *Al Capone*, p. 113; *CT*, September 17, 1928, p. 1; *CT*, February 18, 1926, p. 3; Burns, *The One-Way Ride*, pp. 16, 5, 191, 239. See also Bergreen, *Capone*, pp. 402, 418; and Hoffman, *Scarface Al and the Crime Crusaders*, pp. 131–132. It should be noted that many of these representations of Italian gangsters as savage, swarthy, and simian died hard. As late as 1961, Kenneth Allsop described the Genna brothers as exhibiting "inbred savagery" and Anselmi and Scalise as being "strangely gorilla-like in appearance." Ten years

later, Kobler noted that the Gennas were prone to "lunatic spasms of savagery." See Allsop, *The Bootleggers and Their Era*, pp. 77 (quotation), 84–85, 88 (quotation); Kobler, *Capone*, pp. 15, 89, 162 (quotation). See also Schoenberg, *Mr. Capone*, p. 111.

31. *CD* (national ed.), July 7, 1928, pt. 2, p. 2; Philpott, *The Slum and the Ghetto*, p. 211; Edward A. Kirk, "Park Manor," paper for Sociology 264, 1933, BUR, Box 159, Folder 2. In *Inventing the Public Enemy*, David Ruth argues that "the ethnic gangster, partly through his smooth style, contributed to the replacement of complex, progressive-era racial taxonomies with the emerging conception of a monolithic white race" (p. 73). I would agree with Ruth that gangster imagery did little to ultimately undermine Italians' hold on whiteness. Still, because Italians' criminalization was often so deeply racialized, such imagery increased rather than decreased the importance of racial divisions within the white group.

32. J. G. Militello, "To the Slanderous Critics," *BIANU* (September 1928), p. 1, CFLPS; "Our Mission," *Vita Nuova* (April 1925), pp. 1–2, CFLPS; Andrea Russo to *CT*, December 12, 1928, reprinted in *LTIT*, January 12, 1929, p. 1; "In the Name of Justice," *BIANU* (June 1925), p. 1, CFLPS; *LTIT*, June 21, 1930, p. 1.

33. Mario Manzardo, "Pullman—The Prohibition Era: Zia Emilia Queen of the Stills," n.d. but c. 1973, Mario Manzardo Papers, no boxes, IHRC. For more on Italian women's involvement in alky-cooking at home, see J. O'Malley to Mayor William E. Dever, August 15, 1924, William E. Dever Mayoralty Papers, Box 3, Folder 26, CHS; Interview with DeMarco, p. 30, IAC. On Italian female criminals, see John Landesco, "The Gun Girl," n.d., John P. Landesco Papers, Box 1, Folder 4, UC.

34. On the masculine gendering of gangsters, see Ruth, *Inventing the Public Enemy*, pp. 127–128; Anon., *Life of Al Capone in Pictures!*, p. 1; Enright, *Al Capone on the Spot*, pp. 5, 16.

35. For interviews, see note 19. On the Italian Woman's Club, see Mrs. M. Elsa P. Serra to Frank Loesch, February 16, 1929, reprinted in *LTIT*, March 9, 1929, p. 1.

36. Anthony Sorrentino, "It's an Inside Job," unpublished typed manuscript, 1952, p. 19, Anthony Sorrentino Papers, CHS; Bergreen, *Capone*, p. 203; Landesco, "The Gun Girl." See also Candeloro, "Suburban Italians," p. 263.

37. The Italian-language press was often as critical of the English-language press for their mistreatment of Italians, as it was of compatriot criminals. See, for example, *LIT*, May 12, 1925, p. 1; *LIT*, September 16, 1928, p. 1; *LIT*, May 12, 1929, p. 1; *LIT*, May 15, 1932, p. 1; *LTIT*, December 24, 1927, p. 1; *LTIT*, February 18, 1928, p. 1; *LTIT*, September 15, 1928, p. 1; *LTIT*, September 29, 1928, p. 7; *LTIT*, January 19, 1929, p. 1; *LTIT*, March 22, 1930, p. 3; *LTIT*, March 29, 1930, p. 1; *LTIT*, July 19, 1930, p. 1; *LTIT*, August 9, 1930, p. 2; *LTIT*, September 5, 1931, p. 1; and "Our Mission," *Vita Nuova* (April 1925); "In the Name of Justice," *BIANU* (June 1925); "To the Slanderous Critics," *BIANU* (September 1928); "In Defense of the Sicilian People," *Vita Nuova* (September 1928): 1–4; "News from the News," *BIANU* (October 1928): 1–3; M. G. Farinacci, "Oppressed Sicily," pp. 1–5; "What the Italian Thinks of the Chicago Crime Situation," *Vita Nuova* (June 1930): 1–3; all in CFLPS. In part because the Italian-language press was in constant battle with newspapers like the *CT* regarding its treatment of Italians and crime, I cannot agree with Humbert Nelli's statement that "Any readers who depended solely on *L'Italia* or *La Tribuna Italiana Trans-*

atlantica for news during Prohibition years remained ignorant of the actions and notoriety of John Torrio and Al Capone." The former paper, it is true, relegated most of its news on gangster leaders like Capone and Torrio to its inside pages; but it covered these men with some regularity. *LTIT*, on the other hand, paid a good deal of attention to Capone, when he was arrested in Philadelphia, on trial for tax evasion charges in 1931, and so forth. For Nelli's quotation, see *The Italians in Chicago*, p. 221.

38. *LIT*, December 7, 1919, pp. 1–3, CFLPS; *CT*, February 12, 1926, p. 2; *CT*, February 15, 1926, p. 8; *CT*, February 19, 1926, p. 6. For further examples of Italians' support for American authorities or of their scolding *connazionali* criminals, see *Chicago Italian Chamber of Commerce Bulletin* (May 1926): 1–2, CFLPS; *LIT*, May 12, 1925, p. 1; *LIT*, March 25, 1928, p. 3; *LIT*, September 16, 1928, p. 1; *LIT*, December 6, 1931, p. 3; *LTIT*, November 21, 1925, p. 7; *LTIT*, March 13, 1926, p. 1; *LTIT*, July 23, 1927, p. 1; *LTIT*, September 22, 1928, p. 7; *LTIT*, September 29, 1928, p. 2. See *Il Lavoratore*, October 15, 1925, p. 4 for a similar scolding of Italians for their criminality from an Italian-language communist newspaper.

39. On the Italian consulate's fight against *connazionali* crime in Chicago, see *LTIT*, September 29, 1928, p. 3; *CT*, September 23, 1928, p. 1; *CT*, September 24, 1928, p. 12; *CT*, September 25, 1928, pp. 3, 15; *CT*, February 14, 1926, p. 1.

40. *CT*, February 24, 1926, p. 6. For further evidence of anti-Sicilian feelings and actions among Italians, see Interview with Pandolfi, p. 18, IAC; and Interview with De Falco, p. 14, IAC.

41. *LIT*, March 25, 1928, p. 3; "Our Mission," *Vita Nuova* (April 1925): 1–2; Farinacci, "Oppressed Sicily," *BIANU* (December 1928): 5; "In the Name of Justice," *BIANU* (June 1925): 2.

42. Schiavo, *The Italians in Chicago*, p. 125. See also the similar views of another community activist/intellectual, Cairoli Gigliotti: Cairoli Gigliotti to Julius Rosenwald, July 24, 1929, Julius Rosenwald Papers, Box 20, Folder 18, UC.

43. See *LIT*, September 17, 1922, p. 1; *LIT*, November 15, 1925, p. 1; *LIT*, February 17, 1929, p. 3; *LTIT*, July 4, 1925, p. 2; *LTIT*, September 22, 1928, p. 7; *LTIT*, June 21, 1930, p. 1; *LTIT*, July 19, 1920, p. 1; *LTIT*, September 5, 1931, p. 1. See also Militello, "To the Slanderous Critics," *BIANU* (September 1928): 1–8; "In Defense of the Sicilian People," *Vita Nuova* (September 1928): 1–4; both in the CFLPS.

44. *CT*, February 14, 1926, p. 6; *Il Lavoratore*, December 23, 1924, p. 2. On the left-wing, see also *L'Avanti*, November 15, 1918, pp. 1–3, CFLPS.

45. *CDN* clipping, n.d., but c. August 24, 1938, Roland Libonati Papers, Box "*New Generation* clippings," Envelope "W. Pegler," CHS; *LIT*, September 14, 1938, p. 1. Regarding the continuing criminalization of Italians in Chicago, community leaders in the early 1950s felt compelled to organize the Joint Civic Committee of Italian Americans after a mysterious murder (attributed to the "Mafia" by the *CT*) caused widespread anti-Italian hysteria in Chicago and caused one party to drop from their ticket an Italian candidate for Municipal Court Judge. For more on this story, see Interview with Sorrentino, side 1.

Chapter 5

1. *LTIT*, April 2, 1927, p. 2.

2. *CT*, March 29, 1915, p. 8; Bright, *Hizzoner Big Bill Thompson*, p. 59; Bukowski, *Big Bill Thompson*, p. 28; Green and Holli, *The Mayors*, p. 70; Gosnell,

Negro Politicians, pp. 37–62; Wendt and Kogan, *Big Bill of Chicago*, pp. 94–96, 103–104.

3. *CT*, September 30, 1915, p. 13; *CT*, September 17, 1915, p. 13; Tuttle, *Race Riot*, p. 201. See also Bukowski, *Big Bill Thompson*, p. 80.

4. Tuttle, *Race Riot*, p. 203. See also Spear, *Black Chicago*, pp. 187–189.

5. *LIT*, February 25, 1917; *LIT*, August 18, 1919; *LIT*, September 9, 1918; all in CFLPS. For further evidence of these points, see: *LIT*, October 31, 1920; *LIT*, September 5, 1920; *LIT*, March 9, 1912; *LIT*, September 15, 1912; *LIT*, March 30, 1919; all in CFLPS.

6. *LIT*, February 4, 1923, p. 1 (quotation); see also *LIT*, February 11, 18, 25, 1923; and *LTIT*, February 3, 11, 18, 25, 1923; and March 3, 1923; and Nelli, *The Italians in Chicago*, p. 222.

7. *LIT*, September 12, 1920, CFLPS.

8. Merriam and Gosnell, *Non-Voting*, p. 141; Schiavo, *The Italians in Chicago*, p. 106. On Italians' support for Barasa, see Nelli, *The Italians in Chicago*, p. 223.

9. Harold F. Gosnell, "The Unnaturalized: How to Interest Them in Citizenship," n.d., but c. 1924–1925, Charles E. Merriam Papers, Box 104, Folder 1, UC; Gosnell, "Characteristics of the Non-Naturalized," p. 848. See also "Chicago Commons Report of the Head Resident for the Year Ending September 30, 1933," p. 3, CC, Box 5, Folder "Annual and Other Reports, 1933–1935"; Taylor, *Chicago Commons through Forty Years*, p. 209. Why did so many Italians resist naturalizing? Based on interviews of over 250 Italians conducted in 1924, Harold Gosnell found that "ignorance of law" (31.1 percent), "ignorance of English" (24.4 percent), "indifference towards citizenship" (17.5 percent), and "planning to return to Europe" (9.9 percent) were all significant factors. See table "Reasons for Not Becoming Naturalized by Aliens or Specified Mother Tongue: Per Cent Distribution," Charles E. Merriam Papers, Box 104, Folder 6, UC.

10. Merriam and Gosnell, *Non-Voting*, pp. 224, viii.

11. Merriam and Gosnell, *Non-Voting*, pp. 42, 129–130.

12. Nelli, *The Italians in Chicago*, pp. 88–124; Gosnell, *Machine Politics*, p. 32; Pinderhughes, *Race and Ethnicity in Chicago Politics*, p. 94; [L. W. Crane], "Social Forces Affecting Benton House," May 1, 1942, p. 2, Benton House Papers, Box 3, Folder 15, CHS.

13. Allswang, *A House for All Peoples*, pp. 85–86, 89; Wooddy, *The Chicago Primary of 1926*, p. 185; "Precinct Captain by Party Faction and Father's Birthplace" and "Precinct Captain by Party Faction and Place of Birth"; both n.d., but c. mid-1920s, Charles E. Merriam Papers, Box 98, Folder 16, UC; and *Vita Nuova*, February 1925, and *LIT*, February 21, 1895; both in the CFLPS. It should be noted that Italians in some communities just outside of Chicago were more successful at getting elected to important posts. Melrose Park voters, for instance, elected two different Italians as mayor in the 1930s. See *BIANU* (April 1933); *BIANU* (May 1935); both in the CFLPS.

14. Gosnell, *Machine Politics*, pp. 85–90 (quotation, p. 86). On voter fraud and violence in Italian neighborhoods, see the following: "Poll Watcher's Reports," Citizens Association of Chicago Papers, Box 13, Folders 70–75, CHS; "Ward Committeeman—Progressive (Deneen) Ward 20, Judge Samuel Heller," n.d., pp. 4–6, Charles E. Merriam Papers, Box 99, Folder 2, UC; Interview with Scala, p. 11; Zorbaugh, *The Gold Coast and the Slum*, pp. 175, 178–180; and the following IAC interviews: Pandolfi, p. 20; Clementi, pp. 63–64; Manella, p. 38.

15. Gosnell, *Getting Out the Vote*, p. 66. On recent theory on "strategic mobi-

lization," see Rosenstone and Hansen, *Mobilization, Participation, and Democracy in America.*

16. Andersen, *The Creation of a Democratic Majority*, p. 93.

17. Regarding naturalization rates, in 1924, when Italians were roughly 7 percent of all foreign-born people in Chicago, they comprised more than 12 percent of people seeking to naturalize that year in Chicago courts. See Burgess and Newcomb, *Census Data of the City of Chicago, 1930*, p. 21; Harold F. Gosnell, "Naturalization and Non-Naturalization: A Study in Citizenship," n.d., p. 20, Charles E. Merriam Papers, Box 112, Folder 6, UC. Regarding generational issues, by 1930, the second-generation outnumbered the first by over thiry thousand people (107,901 to 73,960, respectively). See Burgess and Newcomb, *Census Data of the City of Chicago, 1930*, p. xv.

18. "Chicago Commons Report of the Head Resident for the Year Ending September 30, 1933," p. 3, CC, Box 5, Folder "Annual and Other Reports, 1933–1935."

19. Allswang, *A House for All Peoples*, p. 86; and see information on Democratic and Republican Ward committeemen, Box 98, Folders 10–14; and newspaper clippings, Box 101, Folder 6; all in Charles E. Merriam Papers, UC.

20. For evidence of repressive state activism shaping Italians' lives, see *CDN*, February 27, 1926, p. 3; *CT*, February 28, 1926, p. 7. On the state's more benevolent side, see Cohen, *Making a New Deal*, especially p. 258.

21. See the following from RG 196, Entry no. 2, NAII: Josephine Scimeca to Secretary Harold L. Ickes, April 18, 1934; Ann Dovichi to Franklin D. Roosevelt, April 29, 1935; Petition to Franklin D. Roosevelt from Near West Property Owners, n.d.; all in Box 84, Folder H–1400.09. Virginia Di Salvo to Franklin D. Roosevelt, February 20, 1938; Mrs. John Nardi to Franklin D. Roosevelt, January 23, 1938; Frank Riccio to Senator J. Hamilton Lewis, March 30, 1938; in Box 87, Folder H–1400.81. Michaelangelo Laspisa to Mrs. Franklin D. Roosevelt, n.d., but c. September 21, 1935; Property Owners to Franklin D. Roosevelt, petition, October 17, 1935; in Box 101, Folder H-1403.09. Charles Paolucci to Harold Ickes, November 26, 1935, Box 103, H-1405.09. On this point, see also Cohen, *Making a New Deal*, pp. 257–261.

22. Undated, typed William E. Dever speech, c. March–April 1927, William E. Dever Mayorality Papers, Box 8, Folder 61, CHS. For evidence of this debate, see *CHE*, March 23, 1927, p. 8; *CHE*, April 2, 1927, p. 8; *CHE*, April 4, 1927, pp. 8–9; *CT*, March 17, 1927, p. 10; *CT*, March 24, 1927, p. 1; *CT*, April 2, 1927, p. 10; *CD*, April 9, 1927, pt. 2, p. 2 (national ed.); *CDN*, March 26, 1927, p. 6; *CDN*, March 28, 1927, p. 5; and typed, undated Thompson speech, pp. 21, 24, Charles E. Merriam Papers, Box 89, Folder 10, UC.

23. *CT*, April 5, 1927, p. 1; *CHE*, March 27, 1927, p. 1. For more on newspapers' views on the centrality of color in the 1927 campaign, see also: *CDN*, April 4, 1927, p. 1; *CHE*, April 3, 1927, p. 1; *CT*, March 17, 1927, p. 10; *CT*, April 3, 1927, p. 2; *CD*, April 9, 1927, pt. 2, p. 2 (national ed.). See also *New Republic* 50 (April 6, 1927): 186; Bunche, "The Thompson-Negro Alliance," pp. 78–80. No secondary sources have ever dealt too extensively with the race/color aspects of the 1927 mayoral election. For work that has explored it to some degree, see the following: Allswang, *A House for All Peoples*, pp. 145–147; Bukowski, *Big Bill Thompson*, pp. 180–182; Stuart, *The Twenty Incredible Years*, pp. 302–306; Thurner, "The Impact of the Ethnic Groups on the Democratic Party in Chicago, 1920–1928," pp. 250–261; Wendt and Kogan, *Big Bill of*

Chicago, pp. 256–260, 267. For an important primary source, see Gosnell, *Negro Politicians*, pp. 54–55, 369–370.

24. "Equal Rights to All, Special Privileges to None. General Outlines of the Campaign," n.d., but c. March 1927, p. 2, William E. Dever Mayoralty Papers, Box 8, Folder 61, CHS.

25. *CT*, March 1, 1927, p. 1; *Chicago Daily Journal*, March 1, 1927, in DS; *CT*, April 4, 1927, p. 2.

26. *CHE*, March 26, 1927, p. 4; *CHE*, March 29, 1927, p. 1; *CT*, March 24, 1927, p. 2; *CT*, March 29, 1927, p. 3; *CT*, March 30, 1927, pp. 1, 6. See also *CDN*, March 15, 1927, p. 3; *CT*, March 15, 1927, p. 4.

27. *CT*, March 7, 1927, p. 3; *CHE*, March 8, 1927, in DS.

28. *CT*, March 10, 1927, p. 10; *CT*, March 11, 1927, p. 1; *CDN*, March 8, 1927, in DS.

29. *CT*, March 25, 1927, p. 7; *CDN*, March 24, 1927, p. 1.

30. *CT*, March 26, 1927, p. 4 (quotation). On posters, see *CT*, March 24, 1927, p. 1; *CT*, March 26, 1927, p. 5. On the handbill, see "Thompson—America First, Africa First," [1927], Broadside Collection, CHS. On other Thompson campaigners' accusations, see *CDN*, March 23, 1927, p. 5; *CDN*, March 18, 1927, p. 6; *CT*, March 19, 1927, p. 6; *CT*, March 26, 1927, p. 4.

31. *CT*, April 2, 1927, p. 2 (quotation). See also *CDN*, April 1, 1927, p. 5; and Stuart, *The Twenty Incredible Years*, p. 305.

32. *CHE*, April 1, 1927, p. 15; *CHE*, March 19, 1927, p. 9.

33. *CT*, March 29, 1927, p. 3; *CDN*, April 1, 1927, p. 1; *CT*, April 3, 1927, p. 1. For newspaper articles not already cited that spoke generally about many of these tactics, see *CHE*, March 12, 1927, p. 5; *CHE*, March 23, 1927, p. 4; *CHE*, March 28, 1927, p. 1; *CHE*, April 2, 1927, p. 8.

34. *CDN*, March 31, 1927, p. 3; *CDN*, March 14, 1927, p. 1; *CDN*, March 22, 1927, p. 1; *CDN*, March 30, 1927, p. 3; *CT*, March 14, 1927, p. 1; *CT*, March 20, 1927, p. 1; *CT*, March 23, 1927, p. 5; *CT*, March 26, 1927, p. 5; *CT*, March 27, 1927, p. 6. See also *New York Times*, April 1, 1927, pp. 1, 9.

35. *CT*, March 25, 1927, p. 3; *CDN*, April 4, 1927, p. 4; *CHE*, April 2, 1927, p. 9. For more on labor and the Democrats' color campaign, see *CHE*, March 28, 1927, p. 1; and *CT*, March 27, 1927, p. 1.

36. "On Guard White Voters" Flyer, Charles E. Merriam Papers, Box 103, Folder 11, UC; *The Austinite*, March 25, 1927, p. 36 (clipping) in Citizens Association of Chicago Papers, Box 22, Folder 2, CHS. For more on the Peoples Dever for Mayor Committee, see Schmidt, *"The Mayor Who Cleaned Up Chicago,"* pp. 157–158; *CT*, March 8, 1927, p. 2; *CT*, March 13, 1927, p. 14; *CDN*, March 28, 1927, p. 5.

37. *CT*, March 24, 1927, p. 1.

38. *CHE*, March 31, 1927, p. 5; Stuart, *The Twenty Incredible Years*, p. 306. For more on Thompson's and his allies' attacks on Dever and the Democrats, see the following: *CDN*, March 18, 1927, p. 6; *CDN*, March 23, 1927, p. 5; *CHE*, April 3, 1927, p. 4; *CHE*, March 8, 1927, in DS; *CDN*, March 8, 1927, in DS; *CT*, March 18, 1927, p. 6; *CT*, March 24, 1927, p. 1; *CT*, March 23, 1927, p. 6; typed, undated Thompson speech, pp. 21, 24, Charles E. Merriam Papers, Box 89, Folder 10, UC.

39. *CHE*, March 28, 1927, p. 1; *CHE*, March 29, 1927, p. 1; *CHE*, April 2, 1927, p. 8; *CHE*, April 4, 1927, quoted in Stuart, *The Twenty Incredible Years*, p. 314. See also: *CHE*, March 23, 1927, p. 8; *CHE*, April 3, 1927, p. 1.

40. *CDN*, March 24, 1927, p. 1; *CHE*, March 10, 1927, in DS.

41. *CD*, April 9, 1927, p. 2 (national ed.). On Roberts' resolution in Springfield, see *CHE*, March 16, 1927, p. 3. See also *CT*, March 10, 1927, p. 1; *CT*, March 11, 1927, p. 1.

42. *CT*, April 4, 1927, p. 4.

43. Stuart, *The Twenty Incredible Years*, p. 302; *CT*, March 19, 1927, p. 6.

44. *CT*, March 23, 1927, p. 6. For other examples of Thompson vehemently denouncing Democratic cartoons, see *CT*, March 31, 1927, p. 3.

45. *LIT*, April 3, 1927, p. 3; *CHE*, April 2, 1927, p. 9; *CT*, March 26, 1927, p. 5. For more on the Italian Committee for Dever, see *LIT*, March 29, 1927, p. 3; *LIT*, April 3, 1927, p. 6; *LTIT*, March 19, 1927, p. 2; *LTIT*, March 26, 1927, p. 2; *LTIT*, April 2, 1927, p. 2.

46. *LIT*, March 27, 1927, p. 3. On Thompson's *prominenti* allies, see *LIT*, February 6, 1927, p. 3; *LIT*, February 13, 1927, p. 3; *LIT*, February 20, 1927, p. 3; *LIT*, March 13, 1927, p. 3; *LIT*, April 3, 1927, p. 1; *LTIT*, March 19, 1927, p. 3; *LTIT*, February 19, 1927, pp. 6, 8.

47. *LTIT*, March 26, 1927, p. 7. For other pro-Thompson articles and ads in *LTIT*, see note 46.

48. Historian Humbert Nelli and former University of Chicago graduate student George Hoffman have both estimated Italian voting in Chicago's 1927 mayoral election and both have come up with exactly the same results, using voter registration lists to determine heavily Italian electoral precincts and then counting these same precincts' vote totals for Dever, Thompson, and Independent candidate Robertson. See Nelli, *The Italians in Chicago*, pp. 229–231; and Hoffman, "Big Bill Thompson," p. 44. Historian John Allswang has estimated that Thompson received 58 percent of the Italian vote in the 1927 mayoral race. His estimate, however, is less reliable than those of Nelli and Hoffman, because he used census tracts and census data to determine the voting population of particular precincts. The problem with this methodology is that it tells us only about population and nothing about actual voters. Precinct registration lists, by contrast, reveal precisely who was voting in particular units. For Allswang's estimates, see Allswang, *A House for All Peoples*, p. 161; Allswang, *Bosses, Machines, and Urban Voters*, p. 105. Allswang explains his methodology in *A House for All Peoples*, pp. 222–229.

49. Based on Nelli's figures, Thompson/Dever (respectively) vote percentages broke down by neighborhoods as follows: Armour Square 28 percent/71 percent; Near West Side 52 percent /45 percent; Near Northwest Side 70 percent /28 percent; Near North Side 70 percent /26 percent; city at large 51.39 percent /45.69 percent.

50. *CHE*, March 14, 1927, p. 5; *CHE*, April 4, 1927, p. 2. See also *CHE*, March 11, 1927, p. 3; *CDN*, March 16, 1927, p. 7.

51. *CHE*, April 1, 1927, p. 4.

52. *CT*, March 1, 1927, p. 1; *Chicago Daily Journal*, March 1, 1927, in DS. See also *CHE*, March 15, 1927, p. 5; *Chicago American*, March 1, 1927, in DS; Stuart, *The Twenty Incredible Years*, p. 311.

53. *Chicago Post*, March 8, 1927, in DS; *CHE*, February 27, 1927, in DS.

54. *LIT*, April 3, 1927, pp. 3, 6; *LTIT*, March 26, 1927, p. 7. See also *LIT*, February 6, 1927, p. 3; *LIT*, February 13, 1927, p. 3; *LIT*, February 20, 1927, p. 3; *LIT*, March 13, 1927, p. 3; *LIT*, April 3, 1927, p. 1; *LTIT*, March 19, 1927, pp. 3, 7; *LTIT*, February 19, 1927, pp. 4, 6, 8.

55. *CT*, February 2, 1931, p. 2.

56. *CT*, February 13, 1931, p. 4. On the "Lyle or Lawlessness" slogan, see *CT*,

February 5, 1931, pp. 1–2; *CT*, February 2, 1931, p. 2. For more on Capone as Lyle's primary opponent, see *CT*, February 12, 1931, pp. 1–2; *CHE*, February 13, 1931, p. 1; *CHE*, February 15, 1931, p. 1; *CT*, February 15, 1931, p. 3; *CT*, February 16, 1931, pp. 1–2. While Lyle was always primarily concerned with Capone, he often referred to a polyglot group of gangsters as paragons of Chicago lawlessness—Capone, Druggan, Moran, Guzik, O'Donnell, McErlane, and others. See *CT*, February 2, 1931, p. 2; *CT*, February 5, 1931, p. 2; *CT*, February 6, 1931, p. 1; *CT*, February 7, 1931, p. 2; *CT*, February 8, 1931, p. 5; *CT*, February 10, 1931, p. 1; *CT*, February 15, 1931, p. 3.

57. "The Campaign Opens," n.d., p. 6, Charles E. Merriam Papers, Box 90, Folder 4, UC.

58. For the "Thompson Trio" quotation, see *CT*, February 22, 1931, p. 4. For the two political cartoons, see *CT*, February 24, 1931, p. 12; *CT*, February 21, 1931, p. 1. For examples of the *CT* drawing explicit connections between Thompson and Italian gangsters and (allegedly) shady politicians, see the following: *CT*, February 12, 1931, pp. 1–2; *CT*, February 17, 1931, pp. 1, 3; *CT*, February 20, 1931, p. 3; *CT*, February 21, 1931, p. 3; *CT*, February 24, 1931, p. 2. The *CT* was not the only Chicago newspaper to draw these connections. The *CDN*, similarly, deplored the "Caponeization" of Chicago politics. See *CDN*, February 27, 1931, CCC, Al Capone File No. 13190–1. See also the following books on this connection: Allswang, *A House for All Peoples*, pp. 170–171; Nelli, *The Italians in Chicago*, pp. 224–227; Nelli, *The Business of Crime*, pp. 191–192; Pasley, *Al Capone*, p. 153; Peterson, *Barbarians in Our Midst*, pp. 121–151; Wendt and Kogan, *Big Bill of Chicago*, pp. 237–242, 250, 276, 280.

59. *CT*, February 23, 1931, p. 1; *CT*, February 24, 1931, p. 1.

60. *CHE*, February 5, 1931, p. 4; *CHE*, February 19, 1931, p. 3; *CHE*, February 20, 1931, p. 1; *CHE*, February 11, 1931, p. 2.

61. For 1931 primary vote totals, see Bukowski, *Big Bill Thompson*, p. 232. On Italians' voting patterns, *LTIT* reported that all Italian "quartieri" voted for Thompson, though this was only impressionistic. See *LTIT*, February 28, 1931, p. 3.

62. *LIT*, February 15, 1931, p. 1; *LTIT*, February 21, 1931, p. 7.

63. *CT*, March 27, 1931, p. 1; *CT*, April 7, 1931, p. 14.

64. On Serritella's arrest and alleged short-weighting scheme, see *CT*, April 5, 1931, p. 7; Gottfried, *Boss Cermak of Chicago*, pp. 234–235; Bukowski, *Big Bill Thompson*, p. 236; Peterson, *Barbarians in Our Midst*, pp. 153–154.

65. Gottfried, *Boss Cermak of Chicago*, p. 205; *CT*, April 6, 1931, p. 2. Numerous historians have commented on Thompson's "nativist" campaign against Cermak. For a sampling of this work, see the following: Allswang, *A House for All Peoples*, pp. 103–107, 158–160; Allswang, *Bosses, Machines, and Urban Voters*, p. 110; Andersen, *The Creation of a Democratic Majority*, p. 91; Bukowski, *Big Bill Thompson*, pp. 232–235; Cohen, *Making a New Deal*, p. 256; Kantowicz, *Polish-American Politics in Chicago*, pp. 152–153; Wendt and Kogan, *Big Bill of Chicago*, pp. 329–331.

66. Gottfried, *Boss Cermak of Chicago*, p. 226.

67. *CT*, March 24, 1931, p. 1; *CT*, March 27, 1931, p. 2; *CT*, March 29, 1931, p. 1; *CT*, March 24, 1931, p. 4; *CT*, March 30, 1931, p. 1. For more examples of newspapers decrying Thompson's "race bigotry," see *CT*, April 2, 1931, p. 5; *CT*, April 7, 1931, p. 2. For a response from the Thompson camp, see typed, undated speech, but c. March–April 1931, especially p. 5, William D. Saltiel Papers, Box 2, Folder "William Hale Thompson," CHS.

68. Green and Holli, *The Mayors*, p. 99 (quotation); for the five Cermak candidates, see Gottfried, *Boss Cermak of Chicago*, pp. 223–224.

69. Gottfried, *Boss Cermak of Chicago*, pp. 195, 208, 348, 400 n. 90; Allswang, *A House for All Peoples*, pp. 155, 160; Hirsch, "The Cook County Democratic Organization and the Dilemma of Race, 1931–1987," p. 66.

70. "An Appeal to Reason! Why the Negroes Should Vote Democratic Ticket"; Cermak Poster; both in Charles E. Merriam Papers, Box 102, Folder 6, UC. See the material in this folder for more evidence of Cermak's courting of African-American voters. For Cermak's campaigning in the Black Belt and his claims to have suffered from bigotry too, see *CT*, March 26, 1931, p. 3. See also the work cited above and: Biles, *Big City Boss in Depression and War*, pp. 89–90; Bukowski, *Big Bill Thompson*, p. 250; Reed, "Black Chicago Political Realignment during the Great Depression and New Deal," p. 246.

71. Gottfried, *Boss Cermak of Chicago*, p. 205; Republican Flyer, "Don't Bring the South to Chicago," Charles E. Merriam Papers, Box 102, Folder 6; "The Campaign Opens," n.d., p. 13, Charles E. Merriam Papers, Box 90, Folder 4, both in UC.

72. "Wake Up Democrats," Charles E. Merriam Papers, Box 102, Folder 6 UC; *CD*, April 4, 1931, p. 2 (Chicago ed.).

73. George Hoffman estimated that 50 percent of Italians voted for Thompson in the mayoral race of 1931; it can be inferred, therefore, that Cermak received close to 50 percent of the Italian vote as well. Allswang estimated that the Italian vote for Thompson and Cermak was 53 percent and 47 percent, respectively. Citing Allswang, Nelli stated that the Italian vote was 57 percent for Thompson and 43 percent for Cermak. It is likely that he inadvertently transposed these numbers. See Hoffman, "Big Bill Thompson," p. 58; Allswang, *A House for All Peoples*, p. 161; Nelli, *The Italians in Chicago*, p. 234.

74. Nelli, *The Italians in Chicago*, p. 234; *LIT*, April 5, 1931, p. 1. On Serritella's popularity among everyday Italians, see "Demonstrations for Serritella," *Vita Nuova*, February 1930, p. 23, CFLPS.

75. *Chicago Evening American*, March 28, 1931, quoted in Gottfried, *Boss Cermak of Chicago*, p. 223. For Cermak's building of a Democratic base among Italians, see *Il Bolletino Sociale*, March 3, 1931, CFLPS; *Vita Nuova*, May 1931, p. 29, CFLPS; *Vita Nuova*, March 1931, p. 29, CFLPS; *LTIT*, April 4, 1931, p. 4; *LIT*, March 29, 1931, p. 1.

76. *LTIT*, April 4, 1931, p. 4. For examples of pro-Thompson articles, see the following: *LIT*, March 15, 1931, p. 1; *LIT*, March 22, 1931, p. 1; *LIT*, March 29, 1931, p. 1; *LIT*, April 5, 1931, p. 1; *LTIT*, April 4, 1931, p. 3; *LTIT*, April 4, 1931, p. 4.

77. See note 80 below.

78. *LTIT*, February 14, 1931, p. 1. See also *LIT*, March 15, 1931, p. 1.

79. Scholars Geoff Eley, Nicholas Dirks, and Sherry Ortner have recently argued that "politics consists of the effort to domesticate the infinitude of identity. It is the attempt to hegemonize identity, to order it into a strong programmatic statement. If identity is decentered, politics is about the attempt to create a center." See Dirks et al., *Culture/Power/History*, p. 32.

80. *BOSIA* (March 1932), p. 4, CFLPS. For further examples of *Italianita'* not yet cited, see the following in the CFLPS: *Vita Nuova* (April 1930), p. 23; *Vita Nuova* (February 1925); *Vita Nuova* (October 1930), p. 28; *BIANU* (May 1933); *Il Bolletino Sociale* (March 3, 1931); *Il Bolletino Sociale* (November 10, 1930); *Chicago Italian Chamber of Commerce* (March 1929); *Il Bolletino Sociale* (Novem-

ber 24, 1928); *BIANU* (March 1928), p. 3; George Spatuzza, "Wake Up," *BOSIA* (May 1930) pp. 1–3; "To Our Boys and Girls," *BOSIA* (May 15, 1934), pp. 1–4; "Italian Victorious at the Polls," *BIANU* (November 1924), p. 1; "Our Duty towards the Italian Candidates," *BIANU* (October-November 1932), pp. 1–2. See also *LTIT*, August 31, 1929, p. 1.

81. On the Democratic Party's use of similar color campaign strategies at different times and in different places, see: Saxton, *The Rise and Fall of the White Republic*, pp. 127–154; Roediger, *The Wages of Whiteness*, pp. 72–76, 140–143; Goldfield, *The Color of Politics*.

82. Allswang, *A House for All Peoples*, p. 161.

83. *LIT*, September 14, 1924, p. 1.

Chapter 6

1. Smith, *Mussolini's Roman Empire*, p. 75.

2. *LIT*: June 15, 1924, p. 3; April 29, 1923, p. 3; July 15, 1923, p. 3; *LTIT*: March 28, 1925, p. 3; April 4, 1925, p. 1; April 25, 1925, p. 1; October 10, 1925, p. 3; February 27, 1926, p. 3; April 17, 1926, p. 3; January 22, 1927, p. 1; D'Agostino, "Missionaries in Babylon," p. 324; Nelli, *The Italians in Chicago*, p. 242. On Mussolini's views on and policies toward emigration and emigrants, see Finkelstein, "The Johnson Act, Mussolini and Fascist Emigration Policy," pp. 38–55; Gabaccia, *Italy's Many Diasporas*, pp. 141–144; and Cannistraro and Rosoli, "Fascist Emigration Policy in the 1920s," pp. 673–692.

3. Duffield, "Mussolini's American Empire," pp. 661–672.

4. *LIT*, April 2, 1925, p. 3; *LIT*, July 9, 1936, p. 3; *LIT*, August 14, 1932, p. 1; *LIT*, October 16, 1932, p. 1; *Chicago Evening Post*, November 16, 1929; Program for Contest Dance, March 24, 1935, George J. Spatuzza Papers, Box 8, Folder 7, IHRC; Italian Woman's Club Speech, n.d., Rosamond L. Mirabella Papers, Box 1, Folder 1, UIC. For more on the influence/activity of the Italian consul/consulate in Chicago, see *LIT*, August 4, 1929, p. 3; *LIT*, October 13, 1929, p. 2; *LIT*, October 20, 1929, p. 2; *LIT*, June 4, 1933, p. 1; *LIT*, August 6, 1933, p. 1; *BOSIA* (October 1936), CFLPS; "Frustrating the Fascists," n.d. but c. 1942, typescript, p. 4, George L. Quilici Papers, Box 3, Folder 18, IHRC; Interview with Judge George L. Quilici, August 7, 1945, p. 2, Foreign Populations in Chicago Collection, Folder 3, CHS; Program for the "South End Columbus Monument Celebration," October 9, 1932, in Maurice R. Marchello Papers, Box 4, Folder 35, IHRC; D'Agostino, "Missionaries in Babylon," pp. 321–322, 326, 329–333, 342, 361–363, 376, 381; Candeloro, "Chicago's Italians," p. 244.

5. *Vita Nuova*, April–May 1928, p. 8, CFLPS. The best discussion of fascism's infiltration into Chicago's Italian communities is in D'Agostino, "Missionaries in Babylon," pp. 319–397. On the power of fascism within particular Italian institutions in Chicago: on the Catholic Church, see D'Agostino, "Missionaries in Babylon," pp. 9, 333–397; Shaw, "The Catholic Parish as a Way Station of Ethnicity and Americanization," pp. 224–225. On the Italian-language press, *LIT* featured fascist-friendly articles in virtually every issue; for some representative early articles, see November 19, 1922, p. 1; January 23, 1927, p. 1; May 26, 1929, p. 5; October 27, 1929, p. 3; March 27, 1932, p. 1; May 8, 1932, p. 1; on *LIT*'s fascist leanings, see also Norman, "Italo-American Opinion in the Ethiopian Crisis: A Study of Fascist Propaganda," p. 23; George L. Quilici to William J. Connor, July 12, 1944, George L. Quilici Papers, Box 3, Folder 17, IHRC. *LTIT* was as enthralled with fascism as was *LIT*. See, for example, *LTIT*,

January 10, 1925, p. 1; *LTIT*, August 22, 1925, p. 1; *LTIT*, November 6, 1926, p. 1; *LTIT*, September 21, 1929, p. 1. On fraternal orders, see "Frustrating the Fascists," pp. 1–4; *LIT*, August 24, 1929, p. 3; Albert Perry, "The Italian-Americans of Chicago," typed report submitted to the Foreign Nationalities Branch, Office of Strategic Services, October 2, 1942, pp. 9–17, RG 226, INT-17IT-489 (micro), NAII; D'Agostino, "Missionaries in Babylon," pp. 342, 363, 385, 397; Duffield, "Mussolini's American Empire," p. 664; Panunzio, "Italian Americans, Fascism, and the War," pp. 777–778. On schools, see the following fascist textbooks at the IHRC: Direzione Generale degli Italiane all'Estero, *Il Libro della IV Classe Elementare*; Bagaglia, *Letture Classe Prima*; Bagaglia, *Letture Classe Terza*; Direzione Generale Italiani all'Estero e Scuole, *Letture Classe Seconda*.

6. On Americans' enthusiasm for Italian fascism, see Diggins, *Mussolini and Fascism*; and Panunzio, "Italians Americans, Fascism, and the War," p. 777. On the *CT*, see: *CT*, July 24, 1925, p. 8; *CT*, July 29, 1925, p. 8; *CT*, December 11, 1928, p. 20. Evidence of the *CT*'s critical treatment of fascism can also be found in Italian-language newspapers' scathing responses to the *CT* (see, for example, *LIT*, July 26, 1925, p. 1; *LIT*, August 4, 1929, p. 3; *LIT*, August 2, 1925, p. 3; *LTIT*, April 4, 1925, p. 7; *LTIT*, August 22, 1925, p. 3; *LTIT*, November 28, 1925, p. 7; *LTIT*, July 9, 1927, p. 7); as well as in letters between the Italian consul in Chicago and the Italian ambassador in Washington (see, for instance, Castruccio to De Martino, January 4, 1929, RG 242, Mussolini Papers [micro], Series T586, Container 426, frame nos 017324–017326, NAII). On the Hearst-owned Chicago papers, see *CHE*, October 7, 1935, p. 1; *CHE*, October 6, 1935, pt. 4, p. 8; *LIT*, October 4, 1931, p. 2; *LIT*, December 4, 1932, p. 1; *LTIT*, April 25, 1925, p. 10; *LTIT*, September 25, 1926, p. 6; Norman, "Italo-American Opinion," pp. 215–216; Diggins, *Mussolini and Fascism*, pp. 31, 48–49, 300. On Hearst's fascist affections, see RG 242, Mussolini Papers (micro), Series T586, Container 426, frame nos. 013024–013074, NAII. On the *News*, see, for the interview, *CDN*, May 24, 1924, pp. 1, 7; for the reference, see *CDN*, May 26, 1924, p. 8. Another Chicago newspaper enthralled with Mussolini and fascism was the *Chicago Journal*. For examples of their glowing editorials, see their reprints in *LTIT*, April 17, 1926, p. 3; *LTIT*, May 7, 1927, p. 2. Even the *CT* on occasion could treat fascism favorably. See, for example, "Frustrating the Fascists," p. 3; Diggins, *Mussolini and Fascism*, pp. 31, 288. It should be noted that foreign correspondents in Italy at this time were subject to severe censorship and banishment from Italy if fascists disapproved of their writing. George Seldes, a *CT* writer, was forced to leave Italy in 1925 for these reasons. Conversely, writers supporting Italy could receive fascist favors. For more information on fascist censorship and favors, see Diggins, *Mussolini and Fascism* pp. 42–46.

7. Salvemini, *Fascist Activities in the United States*; Diggins, *Mussolini and Fascism*, pp. 78–81; Panunzio, "Italian Americans, Fascism, and the War," p. 775; Nelli, *The Italians in Chicago*, p. 241; Philip V. Cannistraro, "Fascism and Italian Americans," pp. 58–59; Campisi, "The Adjustment of the Italian Americans to the War Crisis," pp. 224–225; "Italian Aliens: Attitudes towards the U.S. and Enemy Alien Status," Bureau of Intelligence, Office of Facts and Figures, May 25, 1942, p. 2, RG 44, Box 1848, Folder 2, NAII.

8. "Italians and Sicilians," *BIANU* (March 1927), p. 2, CFLPS; Castruccio quotation in D'Agostino, "Missionaries in Babylon," p. 361. Examples of Italian-language newspapers' nation/race-building projects are far too numerous to cite here. For some representative examples, see the following articles: *LIT*: April 4, 1920, p. 1; January 1, 1922, p. 1; February 24, 1923, p. 1; March 7, 1926, p. 1;

April 3, 1927, p. 1; November 20, 1927, p. 1; February 19, 1928, p. 2; September 23, 1928, p. 2; November 24, 1928, p. 2; October 27, 1929, p. 3; March 8, 1931, p. 1; January 3, 1932, p. 1; March 27, 1932, p. 1; June 19, 1932, p. 4; August 14, 1932, p. 1; October 16, 1932, p. 1; March 26, 1933, p. 8; August 6, 1933, p. 1. *LTIT*: May 16, 1925, p. 7; May 23, 1925, p. 1; January 1, 1927, p. 1; March 5, 1927, p. 3; March 13, 1927, p. 3; March 19, 1927, p. 3; November 10, 1928, p. 1; April 20, 1929, p. 1; April 27, 1929, p. 1; September 21, 1929, p. 1; October 5, 1929, p. 1; October 12, 1929, p. 1; October 26, 1929, p. 1; November 3, 1929, p. 1; April 19, 1930, p. 1. For secondary sources that stress fascists' attempts to build a "national diaspora," see: Cannistraro, "Fascism and Italian Americans," pp. 51–66; Gabaccia, *Italy's Many Diasporas*, pp. 141–144; Cannistraro, *Blackshirts in Little Italy*, pp. 5–6, 112–113.

9. Schiavo, *The Italians in Chicago*, p. 118; *Chicago Evening Post*, November 16, 1929; Interview with Bertacchi, p. 23, IAC; Interview with De Falco, p. 20, IAC. For further evidence of the popular support of fascism among Italians in Chicago and elsewhere in the United States, see also Interview with Colella, pp. 11–12, IAC; Gaetano Salvemini to George Quilici, September 24, 1942, George L. Quilici Papers, Box 3, Folder 17, IHRC; Campisi, "The Adjustment of the Italian Americans to the War Crisis," pp. 130–163; Panunzio, "Italian Americans, Fascism, and the War," pp. 774–778; Cannistraro, "Fascism and Italian Americans," pp. 51–66; Candeloro, "Chicago's Italians," p. 244.

10. *La Parola Proletaria*, May 3, 1923 and August 4, 1923, cited in Bessie L. Pierce Papers, Box 166, Folder "Italians General," CHS; *La Parola del Popolo*, March 2, 1923; *La Parola del Popolo*, August 4, 1923; *La Parola dei Socialisti*, February 17, 1923; all in CFLPS. On Italian language communist papers, see the Workers' Party of America's *Il Lavoratore*, especially June 27, 1924 (micro), IHRC. On the IWO, see Keeran, "The Italian Section of the International Workers Order, 1930–1950," pp. 25–26; and Rapporto della Conferenza dei Delegati Italiani alla Terza Convenzione Biennale, May 7–9, 1935, pp. 5–8, IWO. On "anti-Fascist terrorists," see John W. Bennett and Herbert Passin, "Major Tension Areas in Chicago," typed Office of War Information report, December 1942, p. 24, RG 44, Box 1840, Folder "Chicago—Passin, Herbert," NAII. On labor union anti-fascism, see Interview with De Maio, November 16, 1970, p. 32, RULOHP; see speeches and clippings in Emilio Grandinetti Papers, Box 1, Folder 15, IHRC. On the "Centro Operaio di Roseland," see "Liberi Cuori," typed manuscript, n.d., p. 7, Mario Manzardo Papers, Box 1, no folders, IHRC; *CT*, October 20, 1935, p. 16. On street battles, see "Study of Non-Delinquents in a Delinquent Area," 1941, p. 27, Anthony Sorrentino Papers, Box 2, Folder 21, CHS.

11. Higham, *Strangers in the Land*, pp. 194–233; Candeloro, "Chicago's Italians," p. 244; see also Hoerder, *The Immigrant Labor Press in North America*, v. 3, pp. 97–98 for how the federal government after World War I forced Italians' most prominent left-wing newspaper in Chicago to change its name multiple times in a few years to avoid suppression.

12. The *Chicago American* and the *Chicago Daily Times* quotations are from *LIT*, July 23, 1933, p. 6. On Chicago's rousing reception of Balbo, see also Colonel Carlo Tempesti to L. H. Shattuck, July 24, 1933, CHS. That a major city street bore Balbo's name gave rise to battles among Italian Americans between those who wanted to change the street's name and those who did not. See George Quilici to Paul Douglas, June 21, 1940; and Paul Douglas to George Quilici, February 24, 1942; both in George L. Quilici Papers, Box 4, Folder 21,

IHRC; V. E. Ferrara to Ralph Argento, December 16, 1946, Near West Side Community Committee Records, Folder 458, UIC; *LIT*, December 22, 1941, p. 1. The street still bears Balbo's name to this day.

13. *CT*, July 16, 1933, p. 2; *LIT*, July 9, 1933, p. 1; *LIT*, July 16, 1933, p. 1; *LIT*, July 23, 1933, p. 6.

14. Interview with De Falco, pp. 19–20, IAC; Interview with Leonardi, p. 4, IAC. On Balbo's landing, see also the following IAC interviews: Cosentino, p. 32; Moreschi, p. 30; Accettura, p. 24; Morandin, p. 35; DeStefano, p. 17; Sister Augustine (Cutrara), p. 44. See, also, photograph of glowing West Side physician, Salvatore Mirabella, posing with Balbo in Rosamond Mirabella Papers, Box 2, Folder 10, UIC; Candeloro, "Chicago's Italians," p. 242; Campisi, "The Adjustment of the Italian Americans to the War Crisis," p. 140; Panunzio, "Italian Americans, Fascism, and the War," p. 777; *CT*, July 16, 1933, p. 2. It should be noted that the fascist state, primarily through Consul General Castruccio and the organizers of the World's Fair, worked together meticulously for over a year to plan Balbo's landing and welcome. See Century of Progress Records, accession nos. 2–1102, 2–1103, UIC.

15. Candeloro, "Chicago's Italians," p. 242; see also clipping of scathing anti-Balbo editorial from Italian socialists that appeared in the *Milwaukee Leader*, June 24, 1933, in George L. Quilici Papers, Box 4, Folder 21, IHRC.

16. The Italian left organized as much opposition to the war as they could muster, marching with African Americans on Chicago's South Side to demonstrate the working-class solidarity of the two communities and writing scathing editorials in their newspapers that condemned fascism and Mussolini for their barbarous imperialism. Still, these efforts proved no match for the jubilant tidal wave of prowar support—both institutional and popular—that washed over Italian-American communities in 1935 and 1936. On the activities of the Italian left, see *CD*, June 22, 1935, p. 1; *Il Proletario*, September 7, 1935, p. 1; *Il Proletario*, August 1, 1935, p. 1; *Il Proletario*, August 15, 1935, p. 2; *Il Proletario*, December 15, 1935, p. 1; *CT*, September 7, 1935, p. 10.

17. *LIT*, May 19, 1935, p. 1; *LIT*, September 22, 1935, p. 3; *LIT*, October 6, 1935, p. 3; *LIT*, March 10, 1935, p. 5; *LIT*, May 12, 1935, p. 6; *LIT*, November 24, 1935, p. 1; *LIT*, October 27, 1935, p. 1; *LIT*, May 10, 1936, p. 3; *LIT*, December 29, 1935, p. 8; *LIT*, June 16, 1935, p. 1; *LIT*, May 3, 1936, p. 1; *LIT*, October 13, 1935, p. 1. On the war coverage of *Il Progresso Italo-Americano*—a New York-based paper that had a wide circulation in Chicago—see the extensive scrapbooks in the Olga Gralton Papers, IHRC.

18. *LIT*, May 10, 1936, p. 3; *LIT*, January 26, 1936, p. 3; *Chicago Italian Chamber of Commerce Bulletin* (October 1935), CFLPS; *BOSIA* (October 1936), CFLPS; *BOSIA* (July 1937), CFLPS; see also George Spatuzza speeches in George J. Spatuzza Papers, Box 11, Folder 11 and Box 13, Folders 4, 6, and 7, IHRC; D'Agostino, "Missionaries in Babylon," pp. 356–358.

19. D'Agostino, "Missionaries in Babylon," pp. 353–358; *Bolletino Parrochiale della Chiesa di Sant'Antonio*, no. 8 (August 1936): 6–7.

20. Chicago Commons Annual Report, 1937, p. 6, CC, Box 5, Folder "Annual and Other Reports, 1937–1940"; "Preliminary Report," n.d. but c. 1936–1937, p. 6, CC, Box 12, Folder "Adult Education, 1937–September 1938"; Glenford W. Lawrence, "Preliminary Workers Education Report, 1937–1938," p. 13, CC, Box 12, Folder "Adult Education October 1938–1939"; *LIT*, September 22, 1935, p. 3; *LIT*, October 20, 1935, p. 3; *LIT*, December 1, 1935, p. 3; *LIT*, December 15, 1935, p. 2; *LIT*, May 17, 1936, p. 3.

21. *CDN*, n.d. but c. May 1936, Community Clippings File, Folder "Ethnic Groups—Italians," CHS; *CT*, May 25, 1936, p. 3; Interview with D'Angelo, pp. 36–37, IAC; Glenford Lawrence, "Significant Statements," typescript, November 1941, CC, Box 12, Folder "Adult Education, 1940–1941"; Interview with Scala, pp. 9–10; *LIT*, May 31, 1936, p. 3; Memo from Glenford Lawrence to Lea Taylor, November 18, 1935, CC, Box 12, Folder "Adult Education, 1934–1936." For more on Italians' popular support for the war in Chicago, see *LIT*, May 31, 1936, p. 2 for a photo of an Italian post-"victory" celebration, which drew, according to the paper, forty thousand people; and Office of War Information, "Group Attitudes and Prejudices in the War Effort: The Italian Minority," typed report, July 27, 1942, p. 1, RG 44, Box 1848, Folder 3, NAII.

22. On civilizing missions, see Adas, *Machines as the Measure of Men*, pp. 199–270; Brantlinger, *Rules of Darkness*, pp. 8, 73–107; McClintock, *Imperial Leather*, pp. 207–231; Ware, *Beyond the Pale*, pp. 126–134.

23. Smith, *Mussolini's Roman Empire*, p. 65; Goglia, *Storia Fotografica dell'Impero Fascista*, pp. 77–78, image nos. 72–77. See also fascist pamphlet published for American consumption, *Italy and Abyssinia*, pp. 45–51; and Carter, *Black Shirt Black Skin*, p. 53.

24. Untitled Scrapbook, no page numbers, Olga Gralton Papers, IHRC. See the Gralton collection for more on the civilizing mission ideology in *Il Progresso Italo-Americano*, especially scrapbooks, v. 1–5 and untitled scrapbooks. These words about "Italy's noble intentions" and so forth were taken verbatim from *Italy and Abyssinia*, pp. 45, 51. For *LIT*, see especially *LIT*, May 19, 1935, p. 1; *LIT*, November 24, 1935, p. 1; *LIT*, March 10, 1935, p. 5.

25. Speech at "Banchetto Coloniale in Celebrazione della Vittoria delle Armi Italiane in Etiopia e della Fondazione del Nuovo Impero Italiano," May 24, 1936, Box 13, Folder 6; see also: "Inaugurazione della Loggia Femminile Regina Elena," typed speech, Box 12, Folder 11; Speech before OSIA in celebration of Columbus Day and of the graduation of Italian university students, 1936, Box 13, Folder 4; Speech in honor of Dr. Eugene Chesrow, October 17, 1936, Box 13, Folder 6; all in George J. Spatuzza Papers, IHRC.

26. *Il Proletario*, November 15, 1935, p. 1.

27. Interview with Bertacchi, p. 23, IAC; *CD*, May 2, 1936, p. 16; Interview with Anonymous; Frazzetta quoted in Vecoli, "The African Connection," p. 15.

28. Bederman, *Manliness and Civilization*.

29. See *Il Progresso Italo-Americano* clippings in Olga Gralton Papers, IHRC; *LIT*, May 10, 1936, p. 3; *LIT*, November 24, 1935, p. 1; Goglia, *Storia Fotografica dell'Impero Fascista, 1935–1941*, p. 38, image no. xi.

30. See note 7 above.

31. *LIT*, October 13, 1935, p. 1.

32. *LIT*, July 21, 1935, p. 8; *LIT*, October 13, 1935, p. 5.

33. Quoted in Padmore, "Ethiopia and World Politics," p. 157. On Italian fascists' drawing of the color line, see Smith, *Mussolini's Roman Empire*, pp. 42–43, 46, 65, 112–113, 123; *CD*, June 29, 1935, p. 16; *CD*, July 13, 1935, p. 12; Peffer, "The White Peril," especially p. 608. After the war Italian fascists became stricter enforcers of the white/black color line in Ethiopia. On the hardening of color lines in colonial Ethiopia, see Sbacchi, *Ethiopia under Mussolini*, pp. 167–175; see also the following *LIT* articles on these developments: *LIT*, February 28, 1937, p. 8; *LIT*, July 27, 1938, p. 1; *LIT*, August 8, 1938, p. 1.

34. Quoted in Norman, "Italo-American Opinion in the Ethiopian Crisis," pp. 79–80.

35. Program for the "Banchetto Coloniale"; *CT*, October 9, 1935, p. 14.

36. Quoted in D'Agostino, "Missionaries in Babylon," p. 357.

37. *Il Proletario*, November 15, 1935, p. 1; "Frustrating the Fascists," p. 3. See also *Il Proletario*, December 15, 1935, p. 1.

38. *CT*, October 2, 1935, p. 4; *LIT*, January 5, 1936, p. 3; *LIT*, February 13, 1936, p. 3; Hansberry quoted in Scott, *The Sons of Sheba's Race*, p. 55; Drake and Cayton, *Black Metropolis*, p. 89.

39. On these activities, see *New York Times*, August 4, 1935, p. 28; Scott, *The Sons of Sheba's Race*, especially pp. 136–146; Harris, *African-American Reactions to War in Ethiopia*, pp. 34–84; Venturini, *Neri e Italiani ad Harlem*, especially pp. 119–209; Ventresco, "Italian-Americans and the Ethiopian Crisis," pp. 8–10; Diggins, *Mussolini and Fascism*, pp. 306–312; Plummer, *Rising Wind*, pp. 44–56.

40. On the Joint Conference, see *CD*, September 7, 1935, p. 1; Arthur G. Falls to the Chicago Federation of Labor, August 12, 1935; Arthur G. Falls to the Chicago Federation of Labor, August 15, 1935; and Petition to "Stop Mussolini's Robber War" and Petititon for "Hands Off Ethiopia"; all in the Chicago Federation of Labor Papers, Box 25, Folder "Negro and Civil Rights Items," CHS. On the Negro World Alliance, see *CD*, June 22, 1935, p. 1; Scott, *The Son's of Sheba's Race*, pp. 59, 101, 138, 215. On the Society, see Scott, *The Sons of Sheba's Race*, pp. 101, 119. See also Storch, "Shades of Red," pp. 165–167; Haywood, *Black Bolshevik*, pp. 447–457; *FN*, September 7, 1935, p. 2. Despite African Americans' and Italians' ardent interests in the war, I have found no evidence of any violence occurring between the two groups in Chicago. This is in contrast to the volatile and violent situation in New York, for instance. On New York, see note 39.

41. *CD*, June 29, 1935, pp. 16, 3; Kelley, *Race Rebels*, p. 129; Scott, *The Sons of Sheba's Race*, pp. 69–80; Harris, *African-American Reactions to War in Ethiopia*, pp. 56–57.

42. *CD*, July 13, 1935, p. 12. See also Du Bois, "Inter-Racial Implications of the Ethiopian Crisis," especially p. 83; Rogers, "Italy over Abyssinia," pp. 38–39, 50.

43. Pierce, "Fascism and the Negro," p. 107; *CD*, October 12, 1935, p. 18. See also Young, "Ethiopia Awakens," p. 262; Haynes, "Negroes and the Ethiopian Crisis," p. 1485.

44. Du Bois, "Inter-Racial Implications of the Ethiopian Crisis," p. 82. For further evidence that African Americans believed Ethiopians to be their "Negro" brothers and sisters, see Haynes, "Negroes and the Ethiopian Crisis," p. 1486; Rogers, "Italy over Abyssinia," p. 50; Scott, *The Sons of Sheba's Race*, pp. xiii, 8, 32, 163, 194–195, 199.

45. Hughes quoted in Roediger, *Black on White*, pp. 124-125; *CD*, November 26, 1938, p. 18. See also Haynes, "Negroes and the Ethiopian Crisis," p. 1485.

46. Haynes, "Negroes and the Ethiopian Crisis," p. 1486; Du Bois, "Inter-Racial Implications of the Ethiopian Crisis," pp. 87–88. See also: *CD*, October 26, 1935, p. 18; *CD*, January 4, 1936, p. 23; *CD*, March 14, 1936, p. 16; *CD*, July 27, 1935, p. 10; Scott, *The Sons of Sheba's Race*, pp. 4–6; Kelley, "'But a Local Phase of a World Problem'," pp. 1066–1067. For more on Du Bois's race/color conceptions in these years, see Guterl, *The Color of Race in America*.

47. Ford, *The Negro and the Democratic Front*, pp. 163–164, 159, 162–163. For more on Ford and the CP's grappling with the Italian-Ethiopian War, see Kelley, *Race Rebels*, p. 131; Scott, *The Sons of Sheba's Race*, pp. 36, 43, 48, 67, 92, 107, 110–112, 126; Diggins, *Mussolini and Fascism*, p. 308; Jacobson, *Whiteness of a Different Color*, p. 319 n. 16; Solomon, *The Cry Was Unity*, pp. 270–272.

48. *CHE*, October 1–10, 1935; quotation from October 6, 1935, pt. 4, p. 8; *CDN*, September 30, 1935, p. 15. See also Courtney, "Blackshirt Heaven," pp. 12–13, 51–52, 54; Courtney, "Dark and Bloody Road," pp. 29–30; and Stoddard, "Men of Color Aroused," pp. 35–36, 57. See also *The New World*, the weekly publication of Chicago's Archdiocese, which never exactly supported Italy's civilizing rhetoric, but nevertheless subtly defended its war with Ethiopia by devoting the bulk of its energy to attacking Italy's opponents—mainly England and France—for their rank "hypocrisy." See, for example, *The New World*: August 30, 1935, p. 4; September 6, 1935, p. 4; September 13, 1935, p. 4; November 8, 1935, p. 4; November 22, 1935, p. 4; and December 6, 1935, p. 4.

49. *CT*, October 8, 1935, p. 12; *CDN*, October 4, 1935, p. 24. See also *CT*, August 20, 1935, p. 1; *CT*, September 7, 1935, p. 10; *CT*, October 29, 1935, p. 1; and *CDN*, July 2, 1935, p. 14. It should be noted that the *CT* initially supported an Italian presence in Ethiopia. See Diggins, *Mussolini and Fascism*, pp. 287–288. For similarly critical views from Chicago's AFL publication—the *FN*—see: May 12, 1934, p. 4; September 14, 1935, p. 4; October 5, 1935, p. 4; May 23, 1936, p. 12; June 20, 1936, p. 3; May 1, 1936, p. 6.

50. Courtney, "Blackshirt Heaven," pp. 52, 54, 52; *New Republic* 84 (October 2, 1935): 197; *New Republic* 84 (October 16, 1935): 253; *New Republic* 84 (September 18, 1935): 141; *Nation* 141 (October 16, 1935): 425; Roosevelt quotation from Schmitz, *The United States and Fascist Italy*, p. 157. For further evidence of Americans' (apart from African Americans already discussed) questioning of Italy's avowed civilizing mission, see *Nation* 141 (July 10, 1935): 34; *Nation* 141 (July 17, 1935): 58; *Nation* 141 (September 4, 1935): 257; *Nation* 141 (October 2, 1935): 368; Stewart, "Mussolini's Dream of Empire," pp. 548–549; Peffer, "The White Peril," pp. 606–609; Carter, *Black Shirt Black Skin*, pp. 159, 178; Coon, "A Realist Looks at Ethiopia," p. 310; Diggins, *Mussolini and Fascism*, pp. 296–302.

51. *CT*, September 22, 1935, pt. 1, p. 20; *CT*, October 18, 1935, p. 16; *CT*, October 9, 1935, p. 14; *LIT*, October 13, 1935, p. 1; *CT*, October 9, 1935, p. 14; *CT*, October 15, 1935, p. 12. See also *CT*, October 23, 1935, p. 14.

52. Stoddard, "Men of Color Aroused," p. 35; Villard, "Issues and Men—War in Ethiopia," p. 287; Carter, *Black Shirt Black Skin*, p. 161. Also, Chicago newspapers, their harsh treatment of Italians notwithstanding, often explicitly categorized them as white. See, for example, *CT*, November 12, 1935, p. 12; and *CDN*, October 31, 1935, p. 1.

53. Coon, "A Realist Looks at Ethiopia," pp. 313–314; Peffer, "The White Peril," p. 609. See also: *Newsweek* 6 (August 10, 1935): 5; *Newsweek* 6 (September 21, 1935): 5.

54. That *Italianita'* was on the rise does not mean that an American identity was not. Becoming Italian and American were not mutually exclusive processes, as we will see in greater detail in the next three chapters. For an example of *Italianita'* and Americanism coexisting, see the following George Spatuzza speeches: Speech at the Victory Banquet for Ethiopia, May 24, 1936, Box 13, Folder 6; Speech at the "Inaugurazione della Loggia Femminile Regina Elena," 1936, Box 12, Folder 11; untitled speech, November 25, 1934, Box 11, Folder 29; all in George J. Spatuzza Papers. On this point, see also the following secondary sources: D'Agostino, "Missionaries in Babylon," 382–383; D'Agostino, "The Scalabrini Fathers, the Italian Emigrant Church and Ethnic Nationalism in America," p. 149; Gabaccia, *Italy's Many Diasporas*, p. 148.

55. For Italy's attempts to harden color lines in Ethiopia, and for *LIT*'s cover-

age of this, see note 33. For important work that talks about empire as a critical site for race/color identity formation, see Stoler, *Race and the Education of Desire*; Holt, *The Problem of Freedom*; McClintock, *Imperial Leather*; Brantlinger, *Rules of Darkness*; Cooper and Stoler, *Tensions of Empire*; Jacobson, *Whiteness of a Different Color*, chap. 6; and Newman, *White Women's Rights*.

Chapter 7

1. "Notes on Letter from Nick Colletta, member of the Animated Arts Club at Chicago Commons," July 22, 1932, CC, Box 25, Folder "March-December 1932"; Cohen, *Making a New Deal*, pp. 217, 243; Newell, *Chicago and the Labor Movement*, pp. 30–34; Halpern, *Down on the Killing Floor*, p. 98.

2. By the time of the crash, there was a small minority of better-off Italians in Chicago, for whom "hard times" were not so hard at all. For this group, see Nelli, *The Italians in Chicago*, pp. 203–204, 208–211.

3. "Report of the Work of the Chicago Commons for the Year Ending September 30, 1932," p. 1, CC, Box 5, Folder "Annual and Other Reports, 1929–1932"; Wirth and Furez, *Local Community Fact Book 1938*, n.p.; *LIT*, June 5, 1932, p. 5. For further information on the Depression's effects on Chicago's Italians, see also Lea Taylor, "Lea Demarest Taylor: Her Life and Work between 1883–1968," typed transcript of autobiographical tapes produced by the National Federation of Settlements and Neighborhood Centers, pp. 55–57, Graham Taylor Papers, NL; and see the following IAC interviews: Avignone, pp. 28–30; De Facci, p. 51; Manella, p. 52; De Falco, p. 7; Penio, pp. 34–36; Perpoli, p. 24; Tonietto, pp. 41–42; Argenzio, p. 41; Patti, pp. 33–35.

4. While this chapter will focus heavily on Italians' workplace and union hall experiences, these were not somehow separate from Italians' lives in their communities and homes, the subject of the following chapter and a companion to this one. For recent work in labor history that moves well beyond the artificial community/workplace boundary, see especially the essays on "Gender and the Reconstruction of Labor History" in *Labor History* 34 (spring-summer 1993); and Baron, *Work Engendered*.

5. On Italian radicalism in Chicago in the pre-Depression years, see Panofsky, "A View of Two Major Centers of Italian Anarchism in the United States," pp. 271–296; Miller and Panofsky, "The Beginnings of the Italian Socialist Movement in Chicago," pp. 55–70; Nelli, *The Italians in Chicago*, pp. 82, 85, 158, 161–164, 167; Vecoli, "Chicago's Italians prior to World War I," pp. 193, 380; see also the various unpublished manuscripts by Eugene Miller and Gianna Panofsky in the Eugene Miller Papers, no boxes or folders, IHRC.

6. On the 24th Street and Oakley neighborhood and its socialist flavor, see Vecoli, "Chicago's Italians prior to World War I," p. 193; Vecoli, "The Formation of Chicago's 'Little Italies,'" p. 13; and the following IAC interviews: Mirabella, pp. 44–45; Petri, pp. 8, 17; Baldacci, pp. 26–34; Fantozzi, pp. 15–20; Gentile, p. 13; Tarabori, pp. 23–33; Valiani, pp. 36–41.

7. On Chicago CP membership statistics, see Storch, "Shades of Red," pp. 40–44. On the Italian communists, see the Ernest De Maio Papers, CHS; Interview with De Maio, RULOHP, Box 8; Mario Manzardo, "Liberi Cuori," typed essay, n.d., but c. early 1970s, especially pp. 14–15, Mario Manzardo Papers, Box 1, Folder "Articles MSS," IHRC (a version of this essay was later published in Lynd and Lynd, *Rank and File*, pp. 131–148); Interview with Cassano,

pp. 26–27, IAC; Zivich, "Fighting Union," p. 10; Bae, "Men's Clothing Workers in Chicago, 1871–1929," p. 305.

8. Lasswell and Bumenstock, *World Revolutionary Propaganda*, pp. 52–53. On the socialists' and communists' movements for the unemployed in Chicago, see, in addition to Lasswell and Blumenstock, Cohen, *Making a New Deal*, 261–267; Storch, "Shades of Red," pp. 83–112; Halpern, *Down on the Killing Floor*, pp. 101–105, 109–112; Taylor, "Lea Demarest Taylor," pp. 57–59; Seymour, "The Organized Unemployed"; Nelson et al., *Steve Nelson*, pp. 70–87. On the Near Northwest Side Workers' Committee, see information on the "Italian Community Association," in CC, Box 25, Folder "Italian Community Association, 1933–1937." This box includes the meeting minutes in Italian of this organization. On Dino Renzi's speech, see *LIT*, October 30, 1932, p. 3. On Italians' involvement in the Illinois Workers Alliance, see "Report of the Meetings of Current Affairs Discussion Group Chicago Commons, October 29, 1935–January 21, 1936, October 20, 1936–March 16, 1937," CC, Box 26, Folder "May–December 1937."

9. For the quotation, see Keeran, "The Italian Section of the International Workers Order, 1930–1950," p. 10. On the membership statistics, see Denning, *The Cultural Front*, p. 75. On the IWO more generally, see, in addition to the works just cited, Keeran, "National Groups and the Popular Front," pp. 23–51; Keeran, "The International Workers Order and the Origins of the CIO," pp. 385–408; Walker, *Pluralistic Fraternity*.

10. On Italians' IWO membership totals and lodges in Chicago, see "Conferenza della Sezione Nazionale Italiana," April 28–29, 1938, Allegati 1–2; "Terza Convenzione dell'Ordine Operaio Internazionale," May 7–9, 1935, p. 5; "Rapporto della Conferenza dei Delegati Italiani alla Terza Convenzione Biennale dell'Ordine Operaio Internazionale," May 7–9, 1935, Allegato A; all in IWO. Many thanks to Jennifer Guglielmo for bringing these documents to my attention. For further information on Chicago Italians' involvement in the IWO, see Interview with Baldacci, p. 26, IAC. On the comparison between membership totals in the IWO, OSIA, and IANU, in the late 1920s: OSIA had nineteen lodges and 1400 members in Illinois; the IANU had thirty-nine lodges and five thousand adult and juvenile members in the Midwest. By the early 1940s, according to a federal government report, OSIA had fifty lodges and 3100 members in Chicago; IANU had seventy lodges and 4700 members in the city. On these totals, see Schiavo, *The Italians in Chicago*, pp. 57–59; Albert Perry, "The Italian-Americans of Chicago," typed report, October 2, 1942, RG 226, U.S. Office of Strategic Services, Foreign Nationalities Branch Files, 1942–1945, INT-17IT-489 (micro), NAII.

11. On labor's woes in the 1920s, see especially Zieger, *The CIO, 1935–1955*, p. 9; Montgomery, *The Fall of the House of Labor*; Cohen, *Making a New Deal*, pp. 159–211; Halpern, *Down on the Killing Floor*, pp. 85–95.

12. On the ILGWU membership totals, see Magee, "The Women's Clothing Industry of Chicago," p. 70. On Chicago and labor more generally in the 1920s, see Newell, *Chicago and the Labor Movement*.

13. On nationwide union membership statistics, see Chafe, *The Unfinished Journey*, p. 9. On USWA District 31 membership totals, see Derber, *Labor in Illinois*, p. 85. On the AFL, see Newell, *Chicago and the Labor Movement*, p. 198.

14. On Chicago Italians' membership in AFL unions, see Schiavo, *The Italians in Chicago*, pp. 115–116; *The Official Labor Union Directory and Buyer's Guide*,

volumes 17–39, January 1930–January 1941, copies at the CHS; "Index of Voting List; Annual Election of Officers and Committees," September 18, 1938, Chicago Federation of Labor Papers, Box 30, Folder 2, CHS; "Italian-American Victory Council," typed list of organizations, pp. 1–3, Ernest De Maio Papers, Box 9, Folder 6, CHS; Mario Manzardo, "Struggles and Growth of Labor in Illinois—Some Italian Contributions: A Sketch Portrait," typed, unpublished essay, pp. 4–5, Mario Manzardo Papers, Box 1, Folder unnamed, IHRC; the following IAC interviews: Moreschi, pp. 12–13; Esposito, pp. 21–25; Penio, pp. 31–42; Ungari, p. 19; Morandin, p. 24; and the following articles in *FN*: January 27, 1934, p. 2; May 26, 1934, p. 2; June 23, 1934, p. 5; December 29, 1934, p. 2; October 19, 1935, p. 9; November 13, 1937, p. 3; June 10, 1939, p. 8; November 11, 1939, p. 5; January 6, 1940, p. 8; January 13, 1940, p. 3; April 6, 1940, p. 9; September 7, 1940, p. 2; December 6, 1941, p. 8; April 25, 1942, p. 12; July 25, 1942, p. 1; January 30, 1943, p. 10; November 14, 1943, p. 11; January 15, 1944, p. 5; February 5, 1944, p. 1.

15. On Chicago Italians' involvement in the CIO generally, see Manzardo, "Struggles and Growth of Labor in Illinois," pp. 3–6; "Italian-American Victory Council," Ernest De Maio Papers, Box 9, Folder 6. On the USWA/SWOC, see "Local Union Officers List, 1942–1943, District no. 31, USWA, CIO," Box 42, Folder 1; "Local Union Officers and Addresses, District no. 31, July 1945, USWA, CIO," Box 42, Folder 7; "District Convention Proceedings of District no. 31," May 8, 1943, pp. 4–5, Box 40, Folder 4; SWOC Field Notes, 1936–1937, Box 124, Folder 4; SWOC subdistrict minutes, 1938–1939, Box 125, Folder 4; Box 184, Folder 3; all in USWA; information on stewards in George Patterson Papers, Box 8, Folder 1, CHS; Kornblum, "Ethnicity, Work, and Politics in South Chicago," p. 112; *Steel Labor*, October 27, 1939, p. 4; *Steel Labor*, June 25, 1943, p. 9; *Steel Labor*, January 21, 1944, p. 12; all (micro), CHS; Interview with Cesario, pp. 18–29, IAC; Interview with Cassano, pp. 46–48, IAC. On UFEMWU, see Gilpin, "Left by Themselves," pp. 88, 185; *Local 101 News*, October-November 1944, pp. 1, 6 (micro), CHS; Interview with Leone, pp. 28–38, IAC; Interview with Petri, pp. 17–19, IAC; Interview with Gentile, pp. 24–27, IAC. On UE, see "UE-CIO Electronics War Conference, March 13, 1944," Box 9, Folder 10, Ernest De Maio Papers; Interview with De Maio, RULOHP; and the following *Chicago UE News* articles (in Ernest De Maio Papers, unboxed material): April 28, 1942, p. 4; May 13, 1942, p. 4; January 12, 1943, p. 4; January 26, 1943, p. 1. On ACWA, see ACWA Local 39 Meeting Minutes, Amalgamated Clothing Workers of America (ACWA) Papers, Box 3, CHS; Interview with Valiani, pp. 44–45. On the UAW, see list of Local 477 officers in Chicago Federation of Labor Papers, Box 35, Folder 8, CHS; Karsh, "The Grievance Process in Union-Management Relations," pp. 26–27; Interview with Tonietto, p. 36, IAC. On Italians' absence from the meatpacking industry, see Sandburg, *The Chicago Race Riots*, p. 75; Vecoli, "Chicago's Italians prior to World War I," pp. 338-341; and Taylor, *Mexican Labor in the Unites States*, pp. 60-61.

16. On the USWA and UE, see note above; on Russo, see "Italian-American Victory Council," Ernest De Maio Papers, Box 8, Folder 6, CHS; on Annunzio, see USWA, Box 105, Folder 5.

17. On Petrillo and Moreschi, see Schiavo, *The Italians in Chicago*, p. 115; Manzardo, "Struggles and Growth of Labor in Illinois," pp. 4–5; *FN*, March 6, 1937, p. 6; *FN*, October 16, 1937, p. 7; *FN*, December 28, 1940, p. 2; . On Italians' underrepresentation among Chicago Federation of Labor and Illinois Federation of Labor officers and committee members, see the following articles in

FN: September 22, 1934, p. 1; January 26, 1935, p. 8; September 21, 1935, p. 2; September 26, 1936, p. 3; September 25, 1937, p. 1; January 8, 1938, p. 10; October 7, 1939, p. 2; January 24, 1942, p. 3; December 26, 1942, p. 3; November 27, 1943, p. 3; June 24, 1944, p. 3.

18. On Diamond Wire and Cable, see *Steel Labor*, January 21, 1944, p. 12 (micro), CHS. On Italian women's involvement in the CIO, see *Loose Leaves* issues; *Women in Steel* 1 (March 1937): 5; *Steel Labor*, June 25, 1943, p. 9; *Chicago UE News*, January 12, 1943, p. 4, all (micro), CHS; Minutes for ACWA Local 39, ACWA Papers, Box 3, no folders, CHS; "Local Union Officers List, 1942–1943, District no. 31, USWA, CIO," Box 42, Folder 1, CHS; and "Local Union Officers and Addresses, District no. 31, July 1945, USWA, CIO," Box 42, Folder 7; both in USWA; information on stewards in George Patterson Papers, Box 8, Folder 1, CHS; Interview with Valiani, pp. 44–45, IAC, ; Interview with Tonietto, p. 36, IAC. On women in the AFL, see Schiavo, *The Italians in Chicago*, p. 116; *The Official Labor Union Directory and Buyer's Guide* 17 (January 1930) and 39 (January 1941), copies at the CHS; "Index of Voting List; Annual Election of Officers and Committees," September 18, 1938, Chicago Federation of Labor Papers, Box 30, Folder 2, CHS; Interview with Morandin, p. 24, IAC; *FN*, April 25, 1942, p. 12; *FN*, January 30, 1943, p. 10. On Italian women's labor activism at the same time in other parts of the country, see Guglielmo, *"Lavoratrici Coscienti"*; and Guglielmo, *"Donne Ribelli."*

19. For Lizabeth Cohen's "culture of unity" thesis, see *Making a New Deal*, pp. 333–349. On the CIO's diverse set of organizers, see "Field Workers, Steel Workers Organizing Committee," attendance sheet, 1937, USWA, Box 124, Folder 6; Interview with Patterson, RULOHP, pp. 52, 63; on "language days" and other CIO "Old World" celebrations, see Zivich, "Fighting Union," p. 25; on the translation of CIO signs, speeches, etc. into foreign languages, see Gilpin, "Left By Themselves," pp. 102–106; Zivich, "Fighting Union," p. 12; *Women in Steel* 2 (October 1937): 4; on the help of "ethnic" community organizations, see Bork, "The Memorial Day 'Massacre' of 1937," p. 63; Keeran, "The International Workers Order and the Origins of the CIO," pp. 385-408; Interview with Petri, p. 18, IAC; "Conferenza della Sezione Nazionale Italiana," April 28-29, 1938, p. 12, IWO.

20. Workers could nuturture class and racial identities simultaneously, of course. For a sampling of work on this point, see Mormino and Pozzetta, *The Immigrant World of Ybor City*, pp. 246–247; Sánchez, *Becoming Mexican American*, chap. 11; Ruiz, *Cannery Women, Cannery Lives*, chap. 2; Hunter, *To 'Joy My Freedom*; Kelley, *Hammer and Hoe*; Lewis, *In Their Own Interests*; Gerstle, *Working-Class Americanism*; Bae, "Men's Clothing Workers in Chicago, 1871–1929," especially pp. 118–119, 132, 187.

21. On CIO mixing in locals, see "Local Union Officers List, 1942–1943, District no. 31, USWA, CIO," Box 42, Folder 1; "Local Union Officers and Addresses, District no. 31, July 1945, USWA, CIO," Box 42, Folder 7; both in USWA; Sofchalk, "The Chicago Memorial Day Incident," pp. 13, 20-21; Meeting Minutes for ACWA Local 39, ACWA Papers, Box 3, CHS; Cohen, *Making a New Deal*, pp. 339–340. On similar mixing beyond the workplace in CIO recreational and social activities, see *Leader* (News of West Pullman Local 107, FE), June 1, 1946, p. 4; *Chicago UE News*, November 18, 1943, p. 1; *Chicago UE News*, December 20, 1943, pp. 1, 3; *Chicago UE News*, April 6, 1944, p. 1; *Chicago UE News*, June 7, 1945, p. 1, all (micro), CHS; Cohen, *Making a New Deal*, pp. 340–341.

22. Zivich, "Fighting Union," pp. 19–20, 40; Cayton and Mitchell, *Black Workers and New Unions*, p. 219.

23. *FN*, January 26, 1930, p. 11. On the mixing of AFL workers both inside and outside the union hall, see also the following articles in *FN*: December 17, 1938, p. 10; January 13, 1940, p. 3; March 29, 1941, p. 8; May 3, 1941, p. 8; April 25, 1942, p. 12; July 25, 1942, p. 1; January 23, 1943, p. 9; November 13, 1943, p. 11; January 15, 1944, p. 5; May 6, 1944, p. 5; July 8, 1944, p. 5; September 23, 1944, p. 9.

24. On European cultural pluralism, see the following *FN* articles: March 4, 1939, p. 3 (quotation); February 8, 1941, p. 9; October 4, 1941, p. 4; November 8, 1941, p. 15; February 19, 1944, pp. 3, 5; October 7, 1944, pp. 1, 3; May 12, 1945, p. 1. For attacks on racial prejudice, see *FN*, January 6, 1940, p. 11 (quotation); *FN*, November 2, 1940, p. 1. On Americanism rallies, see *FN*, June 21, 1941, p. 7 (quotation); *FN*, August 29, 1942, p. 1.

25. On anti-Mussolini attacks, see the following articles and political cartoons in *FN*: January 4, 1930, p. 4; January 18, 1930, p. 16; July 14, 1934, p. 2; May 12, 1934, p. 4 ("wop dictator" quotation); January 19, 1935, p. 2; July 27, 1935, p. 6; August 24, 1935, p. 1; September 7, 1935, p. 2; July 21, 1943, p. 12; August 14, 1943, p. 10.

26. Myers, "The Economic Aspects of the Production of Men's Clothing," p. 34; Gilpin, "Left by Themselves," p. 320.

27. On the CP, see Storch, "Shades of Red," p. 22; and Lasswell and Blumenstock, *World Revolutionary Propaganda*, p. 73. On the anarchists and socialists, see Panofsky, "A View of Two Major Centers of Italian Anarchism in the United States," pp. 271–296; Miller and Panofsky, "The Beginnings of the Italian Socialist Movement in Chicago," pp. 55–70. On the IWO, see Keeran, "The Italian Section of the IWO, 1930–1950"; Keeran, "National Groups and the Popular Front."

28. There is a growing literature on the ways in which immigrant workers "Americanized" themselves through their involvement in organized labor. For some representative texts, see Barrett, "Americanization from the Bottom Up," pp. 996–1020; Barrett, *Work and Community in the Jungle*; Cohen, *Making a New Deal*; Gerstle, *Working-Class Americanism*; Sánchez, *Becoming Mexican American*, especially chap. 11. For more on this historiographical trend, see Kazal, "Revisiting Assimilation," pp. 437–471.

29. Storch, "Shades of Red," pp. 45, 48–51, 67–73, 107–110; Lasswell and Blumenstock, *World Revolutionary Propaganda*, pp. 77–78, 280. For more on the CP and Chicago's African-American community, see Halpern, *Down on the Killing Floor*, pp. 105–112; Cohen, *Making a New Deal*, pp. 261–262, 266; Gosnell, *Negro Politicians*, pp. 319–356; Haywood, *Black Bolshevik*.

30. On the prevalence of the CP's "Black and White, Unite and Fight" organizing strategy, see Lasswell and Blumenstock, *World Revolutionary Propaganda*, pp. 139–140, 197, 200–201; Storch, "Shades of Red," pp. 62, 69, 94–100, 165–167, 184; Drake and Cayton, *Black Metropolis*, pp. 86, 734–737; Gosnell, *Negro Politicians*, pp. 330–331; ILD Scottsboro Defense Fund Poster, Charles E. Merriam Papers, Box 103, Folder 1, UC; Solomon, *The Cry Was Unity*. For this argument, I am indebted to Matthew Frye Jacobson. See *Whiteness of a Different Color*, pp. 248–256. I differ slightly from Jacobson, however, in insisting that the CP had legitimate reasons for organizing workers along "white" and "Negro" lines, since structural realities endowed these categories with powerful meaning for tens of thousands of Chicago workers.

31. For some specific examples of these CIO battles in Chicago, see Gilpin, "Left By Themselves," p. 368; Drake and Cayton, *Black Metropolis*, pp. 324,

333–341; Cayton and Mitchell, *Black Workers and New Unions*, p. 222; Halpern, *Down on the Killing Floor*, pp. 146, 213; Halpern, "Race and Radicalism in the Chicago Stockyards," pp. 75–95; Horowitz, *"Negro and White, Unite and Fight!"*, pp. 73-83.

32. "Local Union Officers List, 1942–1943, District no. 31, USWA, CIO," Box 42, Folder 1; "Local Union Officers and Addresses, District no. 31, July 1945, USWA, CIO," Box 42, Folder 7; both in USWA.

33. Cayton and Mitchell, *Black Workers and New Unions*, pp. 218, 212. For more on the SWOC/USWA's efforts and success at breaking down the color line, see Drake and Cayton, *Black Metropolis*, pp. 317–341; Hutton, "The Negro Worker and the Labor Unions of Chicago," pp. 90-102; *CD*, August 1, 1936, p. 5; *CD*, August 29, 1936, p. 16; *CD*, May 30, 1942, p. 10; Seidman et al., *The Worker Views His Union*, p. 81; Lynd and Lynd, *Rank and File*, p. 169; Stein, "A History of Unionization in the Steel Industry in the Chicago Area," pp. 61-62; Harbison, "Labor Relations in the Iron and Steel Industry," p. 29; SWOC Field Notes, 1936–1937, Box 124, Folder 4, USWA; Baur, "Delinquency among Mexican Boys in South Chicago," pp. 1, 23–24; Cohen, *Making a New Deal*, pp. 334-337.

34. Drake and Cayton, *Black Metropolis*, pp. 325, 324, 333. See also Cayton and Mitchell, *Black Workers and New Unions*, pp. 222, 220; and Hutton, "The Negro Worker and the Labor Unions of Chicago," p. 99. For secondary sources on the Memorial Day Massacre, see Bork, "The Memorial Day 'Massacre' of 1937"; Leab, "The Memorial Day Massacre," pp. 3–17; Sofchalk, "The Chicago Memorial Day Incident," pp. 3–43; and "Remember Memorial Day, May 30, 1937," USWA pamphlet, May 30, 1979, USWA, Box 179, Folder 2.

35. John W. Bennett to E. C. Wilson and Lucien Warner, Memo, "Special Report on Negro Labor in Chicago," February 10, 1943, pp. 2–4, 3 (quotation), RG 44, Entry no. 171, Box 1840, Folder "Chicago—Bennett, John W," NAII.

36. On the UE, see Drake and Cayton, *Black Metropolis*, p. 311; and the following articles in *Chicago UE News* (micro), CHS: September 26, 1942, p. 3; January 12, 1943, p. 1; February 10, 1943, p. 1; December 20, 1943, p. 1; April 6, 1944, p. 1; April 21, 1944, pp. 2, 4; May 11, 1944, p. 3; August 31, 1944, p. 3; December 7, 1944, p. 4; January 4, 1945, p. 4; February 1, 1945, p. 3; March 15, 1945, p. 2; June 7, 1945, p. 1; August 2, 1945, p. 1. On the FE's Local 101, see the following articles in *Local 101 News* (micro), CHS: August 23, 1946, p. 2; February-March, 1944, p. 2; October-November 1944, pp. 2, 6. For the "color question" quotation, see Cayton and Mitchell, *Black Workers and New Unions*, p. 218.

37. For the first quotation, see Drake and Cayton, *Black Metropolis*, p. 332; and Cayton and Mitchell, *Black Workers and New Unions*, p. 221; for the second quotation, see Seidman, et al., *The Worker Views His Union*, p. 222. The problems in Melrose Park described above appear not to have been unique to this plant. As one government official stated about a variety of workplaces in wartime Chicago: "With only one or two exceptions . . . white and black do not mix after hours or at union functions. In some plants, white and colored eat in the same cafeteria, but this is about as far as interracial activity, exclusive of union meetings, etc., will go." See John W. Bennett to E. C. Wilson and Lucien Warner, Memo, "Special Report on Negro Labor in Chicago," February 10, 1943, p. 7, RG 44, Entry no. 171, Box 1840, Folder "Chicago—Bennett, John W., NAII.

38. On the Pullman hate strike, see Memo from Will Maslow to Elmer R. Henderson, December 20, 1944, pp. 1–2 and attached typed chronology, "The Pullman Car Manufacturing Company, Shipbuilding Division Strike, December 5-13, 1944," RG 228, Entry no. 31, Box 404, Folder "Strike Data," NAII. On

other Chicago wartime hate strikes, see *FN*, December 26, 1942, p. 3; *CD*, June 6, 1942, p. 8; and "Strikes Occurring over Racial Issues during Period 7/1943–12/1944"; "Strikes Occurring over Racial Issues during Period 7/1944–7/1945"; Memo from John A . Davis and Joy P. Davis, "Youngstown Sheet and Tube Company—Indiana Harbor, Indiana," March 25, 1944; Memo from Harry H. C. Gibson to Elmer W. Henderson, January 17, 1944; all in RG 228, Entry no. 31, Box 404, Folder "Strike Data," NAII.

39. Zieger, *The CIO, 1935–1955*, pp. 84, 152–162; Gilpin, "Left By Themselves," pp. 378–381. On the problematic nature of certain CIO local leaders, see also Cayton and Mitchell, *Black Workers and New Unions*, p. 207; Seidman et al., *The Worker Views His Union*, pp. 73–74. On labor historians' debates as to who is most responsible for the CIO's shortcomings on color issues—leaders or the rank and file—see esp. Nelson, *Divided We Stand*; Nelson, "Class, Race, and Democracy in the CIO," pp. 351–374; Nelson, "Working-Class Agency and Racial Inequality," pp. 407–420; Faue, "'Anti-Heroes of the Working Class'," pp. 375–388; Sugrue, "Segmented Work, Race-Conscious Workers," pp. 389–406.

40. See the following *Steel Labor* political cartoons, (micro), CHS: September 5, 1936, p. 1; September 25, 1936, p. 2; October 20, 1936, p. 6; November 20, 1936, p. 2; December 5, 1936, pp. 2, 4; December 19, 1936, pp. 6, 8; January 9, 1937, pp. 3, 4; January 23, 1937, p. 3; February 20, 1937, p. 3; June 5, 1937, p. 6; July 7, 1937, p. 4; August 26, 1937, p. 4; September 30, 1937, p. 4; October 15, 1937, p. 8; October 29, 1937, p. 6; November 19, 1937, p. 6; December 13, 1937, pp. 3, 6; December 31, 1937, p. 4; January 21, 1938, p. 4; February 18, 1938, p. 4; June 17, 1938, p. 4; August 19, 1938, p. 4; February 24, 1939, p. 4; April 28, 1939, p. 4; January 26, 1940, p. 4; November 29, 1940, p. 4; June 25, 1941, p. 4; September 25, 1941, p. 4; February 27, 1942, pp. 4, 7; July 31, 1942, p. 3; March 26, 1943, p. 12. For a discussion of labor iconography that focuses on gendered meanings, yet ignores the equally prevalent colorized ones, see Elizabeth Faue, *Community of Suffering and Struggle*, pp. 69–99.

41. *Steel Labor*, May 24, 1940, p. 10; *Chicago UE News*, September 16, 1942, p. 3; both (micro), CHS. On CIO's "Negro/white" rhetoric, see also *CD*, January 2, 1943, p. 6; *Local 101 News*, October-November 1944, p. 2, (micro), CHS; Cohen, *Making a New Deal*, p. 339.

42. *CD*, May 30, 1942, p. 7 on the Hedges sign. For more on the power of employers to structure color in the workplace, see Hutton, "The Negro Worker and the Labor Unions of Chicago," pp. 11–13; Drake and Cayton, *Black Metropolis*, pp. 223, 233, 252–253, 297–298, 321, 324, 334–336; Cayton and Mitchell, *Black Workers and New Unions*, pp. 27, 32–33, 48, 214–217, 222; Memo from Bennett to Wilson and Warner, pp. 1, 3–6; Seidman, et al., *The Worker Views His Union*, pp. 73–74; *CD*, April 11, 1942, p. 28; see also the many FEPC letters to discriminatory employers in RG 228, Entry no. 31, Box 405, Folder "White Copies of Correspondence," NAII. On recent work which has stressed the need for labor historians to take employers seriously, see Sugrue, "Segmented Work, Race-Conscious Workers," pp. 396–406; Arnesen, "Up from Exclusion," p. 156.

43. On the forces that pressured some AFL locals to organize Africans Americans in earnest, see Drake and Cayton, *Black Metropolis*, pp. 337–340; Hutton, "The Negro Worker and the Labor Unions of Chicago," pp. 32, 49–50; and the following articles in *FN*: February 26, 1938, p. 8; July 8, 1939, p. 8; February 1, 1930, pp. 2, 6; June 29, 1939, pp. 1, 3.

44. *FN*, July 6, 1940, p. 1. On Italians' involvement in Local 712, see *FN*, July 25, 1942, p. 1; *FN*, January 25, 1930, p. 11; *FN*, October 19, 1935, p. 9; *FN*,

July 8, 1944, p. 5. For other color-progressive actions, see *FN*, August 19, 1940, p. 10; Weaver, *Negro Labor*, pp. 181–186; Larkin, "Forty-five Years of Collective Bargaining," p. 118; *CD*, January 1, 1943, p. 1.

45. For some examples of these articles and broadcasts, see *FN*, January 4, 1930, p. 4; *FN*, June 30, 1934, p. 1; *FN*, May 4, 1935, p. 4; *FN*, August 3, 1935, p. 11; *FN*, April 3, 1937, p. 8; *FN*, December 31, 1938, p. 4; *FN*, August 19, 1939, p. 3; *FN*, April 6, 1940, p. 1; *FN*, January 11, 1941, p. 11; *FN*, August 29, 1942, p. 1; *FN*, January 9, 1943, p. 12; *FN*, February 19, 1944, p. 3; *FN*, February 26, 1944, p. 1; *FN*, January 6, 1945, p. 4; *FN*, January 27, 1945, p. 5; *FN*, February 10, 1945, p. 3; *FN*, February 24, 1945, p. 2; *FN*, April 7, 1945, p. 8; *FN*, June 16, 1945, p. 4.

46. On AFL locals' exclusionary practices, see Hutton, "The Negro Worker and the Labor Unions of Chicago," pp. 27–60, 118; Newell, *Chicago and the Labor Movement*, pp. 239–240; *CD*, October 7, 1939, p. 1; *CD*, February 2, 1933, p. 14; Drake and Cayton, *Black Metropolis*, pp. 260, 298; Taylor, *Mexican Labor in the United States*, p. 119; A. L. Foster to Thyra [Edwards], March 4, 1937, Welfare Council of Chicago Papers, Box 145, Folder 1, CHS. On Italians' membership and leadership in some of these locals, see *FN*, January 30, 1943, p. 11; *FN*, November 14, 1943, p. 11; *FN*, February 5, 1944, p. 1; *The Chicago Official Labor Union Directory and Buyer's Guide* 26 (January 1934); 29 (January 1936); and 39 (January 1941), CHS.

47. On the "51st Street Riot," see *CD*, September 20, 1930, p. 1; *CT*, September 17, 1930, p. 15. See also Halpern, *Down on the Killing Floor*, p. 111; Halpern, "Race and Radicalism in the Chicago Stockyards," p. 80; Storch, "Shades of Red," p. 95; Reed, "A Study of Black Politics and Protest in Depression-Decade Chicago," pp. 133–134, 266–268. It should be noted that in *Black Metropolis*, Drake and Cayton described this incident as being a violent "attack on white laborers" (p. 85). This may have been the case, although this is not the story that the *Chicago Defender* or the *Chicago Tribune* told. Also interesting to note: if the *CD*'s repeated mention of the "51st Street Riot" is any indication, it seems that this event came to be a popular symbol of the concrete benefits of African-American activism. See *CD*, April 1, 1939, p. 21; *CD*, September 30, 1939, p. 1.

48. *CD*, February 28, 1942, p. 28; *FN*, February 26, 1944, p. 1; see also Drake and Cayton, *Black Metropolis*, p. 299.

49. *FN*, August 1, 1942, p. 7. For further examples of demeaning cartoons of African Americans, see *FN*, September 3, 1938, p. 2; *FN*, October 1, 1938, p. 2; *FN*, November 12, 1938, p. 12. AFL representations of workers as white and male are far too numerous to cite here. For a sampling, see *FN*, September 3, 1934, cover; *FN*, September 15, 1934, p. 1; *FN*, October 31, 1936, p. 1; *FN*, March 20, 1937, p. 3; *FN*, June 26, 1937, p. 1; *FN*, June 11, 1938, p. 1; *FN*, October 12, 1940, p. 1; *FN*, July 4, 1942, p. 8.

Chapter 8

1. Father Louis Giambastiani to Elizabeth Wood, October 7, 1942, SPBPP, Section 2, Folder 68.

2. Wirth and Bernert, *Local Community Fact Book of Chicago*, n.p.; U.S. Department of Commerce, Bureau of the Census, *Population* (1930), vol. 3, pt. 3, p. 640; Bureau of the Census, *Population* (1940), vol. 2, pt. 2, pp. 543–544; Bureau of the Census, *Population* (1950), vol. 2, pt. 13, pp. 97–98.

3. Chicago Commons Neighborhood Housing Survey, CC, Box 30, Folder

"Neighborhood Housing Survey." For the data on housing conditions in Italians' old and new neighborhoods, see Wirth and Bernert, *Local Community Fact Book of Chicago*, n.p. It should be noted, too, that these data are based on large "local communities"; if we were to have information on a smaller neighborhood level, the differences in housing conditions would be even starker. For instance, the Near North Side information is based not only on "Little Sicily" but the Gold Coast as well—Chicago's most elite neighborhood. Also, while on a community-wide level approximately 10 percent of the Near Northwest Side's housing was in need of major repair, a Chicago Commons' study done in 1941 of the local Italian neighborhood of that community found that 40 percent of buildings fit this category. See "A Message from the Chicago Commons," 1941, CC, Box 28, Folder "June-December 1941."

4. *Savings and Homeownership* (August 1947), pp. 1–2 in Hoyt, *According to Hoyt*, pp. 361–362; Jackson, *Crabgrass Frontier*, p. 205; *Savings and Homeownership* (October 1949), p. 3 in Hoyt, *According to Hoyt*, p. 173. On European immigrants' desire to buy homes, see Hirsch, *Making the Second Ghetto*, pp. 187–188; Breckenridge, *New Homes for Old*, p. 71; Abbott, *The Tenements of Chicago*, pp. 362–400. On Italians, in particular, see Addams, *Forty Years at Hull-House*, vol. 2, pp. 231–232; Vecoli, "Chicago's Italians prior to World War I," pp. 216, 232–234; and Nelli, *The Italians in Chicago*, pp. 34, 37. For more on the role of the FHA in promoting home-buying, see Abrams, *The Future of Housing*, pp. 223–238; Tobey et al., "Moving Out and Settling In," pp. 1413–1420.

5. Chicago Plan Commission, *Residential Chicago*, pp. 67–69.

6. On African Americans' population increases during the 1930s and World War II, see Hirsch, *Making the Second Ghetto*, p. 17; Drake and Cayton, *Black Metropolis*, p. 90; Robert C. Weaver, "Racial Tensions in Chicago," CHS.

7. Metropolitan Housing Council, Confidential Report, January 1943, pp. 1–3 (emphasis in original), RG 44, Entry no. 171, Box 1840, Folder "Chicago—Passin, Herbert." For more on African Americans' severe housing problems during the war, see Hirsch, *Making the Second Ghetto*, pp. 18–22.

8. Interview with Domke, p. 4; Interview with DeLiberto, p. 33; Interview with Clementi, p. 84; all in IAC. For further evidence that Italians moved out of older neighborhoods in large part to avoid "colored" groups, mainly African Americans, see: Unsigned Chicago Commons letter, March 22, 1944, Box 29, Folder "January-June 1944"; Handwritten Diary, n.d., but c. 1944–1945, Box 30, Folder "January-November 1945;" both in CC; Candeloro, "Suburban Italians," p. 265; and the following IAC interviews: Lagattuta, pp. 35–36; Mariani, p. 27; Spallitta, pp. 26–27; Zaranti, pp. 33-34; Occhipinti, p. 10; Raia, p. 25; Tonietto, p. 45; Martorano, p. 19; Muzzacavallo, p. 14; Colella, p. 37.

9. Interview with Chidichino, p. 29, IAC. For data on the color composition of Italians' neighborhoods, see Wirth and Bernert, *Local Community Fact Book of Chicago*, n.p.

10. The one minor exception to this point is Mexicans on the Near West Side, where conflict, dating back to the 1920s, was still common in the 1940s. However, this was the only neighborhood where significant Italian-Mexican conflict took place, and even here, evidence suggests that relations were improving. On a citywide level, Italians appear to have treated Mexicans more like their European neighbors than their African-American ones, a pattern that seems to have become more prevalent over time. On Mexican-Italian relations on the Near West Side, see Frank X. Paz, "Mexican-Americans in Chicago: A General Survey," January 1948, Welfare Council of Chicago Papers, Box 147,

Folder 4, CHS; Sherman, "The West Side Community Committee," pp. 24–25; "Mexican Civic Committee on the West Side," n.d., but c. 1944, Welfare Council of Chicago Papers, Box 373, Folder 5, CHS; "Council of Social Agencies, Chicago, Informal Meeting," June 25, 1943, p. 2, Madonna Center Papers, Series 2, Box 2, Marquette University Special Collections, Milwaukee, WI. On Italians' treatment of Mexicans more like "fellow white" neighbors, one Italian noted in an interview in 1980 that "this neighborhood here is a mixed neighborhood. There are a few Italians, a few Germans, a few Polish, a few every damned thing, but no blacks. A few Mexicans. We've got Mexicans in. They're buying but we don't care. They're white." See Interview with DeLiberto, pp. 47–48, IAC. For more on this point, see: "Chicago Commons Annual Report for the Year Ending September 30, 1946," n.d., p. 1, Box 5, Folder "Annual and Other Reports, 1940–1946"; see information in Box 9, Folder "The Spoilers, 1951–1952"; *Community News*, February 2, 1944, clipping, Box 29, Folder "January-June 1944"; "Survey of Negro Population in the Chicago Commons Area, 1946," n.d., p. 2, Box 13, Folder "Adult Education, 1942–1946"; all in CC; see also ACLU confidential reports during the Trumbull Park disturbances in the 1950s in the ACLU Papers, Box 11, Folder 9 and Box 12, Folder 1, UC; Interview with Sorrentino, side 1; Garcia, "History of Chicanos in Chicago Heights," p. 296. On Mexicans' population numbers in Chicago, see Garcia, *Mexicans in the Midwest*, pp. 231–235; and Kerr, "Chicano Settlements in Chicago," p. 25.

11. HOLC, "Area Descriptions—Security Map of Chicago, Illinois," Area no. 41, January 1940, RG 195, Entry no. 39, Box 119, Folder "Metropolitan Chicago, Illinois—Master—Security Map and Area Descriptions, Section 1," NAII. On the neighborhood's housing conditions, see Wirth and Bernert, *Local Community Fact Book of Chicago*, n.p.; Sherman, "The West Side Community Committee," pp. 25–26.

12. On the planning and building of the Addams project, see Metropolitan Housing Council, "Report of the Committee on Public Housing of the Metropolitan Housing Council," n.d., but c. September 1937, pp. 3–4, Graham Aldis Papers, Folder 59, UIC; Federal Emergency Administration of Public Works, PWA Press Section, Immediate Release, Release No. 1315, n.d., Jane Addams Papers (micro), Reel 34, UIC; and see clippings: *CDN*, April 11, 1935; *CT*, April 12, 1935; *CHE*, April 12, 1935; all in RG 196, Entry no. 2, Box 84, Folder H-1400.09, NAII.

13. David A. Wallace argued in his dissertation that this neighborhood composition rule was formed first with regard to the Jane Addams Houses and only after this became federal policy nationwide. Wallace writes: "A meeting of national housing officials was held in Chicago with a representative of Administrator Ickes and a number of race relations advisors. The decision on the Jane Addams Homes [*sic*] set the national policy that no housing project should change the racial complexion of the neighborhood in which it was located." See Wallace, "Residential Concentration of Negroes in Chicago," p. 225 n. 2.

14. On CHA's deliberate attempts to keep Lathrop and Trumbull Park lily-white, see Edward Holmgern Affidavit, n.d., Box 1, Folder "Holmgern"; and "Data from Chicago Housing Authority records showing Negro and white occupancy, by numbers of families, of specified housing project," n.d., Box 5, Folder "Racetrack Research"; Chicago Housing Authority Memo, April 13, 1940, Box 6, Green CHS Folder; all in BPPPI; Simon, "The First Tenants of the Trumbull Park Homes," p. 16; Hirsch, *Making the Second Ghetto*, pp. 14, 230. On questions about Mexican tenancy at Trumbull Park, see E. K. Burlew, Federal

Emergency Administrator of Public Work Administration, Memorandum for Mr. Clas, May 8, 1936; and A. R. Clas, Director of Housing, Trumbull Park Homes, Memorandum for Mr. Burlew, May 12, 1936; both in RG 196, Entry no. 2, Box 86, Folder 1400.81.

15. There was a slight difference of opinion between the CHA and the CD as to the number of African-American families prior to demolition on the Addams's site. The CD claimed that there were thirty families, the CHA claimed twenty-five. See CD, February 12, 1938, p. 1; Elizabeth Wood to R. A. Voight, October 2, 1940, Box 3, Folder "CHA Working"; and Elizabeth Wood to R. A. Voight, October 28, 1940, Box 6, Green CHS Folder; both in BPPPI. For the PWA survey, see "West Side Project No. H-1401—Block Summary of Social Survey—Dwellings," n.d., but c. 1935, RG 196, Entry no. 2, Box 92, Folder H-1401.4. On Mexicans' underrepresentation at Addams: According to the survey cited above, they represented 3.8 percent of the future project's neighborhood but, in 1939, made up only 1.9 percent of the Addams's tenants (11/1029). For these numbers, see Fromer, "The First Tenants of the Jane Addams Houses," p. 23.

16. A. L. Foster to Harold L. Ickes, April 14, 1937, Box 84, Folder H-1400.09; Harry Slattery to A. L. Foster, April 22, 1937, Box 84, Folder H-1400.09; A. L. Foster to Harold L. Ickes, May 3, 1937, Box 86, Folder H-1400.81; Harry Slattery to A. L. Foster, May 7, 1937, Box 86, Folder H-1400.81; all in RG 196, Entry no. 2.

17. Dorothy K. Toms, "Executive Committee, Division on Education and Recreation," Meeting of March 15, 1939, Welfare Council Papers, Box 145, Folder 1, CHS. On anti-African-American discrimination by the JAH management office, see Sherman Aldrich to H. A. Gray, September 7, 1937, Box 93, Folder H-1401.81; Sherman Aldrich [by Charles C. Weinz] to A. L. Foster, October 1, 1937, Box 84, Folder 1400.81; Edward Spurlin to Department of Interior, May 7, 1937, Box 86, Folder H-1400.81; Joseph H. Jefferson to Harold Ickes, January 31, 1938, Box 86, Folder H-1400.81; J. Jones to Franklin D. Roosevelt, February 22, 1938, Box 87, Folder H-1400.81; Nathan Straus to John R. Fugard, March 4, 1938, Box 87, Folder 1400.81; all in RG 196, Entry no. 2; Elizabeth Wood to Mary Lumsden, May 23, 1938, BPPPI, Box 3, Folder "Tenant Assignment"; A. L. Foster to Lea Taylor, November 24, 1937, Box 17, Folder "Housing, 1927–1940," Lea Taylor Papers, CHS; and the following CD articles: September 18, 1937, p. 1; February 12, 1938, p. 1; February 26, 1938, p. 1.

18. J. Jones to Franklin D. Roosevelt, February 22, 1938, Box 87, Folder H-1400.81, RG 196, Entry no. 2. On African-American mobilization, see note 23.

19. For the CHA resolution, see BPPPI memorandum from Bob Vollen, Bob Howard, and Dick Hirsch to CHA Team, April 3, 1968, BPPPI, Box 3, Folder "CHA Working." On African Americans finally being accepted at and moving into Addams, see John R. Fugard to Nathan Straus, March 16, 1938, Box 87, Folder H-1400.81; John R. Fugard to Nathan Straus, March 29, 1938, Box 103, Folder H-1405.81; both in RG 196, Entry no. 2; and the following CD articles: February 26, 1938, p. 1; March 19, 1938, p. 1; March 26, 1938, p. 1.

20. For the CHA's alternative conceptions of "neighborhood" and "neighborhood composition rule," see Regular Meeting of the Commissioners of the Chicago Housing Authority, January 17, 1938, in BPPPI memorandum from Bob Vollen, Bob Howard, and Dick Hirsch to CHA Team, April 3, 1938; and Elizabeth Wood to R. A. Voight, October 28, 1940, Box 6, Green CHS Folder; both in BPPPI. For Cayton and Scott's study, see CD, January 29, 1938, p. 2. See also Wallace, "Residential Concentration of Negroes in Chicago," p. 227.

21. For Poles' neighborhood numbers, see "West Side Project No. H-1401—Block Summary of Social Survey—Dwellings." On CHA's deliberate limiting of African Americans' numbers at Addams, see Elizabeth Wood to R. A. Voight, October 2, 1940, Box 3, Folder "CHA Working"; Elizabeth Wood to R. A. Voight, October 28, 1940, Box 6, Green CHS Folder; Elizabeth Wood to Catherine Henck, September 10, 1942, Box 3, Folder "Tenant Assignment"; CHA Interoffice Memo, Elizabeth Wood to the Commissioners, Box 3, Folder "CHA Working"; all in BPPPI. On CHA's increasing the number of African-American families at Addams to sixty and on postwar numbers, see Emil G. Hirsch to Priscilla Gray, February 16, 1943, Box 1, Folder "Hirsch"; "Data from Chicago Housing Authority records showing Negro and white occupancy, by numbers of families, of specified housing project," n.d., Box 5, Folder "Racetrack Research"; both in BPPPI.

22. Elizabeth Wood to Catherine Henck, September 10, 1942, Box 3, Folder "Tenant Assignment," BPPPI; Robert C. Weaver to A. L. Foster, September 2, 1939, RG 196, Entry no. 2, Box 87, Folder H-1400.81. For more evidence that the CHA deliberately segregated "white" and "Negro" families at Addams, see: John R. Fugard to Nathan Straus, March 29, 1938, Box 103, Folder H-1405.81, RG 196, Entry no. 2; Elizabeth Wood to May Lumsden, May 23, 1938, Box 3, Folder "Tenant Assignment," BPPPI; CD, January 29, 1938, p. 1; CD, February 12, 1938, p. 1; CD, February 19, 1938, p. 1. It should be noted that the Federal Housing Act of 1937, in its insistence on local control, impinged on what federal officials like Robert Weaver could do about segregation in Chicago's projects. On this point, see McDonnell, "The New Deal Makes a Public Housing Law", Wheaton, "The Evolution of the Federal Housing Programs."

23. On African-American protest against CHA segregation policies, see: A. L. Foster to Lea Taylor, January 28, 1938, Lea Taylor Papers, Box 17, Folder "Housing, 1927–1940"; A. L. Foster to Robert C. Weaver, August 10, 1939, RG 196, Entry no. 2 Box 87, Folder H-1400.81, and A. L. Foster to Robert C. Weaver, August 23, 1939, RG 196, Entry no. 2, Box 87, Folder H-1400.81, CD, January 29, 1938, p. 1; CD, February 12, 1938, p. 1; CD, February 19, 1938, p. 1. For CHA's anti-segregation resolution, see CD, July 22, 1939, p. 1; CD, October 21, 1939, p. 1; Regular Meeting of the Commissioners of the Chicago Housing Authority, January 9, 1939, attached to Elizabeth Wood to Thomas Wright, December 14, 1949, Box 3, Folder "Tenant Assignment," BPPPI.

24. All quotations from Wood to Henck, September 9, 1942, Box 3, Folder "Tenant Assignment," BPPPI. For more on the rioting, see A. L. Foster to Robert C. Weaver, August 10, 1939, RG 196, Entry no. 2, Box 87, Folder H-1400.81; Interview with Fumarolo, p. 30, IAC. Brooks's color composition in 1940 was 82 percent African American; ten years later it was over 95 percent. As for Addams, CHA kept African Americans' numbers under 10 percent until the mid-1950s. Once they broke this barrier, African Americans' numbers increased quickly. By the early 1960s, African Americans made up roughly three-quarters of Addams tenants. See CHA charts of African Americans' numbers by project in Box 1, Folder "Baron Material," BPPPI; Wallace, "Residential Concentration of Negroes in Chicago," p. 231. On Italians and color succession at Addams in the 1960s, see Suttles, The Social Order of the Slum, p. 16 n. 5.

25. Fromer, "The First Tenants of the Jane Addams Houses," p. 23; New Generation, March 1938, clipping, in Roland Libonati Papers, New Generation Clippings Box, no folders, CHS.

26. Interview with Fumarolo, p. 30, IAC; Wallace, "Residential Concentra-

tion of Negroes in Chicago," p. 133 n. 1. See also *LIT*, November 11, 1945, p. 3; *LIT*, June 5, 1945, p. 4.

27. HOLC, "Area Descriptions—Security Map of Chicago, Illinois," Area no. 30, March 1940, RG 195, Entry no. 39, Box 119, Folder "Metropolitan Chicago, Illinois—Master—Security Map and Area Descriptions, Section 1." See also Inter-Office Memo, C. L. Gardner to Howard Fenton, January 9, 1941, United Charities of Chicago Papers, Box 8, Folder 10, CHS.

28. On initial plans for and opposition to the "Blackhawk Project," see Metropolitan Housing Council, "Report of the Committee on Public Housing of the Metropolitan Housing Council," p. 6, Graham Aldis Papers, Folder 59, UIC; Joshua D'Esposito to Harold Ickes, December 29, 1934, RG 196, Entry no. 2, Box 84, Folder H-1400.09. For Italians' desires to have a project built on the Near North Side, see some of their letters to federal officials and politicians in RG 196, Entry no. 2, Box 101, Folder H-1403.09.

29. Letter draft by Elizabeth Wood, attached to CHA Inter-Office Memo, H. A. White to Elizabeth Wood, January 28, 1944, BPPPI, Box 3, Folder "CHA Working." On CHA's maintenance of the neighborhood composition rule on the Near North Side, see Emil G. Hirsch to Priscilla Gray, February 16, 1943, BPPPI, Box 6, Green CHS Folder.

30. Graham Aldis to George A. Bates, April 17, 1941; John B. Denell to Russell Tyson, April 16, 1941; see also Elizabeth Wood to Russell Tyson, April 21, 1941; all in Graham Aldis Papers, Folder 56, UIC. For more on the NNSPOA, see Plotkin, "Deeds of Mistrust," pp. 75–77.

31. I have made this determination based on the fact that the streets that the organization successfully restricted were not those in the heart of Little Sicily. See Pierce W. Jones to L. H. Shattuck, February 18, 1936, CHS.

32. Father Luigi Giambastiani, Invocation for the Dedication of the New Project, Frances Cabrini Homes, Chicago, Illinois, August 29, 1942, SPBPP, Section 2, Folder 68. On Giambastiani's initially friendly relationship with the CHA, see: Giambastiani to CHA, January 5, 1941; Wood to Giambastiani, January 15, 1941; Wood to Giambastiani, March 31, 1941; Wood to Giambastiani, May 21, 1941; Warren Shumard to Giambastiani, October 20, 1941; Wood to Giambastiani, April 22, 1942; Wood to Giambastiani, July 25, 1942; all in LG, Box 7, Folder 99. See also *New World*, January 23, 1942, p. 1.

33. Giambastiani to Wood, October 7, 1942, SPBPP, Section 2, Folder 68; *CD*, March 13, 1943, p. 2. For more on Giambastiani's opposition to the CHA, see: Giambastiani to Wood, January 10, 1944, SPBPP, Section 2, Folder 68; Giambastiani to Wood, October 11, 1943, LG, Box 7, Folder 99; *Monthly Report of the Executive Secretary to the Commissioners of the CHA* 4 (October 9, 1944): 2–4.

34. *CD*, August 23, 1941, p. 5; *CD*, September 6, 1941, p. 9. See also Desmond, "The Lower North Community Council," pp. 55–56; "Excerpt from Chicago Recreation Commission, 'Recreation and Delinquency,'" n.d., but c. 1940, Olivet Community Center Papers, Box 1, Folder 2, CHS. For the history of troubled African-American–Italian relations in this area, see chap. 2.

35. On the color composition of those families forced to move for the Cabrini construction, see CHA, *Bulletin* 1 (March 25, 1941): 2. There were 538 relocated families total—among them 380 Italian, 135 African American, 9 Polish, 5 Swedish, 3 Jewish, 2 "American," and 1 Chinese. David Wallace argues that 170 African Americans were displaced. See "Residential Concentration," p. 227. For explanations for the Near North Side color conflict that have

stressed the changing status of Cabrini, see MHC, "Preliminary Report of the Race Relations Committee of the Metropolitan Housing Council of Chicago," May 4, 1943, p. 1, MHPC, Box 53, Folder 6; Hirsch, *Making the Second Ghetto*, pp. 45–46. It should also be noted that this "change in status" argument assumes (wrongfully, I think) that Italians wished to return to the neighborhood. In part because the CHA refused to segregate, it appears that many Italians had little desire to return. On this point and on CHA's continual efforts to attract Italians to the project, see Harry A. White to Giambastiani, February 18, 1943; W. Gerhardt to Giambastiani, April 28, 1943; W. Gerhardt to Giambastiani, May 12, 1943; Harry A. White to Giambastiani, July 17, 1943; all in LG, Box 7, Folder 99; Metropolitan Housing Council, "Preliminary Report of the Race Relations Committee of the Metropolitan Housing Council of Chicago," p. 2, MHPC, Box 53, Folder 6; and the following IAC interviews: Lagattuta, p. 35; Spallitta, p. 26; Penio, p. 60.

36. Wood to Henck, September 10, 1942, BPPPI, Box 3, Folder "Tenant Assignment."

37. Ibid.; *Chicago Defender*, March 13, 1943, p. 16; MHC, "Preliminary Report of the Race Relations Committee of the Metropolitan Housing Council of Chicago," p. 2, MHPC, Box 53, Folder 6. For more on Italians' resistance to African Americans, see "The Chicago Urban League in 1943: Summary of Activities of a Critical Year," n.d., n.p., Chicago Urban League Annual Reports File, Chicago Urban League Papers, UIC; John W. Bennett and Herbert Passin, "Major Tensions in the Chicago Area, March 7–13," March 1943, n.p., RG 44, Entry no. 171, Box 1840, Folder "Chicago—Bennett, John W"; Mayor's Commission on Human Relations, "Race Relations in Chicago: Report of the Mayor's Commission on Human Relations, 1945," n.d., p. 41, Municipal Reference Library, Harold Washington Public Library; Minutes of the Regular Meeting of the Board of Governors, May 4, 1943; and Minutes of the Regular Meeting of the Board of Governors, August 3, 1943; both in MHPC, Accession 74–20, Box 3, Folder 33. On the Sojourner Truth riot, see Crawford, "Daily Life on the Home Front," pp. 108–113; Sugrue, "Crabgrass-Roots Politics," p. 563.

38. CHA, "Cabrini Extension Area: Portrait of a Chicago Slum," 1951, p. 5, CHS. On color proportions at Cabrini, see CHA charts of African-American numbers by project in Box 1, Folder "Baron Material"; and "Data from CHA records showing Negro and white occupancy, by numbers of families, of specified housing projects," Box 5, Folder "Racetrack Research"; both in BPPPI.

39. On the neighborhood's poor housing conditions, see HOLC, "Area Descriptions—Security Map of Chicago, Illinois," Area no. 32, March 1940, RG 195, Entry no. 39, Box 119, Folder "Metropolitan Chicago, Illinois—Master—Security Map and Area Descriptions, Section 1"; "A Message from the Chicago Commons," 1941, CC, Box 28, Folder "June-December 1941."

40. "Chicago Commons Farm Camp, New Buffalo, MI, 1940," n.d., p. 3, Box 5, Folder "Annual and Other Reports, 1937–1940"; 1940–1941 Report, n.d., pp. 24–25, Box 12, Folder "Adult Education, 1940–1941"; both in CC. On African-American population numbers, see Chicago Commons map based on 1940 census figures, CC, Box 30, Folder "January-May, 1946."

41. Typed Meeting Notes for Eagles Club, January 20, 1942, CC, Box 7, Folder "Clubs and Groups, 1940–1942"; Interview with Tonietto, p. 28, IAC. I am not arguing here that contact alone causes conflict. I would agree with both parts of the following Drake and Cayton quotation: "It is undoubtedly true that mere contact is likely to result in some degree of understanding and

friendliness. It is equally true, however, that contact can produce tension and reinforcement of folk-prejudices." The critical point, to my mind, is that given the structural *context* in which Chicago Italians lived, close contact with "Negroes" was bound to cause some problems. Thus, contact alone produces nothing inevitable for it does not occur in a vacuum; it is the context that is critical. For the quotation, see Drake and Cayton, *Black Metropolis*, pp. 281–282.

42. "Survey of the Negro Population in the Chicago Commons Area, 1946," n.d., pp. 2–3, CC, Box 13, Folder "Adult Education, 1942–1946."

43. Lea Taylor, "Lea Demarest Taylor: Her Life and Work between 1883–1968," typed transcript of autobiographical tapes produced by the National Federation of Settlements and Neighborhood Centers, p. 65, Graham Taylor Papers, Folder "Lea Taylor," NL; "Analysis of Neighborhood Needs," typed report, n.d., but c. 1945–1946, p. 2, CC, Box 13, Folder "Adult Education, 1942–1946"; "Additional Information Obtained from Interviews," typed notes, CC, Box 7, Folder "Clubs and Groups, 1943–1947."

44. Unsigned Chicago Commons letter, March 22, 1944, Box 29, Folder "January-June 1944"; "Housing as it Relates to Negroes Who are Living in Italian and Polish Neighborhoods," June 16, 1944, Box 13, Folder "Adult Education, 1942–1946"; *CD*, March 18, 1944, pp. 1–2, clipping, Box 29, Folder "January-June 1944"; all in CC. The Chicago Commons Papers are loaded with the richest of information on neighborhood relations at this time. It would be very difficult, then, to list all relevant documents. For some representative and particularly helpful documents see, in addition to those already cited: "Chicago Commons Association: Report of Work for the Year ending September 30, 1944," p. 2, Box 5, Folder "Annual and Other Reports, 1940–1946"; "Chicago Commons Association: Report of Work for the Year 1944–1945," pp. 1–3, Box 5, Folder "Annual and Other Reports, 1940–1946"; "Chicago Commons Association: Report of Work for the Year 1945–1946," pp. 9–11, Box 5, Folder "Annual and Other Reports, 1940–1946"; "Homes West of Morgan St. Which Have Been Damaged or Destroyed in the Inter-Racial Situation," December 3, 1946, Box 30, Folder "June-December, 1946"; Lea Taylor, Typed meeting minutes, n.d., Box 13, Folder "Adult Education, 1942–1946"; Harvey Seeds, "Report October-December 1945," Box 13, Folder "Adult Education, 1942–1946"; Marion Blackwell, "January Report 1946," Box 7, Folder "Clubs and Groups, 1943–1947"; Marion Blackwell, "Fall Report on Evening Work," n.d. but c. fall 1945, Box 7, Folder "Clubs and Groups, 1943–1947"; finally, see more generally boxes 13, 29, and 30; all in CC.

45. Homer A. Jack, "Documented Memorandum XI*: 1947 School Race Strike at Wells High in Chicago," p. 2 (quotation), Welfare Council Papers, Box 145, Folder 5, CHS; Lea Taylor, "Lea Demarest Taylor," p. 67. For more on the strike, see handwritten notes by D. "Moose" Brindisi, 1947, Chicago Area Project, Box 29, Folder 6, CHS; "Report of Adult Workers Education Department, 1946–1947," p. 8, CC, Box 13, Folder "Adult Education, 1947." For more on the fire, see Lea Taylor, "The Fire at 940–942 West Ohio Street: Midnight Thursday, October 9, 1947"; "Later Reactions to the Fire at 940–942 W. Ohio St.," October 15, 1947; and "Visiting," typed notes on neighborhood people's responses to the fire, October 14, 1947 (see p. 2 of this document for evidence that the fire was set intentionally); all in CC, Box 13, Folder "Adult Education, 1947."

46. For the CHA's application, see CHA, "The Procedure for Tenant Selection," typed manuscript, January 17, 1938, RG 196, Entry no. 2, Box 87, Folder

H-1400.81; on Japanese, Mexican, and Filipino tenants at Addams, see Fromer, "The First Tenants of the Jane Addams Houses," p. 23.

47. For good examples of the Chicago School's connection between geographical mobility and assimilation, see Cressey, "The Succession of Cultural Groups in the City of Chicago; Cressey, "Population Succession in Chicago: 1898–1930"; Ford, "Population Succession in Chicago," pp. 156–160.

48. Interview with "A Priest in an Italian Church" [Giambastiani], Document no. 27, pp. 2–3, "History of Lower North Side Community."; both in vol. 3, pt. 2, LCRC, CHS; Abbott, *The Tenements of Chicago*, p. 381.

49. *CDN*, May 18, 1942, clipping, LG, Box 7, Folder 99; excerpt from Chicago Recreation Commission, "Recreation and Delinquency," n.d., but c. 1940, Olivet Community Center Papers, Box 1, Folder 2, CHS; P. V. Interview, n.d. c. 1948–1949, p. 4, Chicago Area Project Papers, Box 118, CHS.

50. Interview with Spallitta, pp. 43, 18, IAC. For more evidence of Italians returning to the old neighborhood, see Interview with Clementi, p. 84, IAC; Interview with Domke, p. 55, IAC.

51. Interview with De Falco, p. 35; Interview with Martorano, pp. 18, 20–27; see also Interview with Spallitta, pp. 4–5; Interview with Giuliano, p. 74.; all in IAC.

52. Hoyt, *One Hundred Years of Land Values in Chicago*, p. 316. On the influence of Hoyt's hierarchy, see Abrams, *Forbidden Neighbors*, pp. 160–161; and Bradford, "Financing Home Ownership," p. 322.

53. "Residential Security Map, Metropolitan Chicago, Illinois, Explanation," p. 2, Box 121, Folder "Metropolitan Chicago, IL—Security Map and Area Descriptions, Section II, #1", "Confidential Report of a Re-Survey of Metropolitan Chicago, Illinois for the Division of Research and Statistics, Home Owners' Loan Corporation, Washington, D.C.," June 1, 1940, p. 35, Box 85, Folder "Chicago Resurvey Report, #2, v. I (5)"; HOLC, "Area Descriptions—Security Map of Chicago, Illinois," Area no. 89, December 1939, Box 119, Folder "Metropolitan Chicago, Illinois—Master—Security Map and Area Descriptions, Section 1"; HOLC, "Area Descriptions—Security Map of Chicago, Illinois," Area no. 106, Box 119, Folder "Metropolitan Chicago, Illinois—Master—Security Map and Area Descriptions, Section 1"; all in RG 195, Entry no. 39.

54. Hoyt, *One Hundred Years of Land Values*, pp. 314, 376; NAREB's code of ethics cited in Helper, *Racial Policies and Practices of Real Estate Brokers*, p. 201. For more on the real estate industry's race/color creed, see, in addition to Helper, Abrams, *Forbidden Neighbors*, pp. 155–168; Jackson, *Crabgrass Frontier*, pp. 198–199; Bradford, "Financing Home Ownership," 322-323.

55. Philpott, *The Slum and the Ghetto*, p. 193; Helper, *Racial Policies and Practices*, p. 150. On Chicago's real estate industry, see also Massey and Denton, *American Apartheid*, p. 50; Molotch, *Managed Integration*; Mikva, "The Neighborhood Improvement Association," pp. 4–6; Drake and Cayton, *Black Metropolis*, pp. 179-180, 202, 207.

56. Philpott, *The Slum and the Ghetto*, p. 195. On the 1950 figure, see Mikva, "The Neighborhood Improvement Association," p. 72. For other estimates and more on improvement associations, see Chicago Council Against Racial and Religious Discrimination, "Terrorism Against Negroes in Chicago: Since V-J Day—August 1945 to April 1948," map, Near West Side Community Committee Records, Folder 172, UIC; Long and Johnson, *People vs. Property*, pp. 39-55; Plotkin, "Deeds of Mistrust."

57. Long and Johnson, *People vs. Property*, p. 18. For more on restrictive

covenants in Chicago, see note 56 and: Washington, "A Study of Restrictive Covenants in Chicago"; MHC Board of Governors Minutes, June 19, 1944 and November 1, 1944, MHPC, Box 3, Folder 34; MHC, Confidential Report, January 1943, p. 2, RG 44, Entry no. 171, Box 1840, Folder "Chicago—Passin, Herbert"; Drake and Cayton, *Black Metropolis*, p. 184; Abrams, *The Future of Housing*, p. 25; Abrams, *Forbidden Neighbors*, p. 218; Schietinger, "Real Estate Transfers during Negro Invasion."

58. Mikva, "The Neighborhood Improvement Association," p. 85; Philpott, *The Slum and the Ghetto*, pp. 197–198; T.W. Wysacker, "Keeping Uptown Chicago 99 44/100% Pure (White)," Paper for Sociology 110, 1930, BUR, Box 154, Folder 2; Hirsch, *Making the Second Ghetto*, pp. 199, 208. Regarding restrictive covenants, Paul Campisi discovered in the 1940s that in Rockford, Illinois, an industrial community eighty miles northwest of Chicago, "Southern Italians are legally excluded by discriminatory clauses in abstracts from buying real estate in certain parts of X community [Rockford]." See Campisi, "The Adjustment of the Italian Americans to the War Crisis," p. 72.

59. Schietinger, "Real Estate Transfers During Negro Invasion," pp. 15–17; Long and Johnson, *People vs. Property*, p. 35.

60. Abrams, *Forbidden Neighbors*, p. 228.

61. Federal Housing Administration, *Underwriting Manual* (1936), pt. 2, paragraph 233; Federal Housing Administration, *Underwriting Manual* (1938), paragraph 980.

62. Gelfand, *A Nation of Cities*, p. 123; Jackson, *Crabgrass Frontier*, p. 215. For more on the FHA's problematic racial policies, see Federal Housing Administration, *Underwriting Manual* (1938), paragraphs 935, 980; Lipsitz, *The Possessive Investment in Whiteness*, pp. 5–6; Oliver and Shapiro, *Black Wealth/White Wealth*, pp. 18–19, 39–41, 51–52; Jackson, *Crabgrass Frontier*, pp. 203–218; Massey and Denton, *American Apartheid*, pp. 51–54; Bradford, "Financing Home Ownership," pp. 318–325; Abrams, *The Future of Housing*, p. 24.

63. On the importance of place in racial identity formation, see Hartigan, *Racial Situations*; Haas, *Conquests and Historical Identities in California*; Sugrue, *The Origins of the Urban Crisis*.

64. Minutes of Meeting of Board of Directors of the Olivet Institute, November 21, 1939, Olivet Community Center Papers, Box 1, Folder 1, CHS.

65. See note 14.

66. [Lea Taylor], "Race Situation," handwritten notes, 1944, Box 29, Folder "July-December 1944"; Marion Blackwell, "Report of Afternoon Work for January 1946," p. 1, Box 7, Folder "Clubs and Groups, 1943–1947"; [Lea Taylor], Handwritten notes from summer 1945, Box 30, Folder "December 1945 and 1945 Undated"; "Quotations for Annual Report," October 24, 1947, Box 13, Folder "Adult Education, 1947"; [Lea Taylor], handwritten diary of neighborhood "race situation," 1943–1945, n.p., entry for January 21, 1944 on "white tenants only" sign; all in CC. See also Chicago Commons Committee Meeting, November 7, 1946, handwritten minutes; and Untitled typescript, n.d., but c. 1945, p. 1; both in CC, Box 13, Folder "Adult Education, 1942–1946."

67. *Il Calendario Italiano* (June 1922), pp. 8–9, quoted in Shaw, "The Catholic Parish," pp. 214–215 n. 3; *CT*, September 23, 1928, p. 2; *CD*, April 6, 1935, p. 2.

68. Handwritten Notes, n.d., Box 7, Folder 99; Giambastiani to Wood, October 11, 1943, Box 7, Folder 99; both in LG; *CD*, March 13, 1943, p. 1.

69. Chicago Commons Committee Meeting, handwritten minutes, Febru-

ary 7, 1944, Box 12, Folder "Adult Education, 1942–1946"; [Lea Taylor], Handwritten diary on neighborhood color relations, 1943–1945, Mother's Club discussion under October 4, 1944 entry, Box 30, Folder "January-November 1944"; both in CC; *New Generation*, (October 1940): 4 (micro), Harold Washington Public Library, Chicago, IL. See also Carl Harris, "Jane Addams Residents Find a New Life in US Houses," *Mid-West Record*, reproduced in Fontana, "A Community Center in Relation to Its Neighborhood," pp. 46–48; Marion Blackwell, "Fall Report on Afternoon Work," pp. 2–3, Box 7, Folder "Clubs and Groups, 1943–1947"; and Jeanne Blacker, "Summary Record," March 3, 1948, pp. 1–2, Box 7, Folder "Red Peppers Club"; both in CC.

Conclusion

1. Numerous scholars have seen World War II as a crucial moment in European immigrants' and "ethnics'" developing white consciousness. For a sample, see Gerstle, *American Crucible*, chap. 5; McGreevy, *Parish Boundaries*, especially p. 78; Barrett and Roediger, "Inbetween Peoples," pp. 33–34; Denning, *The Cultural Front*, pp. 36, 451; Sugrue, *The Origins of the Urban Crisis*, p. 22; Nelson, *Divided We Stand*, p. xxxiv.

2. One newspaper claimed that Italian Americans constitued 10 percent of Chicago's servicemen. See *Chicago Herald American*, July 25, 1943, p. 1. For an extensive list of Chicago Italians who were injured or killed in World War II, see *LIT*'s regular column, beginning on March 7, 1943 and contuining throughout the war. On Italian Americans' representation in the armed forces nationally, see Memorandum from [Dr. Frank Stanton] to Archibald MacLeish, May 25, 1942, p. 5, RG 44, Entry no. 171, Box 1848, Folder 2, NAII; and *L'Unita del Popolo*, October 24, 1942, p. 1.

3. On Italian Americans' many win-the-war efforts in Chicago, see virtually every *LIT* issue during the war, especially the following: December 14, 1941, p. 1; Decemeber 24, 1941, p. 2; May 24, 1942, p. 3; August 29, 1943, p. 4; March 19, 1944, p. 3. See also: *L'Unita del Popolo*, December 26, 1942, p. 1; *L'Unita del Popolo*, October 1, 1942, p. 1; *L'Unita del Popolo*, October 10, 1942, p. 1; *CT*, June 15, 1942, p. 16; *CT*, October 10, 1943, pt. 3, p. 1; "Report of the Work of the Chicago Commons for the Year ending September 30, 1942," CC, Box 5, Folder "Annual and Other Reports, 1940–1946," p. 2; Renzo Sereno, "Italian American Committee for Victory in Chicago," September 25, 1942, RG 44, Entry no. 177, Box 1848, Folder 5; "Press Release, Italian-American Victory Council," September 23, 1942, Ernest De Maio Papers, Box 9, Folder 6, CHS; "Frustrating the Fascists," n.d., but c. late 1942, George L. Quilici Papers, Box 3, Folder 18; George Quilici to Ugo Carusi, September 16, 1943, George L. Quilici Papers, Box 3, Folder 17; both in IHRC.

4. There were, of course, exceptions to this point. In late 1941, for example, one government agent observed: "Most companies in the Chicago area are refusing to hire aliens and . . . some are discharging aliens now employed. The discrimination often extends to second-generation Americans, especially Italians." See H. Johnson to Files, Re: Sara Southall, November 25, 1941, Records of the INS, 146-13-5, sec. 3, accession no. 53A10, NAI. See also J. W. Innes, "Exclusions from Defense Employments of National and Racial Populations and the Press Reactions of the Excluded Groups," typed report, attached to Lawrence M. C. Smith to Lowell Mellett, December 4, 1941, Lowell Mellett Papers, Box 3, Folder "Special War Policies Unit," Franklin Delano Roosevelt Library, Hyde

Park, NY; and Steele, "'No Racials'," pp. 66–90. For more on wartime anti-Italian discrimination and prejudice, see *Public Opinion Quarterly* (March 1940): 95. One public opinion poll from 1939 found that Americans nationwide deemed Italians their least favorite immigrants overwhelmingly. The poll included immigrants of "color."

5. Lewis, *Cass Timberlaine*, pp. 44–45. On Italian-American soldiers in plural platoons, see the following books: Pyle, *Here is Your War*; Brown, *A Walk in the Sun*; Hersey, *A Bell for Adano*; Tregaskis, *Guadalcanal Diary*; Miller, *Situation Normal*. For movies, see *Back to Bataan* (1945); *The Purple Heart* (1944). For secondary sources on these themes, see Gerstle, "The Working Class Goes to War," p. 316; Gerstle, *American Crucible*, pp. 204–210; Black and Koppes, *Hollywood Goes to War*; Dick, *The Star-Spangled Screen*; Doherty, *Projections of War*.

6. On the "I Am American Day" celebrations, see *LIT*, May 16, 1943, p. 1; *LIT*, May 13, 1945, p. 3; *LIT*, May 20, 1945, p. 1. On newspapers, see *CT*, June 15, 1942, p. 16 (quotation) and the following clippings in the George L. Quilici Papers, Scrapbooks, v. 4, IHRC: *Chicago Sun*, September 19, 1942, p. 8; *Chicago Herald American*, July 25, 1943; *Chicago Daily Times*, July 26, 1943, p. 4; *CDN*, July 26, 1943; *CT*, July 26, 1943; *Chicago Sun*, July 26, 1943; v. 5: *CDN*, August 30, 1943. For an example of union publications pushing the same themes, see: *The Chicago UE News*, October 19, 1944, p. 4; *FN*, November 2, 1940, p. 1; *FN*, June 21, 1941, p. 7; *FN*, August 29, 1942, p. 1; *FN*, September 4, 1943, p. 92; *FN*, May 12, 1945, p. 1.

7. *The New York Times Magazine*, September 5, 1943, pp. 16–17. For other examples, see the secondary sources cited in note 5 above. On the general wartime expansion of Americanness, see Higham, *Send These to Me*; Gleason, *Speaking of Diversity*, pp. 153–206; Gleason, "American Identity and Americanization," pp. 31–58; Steele, "The War on Intolerance," pp. 9–35; Weiss, "Ethnicity and Reform," pp. 566–585; Gerstle, *Working-Class Americanism*, pp. 289–302. On the 1930s roots of these changes, see also Denning, *The Cultural Front*, chap. 3; and Savage, *Broadcasting Freedom*, chap. 1.

8. Glenford W. Lawrence, "Chicago Commons Celebrates Pan-American Week," n.d., but c. early 1942, CC, Box 28, Folder "January-July 1942"; Lea Taylor to Chicago Commons Board, January 23, 1945, CC, Box 30, Folder "January-November 1945"; *Hull House Bulletin* 19 (June 15, 1942) in Hull-House Records, Folder 467, UIC; *LIT*, June 28, 1942, p. 4; *LIT*, August 23, 1942, p. 1; *LIT*, May 16, 1943, p. 1; *LIT*, May 13, 1945, p. 3.

9. Gerstle, *American Crucible*, p. 231.

10. [Dr. Frank Stanton], Bureau of Intelligence, Office of Facts and Figures, Memorandum to Archibald MacLeish, May 25, 1942, p. 1, RG 44, Entry no. 171, Box 1848, Folder 2; Albert Perry, "The Italian-Americans of Chicago," RG 226 (micro), INT—17IT—489, NAII.

11. There is no consensus on how many Chicago Italians were arrested and/or interned. *L'Italia* reported in December 1941 that federal agents in Chicago picked up forty-eight aliens, most of whom were Germans and Italians. One federal government report noted that only three to four had been interned. The *CT* reported five Italian aliens had been arrested by June 1942. See *LIT*, December 16, 1941, p. 3; "Frustrating the Fascists," p. 6; *CT*, June 15, 1942, p. 16. On Italians' relocation and internment experience, see Fox, *The Unknown Internment*; DiStasi, *Una Storia Segreta*; Scherini, "When Italian Americans Were 'Enemy Aliens'"; and Scherini, "Executive Order 9066 and Italian Americans," pp. 367–377. America's differential treatment of "enemy aliens" ex-

tended to pop culture representations. On this point, see Guglielmo, "The Forgotten Enemy," pp. 5–22; Dower, *War Without Mercy*, pp. 15–32; Blum, *V Was for Victory*; Doherty, *Projections of War*; Black and Koppes, *Hollywood Goes to War*.

12. Lemuel B. Schofield to District Director, June 26, 1941, RG 85, Entry no. 26, Box 1041, File 44/5, pt. 2, NAI. For more on government discussions of race/color confusions and their decisions to make changes in their forms regarding these categories, see Charles P. Mueller to Mr. T. B. Shoemaker, June 3, 1941; Francis Biddle to Arthur Hays Schulzberger, August 20, 1943; Lemuel B. Schofield to Assistant District Director, INS, New York, August 19, 1941; Arthur Hays Schulzberger to Francis Biddle, July 25, 1941; all in RG 85, Entry no. 26, Box 1041, File 44/5, pt. 2, NAI. For copies of Declarations of Intention, in which one can see race/color answers change over time, see RG 21, U.S. District Court, Northern District of Illinois, Naturalizations, vols. 1026–1027, National Archives, Great Lakes Branch, Chicago, IL.

13. See, for instance, Mayor's Conference on Race Relations, *City Planning in Race Relations*; Mayor's Conference on Race Relations, *Race Relations in Chicago*; Mayor's Committee on Human Relations, *Human Relations in Chicago: Report for the Year 1946*; Mayor's Commission on Human Relations memorandum from Thomas H. Wright to Members of the Commission and all Committee Members, September 18, 1946, Lea Taylor Papers, Box 20, Folder 110, CHS. On the "Neighbors Around the World" Project, see Chicago Federation of Settlements and Neighborhood Centers, "Notes of Social Education Projects For Summer Schools," typed report, July 1, 1946, Madonna Center Records, Series 2, Box 2, Folder "Chicago Federation of Settlements," Marquette University, Memorial Library, Milwaukee, WI. Further examples of local race/color melding can be found throughout the CC and are far too numerous to cite here. See especially Boxes 12–13, 28–30.

14. *LIT*, March 26, 1942, p. 2 (quotation); *LIT*, March 19, 1942, p. 2; *LIT*, April 2, 1942, p. 2; *LIT*, April 9, 1942, p. 2. For references to "il nostro gruppo etnco," see the following *LIT* citations: July 25, 1943, pp. 3–4; August 8, 1943, p. 1; August 29, 1943, p. 1; June 26, 1940, p. 1. Terms such as "la nostra razza" hardly disappeared in *LIT*, however. See *LIT*: April 4, 1943, p. 1; October 10, 1943, p. 1; April 9, 1944, p. 1; January 14, 1945, p. 3; July 22, 1945, p. 3; September 23, 1945, p. 1.

15. Polenberg, *One Nation Divisible*, p. 44. For evidence that Italians, as an "enemy group," felt particularly uneasy during the war years, see the following: [Dr. Frank Stanton], Bureau of Intelligence, Office of Facts and Figures, Memorandum to Archibald MacLeish, May 25, 1942, p. 3, RG 44, Entry no. 171, Box 1848, Folder 2; Campisi, "The Adjustment of the Italian Americans to the War Crisis."

16. Jacobson, *Whiteness of a Different Color*, p. 8.

17. Quilici's address reprinted in *Mayor's Committee on Home Front Unity* (Program), May 29, 1945, p. 16, Chicago Urban League Papers, Folder 231 (supplement), UIC (my emphasis).

BIBLIOGRAPHY

Primary Sources

Archival and Manuscript Collections

Archdiocese of Chicago's Joseph Cardinal Bernardin Archives and Records
    Center, Chicago, IL
        Chancery Correspondence
        George Cardinal Mundelein Papers
        Bishop Bernard Sheil Papers
        Samuel Cardinal Strich Papers
Chicago Crime Commission, Chicago, IL
        Clippings File
Chicago Historical Society, Chicago, IL
        Amalgamated Clothing Workers of America Papers
        Benton House Papers
        Broadside Collection
        Business and Professional People for the Public Interest Papers
        Alphonse Capone Papers
        Catholic Interracial Council Papers
        Chicago Area Project Papers
        Chicago Boys Club Papers
        Chicago Commons Papers
        Chicago Federation of Labor Papers
        Citizens Association of Chicago Papers
        Community Clippings File
        Ernest De Maio Papers
        William E. Dever Mayoralty Papers
        Emerson House Papers
        Erie Neighborhood House Papers
        Foreign Populations Collection
        James Berwick Forgan Papers
        Joint Civic Committee of Italian Americans Papers
        Roland Libonati Papers
        Local Community Research Committee Papers

Arthur Mitchell Papers
Olivet Community Center Papers
George Patterson Papers
Bessie L. Pierce Papers
William D. Saltiel Papers
Anthony Sorrentino Papers
Lea Taylor Papers
United Charities of Chicago Papers
United Steelworkers of America Papers
Welfare Council of Chicago Papers
Cornell University, Labor Management Documentation Center, Ithaca, NY
International Workers Order Papers
Franklin Delano Roosevelt Library, Hyde Park, NY
Lowell Mellett Papers
Harold Washington Public Library, Special Collections, Chicago, IL
Municipal Reference Library Collection
Immigration History Research Center, Minneapolis, MN
Egidio Clemente Papers
Joseph Fucilla Papers
Olga Gralton Papers
Emilio Grandinetti Papers
Mario Manzardo Papers
Maurice R. Marchello Papers
Eugene Miller Papers
Order of the Sons of Italy, Illinois Grand Lodge Records
George L. Quilici Papers
George J. Spatuzza Papers
Labadie Collection, University of Michigan Special Collections, Ann Arbor, MI
Marquette University, Memorial Library, Special Collections and University Archives, Milwaukee, WI
Madonna Center Records
National Archives I, Washington, D.C.
Records of the Bureau of the Census, RG 29
Records of the Immigration and Naturalization Service, RG 85
National Archives II, College Park, MD
General Records of the Department of Housing and Urban Development, RG 207
General Records of the Department of Justice, RG 60
General Records of the Department of Labor, RG 174
National Archives Collection of Foreign Records Seized, RG 242 (micro)
Records of the Committee on Fair Employment Practice, RG 228
Records of the Federal Home Loan Bank Board, RG 195
Records of the Office of Government Reports, RG 44
Records of the Office of Strategic Services, RG 226 (micro)
Records of the Public Housing Administration, RG 196
National Archives, Great Lakes Branch, Chicago, IL
Records of the U.S. District Court, Northern District of Illinois, RG 21
Newberry Library, Chicago, IL
Victor Lawson Papers
Pullman Company Records

Graham Taylor Papers
Our Lady of Sorrows Basilica Archives, Chicago, IL
Fr. Luigi Giambastiani, OSM Papers, The Morini Memorial Collection
Fr. Pellegrino M. Giangrandi, OSM Papers
St. Philip Benizi Parish Papers
University of Chicago, Department of Special Collections, Chicago, IL
Grace and Edith Abbott Papers
Jane Addams Letters and Hull-House Materials
American Civil Liberties Union Papers
Ernest W. Burgess Papers
Chicago Foreign Language Press Survey
Harold F. Gosnell Papers
John P. Landesco Papers
Charles E. Merriam Papers
Julius Rosenwald Papers
University of Illinois at Chicago, Special Collections, Richard J. Daley University
Library, Chicago, IL
Jane Addams Papers (micro)
Graham Aldis Papers
Martin Bickham Papers
Century of Progress Records
Chicago Urban League Papers
Egidio Clemente Papers
Hull-House Records
Immigrant Protective League Records
Italian-American Oral History Collection
Juvenile Protective Association Records
Metropolitan Housing and Planning Council Papers
Rosamond L. Mirabella Papers
Near West Side Community Committee Records
Vivien G. Harsh Research Collection, Carter G. Woodson Regional Library,
Chicago, IL
Negro in Illinois Papers

Federal Government Publications

Federal Housing Administration. *Underwriting Manual*. Washington, D.C.: Government Printing Office, 1936.
———. *Underwriting Manual*. Washington, D.C.: Government Printing Office, 1938.
Gries, John M. and James Ford, eds. *Publications of the President's Conference on Home Building and Home-Ownership*, 11 vols. Washington, D.C.: Government Printing Office, 1932.
Kelley, Florence. "Italians in Chicago." *Bulletin of the Department of Labor* (United States Bureau of Labor) 2 (1897): 691–727.
U.S. Commissioner of Labor. *Seventh Special Report: The Slums of Baltimore, Chicago, New York and Philadelphia*. Washington, D.C.: Government Printing Office, 1894.
U.S. Congress. *Congressional Record*, vol. 58. 66th Cong., 1st sess. Washington, D.C.: Government Printing Office, 1919.

———. *Congressional Record*, vol. 65. 68th Cong., 1st sess. Washington, D.C.: Government Printing Office, 1924.

———. *Congressional Record*, vol. 67. 69th Cong., 1st sess. Washington, D.C.: Government Printing Office, 1924.

U.S. Congress. House. Committee on Immigration and Naturalization. *Hearings Relative to the Further Restriction of Immigration*. 62nd Cong., 2nd sess. Washington, D.C.: Government Printing Office, 1912.

———. Committee on Immigration and Naturalization. *Hearings: Restriction of Immigration*. 68th Cong., 1st sess. Washington, D.C.: Government Printing Office, 1924.

U.S. Congress. Senate. Committee on Immigration. *Hearings: Selective Immigration Legislation*. 68th Cong., 1st sess. Washington, D.C.: Government Printing Office, 1924.

U.S. Department of Commerce. Bureau of Census. *Eleventh Census of the United States, 1890. Population*. Washington, D.C.: Government Printing Office, 1895.

———. *Twelfth Census of the United States, 1900. Population*. Washington, D.C.: Government Printing Office, 1901.

———. *Thirteenth Census of the United States, 1910. Population*. Washington, D.C.: Government Printing Office, 1913.

———. *Fifteenth Census of the United States, 1930. Population*. Washington, D.C.: Government Printing Office, 1932.

———. *Sixteenth Census of the United States, 1940. Population*. Washington, D.C.: Government Printing Office, 1943.

———. *Seventeenth Census of the United States, 1950. Population*. Washington, D.C.: Government Printing Office, 1952.

U.S. Immigration Commission. *Abstracts of the Reports of the Immigration Commission*. Washington, D.C.: Government Printing Office, 1911.

———. *Bituminous Coal Mining*. Washington, D.C.: Government Printing Office, 1911.

———. *Clothing Manufacturing*. Washington, D.C.: Government Printing Office, 1911.

———. *Dictionary of Races and Peoples*. Washington, D.C.: Government Printing Office, 1911.

———. *Immigrants in the Cities*. Washington, D.C.: Government Printing Office, 1911.

———. *Iron and Steel Manufacturing*. Washington, D.C.: Government Printing Office, 1911.

———. *Slaughtering and Meatpacking*. Washington, D.C.: Government Printing Office, 1911.

Wright, Caroll D. *The Italians in Chicago*. Washington, D.C.: Government Printing Office, 1896.

———. "Ninth Special Report of the Italians in Chicago," *U.S. Department of Labor Bulletin*, No. 13 (November 1897).

Newspapers and Periodicals

The American Mercury
Atlantic Monthly
Bolletino Parocchiale della Chiesa di Sant'Antonio
Bulletin of the Italo-American National Union

Bulletin of the Order of the Sons of Italy of Illinois
By Archer Road
Il Calendario Italiano
Chicago American
Chicago Daily Journal
Chicago Daily News
Chicago Defender
Chicago Evening American
Chicago Evening Post
Chicago Herald Examiner
Chicago Housing Authority Bulletin
Chicago Italian Chamber of Commerce Bulletin
Chicago Record-Herald
Chicago Times
Chicago Tribune
Chicago UE News
Christian Century
Collier's
The Crisis
Current Opinion
Daily Inter-Ocean
Dawn
Federation News
Foreign Affairs
The Forum
Harper's Monthly Magazine
Journal of Criminal Law and Criminology
Journal of Negro History
Journal of the Chicago Crime Commission
L'Avanti
Il Lavoratore
Leader
L'Italia
Literary Digest
Local 101 News
Loose Leaves
L'Unita del Popolo
Mid-West Record
The Nation
Newsweek
New Generation
New Republic
New York Times
New World
North American Review
La Parola del Popolo
La Parola dei Socialisti
La Parola Proletaria
Il Progresso Italo-Americano
Il Proletario
Race Relations

Review of Reviews
Saturday Evening Post
Steel News
Survey Graphic
La Tribuna Italiana Transatlantica
Vita Nuova
Women in Steel
World's Work
Yale Review

Interviews

Italian-American Oral History Collection, Richard J. Daley University Library, Special Collections, University of Illinois at Chicago

Nick Accettura, July 19, 1979
Joseph Amella, February 8, 1980
Mary Argenzio, July 2, 1980
Rita (Mattioni) Arrow, March 31, 1980
Rosalie Augustine, August 5, 1980
Mario Avignone, July 12 and 14, 1979
Gloria A. Bacci, April 9, 1980
Sam Baio, May 31, 1980
Edward Baldacci, May 29, 1980
Aldo Bertacchi, April 15, 1980
Frank Bertucci, May 3, 1980
Mildred Bonevolenta, July 21, 1980
Mario Bruno, March 20, 1980
Vito Cali, April 22, 1980
Jean Carsello, February 3, 1980
Anthony Cassano, March 22, 1980
Frank Catrambone, December 20, 1979
Joseph Cesario, December 18, 1979
Agnes Chidichino, May 7, 1980
Rose Clementi, April 7, 1980
Leonard Colella, July 2, 1980
Frank Coradetti, May 13, 1980
Salvatore Cosentino, July 13, 1979
Sister Augustine (Cutrara), August 7, 1980
Nina Dal Cason, December 3, 1979
Ernest Dalle Molle, April 30, 1980
Rosa D'Angelo, July 16, 1979
Robert De Facci, March 20, 1980
Teresa De Falco, April 28, 1980
Jennie DiFalco DeFiglio, November 28, 1979
Frank DeLiberto, April 17, 1980
Antoinette DeMarco, March 7, 1980
Marco DeStefano, January 4, 1980
Anthony DiCicco, August 9, 1980
Domenick DiMucci, July 19, 1979
Umberto J. Dini, July 16, 1979
Rena Domke, April 28, 1980

Louis Esposito, April 8, 1980
Alfred Fantozzi, May 27, 1980
Antonio Faustini, February 11, 1980
Donald Fumarolo, May 1, 1980
Joseph Gentile, June 2, 1980
Theresa Giannetti, April 16, 1980
Leonard Giuliano, January 2, 1980
Victor Giustino, January 5, 1980
Dante A. Greco, April 25, 1980
Marietta Magnuco Interlandi, October 17, 1979
Olivia Kowalski, February 19, 1980
Sarah Lagattuta, January 5, 1981
Valentino Lazzaretti, July 12, 1979
Emilio Leonardi, January 24, 1980
Alphonse Leone, February 29, 1980
Grace Licata, March 1, 1979
Carmela Lizzo, December 21, 1979 and January 10, 1980
Joseph Loguidice, July 21, 1980
Mary Manella, April 14, 1980
Frank Mariani, November 19, 1979
Joachim Martorano, July 9, 1980
Philomena Mazzei, April 22, 1981
Rosamond Mirabella, May 23, 1980
Rena Morandin, July 22, 1980
Americo Moreschi, July 14, 1979
Umberta Mugnaini, July 17, 1979
Constance Muzzacavallo, June 12, 1980
Joe Muzzarelli, April 23, 1980
James Neri, September 17, 1980
Salvatore Occhipinti, April 10, 1980
Domenic Pandolfi, February 20, 1980
Angelo Pane, July 30, 1980
Louis Panico, March 25, 1980
Florence Parise, June 20, 1980
Daniel Passarella, August 11, 1980
Angelo Patti, July 14, 1980
Paul Penio, June 30, 1980
Thomas Perpoli, June 26, 1980
Sylvio Petri, May 20, 1980
Joseph Provenzano, March 17, 1980
Carlo Pulcini, March 13, 1980
Phil Rafaelli, June 23, 1980
Susan Rago, November 8, 1980
Louis Raia, September 19, 1979
Joe Rosa, August 9, 1980
Florence Roselli, April 4, 1979
Lois Roth (Clarizio), April 1, 1980
Margaret Sabella, April 15, 1980
Emilia Scarpelli, July 2, 1980
Nella Schnaufer, May 16, 1980
Lawrence Spallitta, December 30, 1979 and January 2, 1980

Pasqua Sparvieri, February 28, 1980
Lina Tarabori, June 5, 1980
Rose Tellerino, February 12, 1980
Nick Tieri, February 21, 1980
Angeline Tonietto, July 1, 1980
Joe Ungari, March 8, 1980
Caterina Valente, May 6, 1980
Maria Valiani, June 10, 1980
Amadeo Yelmini, May 4, 1980
Nick Zaranti, March 5, 1980
Carmella Zoppetti, June 9, 1980

Roosevelt University Labor Oral History Project, Roosevelt University, Chicago, IL

Ernest De Maio, November 16, 1970, February 23, 1971
Joe Martin, n.d.
George Patterson, December 1970, January 1971

Interview with Timothy B. Neary (in author's possession)

Florence Scala, November 7, 1997

Interviews with Author (in author's possession)

Anonymous, February 10, 1999
Anthony Sorrentino, January 29, 1999

Other Primary Sources

Abbott, Edith. *Immigration.* Chicago: University of Chicago Press, 1926.
———. *The Tenements of Chicago, 1908–1935.* Chicago: University of Chicago Press, 1936.
Addams, Jane. "Foreign-born Children in the Primary Grades; Italian Families in Chicago." *National Education Association; Journal of Proceedings and Addresses* 36 (1897): 104–112.
———. "The Housing Problem in Chicago." *Annals of the American Academy of Political and Social Science* 20 (July 1902): 99–103.
———. *Forty Years at Hull-House,* 2 vols. New York: Macmillan, 1935.
———. *Twenty Years at Hull-House.* Reprint ed. New York: Macmillan, 1981.
Amberg, Mary A. *Madonna Center.* Chicago: Loyola University Press, 1975.
Bagaglia, Clementina. *Letture Classe Prima.* Rome: Libreria dello Stato, 1933.
———. *Letture Classe Terza.* Rome: Libreria dello Stato, 1933.
Barnes, Charles B. *The Longshoremen.* New York: Survey Associates, 1915.
Beck, Frank O. "The Italian in Chicago." *Bulletin of the Chicago Department of Public Welfare* 2 (February 1919).
Boas, Franz. "Human Faculty as Determined by Race." *American Academy of Arts and Sciences Proceedings* 43 (1894): 301–327.
———. *The Mind of Primitive Man.* New York: Macmillan, 1911.
———. "The Rising Tide of Color." *The Nation* 111 (December 8, 1920): 656.
———. "The Question of Racial Purity." *The American Mercury* 111 (October 1924): 163–169.
———. "What Is a Race?" *The Nation* 120 (January 28, 1925): 89–91.
———. "This Nordic Nonsense." *The Forum* 74 (October 1925): 502–511.

Boas, Franz, with Helen M. Boas. "The Head Forms of Italians as Influenced by Heredity and Environment." *American Anthropologist* 15 (1913): 163–188.

Breckenridge, Sophonisba. *New Homes for Old.* Reprint ed. Montclair, NJ: Patterson Smith, 1971.

Breckenridge, Sophonisba, and Edith Abbott. "Chicago Housing Conditions, IV: The West Side Revisited." *American Journal of Sociology* 17 (July 1911): 1–34.

——— "The Color Line in the Housing Problem." *Survey* 29 (February 1, 1913): 575–576.

Brigham, Carl C. *A Study of American Intelligence.* Princeton, NJ: Princeton University Press, 1923.

Brown, Harry. *A Walk in the Sun.* New York: Alfred A. Knopf, 1944.

Bunche, Ralph J. "The Thompson-Negro Alliance." *Opportunity* 7 (March 1929): 78–80.

Burgess, Ernest W., and Charles Newcomb, eds. *Census Data of the City of Chicago, 1920.* Chicago: University of Chicago Press, 1931.

———. *Census Data of the City of Chicago, 1930.* Chicago: University of Chicago Press, 1933.

Burns, Walter N. *The One-Way Ride: The Red Trail of Chicago Gangland from Prohibition to Jake Lingle.* Garden City, NY: Doubleday, Doran & Co., 1931.

Burr, Clinton Stoddard. *America's Race Heritage.* New York: The National Historical Society, 1922.

Carter, Boake. *Black Shirt Black Skin.* Harrisburg, PA: Telegraph Press, 1935.

Cavan, Ruth Shonle, and Katherine Howland Ranck. *The Family and the Depression: A Study of One Hundred Chicago Families.* Chicago: University of Chicago Press, 1938.

Cayton, Horace R., and George S. Mitchell. *Black Workers and New Unions.* Chapel Hill: University of North Carolina Press, 1939.

Chicago Commission on Race Relations. *The Negro in Chicago: A Study of Race Relations and a Riot.* Chicago: University of Chicago Press, 1922.

Chicago Housing Authority. "Low Rent Housing in Chicago." Chicago: n.p. 1941.

———. "Cabrini Extension Area; Portrait of a Chicago Slum." Chicago: n.p. 1951.

Chicago Plan Commission. *Residential Chicago.* Chicago: University of Chicago Press, 1943.

Cipriani, Lisi. *Selected Directory of the Italians in Chicago, 1930 & 1933-34.* Chicago: Italian Labor Publishing Co., 1933.

Coon, Carleton S. "A Realist Looks at Ethiopia." *Atlantic Monthly* 156 (September 1935): 310–315.

Courtney, W. B. "Blackshirt Heaven." *Collier's* 97 (May 16, 1936): 12–13, 51–52, 54.

———. "Dark and Bloody Road." *Collier's* 97 (May 21, 1936): 29–30.

Creel, George. "Melting Pot or Dumping Ground." *Collier's* 68 (September 3, 1921): 9–10.

———. "Close the Gates! The Way to Shut the Door Is to Shut It." *Collier's* 69 (May 6, 1922): 9–10.

Cressey, Paul G. *Taxi Dance Halls.* Chicago: University of Chicago Press, 1932.

Curran, H. H. "Fewer and Better, or None." *Saturday Evening Post* 196 (November 15, 1924): 8–9.

Davie, Maurice R. *A Constructive Immigration Policy.* New Haven, CT: Yale University Press, 1923.

De Palma Castiglione, G. E. "Italian Immigration into the United States, 1901–1904." *American Journal of Sociology* 11 (September 1905): 183–206.

Direzione Generale degli Italiane all'Estero. *Il Libro della IV Classe Elementare: Scuole Italiane all'Estero.* Rome: Libreria dello Stato, 1933.

Direzione Generale Italiani all'Estero e Scuole. *Letture Classe Seconda.* Rome: Libreria dello Stato, 1929.

Divers, Vivia H. *'The Black Hole'; or The Missionary Experience of a Girl in the Slums of Chicago, 1891–1892.* N.p., 1893.

Does Crime Pay? No! As Shown by the Uncensored Photos in This Book. Life Story of Al Capone in Pictures. Chicago: n.p., n.d. [1931].

Drake, St. Clair, and Horace R. Cayton. *Black Metropolis: A Study of Negro Life in a Northern City.* Rev. ed. Chicago: University of Chicago Press, 1993.

Du Bois, W. E. B. "Inter-Racial Implications of the Ethiopian Crisis: A Negro View." *Foreign Affairs* 14 (October 1935): pp. 82–93.

Duffield, Marcus. "Mussolini's American Empire: The Fascist Invasion of the United States." *Harper's Magazine* 159 (November 1929): 661–672.

Dunne, Edmund M. *Memoirs of "Zi Pre."* St. Louis: B. Herder, 1914.

Editor. "The Man Who Broke Chicago's Gang Rule." *Real Detective* (October 1933): 33–34.

Embree, Edwin R. *Summary of Mayor's Conference on Race Relations.* Chicago: n.p., 1944.

Enright, Richard T. *Al Capone on the Spot: The Inside Story of Chicago's Master Criminal.* Chicago: Graphic Arts Corp., 1931.

Evans, Hiram Wesley. "The Klan's Fight for Americanism." *North American Review* 223 (March-April-May 1924): 33–63.

Fairchild, Henry Pratt. *Immigration: A World Movement and Its American Significance.* Rev. ed. New York: Macmillan, 1925.

Farinacci, M. G. "Oppressed Sicily." *Bulletin of the Italo-American National Union* (October 1928): 1–5.

Farrell, James T. *Studs Lonigan: A Trilogy.* New York: The Modern Library, 1938.

Foerster, Robert F. *The Italian Emigration of Our Times.* Cambridge, MA: Harvard University Press, 1919.

Ford, James W. *The Negro and the Democratic Front.* New York: International Publishers, 1935.

Frazer, Elizabeth. "Our Foreign Cities: Chicago." *Saturday Evening Post* 196 (August 25, 1923): 14–15, 102–105.

Frazier, E. Franklin. *The Negro Family in Chicago.* Chicago: University of Chicago Press, 1932.

Garis, Roy L. *Immigration Restriction: A Study of the Opposition to and the Regulation of Immigration into the United States.* New York: Macmillan, 1927.

Gavit, J. P. "So This Is Civilization?" *Survey Graphic* 24 (November 1935): 548–549.

Gerould, Katherine Fullerton. "Jessica and Al Capone." *Harper's Monthly Magazine* 163 (June 1931): 92–97.

Giacosa, Giuseppe. "Gli Italiani a New York ed a Chicago." *Nuova Antalogia* 15 (August 16, 1892): 618–640.

Gosnell, Harold F. *Getting Out the Vote: An Experiment in the Stimulation of Voting.* Chicago: University of Chicago Press, 1927.

———. "Characteristics of the Non-Naturalized." *American Journal of Sociology* 34 (March 1929): pp. 847–855.

———. *Negro Politicians: The Rise of Negro Politicians in Chicago.* Chicago: University of Chicago Press, 1935.

———. *Machine Politics: Chicago Model.* Chicago: University of Chicago Press, 1937.

Grant, Madison. *The Passing of the Great Race or the Racial Basis of European History.* 4th ed. New York: Charles Scribner's Sons, 1921.

Haile, Makonnen. "Last Gobble of Africa." *The Crisis* 42 (March 1935): 70–71, 90.

Haynes, George Edmund. "Negroes and the Ethiopian Crisis." *Christian Century* 52 (November 20, 1935): 1485–1486.

Hersey, John. *Into the Valley.* New York: Alfred A. Knopf, 1943.

———. *A Bell for Adano.* New York: Alfred A. Knopf, 1944.

Houghteling, Leila. *The Income and Standard of Living of Unskilled Laborers in Chicago.* Chicago: University of Chicago Press, 1927.

Hoyt, Homer. *One Hundred Years of Land Values in Chicago.* Chicago: University of Chicago Press, 1933.

———. *According to Hoyt: 50 Years of Homer Hoyt.* Washington, D.C.: n.p., 1966.

Hughes, Elizabeth A. *Living Conditions for Small-Wage Earners in Chicago.* Chicago: Department of Public Welfare, City of Chicago, 1925.

Human Relations in Chicago: Report of Commissions and Charter of Human Relations. Chicago: n.p., 1945.

Hunter, Robert. *Tenement Conditions in Chicago: Report by the Investigating Committee of the City Homes Association.* Chicago: City Homes Association, 1901.

Huntington, Ellsworth. *The Character of Races as Influenced by Physical Environment, Natural Selection, and Historical Development.* New York: Charles Scribner's Sons, 1927.

Italy and Abyssinia. Rome: Societa' Editrice di Novissima, n.d [1936?].

Kallen, Horace. *Culture and Democracy in the United States: Studies in the Group Psychologies of the American Peoples.* New York: Boni and Liveright, 1924.

Kirkpatrick, Clifford. *Intelligence and Immigration with Special Reference to Certain New England Groups.* Baltimore, MD: Williams and Wilkins, 1925.

Landesco, John. *Organized Crime in Chicago.* Chicago: University of Chicago Press, 1928.

———. "Life History of a Member of the Forty-Two Gang." *Journal of Criminal Law and Criminology* 23 (July 1932): 964–998.

———. "Prohibition and Crime." *The Annals of the American Academy of Political and Social Science* 163 (September 1932): 120–129.

———. "Crime and the Failure of Institutions in Chicago's Immigrant Areas." *Journal of Criminal Law and Criminology* 23 (March 1933): 964–998.

Leiserson, William M. *Adjusting Immigrant and Industry.* New York: Harper and Brothers, 1924.

Lewis, Sinclair. *Babbitt.* Reprint ed. New York: Signet Classic, 1992.

———. *Cass Timberlaine.* New York: Random House, 1945.

Life of Al Capone in Pictures! And Chicago's Gang Wars. Chicago: Lake Michigan Publishing Co., 1931.

Lord, Eliot. *The Italian in America.* New York: B. F. Buck Co., 1905.

Mannheim, Frank J. "The United States and Ethiopia." *Journal of Negro History* 17 (April 1932): 141–155.

Marimpietri, A. D. *From These Beginnings: The Making of the Amalgamated.* Chicago: Chicago Joint Board, Amalgamated Clothing Workers, 1928.

Mastro-Valerio, Alessandro. "Remarks upon the Italian Colony in Chicago." In *Hull-House Maps and Papers*, edited by Residents of Hull-House. New York: T.Y. Cromwell & Co., 1895.

Mayor's Conference on Race Relations. *City Planning in Race Relations.* Chicago: n.p., 1944.

———. *Race Relations in Chicago.* Chicago: Committee on Race Relations, 1944.

Mayor's Committee on Human Relations. *Human Relations in Chicago: Report for the Year 1946.* Chicago: Chicago Commission on Human Relations, n.d.

McDougall, William. *Is America Safe for Democracy?* New York: Charles Scribner's Sons, 1921.

Merriam, Charles E. *Chicago: A More Intimate View of Urban Politics.* New York: Macmillan, 1929.

———. *The Government of the Metropolitan Region of Chicago.* Chicago: University of Chicago Press, 1933.

Merriam, Charles E., and Harold Foote Gosnell. *Non-Voting: Causes and Methods of Control.* Chicago: University of Chicago Press, 1924.

Miller, Arthur. *Situation Normal.* New York: Reynal and Hitchcock, 1944.

Myrdal, Gunnar. *An American Dilemma: The Negro Problem and Modern Democracy.* New York: Harper, 1944.

Newcomb, Charles, and Richard Lang, eds. *Census Data of the City of Chicago, 1934.* Chicago: University of Chicago Press, 1934.

Norton, Grace P. "Chicago Housing Conditions, VII: Two Italian Districts." *American Journal of Sociology* 18 (January 1913): 509–542.

Padmore, George. "Ethiopia and World Politics." *The Crisis* 42 (March 1935): 138–139, 156–157.

Panunzio, Constantine. "Italian Americans, Fascism, and the War." *Yale Review* 31 (Summer 1942): 771–782.

Park, Robert E. *Race and Culture.* Glencoe, IL: The Free Press, 1950.

Park, Robert E., and Herbert A. Miller. *Old World Traits Transplanted.* New York: Harper and Brothers, 1921.

Pasley, Fred D. *Al Capone: The Biography of a Self-Made Man.* New York: Ives Washburn, 1930.

Peffer, Nathaniel. "The White Peril: Is Italy Forcing the Race Issue Upon Africa As Well as Asia?" *Asia* 35 (October 1935): 606–609.

Pierce, David. "Fascism and the Negro." *The Crisis* 42 (April 1935): 107, 114.

Preece, Harold. "Fascism and the Negro." *The Crisis* 41 (December 1934): 355, 366.

Prindiville, Kate G. "Italy in Chicago." *Catholic World* 77 (July 1903): 452–461.

Provana del Sabbione, L. "Condizione della Emigrazione nel R. Distretto Consolare in Chicago." *Bolletino dell'Emigrazione* 1 (1913): 27-33.

Pyle, Ernie. *Here is Your War.* Cleveland: World Publishing Co., 1945.

Randolph, Robert Isham. "How to Wreck Capone's Gang." *Collier's* 87 (March 7, 1931): 7–9.

Ripley, William Z. "Races in the United States." *Atlantic Monthly* 102 (December 1908): 745–759.

Roberts, Kenneth. *Why Europe Leaves Home.* New York: Bobbs-Merrill, 1922.

———. "Slow Poison." *Saturday Evening Post* 196 (February 2, 1924): 8–9, 54, 56, 58.

Rogers, J. A. "Italy over Abyssinia." *The Crisis* 42 (February 1935):38–39, 50.

Ross, Edward A. *The Old World in the New: The Significance of Past and Present Immigration to the American People*. New York: Century, 1914.

———. "Italians in America." *Century Magazine* 87 (July 1914): 443–445.

Salvemini, Gaetano. *Fascist Activities in the United States*, edited by Philip V. Cannistraro. New York: Center for Migration Studies, 1977.

Sandburg, Carl. *The Chicago Race Riots, July, 1919*. Reprint ed. New York: Harcourt, Brace, and World, 1969.

Schiavo, Giovanni. *The Italians in Chicago: A Study in Americanization*. Chicago: Italian American Publishing Co., 1928.

Shaw, Clifford R. *Delinquency Areas: A Study of the Geographic Distribution of School Truants, Juvenile Delinquents, and Adult Offenders in Chicago*. Chicago: University of Chicago Press, 1929.

———. *The Jack-Roller: A Delinquent Boy's Own Story*. Chicago: University of Chicago Press, 1930.

Shaw, Clifford R., and Henry D. McKay. *Social Factors in Juvenile Delinquency*. Washington, D.C.: Government Printing Office, 1931.

Skidmore, Hubert. *Valley of the Sky*. Boston, MA: Houghton Mifflin, 1944.

Speranza, Gino C. "How It Feels to Be a Problem." *Charities* 12 (May 7, 1904): 457–463.

———. "The Immigration Peril." Series of articles in the *World's Work* 47–48 (November 1923–May 1924).

———. *Race or Nation: A Conflict of Divided Loyalties*. Indianapolis, IN: Bobbs-Merrill, 1925.

Spatuzza, George. "Wake Up." *Bulletin of the Order of the Sons of Italy of Illinois* (May 15, 1934). 1–3.

Stella, Antonio. *Some Aspects of Italian Immigration*. New York: G.P. Putnam's Sons, 1924.

Stewart, Maxwell S. "Mussolini's Dream of Empire." *The Nation* 141 (September 4, 1935): 402–405.

Stoddard, Lothrop. *The Rising Tide of Color Against White World Supremacy*. New York: Charles Scribner's Sons, 1920.

———. "Men of Color Aroused." *Review of Reviews* 92 (November 1935): 35–36, 57.

Sullivan, Edward D. *Rattling the Cup on Chicago Crime*. New York: The Vanguard Press, 1929.

———. *Chicago Surrenders*. New York: Vanguard Press, 1930.

Sweeney, Arthur. "Mental Tests for Immigrants." *North American Review* 215 (May 1922): 600–612.

Tannenbaum, Frank. *Darker Phases of the South*. New York: G. P. Putnam's Sons, 1924.

Taylor, Graham. *Pioneering on Social Frontiers*. Chicago: University of Chicago Press, 1926.

———. *Chicago Commons through Forty Years*. Chicago: University of Chicago Press, 1936.

Taylor, Paul S. *Mexican Labor in the United States: Chicago and the Calumet Region*. vol. 7. Berkeley: University of California Press, 1932.

Thrasher, Frederic M. *The Gang: A Study of 1,313 Gangs in Chicago*. Chicago: University of Chicago Press, 1927.

Thwaites, Rueben Gold. *Afloat on the Ohio: An Historical Pilgrimage of a Thousand Miles in a Skiff, from Redstone to Cairo*. New York: Doubleday and McClure, 1900.

Tregaskis, Richard. *Guadalcanal Diary*. New York: Random House, 1943.

Villard, Oswald Garrison. "Issues and Men—War in Ethiopia." *The Nation* 141 (September 11, 1935): 287.

Walker, Natalie. "Chicago Housing Conditions, X: Greeks and Italians in the Neighborhood of Hull House." *American Journal of Sociology* 21 (November 1915): 285–316.

Weaver, Robert C. *Negro Labor: A National Problem*. Reprint ed. Port Washington, NY: Kennikat Press, 1969.

Wirth, Louis. *The Ghetto: A Study in Isolation*. Chicago: University of Chicago Press, 1928.

Wirth, Louis, and Margaret Furez, eds. *Local Community Fact Book 1938*. Chicago: University of Chicago Press, 1938.

———, and Eleanor Bernert, eds. *Local Community Fact Book of Chicago*. Chicago: University of Chicago Press, 1949.

Wolfert, Ira. *Battle of the Solomons*. Boston: Houghton Mifflin, 1943.

Woody, Carroll Hill. *The Chicago Primary of 1926: A Study in Election Methods*. Chicago: University of Chicago Press, 1926.

Young, Rueben S. "Ethiopia Awakens." *The Crisis* 42 (September 1935): 262–263, 283.

Zorbaugh, Harvey Warren. *The Gold Coast and the Slum*. Chicago: University of Chicago Press, 1929.

Secondary Sources

Books, Pamphlets, Articles

Abrams, Charles. *The Future of Housing*. New York: Harper and Brothers, 1946.

———. *Forbidden Neighbors: A Study of Prejudice in Housing*. New York: Harper and Brothers, 1955.

Adas, Michael. *Machines as the Measure of Men: Science, Technology, and Ideologies of Western Dominance*. Ithaca, NY: Cornell University Press, 1989.

Allen, Theodore. *The Invention of the White Race*. 2 vols. London: Verso, 1994 and 1997.

Allsop, Kenneth. *The Bootleggers and Their Era*. Garden City, NY: Doubleday, 1961.

Allswang, John M. *A House for All Peoples: Ethnic Politics in Chicago, 1890–1936*. Lexington: University of Kentucky Press, 1971.

———. *Bosses, Machines, and Urban Voters*. Rev. ed. Baltimore, MD: Johns Hopkins University Press, 1986.

Almaguer, Tomás. *Racial Fault Lines: The Historical Origins of White Supremacy in California*. Berkeley: University of California Press, 1994.

Andersen, Kristi. *The Creation of a Democratic Majority, 1928–1936*. Chicago: University of Chicago Press, 1979.

Anderson, Benedict. *Imagined Communities: Reflections on the Origin and Spread of Nationalism*. Rev. ed. London: Verso, 1991.

Arnesen, Eric. "Up From Exclusion: Black and White Workers, Race, and the State of Labor History." *Reviews in American History* 26 (March 1998): 146–174.

———. "Whiteness and the Historians' Imagination." *International Labor and Working-Class History* 60 (Fall 2001): 3–32.

Asbury, Herbert. *Gem of the Prairie: An Informal History of the Chicago Underworld*. New York: Alfred A. Knopf, 1940.

Avrich, Paul. *Sacco and Vanzetti: The Anarchist Background*. Princeton, NJ: Princeton University Press, 1991.

Baiamonte, John V., Jr. *Spirit of Vengeance: Nativism and Louisiana Justice, 1921–1924*. Baton Rouge: Louisiana State University Press, 1986.

————. "'Who Killa de Chief?' Revisited: The Hennessey Assassination and Its Aftermath, 1890–1891." *Louisiana History* 33 (Spring 1992): 117–146.

Baily, Samuel L. *Immigrants in the Lands of Promise: Italians in Buenos Aires and New York City, 1870–1914*. Ithaca, NY: Cornell University Press, 1999.

Baker, Lee D. *From Savage to Negro: Anthropology and the Construction of Race, 1896–1954*. Berkeley: University of California Press, 1998.

Baron, Ava, ed. *Work Engendered: Toward a New History of American Labor*. Ithaca, NY: Cornell University Press, 1991.

Barrett, James R. *Work and Community in the Jungle: Chicago's Packinghouse Workers, 1894–1922*. Urbana: University of Illinois Press, 1987.

————. "Americanization from the Bottom Up: Immigration and the Remaking of the Working Class in the United States, 1880–1930." *Journal of American History* 79 (December 1992): 996-1020.

Barrett, James, and David Roediger. "Inbetween Peoples: Race, Nationality and the 'New Immigrant' Working Class." *Journal of American Ethnic History* 16 (Spring 1997): 3–44.

Battacchi, Marco Walter. *Meridionali e Settentrionale nella Struttura del Pregiudizio Etnico in Italia*. 2d ed. Bologna: Il Mulino, 1972.

Bederman, Gail. *Manliness and Civilization: A Cultural History of Gender and Race in the United States, 1880–1917*. Chicago: University of Chicago Press, 1995.

Bergreen, Laurence. *Capone: The Man and the Era*. New York: Simon and Schuster, 1994.

Biles, Roger. *Big City Boss in Depression and War: Mayor Edward J. Kelly of Chicago*. DeKalb: Northern Illinois University Press, 1984.

Black, Gregory D., and Clayton R. Koppes. *Hollywood Goes to War: How Politics, Profits, and Propaganda Shaped World War II Movies*. New York: The Free Press, 1987.

Blalock, Hubert M., Jr. *Toward a Theory of Minority Group Relations*. New York: John Wiley and Sons, 1967.

————. *Race and Ethnic Relations*. Englewood Cliffs, NJ: Prentice-Hall, 1982.

Blee, Kathleen. *Women of the Klan: Racism and Gender in the 1920s*. Berkeley: University of California Press, 1991.

Blum, John M. *V Was for Victory: Politics and American Culture during World War II*. San Diego, CA: Harcourt, Brace, Jovanovich, 1976.

Blumer, Herbert. "Reflections on Theory of Race Relations." In *Race Relations in World Perspective*, edited by A. W. Lind. Honolulu: University of Hawaii Press, 1955.

————. "Race Prejudice as a Sense of Group Position." *Pacific Sociological Review* 1 (Spring 1958): 3–7.

Bohme, Frederick G., and Walter C. Odom, eds. *200 Years of United States Census Taking: Population and Housing Questions, 1790–1990*. Washington, D.C.: Government Printing Office, 1989.

Bonacich, Edna. "A Theory of Ethnic Antagonism: The Split Labor Market." *American Sociological Review* 37 (October 1972): 547–559.

Bongiovanni, Bruno. "The Question of the South." In *Modern Italy: Images and History of a National Identity*, edited by Carlo Pirovano. Milan: Electra Editrice, 1982.

———. "Anthology of the Problem of the South." In *Modern Italy: Images and History of a National Identity*, edited by Carlo Pirovano. Milan: Electra Editrice, 1982.

Bonilla-Silva, Eduardo. "Rethinking Racism: Toward a Structural Interpretation." *American Sociological Review* 62 (June 1996): 465–480.

Bonilla-Silva, Eduardo, and Amanda Lewis. "The 'New Racism': Toward an Analysis of the U.S. Racial Structure, 1960s–1990s." In *Race, Ethnicity, and Nationality in the United States: Toward the Twenty-First Century*, edited by Paul Wong. Boulder, CO: Westview Press, 1999.

Bonnett, Alastair. "Who Was White? The Disappearance of Non-European White Identities and the Formation of European Racial Whiteness." *Ethnic and Racial Studies* 21 (November 1998): 1029–1055.

Botein, Barbara. "The Hennessy Case: An Episode in Anti-Italian Nativism." *Louisiana History* 20 (Summer 1979): 261–279.

Bradford, Calvin. "Financing Home Ownership: The Federal Role in Neighborhood Decline." *Urban Affairs Quarterly* 14 (March 1979): 313–335.

Brandfon, Robert L. "The End of Immigration to the Cotton Fields." *Mississippi Valley Historical Review* 50 (March 1964): 591–611.

Brantlinger, Patrick. *Rules of Darkness: British Literature and Imperialism, 1830–1914*. Ithaca, NY: Cornell University Press, 1989.

Brattain, Michelle. *The Politics of Whiteness: Race, Workers, and Culture in The Modern South*. Princeton, NJ: Princeton University Press, 2001.

Bright, John. *Hizzoner Big Bill Thompson: An Idyll of Chicago*. New York: Jonathan Cape and Harrison Smith, 1930.

Brodkin, Karen. *How Jews Became White Folks and What That Says About Race in America*. New Brunswick, NJ: Rutgers University Press, 1998.

Brundage, W. Fitzhugh, ed. *Under Sentence of Death: Lynching in the South*. Chapel Hill: University of North Carolina Press, 1997.

Buhle, Mari Jo. "Socialist Women and the 'Girl Strikers,' Chicago, 1910." *Signs* 1 (Summer 1976): 1039–1051.

Bukowski, Douglas. *Big Bill Thompson, Chicago, and the Politics of Image*. Urbana: University of Illinois Press, 1998.

Burnham, J. C. "New Perspectives on the Prohibition 'Experiment' of the 1920s." *Journal of Social History* 2 (Fall 1968): 51–68.

Candeloro, Dominic. "Suburban Italians: Chicago Heights, 1890–1975." In *Ethnic Chicago*, edited by Melvin G. Holli and Peter d'A. Jones. Rev. ed. Grand Rapids, MI: William B. Eerdman's Publishing Co., 1984.

———. "Chicago's Italians: A Survey of the Ethnic Factor, 1850–1990." In *Ethnic Chicago: A Multicultural Portrait*, edited by Melvin G. Holli and Peter d'A. Jones. 4th ed. Grand Rapids, MI: William B. Eerdman's, 1995.

Cannistraro, Philip V. "Fascism and Italian Americans." In *Perspectives in Italian Immigration and Ethnicity*, edited by S. M. Tomasi. New York: Center for Migration Studies, 1977.

———. *Blackshirts in Little Italy: Italian Americans and Fascism, 1921–1929*. West Lafayette, IN: Bordighera, 1999.

Cannistraro, Philip V., and Gianfausto Rosoli. "Fascist Emigration Policy in the 1920s." *International Migration Review* 13 (Winter 1979): 673–692.

Carter, Hodding. *Southern Legacy*. Baton Rouge: Louisiana State University Press, 1950.

Casillo, Robert. "Moments in Italian-American Cinema: From *Little Caesar* to Scorcese." In *From the Margin: Writings in Italian Americana*, edited by Anthony Julian Tamburri et al. West Lafayette, IN: Purdue University Press, 1991.

Chafe, William. *The Unfinished Journey: America Since World War II*. 3rd ed. New York: Oxford University Press, 1996.

Cinel, Dino. *From Italy to San Francisco: The Immigrant Experience*. Stanford, CA: Stanford University Press, 1982.

———. *The National Integration of Return Migration, 1870–1929*. Cambridge: Cambridge University Press, 1990.

———. "Sicilians in the Deep South: The Ironic Outcome of Isolation." *Studi Emigrazione* 27 (May 1990): 55–86.

———. "Italians in the South: The Alabama Case." *Italian Americana* 9 (Fall/Winter 1990): 7–24.

Cleaver, Kathleen Neal. "The Antidemocratic Power of Whiteness." In *Critical White Studies: Looking Behind the Mirror*, edited by Richard Delgado and Jean Stefancic. Philadelphia, PA: Temple University Press, 1997.

Cobb, James C. *The Most Southern Place on Earth: The Mississippi Delta and the Roots of Regional Identity*. New York: Oxford University Press, 1992.

Cohen, Lizabeth. *Making a New Deal: Industrial Workers in Chicago, 1919–1939*. Cambridge: Cambridge University Press, 1990.

Cohen, Miriam. *Workshop to Office: Two Generations of Italian Women in New York City, 1900–1950*. Ithaca, NY: Cornell University Press, 1992.

Colley, Linda. *Britons: Forging the Nation, 1707–1837*. New Haven, CT: Yale University Press, 1992.

———. "Britishness and Otherness: An Argument." *Journal of British Studies* 31 (October 1992): 309–329.

Cooper, Frederick, and Ann Stoler, eds. *Tensions of Empire: Colonial Cultures in a Bourgeois World*. Berkeley: University of California Press, 1997.

Count, Earl W., ed. *This Is Race: An Anthology Selected from the International Literature on the Races of Man*. New York: Henry Schuman, 1950.

Covello, Leonard. *The Social Background of the Italo-American School Child*. Leiden: E. J. Brill, 1967.

Crawford, Margaret. "Daily Life on the Home Front: Women, Blacks, and the Struggle for Public Housing." In *World War II and the American Dream*, edited by Donald Albrecht. Cambridge, MA: Massachusetts Institute of Technology Press, 1995.

Cressey, Paul F. "Population Succession in Chicago: 1898–1930." *American Journal of Sociology* 44 (July 1938): 59–69.

Cronon, William. *Nature's Metropolis: Chicago and the Great West*. New York: W. W. Norton, 1992.

Cunningham, George E. "The Italian, A Hindrance to White Solidarity, 1890–1898." *Journal of Negro History* 50 (June 1965): 22–36.

D'Agostino, Peter R. "The Scalabrini Fathers, the Italian Emigrant Church and Ethnic Nationalism in America." *Religion and American Culture* 7 (Winter 1997): 121–159.

DeConde, Alexander. *Half Bitter, Half Sweet: An Excursion into Italian American History*. New York: Charles Scribner's Sons, 1971.

Denning, Michael. *The Cultural Front: The Laboring of American Culture in the Twentieth Century*. London: Verso, 1997.

Derber, Milton. *Labor in Illinois: The Affluent Years, 1945–1980*. Urbana: University of Illinois Press, 1989.

Dick, Bernard. *The Star-Spangled Screen*. Lexington: University of Kentucky Press, 1985.

Dickie, John. "Stereotypes of the Italian South, 1860–1900." In *The New History of the Italian South: The Mezzogiorno Revisited*, edited by Robert Lumley and Jonathan Morris. Devon: University of Exeter Press, 1997.

———. *Darkest Italy: The Nation and the Stereotypes of the Mezzogiorno, 1860–1900*. New York: St. Martin's Press, 1999.

Diggins, John P. *Mussolini and Fascism: The View from America*. Princeton, NJ: Princeton University Press, 1972.

Dirks, Nicholas B., Geoff Eley, and Sherry B. Ortner, eds. *Culture/Power/History: A Reader in Contemporary Social Theory*. Princeton, NJ: Princeton University Press, 1995.

DiStasi, Lawrence, ed. *Una Storia Segreta: The Secret History of Italian American Evacuation and Internment during World War II*. Berkeley, CA: Heyday Books, 2001.

Doherty, Thomas. *Projections of War: Hollywood, American Culture and World War II*. New York: Columbia University Press, 1994.

Douglass, William A. *Emigration in a South Italian Town: An Anthropological History*. New Brunswick, NJ: Rutgers University Press, 1984.

Dower, John W. *War Without Mercy: Race and Power in the Pacific War*. New York: Pantheon Books, 1986.

Escobar, Edward J. *Race, the Police, and the Making of a Political Identity: Mexican Americans and the Los Angeles Police Department, 1900–1945*. Berkeley: University of California Press, 1999.

Faue, Elizabeth. *Community of Suffering and Struggle: Women, Men, and the Labor Movement in Minneapolis, 1915–1945*. Chapel Hill: University of North Carolina Press, 1991.

———, ed. *Labor History* (special issue on gender and labor history) 34 (Spring-Summer 1993).

———. "'Anti-Heroes of the Working Class': A Response to Bruce Nelson." *International Review of Social History* 41 (1996): 375–388.

Feagin, Joe R. *Racist America: Roots, Current Realities, and Future Reparations*. New York: Routledge, 2000.

Finkelstein, Monte S. "The Johnson Act, Mussolini and Fascist Emigration Policy: 1921–1930." *Journal of American Ethnic History* 8 (Fall 1988): 38–55.

Foley, Neil. *The White Scourge: Mexicans, Blacks, and Poor Whites in Texas Cotton Culture*. Berkeley: University of California Press, 1997.

Ford, Richard G. "Population Succession in Chicago." *American Journal of Sociology* 56 (September 1950): 156–160.

Fox, Stephen. *The Unknown Internment: An Oral History of the Relocation of Italian Americans during World War II*. Boston, MA: Twayne Publishers, 1990.

Frank, Dana. "White Working-Class Women and the Race Question." *International Labor and Working-Class History* 54 (Fall 1998): 80–102.

Frankenberg, Ruth. *White Women, Race Matters: The Social Construction of Whiteness*. Minneapolis: University of Minnesota Press, 1994.

Gabaccia, Donna R. *From Sicily to Elizabeth Street: Housing and Social Change among Italian Immigrants, 1880–1930*. Albany: State University of New York Press, 1984.

———. *Militants and Migrants: Rural Sicilians Become Italian Workers*. New Brunswick, NJ: Rutgers University Press, 1988.

———. "Is Everywhere Nowhere? Nomads, Nations, and the Immigrant Paradigm of United States History." *Journal of American History* 86 (December 1999): 1115–1134.

———. "The 'Yellow Peril' and the 'Chinese of Europe': Global Perspectives on Race and Labor, 1815–1930." In *Migration, Migration History, History: Old Paradigms and New Perspectives*, edited by Jan and Leo Lucassen. New York: Berg and International Institute for Social History, 1999.

———. *Italy's Many Diasporas*. London: University College London Press, 2000.

Gaines, Kevin. *Uplifting the Race: Black Leadership, Politics, and Culture in the Twentieth Century*. Chapel Hill: University of North Carolina Press, 1996.

Galasso, Giuseppe. *Il Mezzogiorno nella Storia d'Italia*. Firenze: Le Monnier, 1977.

Gambino, Richard. *Blood of My Blood: The Dilemma of the Italian Americans*. Garden City, NY: Anchor Books, 1974.

Gamm, Gerald. *Mass Exodus: Why the Jews Left Boston and the Catholics Stayed*. Cambridge, MA: Harvard University Press, 1999.

Garcia, Juan R. "History of Chicanos in Chicago Heights." *Aztlan* 7 (Summer 1976): 291–306.

———. *Mexicans in the Midwest, 1900–1932*. Tuscon: University of Arizona Press, 1996.

Gatewood, William B., Jr. "Strangers and the South Eden: The South and Immigration, 1900–1920." In *Ethnic Minorities in Gulf Coast Society*, edited by Jerrel H. Shofner and Linda V. Ellsworth. Pensacola, FL: Gulf Coast History and Humanities Conference, 1979.

Gelfand, Mark I. *A Nation of Cities: The Federal Government and Urban America, 1933–1965*. New York: Oxford University Press, 1975.

Gerstle, Gary. *Working-Class Americanism: The Politics of Labor in a Textile City, 1914–1960*. Cambridge: Cambridge University Press, 1989.

———. "The Working Class Goes to War." *Mid-America* 75 (October 1993): 303–322.

———. "Working-Class Racism: Broaden the Focus." *International Labor and Working-Class History* 44 (Fall 1993): 33–40.

———. "Race and the Myth of the Liberal Consensus." *Journal of American History* 82 (September 1995): 579–586.

———. "Liberty, Coercion and the Making of Americans." *Journal of American History* 84 (September 1997): 524–558.

———. *American Crucible: Race and Nation in the Twentieth Century*. Princeton, NJ: Princeton University Press, 2000.

Gleason, Philip. "American Identity and Americanization." In *Harvard Encyclopedia of American Ethnic Groups*, edited by Stephan Thernstrom et al. Cambridge, MA: Belknap Press, 1980.

———. *Speaking of Diversity*. Baltimore, MD: Johns Hopkins University Press, 1992.

Glickman, Lawrence B. "The 'Ism' That Won the Century." *The Nation* 271 (December 4, 2000): 36–38.

Goglia, Luigi, ed. *Storia Fotografica dell'Impero Fascista, 1935–1941*. Rome-Bari: Editori Laterza, 1985.

Goldfield, Michael. *The Color of Politics: Race and the Mainsprings of American Politics*. New York: The New Press, 1997.

Gordon, Linda. *The Great Arizona Orphan Abduction*. Cambridge, MA: Harvard University Press, 1999.

Gossett, Thomas F. *Race: The History of an Idea in America*. Dallas, TX: Southern Methodist University Press, 1963.

Gottfried, Alex. *Boss Cermak of Chicago: A Study of Political Leadership*. Seattle: University of Washington Press, 1962.

Green, Paul M., and Melvin G. Holli, eds. *The Mayors: The Chicago Political Tradition*. Carbondale: Southern Illinois University Press, 1987.

Gribaudi, Gabriella. "Images of the South: The *Mezzogiorno* as seen by Insiders and Outsiders." In *The New History of the Italian South: The Mezzogiorno Revisited*, edited by Robert Lumley and Jonathan Morris, eds. Devon: University of Exeter Press, 1997.

Grossman, James R. *Land of Hope: Chicago, Black Southerners, and the Great Migration*. Chicago: University of Chicago Press, 1989.

Guglielmo, Jennifer M. "*Lavoratrici Coscienti*: Italian Women Garment Workers and the Politics of Labor Organizing in New York City, 1890s–1940s." In *Women, Gender, and Transnational Lives: Italian Workers of the World*, edited by Donna Gabaccia and Franca Iacovetta. Toronto: University of Toronto Press, 2002.

———. "*Donne Ribelli*: Recovering the History of Italian Women's Radicalism in the United States." In *The Lost World of Italian-American Radicalism: Politics, Culture, History*, edited by Philip V. Cannistraro and Gerald Meyer. Albany: State University of New York Press, forthcoming.

Guglielmo, Thomas A. "Toward Essentialism, Toward Difference: Gino Speranza and Conceptions of Race and Italian-American Racial Identity, 1900–1925." *Mid-America* 81 (Summer 1999): 169–213.

———. "The Forgotten Enemy: Wartime Representations of Italians in American Popular Culture, 1941–1945." *Italian Americana* 18 (Winter 2000): 5–22.

Guterl, Matthew Pratt. *The Color of Race in America, 1900–1940*. Cambridge, MA: Harvard University Press, 2001.

Haas, Edward F. "Guns, Goats, and Italians: The Tallulah Lynching of 1899." *North Louisiana Historical Association Journal* 13 (1982): 45–58.

Haas, Lisabeth. *Conquests and Historical Identities in California, 1769–1936*. Berkeley: University of California Press, 1995.

Hale, Grace Elizabeth. *Making Whiteness: The Culture of Segregation in the South, 1890–1940*. New York: Pantheon, 1998.

Halpern, Rick. *Down on the Killing Floor: Black and White Workers in Chicago's Packinghouses, 1904–1954*. Urbana: University of Illinois Press, 1997.

———. "Race and Radicalism in the Chicago Stockyards: The Rise of the Chicago Packinghouse Workers Organizing Committee." In *Unionizing the Jungles: Labor and Community in the Twentieth-Century Meatpacking Industry*, edited Shelton Stromquist and Marvin Bergman. Iowa City: University of Iowa Press, 1997.

Haney Lopez, Ian F. *White by Law: The Legal Construction of Race*. New York: New York University Press, 1996.

Harris, Cheryl I. "Whiteness as Property." *Harvard Law Review* 106 (June 1993): 1709–1791.

Harris, Joseph E. *African-American Reactions to War in Ethiopia, 1936–1941.* Baton Rouge: Louisiana State University Press, 1994.

Hartigan, John M. *Racial Situations: Class Predicaments of Whiteness in Detroit.* Princeton, NJ: Princeton University Press, 1999.

Hayden, Tom. *Irish on the Inside: In Search of the Soul of Irish America.* London: Verso, 2000.

Haywood, Harry. *Black Bolshevik: Autobiography of a Black Bolshevik.* Chicago: Liberator Press, 1978.

Helper, Rose. *Racial Policies and Practices of Real Estate Brokers.* Minneapolis: University of Minnesota Press, 1969.

Higham, John. *Strangers in the Land: Patterns of American Nativism, 1860–1925.* 2d ed. New Brunswick, NJ: Rutgers University Press, 1988.

———. *Send These to Me: Jews and Other Immigrants in Urban America.* Rev. ed. Baltimore, MD: Johns Hopkins University Press, 1992.

Hirsch, Arnold R. "The Cook County Democratic Organization and the Dilemma of Race, 1931–1987." In *Snowbelt Cities: Metropolitan Politics in the Northeast and Midwest since World War II,* edited by Richard M. Bernard. Bloomington: Indiana University Press, 1990.

———. "Massive Resistance in the Urban North: Trumbull Park, Chicago, 1953–1966." *Journal of American History* 82 (September 1995): 522–550.

———. *Making the Second Ghetto: Race and Housing in Chicago, 1940–1960.* New ed. Chicago: University of Chicago Press, 1998.

Hoerder, Dirk, ed. *The Immigrant Labor Press in North America, 1840–1870s,* 3 vols. New York: Greenwood Press, 1987.

Hoffman, Dennis E. *Scarface Al and the Crime Crusaders: Chicago's Private War Against Capone.* Carbondale: Southern Illinois University Press, 1993.

Holt, Thomas C. *The Problem of Freedom: Race, Labor, and Politics in Jamaica and Britain, 1832–1938.* Baltimore, MD: Johns Hopkins University Press, 1992.

Horowitz, Roger. *"Negro and White, Unite and Fight!": A Social History of Industrial Unionism in Meatpacking, 1930–1990.* Urbana: University of Illinois Press, 1997.

Hunter, Tera W. *To 'Joy My Freedom: Southern Black Women's Lives and Labors after the Civil War.* Cambridge, MA: Harvard University Press, 1997.

Hyde, Cheryl. "The Meaning of Whiteness." *Qualitative Sociology* 18 (Spring 1995): 87–95.

Ignatiev, Noel. *How the Irish Became White.* New York: Routledge, 1995.

Ingalls, Robert P. "Lynching and Establishment Violence in Tampa, 1858–1935." *Journal of Southern History* 53 (November 1987): 613-644.

Iorizzo, Luciano J., and Salvatore Mondello. *The Italian-Americans.* New York: Twayne, 1971.

Jackson, Kenneth T. *The Ku Klux Klan in the City, 1915–1930.* New York: Oxford University Press, 1967.

———. *Crabgrass Frontier: The Suburbanization of the United States.* New York: Oxford University Press, 1985.

Jacobson, Matthew Frye. *Special Sorrows: The Diasporic Imagination of Irish, Polish, and Jewish Immigrants in the United States.* Cambridge, MA: Harvard University Press, 1994.

———. *Whiteness of a Different Color: European Immigrants and the Alchemy of Race.* Cambridge, MA: Harvard University Press, 1998.

Janowitz, Morris, ed. *W. I. Thomas on Social Organization and Social Personality: Selected Papers*. Chicago: University of Chicago Press, 1966.

Jenkins, Richard. *Rethinking Ethnicity: Arguments and Explorations*. London: Sage, 1997.

Kantowicz, Edward R. *Polish-American Politics in Chicago, 1880–1940*. Chicago: University of Chicago Press, 1975.

Karlin, J. Alexander. "The Italo-American Incident of 1891 and the Road to Reunion." *Journal of Southern History* 8 (May 1942): 242–246.

Kazal, Russel A. "Revisiting Assimilation: The Rise, Fall, and Reappraisal of a Concept in American Ethnic History." *American Historical Review* 100 (April 1995): 437–471.

Keeran, Roger. "The International Workers Order and the Origins of the CIO." *Labor History* 30 (Summer 1989): 385–408.

——. "National Groups and the Popular Front: The Case of the International Workers Order." *Journal of American Ethnic History* 14 (Spring 1995): 23–51.

Kelley, Robin D. G. *Hammer and Hoe: Alabama Communists during the Great Depression*. Chapel Hill: University of North Carolina Press, 1990.

——. "'We Are Not What We Seem': Rethinking Black Working-Class Opposition in the Jim Crow South." *Journal of American History* 80 (June 1993): 75–112.

——. *Race Rebels: Culture, Politics, and the Black Working Class*. New York: The Free Press, 1994.

——. "'But a Local Phase of a World Problem': Black History's Global Vision, 1883–1950." *Journal of American History* 86 (December 1999): 1045–1078.

Kendall, John S. "Who Killa de Chief." *Louisiana Historical Quarterly* 22 (1939): 492–530.

Kerr, Louise Ano Nuevo de. "Chicano Settlements in Chicago: A Brief History." *Journal of Ethnic Studies* 2 (Winter 1975): 22–32.

King, Desmond S. *Making Americans: Immigration, Race, and the Origins of the Diverse Democracy*. Cambridge, MA: Harvard University Press, 2000.

Kobler, John. *Capone: The Life and World of Al Capone*. New York: G.P. Putnam's Sons, 1971.

Kolchin, Peter. "Whiteness Studies: The New History of Race in America." *Journal of American History* 81 (June 2002): 154–173.

Lasswell, Harold D., and Dorothy Blumenstock. *World Revolutionary Propaganda: A Chicago Study*. New York: Alfred A. Knopf, 1939.

Lay, Shawn, ed. *The Invisible Empire in the West: Toward a New Historical Appraisal of the Ku Klux Klan of the 1920s*. Urbana: University of Illinois Press, 1991.

Leab, Daniel J. "The Memorial Day Massacre." *Midcontinent American Studies Journal* 8 (Fall 1967): 3–17.

Lewis, Earl. *In Their Own Interests: Race, Class, and Power in Twentieth-Century Norfolk, Virginia*. Berkeley: University of California Press, 1991.

——. "'To Turn as on a Pivot': Writing African Americans into a History of Overlapping Diasporas." *American Historical Review* 100 (June 1995): 765–785.

Lieberson, Stanley. *A Piece of the Pie: Blacks and White Immigrants Since 1880*. Berkeley: University of California Press, 1980.

Lipsitz, George. "The Possessive Investment in Whiteness: Racialized Social

Democracy and the 'White' Problem in American Studies." *American Quarterly* 47 (September 1997): 369–427.

———. *The Possessive Investment in Whiteness: How White People Profit from Identity Politics.* Philadelphia: Temple University Press, 1998.

Loewen, James W. *The Mississippi Chinese: Between Black and White.* Cambridge, MA: Harvard University Press, 1971.

Long, Herman H., and Charles S. Johnson. *People vs. Property: Race Restrictive Covenants in Housing.* Nashville, TN: Fisk University Press, 1947.

Lott, Eric. *Love and Theft: Blackface Minstrelsy and the American Working Class.* New York: Oxford University Press, 1993.

Lumley, Robert, and Jonathan Morris, eds. *The New History of the Italian South: The Mezzogiorno Revisited.* Devon: University of Exeter Press, 1997.

Lynd, Alice, and Staughton Lynd, eds. *Rank and File: Personal Histories by Working-Class Organizers.* Boston, MA: Beacon Press, 1975.

Mangione, Jerre and Ben Morreale. *La Storia: Five Centuries of the Italian American Experience.* New York: HarperCollins, 1992.

Massey, Douglas S., and Nancy A. Denton. *American Apartheid: Segregation and the Making of the Underclass.* Cambridge, MA: Harvard University Press, 1993.

Matthews, Fred H. *Quest for an American Sociology: Robert E. Park and the Chicago School.* Montreal: McGill-Queen's University Press, 1977.

Mayer, Harold M., and Richard C. Wade. *Chicago: Growth of a Metropolis.* Chicago: University of Chicago Press, 1969.

McClintock, Anne. *Imperial Leather: Race, Gender, and Sexuality in the Colonial Contest.* New York: Routledge, 1995.

McGreevy, John T. *Parish Boundaries: The Catholic Encounter with Race in the Twentieth-Century Urban North.* Chicago: University of Chicago Press, 1996.

McMahon, Eileen M. *What Parish Are You From?* Lexington: University of Kentucky Press, 1995.

Meyerson, Martin, and Edward C. Banfield. *Politics, Planning, and the Public Interest.* New York: The Free Press, 1955.

Miller, Eugene, and Gianna Sommi Panofsky. "The Beginning of the Italian Socialist Movement in Chicago." In *Support and Struggle,* edited by Joseph Tropea et al. New York: American Italian Historical Association, 1986.

Molotch, Harvey Luskin. *Managed Integration: Dilemmas of Doing Good in the City.* Berkeley: University of California Press, 1972.

Montgomery, David. *The Fall of the House of Labor.* Cambridge: Cambridge University Press, 1987.

Moore, Leonard J. "Historical Interpretations of the 1920s Klan: The Traditional View and the Populist Revision." *Journal of Social History* 24 (Winter 1990): 341–357.

———. *Citizen Klansmen: The Ku Klux Klan in Indiana, 1921–1928.* Chapel Hill: University of North Carolina Press, 1991.

Morawska, Ewa. "The Sociology and Historiography of Immigration." In *Immigration Reconsidered: History, Sociology, and Politics,* edited by Virginia Yans McLaughlin. New York: Oxford University Press, 1990.

Morgan, Edmund S. *American Slavery, American Freedom: The Ordeal of Colonial Virginia.* New York: W. W. Norton, 1976.

Mormino, Gary R., and George E. Pozzetta. *The Immigrant World of Ybor City.* Urbana: University of Illinois Press, 1987.

Morrison, Toni. *Playing in the Dark: Whiteness and the Literary Imagination*. Cambridge, MA: Harvard University Press, 1992.

Mumford, Kevin J. *Interzones: Black/White Sex Districts in Chicago and New York in the Early Twentieth Century*. New York: Columbia University Press, 1997.

Nelli, Humbert S. "Italians and Crime in Chicago: The Formative Years, 1890–1920." *American Journal of Sociology* 74 (1969): 373–391.

———. *The Italians in Chicago, 1880–1930: A Study in Ethnic Mobility*. New York: Oxford University Press, 1970.

———. "John Powers and the Italians: Politics in a Chicago Ward, 1896–1921." *Journal of American History* 57 (June 1970): 67–84.

———. "Chicago's Italian-Language Press and World War I." In *Studies in Italian American Social History*, edited by Francesco Cordasco. Totowa, NJ: Rowman and Littlefield, 1975.

———. *The Business of Crime: Italians and Syndicate Crime in the United States*. New York: Oxford University Press, 1976.

Nelson, Bruce. "Class, Race and Democracy in the CIO: The 'New' Labor History Meets the 'Wages of Whiteness'." *International Review of Social History* 41 (1996): 351–374.

———."Working-Class Agency and Racial Equality." *International Review of Social History* 41 (1996): 407–420.

———. *Divided We Stand: American Workers and the Struggle for Black Equality*. Princeton, NJ: Princeton University Press, 2001.

Nelson, Steve, James R. Barrett, and Rob Ruck. *Steve Nelson: American Radical*. Pittsburgh, PA: University of Pittsburgh Press, 1981.

Newell, Barbara Warne. *Chicago and the Labor Movement: Metropolitan Unionism in the 1930s*. Urbana: University of Illinois Press, 1961.

Newman, Louise Michele. *White Women's Rights: The Racial Origins of Feminism in the United States*. New York: Oxford University Press, 1999.

Ngai, Mae. "The Architecture of Race in American Immigration Law: A Reexamination of the Immigration Act of 1924." *Journal of American History* 86 (June 1999): 67–92.

Oliver, Melvin L., and Thomas M. Shapiro. *Black Wealth/White Wealth: A New Perspective on Racial Inequality*. New York: Routledge, 1995.

Omi, Michael, and Howard Winant. *Racial Formation in the United States from the 1960s to the 1990s*. 2d ed. New York: Routledge, 1994.

Orsi, Robert. *The Madonna of 115th Street: Faith and Community in Italian Harlem, 1880–1950*. New Haven, CT: Yale University Press, 1985.

———. "The Religious Boundaries of an Inbetween People: Street *Feste* and the Problem of the Dark-Skinned Other in Italian Harlem, 1920–1990." *American Quarterly* 44 (September 1992): 313–347.

Pacyga, Dominic A. "Polish-America in Transition: Social Change and the Chicago Polonia, 1945–1980." *Polish American Studies* 44 (Spring 1987): 38–55.

———. *Polish Immigrants and Industrial Chicago: Workers on the South Side, 1880–1922*. Columbus: Ohio State University Press, 1991.

———. "To Live Amongst Others: Poles and Their Neighbors in Industrial Chicago, 1865–1930." *Journal of American Ethnic History* 16 (Fall 1996): 55–73

———. "Chicago's 1919 Race Riot: Ethnicity, Class, and Urban Violence." In *The Making of Urban America*, edited Raymond A. Mohl. 2d ed. Wilmington, DE: Scholarly Resources, 1997.

Panofsky, Gianna S. "A View of Two Major Centers of Italian Anarchism in the United States: Spring Valley and Chicago, Illinois." In *Italian Ethnics*, edited by Dominic Candeloro. New York: American Italian Historical Association, 1988.

Pascoe, Peggy. "Miscegenation Law, Court Cases, and Ideologies of 'Race' in Twentieth-Century America." *Journal of American History* 83 (June 1996): 44–69.

Peck, Gunther. *Reinventing Free Labor: Padrone and Immigrant Workers in the North American West, 1880–1930*. Cambridge: Cambridge University Press, 2000.

Person, Stowe. *Ethnic Studies at Chicago, 1905–1945*. Urbana: University of Illinois Press, 1987.

Peterson, Virgil W. *Barbarians in our Midst: A History of Chicago Crime and Politics*. Boston, MA: Little, Brown, 1952.

Philpott, Thomas Lee. *The Slum and the Ghetto: Immigrants, Blacks, and Reformers in Chicago, 1880–1930*. 2d ed. Belmont, CA: Wadsworth, 1991.

Pinderhughes, Dianne M. *Race and Ethnicity in Chicago Politics: A Reexamination of Pluralist Theory*. Urbana: University of Illinois Press, 1987.

Plummer, Brenda Gayle. *Rising Wind: Black Americans and U.S. Foreign Affairs, 1935–1960*. Chapel Hill: University of North Carolina Press, 1996.

Polenberg, Richard. *One Nation Divisible: Class, Race, and Ethnicity in the United States since 1938*. New York: Penguin Books, 1980.

Posadas, Barbara M. "Crossed Boundaries in Interracial Chicago: Filipino American Families since 1925." *Amerasia Journal* 8 (Fall/Winter): 31–52.

Posadas, Barbara M., and Roland L. Guyotte. "Unintentional Immigrants: Chicago's Filipino Foreign Students Become Settlers, 1900–1941." *Journal of American Ethnic History* 9 (Spring 1990): 26–48.

Pozzetta, George E., "Foreigners in Florida: A Study of Immigration Promotion, 1865–1910." *Florida Historical Quarterly* 53 (October 1974): 164–180.

Prashad, Vijay. *The Karma of Brown Folk*. Minneapolis: University of Minnesota Press, 2000.

Radzialowski, Thaddeus. "The Competition for Jobs and Racial Stereotypes: Poles and Blacks in Chicago." *Polish American Studies* 32 (Autumn 1976): 5–18.

Reed, Christopher Robert. "Black Chicago Political Realignment during the Great Depression and New Deal." *Illinois Historical Journal* 78 (Winter 1985): 242–256.

Richards, David A. J. *Italian American: The Racializing of an Ethnic Identity*. New York: New York University Press, 1999.

Rimanelli, Marco, and Sheryl L. Postman, eds. *The 1891 New Orleans Lynching and U.S.-Italian Relations: A Look Back*. New York: Peter Lang, 1992.

Rodriguez, Clara E. *Changing Race: Latinos, the Census, and the History of Ethnicity in the United States*. New York: New York University Press, 2000.

Roediger, David R. *The Wages of Whiteness: Race and the Making of the American Working Class*. London: Verso, 1991.

———. *Towards the Abolition of Whiteness: Essays on Race, Politics, and Working Class History*. London: Verso, 1994.

———, ed. *Black on White: Black Writers on What It Means to Be White*. New York: Shocken Books, 1998.

Rogin, Michael. *Blackface, White Noise: Jewish Immigrants in the Hollywood Melting Pot*. Berkeley: University of California Press, 1996.

Rose, Kenneth D. *American Women and the Repeal of Prohibition*. New York: New York University Press, 1996.

Rosenstone, Steven J., and John Mark Hansen. *Mobilization, Participation, and Democracy in America*. New York: Macmillan, 1993.

Rostow, Eugene. *Born to Lose: The Gangster Film in America*. New York: Oxford University Press, 1978.

Roy, William G. *Making Societies: The Historical Construction of Our World*. Thousand Oaks, CA: Forge Press, 2001.

Ruiz, Vicki. *Cannery Women, Cannery Lives: Mexican Women, Unionization, and the California Food Processing Industry*. Albuquerque: University of New Mexico Press, 1987.

Ruth, David E. *Inventing the Public Enemy: The Gangster in American Popular Culture, 1918–1934*. Chicago: University of Chicago Press, 1996.

Sacks, Karen Brodkin. "How Did the Jews Become White Folks?" In *Race*, edited by Steven Gregory and Roger Sanjek. New Brunswick, NJ: Rutgers University Press, 1994.

Sánchez, George J. *Becoming Mexican American: Ethnicity, Culture and Identity in Chicano Los Angeles, 1900–1945*. New York: Oxford University Press, 1993.

———. "Race, Nation, and Culture in Recent Immigration Studies." *Journal of American Ethnic History* 19 (Summer 1999): 66–84.

Savage, Barbara Dianne. *Broadcasting Freedom: Radio, War, and the Politics of Race, 1938–1948*. Chapel Hill: University of North Carolina Press, 1999.

Saxton, Alexander. *The Rise and Fall of the White Republic: Class Politics and Mass Culture in Nineteenth-Century America*. London: Verso, 1990.

Sbacchi, Alberto. *Ethiopia Under Mussolini: Fascism and the Colonial Experience*. London: Zed Books, 1985.

Scarpaci, Jean. "Immigrants in the New South: Italians in Louisiana's Sugar Parishes, 1880–1910." In *Studies in Italian American Social History*, edited by Francesco Cordasco. Totowa, NJ: Rowman and Littlefield, 1975.

———. "A Tale of Selective Accommodation: Sicilians and Native Whites in Louisiana." *Journal of Ethnic Studies* 5 (Fall 1977): 37–50.

Scherini, Rose. "Executive Order 9066 and Italian Americans: The San Francisco Story." *California History* 70 (Winter 1991–1992): 367–377.

———. "When Italian Americans Were 'Enemy Aliens'." In *Enemies Within: Italian and Other Internees in Canada and Abroad*, edited by Franca Iacovetta, Roberto Perin, and Angelo Principe. Toronto: University of Toronto Press, 2000.

Schermerhorn, Richard. *Comparative Ethnic Relations: A Framework for Theory and Research*. New York: Random House, 1970.

Schmidt, John R. *"The Mayor Who Cleaned Up Chicago": A Political Biography of William E. Dever*. DeKalb: Northern Illinois University Press, 1989.

Schmitz, David F. *The United States and Fascist Italy, 1922–1940*. Chapel Hill: University of North Carolina Press, 1988.

Schneider, Jane, ed. *Italy's 'Southern Question': Orientalism in One Country*. New York: Berg, 1998.

Schoenberg, Robert J. *Mr. Capone*. New York: William Morrow, 1992.

Scott, William R. *The Sons of Sheba's Race: African-Americans and the Italo-Ethiopian War, 1935–1941*. Bloomington: Indiana University Press, 1993.

Seidman, Joel, Jack London, Bernard Karsh, and Daisy L. Tagliacozzo. *The Worker Views His Union*. Chicago: University of Chicago Press, 1958.

Seton-Watson, Christopher. *Italy from Liberalism to Fascism, 1870-1925*. London: Methuen and Co., 1967.

Shah, Nayan. *Contagious Divides: Epidemics and Race in San Francisco's Chinatown*. Berkeley: University of California Press, 2001.

Shankman, Arnold. *Ambivalent Friends: Afro-Americans View the Immigrant*. Westport, CT: Greenwood Press, 1982.

Shibutani, Tamotsu, and Kian M. Kwan. *Ethnic Stratification: A Comparative Approach*. New York: Macmillan, 1965.

Shufelt, Gordon H. "Jim Crow among Strangers: The Growth of Baltimore's Little Italy and Maryland's Disfranchisement Campaigns." *Journal of American Ethnic History* 19 (Summer 2000): 49–78.

Sofchalk, Donald G. "The Chicago Memorial Day Incident: An Episode of Mass Action." *Labor History* 6 (Winter 1965): 3-43.

Solomon, Mark I. *The Cry Was Unity: Communists and African Americans, 1917–1936*. Jackson: University of Mississippi Press, 1998.

Smith, Denis Mack. "Regionalism." In *Modern Italy: A Topical History since 1861*, edited by Edward Tannenbaum and Emiliana Noether. New York: New York University Press, 1974.

———. *Mussolini's Roman Empire*. New York: Penguin Books, 1976.

Spear, Allan H. *Black Chicago: The Making of the Negro Ghetto, 1890–1920*. Chicago: University of Chicago Press, 1967.

Steele, Richard W. "The War on Intolerance: The Reformulation of American Nationalism, 1939–1941." *Journal of American Ethnic History* 9 (Fall 1989): 9-35.

———. "'No Racials'. Discrimination against Ethnics in American Defense Industry, 1940–1942." *Labor History* 32 (Winter 1991): 66–90.

Sterba, Christopher M. "'More Than Ever, We Feel Proud to be Italians': World War I and the New Haven *Colonia*, 1917–1918." *Journal of American Ethnic History* 20 (Winter 2001): 70–106.

Stocking, George W., Jr. *Race, Culture, and Evolution: Essays in the History of Anthropology*. New York: The Free Press, 1996.

Stoler, Ann. *Race and the Education of Desire: Foucault's History of Sexuality and the Colonial Order of Things*. Durham, NC: Duke University Press, 1995.

———. "Sexual Affronts and Racial Frontiers: European Identities and the Cultural Politics of Exclusion in Colonial Southeast Asia." In *Becoming National: A Reader*, edited by Geoff Eley and Ronald Grigor Suny. New York: Oxford University Press, 1996.

Stuart, William H. *The Twenty Incredible Years*. Chicago: M. A. Donahue, 1935.

Sugrue, Thomas J. "Crabgrass-Roots Politics: Race, Rights and the Reaction against Liberalism in the Urban North, 1940–1964." *Journal of American History* 82 (September 1995): 551-578.

———. *The Origins of the Urban Crisis: Race and Inequality in Postwar Detroit*. Princeton: Princeton University Press, 1996.

———. "Segmented Work, Race-Conscious Workers: Structure, Agency, and Division in the CIO Era." *International Review of Social History* 41 (1996): 389–406.

Suttles, Gerald. *The Social Order of the Slum: Ethnicity and Territory in the Inner City*. Chicago: University of Chicago Press, 1968.

Tebbel, John. *George Horace Lorimer and the Saturday Evening Post*. Garden City, NY: Doubleday, Inc., 1948.

Teti, Vito. *La Razza Maledetta: Origini del Pregiudizio Antimeridionale*. Rome: Manifestolibri, 1993.

Tobey, Ronald, Charles Wetherell, and Jay Brigham. "Moving Out and Settling In: Residential Mobility, Home Owning, and the Public Enframing of Citizenship, 1921–1950." *American Historical Review* 95 (December 1990): 1395–1422.

Trotter, Joe W. *Coal, Class, Color: Blacks in Southern West Virginia, 1915–1932*. Urbana: University of Illinois Press, 1990.

Tuttle, William M., Jr. *Race Riot: Chicago in the Red Summer of 1919*. New York: Atheneum, 1970.

Vecoli, Rudolph J. "*Contadini* in Chicago: A Critique of the Uprooted." *Journal of American History* 51 (December 1964): 404–417.

———. "Prelates and Peasants," *Journal of Social History* 2 (Spring 1969): 217–268.

———. "'Ethnic versus Black Metropolis': A Comment." *Polish American Studies* 29 (Spring-Autumn 1972): 34–39.

———. "The Formation of Chicago's 'Little Italies'." *Journal of American Ethnic History* 2 (Spring 1983): 5–20.

———. "An Inter-Ethnic Perspective on American Immigration History." *Mid-America* 75 (April–July 1993): 223–235.

———. "Are Italians Just White Folks?" *Italian Americana* 13 (Summer 1995): 149–165

Ventresco, Fiorello B. "Italian-Americans and the Ethiopian Crisis." *Italian Americana* 6 (Fall-Winter 1980): 4–27.

Venturini, Nadia. *Neri e Italiani ad Harlem: Gli Anni Trenta e la Guerra d'Etiopia*. Rome: Edizione Lavoro, 1990.

Verdicchio, Pasquale. *Bound by Distance: Rethinking Nationalism through the Italian Diaspora*. Madison, NJ: Fairleigh Dickinson University Press, 1997.

Wacker, R. Fred. *Ethnicity, Pluralism, and Race: Race Relations Theory in America Before Myrdal*. Westport, CT: Greenwood Press, 1983.

Waldron, Caroline. "'Lynch Law Must Go!': Race, Citizenship, and the Other in an American Coal Mining Town." *Journal of American Ethnic History* 20 (Fall 2000): 50–77.

Walker, Thomas J. E. *Pluralistic Fraternity: The History of the International Workers Order*. New York: Garland Press, 1991.

Ware, Vron. *Beyond the Pale: White Women, Racism, and History*. London: Verso, 1992.

Warren, Jonathan W., and Frank Winndance Twine. "White Americans, the New Minority? Non-Blacks and the Ever-Expanding Boundaries of Whiteness." *Journal of Black Studies* 28 (November 1997): 200–218.

Waters, Mary C. *Ethnic Options: Choosing Identities in America*. Berkeley: University of California Press, 1990.

———. *Black Identities: West Indian Immigrant Dreams and American Realities*. Cambridge, MA: Harvard University Press, 1999.

Weiss, Richard. "Ethnicity and Reform: Minorities and the Ambiance of the Depression Years." *Journal of American History* 66 (December 1979): 566–585.

Wellman, David T. *Portraits of White Racism*. 2d ed. Cambridge: Cambridge University Press, 1993.

Wendt, Lloyd, and Herman Kogan. *Big Bill of Chicago*. Indianapolis, IN: Bobbs-Merrill, 1953.

West, Cornel. *Race Matters*. New York: Vintage Books, 1994.

X, Malcolm with Alex Haley. *The Autobiography of Malcolm X*. New York: Ballantine Books, 1993.

Yu, Henry. *Thinking Orientals: Migration, Contact, and Exoticism in Modern America*. New York: Oxford University Press, 2000.

Zieger, Robert H. *The CIO, 1935–1955*. Chapel Hill: University of North Carolina Press, 1995.

Zunz, Olivier. *The Changing Face of Inequality: Urbanization, Industrial Development and the Immigrants of Detroit, 1880–1920*. Chicago: University of Chicago Press, 1982.

Dissertations, Theses, and Unpublished Papers

Adams, Mary. "Present Housing Conditions in South Chicago, South Deering, and Pullman." Master's thesis, University of Chicago, 1926.

Arredondo, Gabriela. "'What!' The Mexicans, Americans?: Race and Ethnicity, Mexicans in Chicago, 1916–1939." Ph.D. diss., University of Chicago, 1999.

Bae, Young-so. "Men's Clothing Workers in Chicago, 1871–1929: Ethnicity, Class, and a Labor Union." Ph.D. diss., Harvard University, 1988.

Barrows, Emily. "Trade Union Organization among Women in Chicago." Master's thesis, University of Chicago, 1927.

Bate, Phyllis. "The Development of the Iron and Steel Industry of the Chicago Area, 1900–1920." Ph.D. diss., University of Chicago, 1948.

Baur, Edward J. "Delinquency among Mexican Boys in South Chicago." Master's thesis University of Chicago, 1938

Bertellini, Giorgio. "Southern Crossings: Italians, Cinema, and Modernity." Ph.D. diss., New York University, 2001.

Bork, William Hal. "The Memorial Day 'Massacre' of 1937 and Its Significance in the Unionization of the Republic Steel Corporation." Master's thesis, University of Illinois, 1975.

Campisi, Paul. "The Adjustment of the Italian Americans to the War Crisis." Master's thesis, University of Chicago, 1942.

———. "A Scale for the Measurement of Acculturation." Ph.D. diss., University of Chicago, 1947.

Cotton, Lexie Lucille. "Families Who Moved from the Jane Addams Houses, 1939." Master's thesis, University of Chicago, 1941.

Cressey, Paul F. "The Succession of Cultural Groups in the City of Chicago." Ph.D. diss., University of Chicago, 1930.

D'Agostino, Peter D. "Missionaries in Babylon: The Adaptation of Italian Priests to Chicago's Church, 1870–1940." Ph.D. diss., University of Chicago, 1993.

Davis, Berenice Davida. "Housing Conditions in the District of Burnside." Master's thesis, University of Chicago, 1924.

Dee, William Louis Jolly. "The Social Effects of a Public Housing Project on the Immediate Community." Ph.D. diss., University of Chicago, 1949.

Desmond, Thomas. "The Lower North Community Council." Master's thesis, Loyola University, 1942.

Ferguson, Yvonne Mary. "The Chicago Housing Authority." Master's thesis, University of Chicago, 1942.

Fontana, James. "A Community Center in Relation to Its Neighborhood." Master's thesis, University of Chicago, 1942.

Fromer, Milton. "The First Tenants of the Jane Addams Houses." Master's thesis, University of Chicago, 1939.

Gilpin, Toni. "Left by Themselves: A History of the United Farm Equipment and Metal Workers Union, 1938–1955." Ph.D. diss., Yale University, 1992.

Gower, Charlotte Day. "The Supernatural Patron in Sicilian Life." Ph.D. diss., University of Chicago, 1928.

Guglielmo, Thomas. "Americans All?: Ethnicity and National Identity in American Wartime Popular Culture, 1941-1945." Unpublished essay (in author's possession), 1996.

Gutowski, Thomas. "The High School as an Adolescent-Raising Institution: An Inner History of Chicago Public Secondary Education, 1856–1940." Ph.D. diss., University of Chicago, 1978.

Harbison, Frederick Lewis. "Labor Relations in the Iron and Steel Industry, 1936 to 1939," Ph.D. diss., Princeton University, 1942.

Hart, Ann Webster. "Lower Income Groups Admitted to the Jane Addams Houses." Master's thesis, University of Chicago, 1941.

Hirsch, Arnold R. "Making the Second Ghetto: Race and Housing in Chicago, 1940–1960." Ph.D. diss., University of Illinois, Chicago, 1978.

Hoffman, George C. "Big Bill Thompson: His Mayoral Campaigns and His Voting Strength." Master's thesis, University of Chicago, 1956.

Hutton, Oscar D., Jr. "The Negro Worker and the Labor Unions of Chicago." Master's thesis, University of Chicago, 1939.

Jenkins, Thomas Harrison. "Changes in Ethnic and Racial Representation among Professional Boxers: A Study in Ethnic Succession." Master's thesis, University of Chicago, 1955.

Jones, Anita Edgar. "Conditions Surrounding Mexicans in Chicago." Master's-thesis, University of Chicago, 1929.

Karsh, Bernard. "The Grievance Process in Union-Management Relations: Buick Melrose Park and the UAW-CIO Local 6." Master's thesis, University of Chicago, 1950.

Keeran, Roger. "The Italian Section of the International Workers Order, 1930–1950." Unpublished essay (in author's possession), 1997.

Kerr, Louise Ano Nuevo de. "The Chicano Experience in Chicago, 1920-1970." Ph.D. diss., University of Illinois, Chicago, 1976.

Kornblum, William S. "Ethnicity, Work, and Politics in South Chicago." Ph.D. diss., University of Chicago, 1972.

Kornhauser, William Alan. "Labor Unions and Race Relations." Master's thesis, University of Chicago, 1950.

Larkin, William Donald. "Forty-Five Years of Collective Bargaining and Arbitration between Chicago Surface Lines and Its Trainmen." Master's thesis, Loyola University, 1948.

Mackelmann, Detlef Ernest. "Housing Conditions of 906 Families Known in the United Charities." Master's thesis, University of Chicago, 1936.

Magee, Mabel Agnes. "The Women's Clothing Industry of Chicago with Special Reference to Relations between the Manufacturers and the Union." Ph.D. diss., University of Chicago, 1927.

McCluer, Franc Lewis. "Living Conditions among Wage Earning Families in Forty-One Blocks in Chicago." Ph.D. diss., University of Chicago, 1928.

McDonnell, Timothy L. "The New Deal Makes a Public Housing Law: A Case Study of the Wagner Housing Bill of 1937." Ph.D. diss., St. Louis University, 1953.

Mikva, Zorita Wise. "The Neighborhood Improvement Association." Master's thesis, University of Chicago, 1951.

Myers, Robert James. "The Economic Aspects of the Production of Men's Clothing, with Particular Reference to the Industry of Chicago." Ph.D. diss., University of Chicago, 1937.

Nelli, Humbert. "The Role of the 'Colonial' Press in the Italian-American Community of Chicago, 1886–1921." Ph.D. diss., University of Chicago, 1965.

Nelson, Raymond Edward. "A Study of An Isolated Industrial Community: Based on Personal Documents Secured by the Participant Observer Method." Master's thesis, University of Chicago, 1929.

Norman, John. "Italo-American Opinion in the Ethiopian Crisis: A Study of Fascist Propaganda." Ph.D. diss., Clark University, 1942.

Overton, Alice. "Social Services of the Amalgamated Clothing Workers of Chicago." Master's thesis, University of Chicago, 1938.

Palmer, Vivien M. "The Primary Settlement Area as a Unit of Urban Growth and Organization." Ph.D. diss., University of Chicago, 1932.

Plotkin, Wendy. "Deeds of Mistrust: Race, Housing, and Restrictive Covenants in Chicago, 1900–1953." Ph.D. diss., University of Illinois at Chicago, 1999.

Puzzo, Virgil P. "The Italians in Chicago, 1890–1930." Master's thesis, University Chicago, 1937.

Quaintance, Esther Crockett. "Rents and Housing Conditions in the Italian District of the Lower North Side of Chicago, 1924." Master's thesis, University of Chicago, 1925.

Reed, Christopher Robert. "A Study of Black Politics and Protest in Depression-Decade Chicago: 1930–1939." Ph.D. diss., Kent State University, 1982.

Roberts, Robert Edward T. "Negro-White Marriages in Chicago." Master's thesis, University of Chicago, 1939.

Rogoff, Natalie. "Racial Attitudes in a White Community Bordering on the Negro District." Master's thesis, University of Chicago, 1947.

Sager, Gertrude. "Immigration Based Upon a Study of the Italian Women and Girls of Chicago." Master's thesis, University of Chicago, 1914.

Schietinger, Egbert F. "Real Estate Transfers during Negro Invasion: A Case Study, 1948." Master's thesis, University of Chicago, 1948.

———. "Racial Succession and Changing Property Values in Residential Chicago." Ph.D. diss., University of Chicago, 1953.

Seymour, Helen. "The Organized Unemployed." Master's thesis, University of Chicago, 1937.

Shanabruch, Charles. "The Catholic Church's Role in the Americanization of Chicago's Immigrants, 1853–1928." Ph.D. diss., University of Chicago, 1975.

Shaw, Stephen Joseph. "The Catholic Parish as a Way-Station of Ethnicity and Americanization." Ph.D. diss, University of Chicago, 1981.

Sheldon, Eleanor Harriet. "The Chicago Labor Force, 1910–1940." Ph.D. diss., University of Chicago, 1949.

Sherman, Rochelle Dubory. "The West Side Community Committee: A People's Organization in Action." Master's thesis, University of Chicago, 1946.

Shufelt, Gordon H. "Strangers in a Middle Land: Italian Immigrants and Race Relations in Baltimore, 1890–1920." Ph.D. diss., American University, 1998.

Simon, Bernece Kern. "The First Tenants of the Trumbull Park Homes." Master's thesis, University of Chicago, 1942.

Star, Shirley A. "Interracial Tensions in Two Areas of Chicago: An Exploratory Approach to the Measurement of Interracial Tension." Ph.D. diss., University of Chicago, 1950.

Stein, Jack M. "A History of Unionization in the Steel Industry in the Chicago Area." Master's thesis, University of Chicago, 1948.

Storch, Randi Jill. "Shades of Red: The Communist Party and Chicago's Workers, 1928–1939." Ph.D. diss., University of Illinois, 1998.

Thurner, Arthur W. "The Impact of Ethnic Groups on the Democratic Party in Chicago, 1920–1928." Ph.D. diss., University of Chicago, 1966.

Vecoli, Rudolph J. "Chicago's Italians Prior to World War I: A Study of Their Social and Economic Adjustment." Ph.D. diss., University of Wisconsin, 1963.

———. "The African Connection: Italian Americans and Race." Unpublished essay (in author's possession), 1997.

Wallace, David A. "Residential Concentration of Negroes in Chicago." Ph.D. diss., Harvard University, 1953.

Walsh, John P. "The Catholic Church in Chicago and Problems of an Urban Society." Ph.D. diss., University of Chicago, 1948.

Washington, Louis C. "A Study of Restrictive Covenants in Chicago." Master's thesis, University of Chicago, 1948.

Wheaton, William. "The Evolution of the Federal Housing Programs." Ph.D. diss., University of Chicago, 1954.

Williams, Luther. "The People of Tangipahoa Parish: A Sociological Comparison of Two Ethnic Groups." Master's thesis, Louisiana State University, 1951.

Winder, Alvin. "White Attitudes towards Negro-White Interaction in an Area of Changing Racial Composition." Ph.D. diss., University of Chicago, 1952.

Young, Kimball. "A Sociological Study of a Disintegrated Neighborhood." Master's thesis, University of Chicago, 1918.

Zaloha, Anna. "A Study of the Persistence of Italian Customs among 143 Families of Italian Descent, Members of Social Clubs at Chicago Commons." Master's thesis, Northwestern University, 1937.

Zivich, Edward Andrew. "Fighting Union: The CIO at Inland Steel, 1936–1942." Master's thesis, University of Wisconsin, Milwaukee, 1972.

INDEX